OUR VICHY GAMBLE

Our Vichy Gamble

BY

WILLIAM L. LANGER

Coolidge Professor of History, Harvard University

1 9 4 7

ALFRED · A · KNOPF

NEW YORK

TO ROWENA

PREFACE

THE publication of this book calls particularly for some words of prefatory explanation. It is based in large measure upon official documents of the United States government; that is, upon materials which would not normally become available to the public for many years. Since its publication has been authorized by the Department of State, by the War Department and by the Director of the former Office of Strategic Services, it is only fitting and proper that something should be said about its origin and history.

Some three years ago Secretary Hull, who had been violently attacked in the press because of our policy toward Vichy France, requested me to make a detailed and altogether independent study of that policy from the time of the Franco-German armistice to the assassination of Admiral Darlan in December 1942. I told the Secretary that his proposition was a challenging one for any professional historian and that I would be glad to work on the project in my spare time, but on the explicit understanding that I could serve only as a dispassionate scholar, not as an apologist. Mr. Hull reiterated in the strongest terms his desire for an outside evaluation by a professional historian and promised to make available all relevant materials in the State Department.

My plan was to work originally from the records and to trouble busy Washington officials only after a preliminary survey had revealed gaps in the materials or irreconcilable contradictions in the evidence. I sifted an immense number of documents in the State Department and, through the generosity of General William J. Donovan, was given full access to the records of my own agency, the Office of Strategic Services. At Secretary Hull's request the War Department made available a detailed digest of such military records as had political importance in connection with the invasion of North Africa. Admiral William D. Leahy, formerly our ambassador to Vichy France, also took an interest in the work and very kindly aided me with some of his papers.

A first draft of the study was completed in the summer of 1944 and was read by a number of officials who were connected with the problem—Secretary Hull, Admiral Leahy, General Donovan, Colonel William A. Eddy, and, within the Department, Mr. Ray Atherton, Mr. H. Freeman Mathews, Mr. Robert D. Murphy, Mr. Wallace Murray, Mr. Henry S. Villard, Mr. Woodruff Wallner, and Mr. Carlton W. Savage. All took a lively interest in the project and gave me the benefit of extended comment and criticism.

In the meanwhile my labors had been called to the attention of President Roosevelt, who at once offered to help in any way possible. The President instructed his aides to prepare an abstract of such of his papers as bore upon the problem, and he himself checked these notes at Warm Springs just before his death. I am deeply indebted to him for some very illuminating details.

During the winter and spring of 1944–5 I continued my conferences with various participants and in particular discussed the initial chapters with Mr. William C. Bullitt. At the same time I followed carefully the vast amount of new material that came to light after the Allied victory in Europe. The extensive record of the Pétain trial, for example, is an invaluable fund of information on the French side. In like manner the interrogations of prominent German leaders by Mr. DeWitt C. Poole and the Special Interrogation Mission of the State Department gave us for the first time an adequate picture of Nazi plans and policies. Finally, among the captured German documents there were many of great interest, such as the records of the conferences between Hitler, Pétain, Laval, Darlan, and Franco.

This great accretion of new evidence made necessary complete revision of the original draft, and it is this new version that is presented herewith. Secretary Hull and the Department of State have agreed to its publication chiefly because of continued demands from the public for more information regarding our objectives and our achievements with respect to France and the French problem. For example, on August 3, 1945 the *Washington Post* in an editorial declared: "American policy toward Vichy should be opened to the light of day. With the Vichy regime long since cast into limbo, with the war over, the occasion for further secrecy simply does not exist and, if continued, will only deepen long-standing American suspicion that our Vichy policy was a far from creditable episode in our diplomacy."

It is hoped that the present study will help to dispel many misunderstandings and to set forth not only the aims of our policy but the difficulties and uncertainties with which it had to deal. I cannot emphasize too strongly that this is an altogether independent analysis and that it in no sense reflects or records official opinion or judgment. Members of the State Department and of the government generally have been of great help to me and I am grateful for their interest. But none of them has ever attempted to sway my conclusions or in any way to influence my work. This is a purely historical study, for which I personally bear the entire responsibility.

Like all authors, I am indebted to others for help. Mr. Savage and Mr. Wallner of the Department were unflagging in their efforts to locate the necessary materials. My wife devoted herself to the thankless job of plowing through newspaper and other printed matter, and my secretary, Miss Frances Douglas, took care of the clerical aspects with her wonted efficiency. To them all I am more grateful than I can say, for the assignment, undertaken in the midst of a heavy program of war work, was not easily manageable for any of us.

WILLIAM L. LANGER

CONTENTS

OUR VICHY GAMBLE

CHAPTER I

The Collapse of France

M ODERN HISTORY has recorded but few events so cataclysmic as the defeat and surrender of the French Republic in June 1940. Not since the lightning-like campaign of Napoleon against Prussia in 1806 had a great military power met its doom so quickly and inexorably. In the brief span of less than six weeks one of the world's leading powers was erased from the international scene, thereby upsetting whatever balance of power had previously remained in world affairs and confronting the United States as well as other nations with a host of new problems, none of which could be ignored or postponed. It is the purpose of the present study to examine the implications of France's defeat and surrender and to analyze the objectives and methods of United States policy toward the French problem from the time of the armistice to the invasion of North Africa and the assassination of Darlan at the very end of 1942.

The drama of the French defeat began with the assault of the Nazi armies on the Low Countries on May 10, 1940. During the preceding six months the British and French Allies had been obliged to look on helplessly while Poland was engulfed and while they sought hectically for some plan by which the Nazi enemy's supplies could be cut off and his armies worn down in futile campaigning. While popular humor indulged in quips about the "phony war," the French and British staffs elaborated schemes for opening fronts in Norway, in the Balkans, and against the Russians in the Caucasian oilfields. The details of these plans need not concern us here, for none of them materialized in time.[1] All we need say is that they were

[1] The Germans published a large number of documents on these plans, which were captured at La Charité in 1940. See *Auswärtiges Amt*, 1939-41, No. 6: *Die Geheimakten des französischen Generalstabes* (Berlin, 1941).

[3]

far too ambitious and optimistic, as the Allies soon learned
when they got their own first taste of Nazi power during the
Norwegian campaign. Hardly had that unhappy interlude
come to its bungling close when the full fury of German air
power and mechanized might broke over the Netherlands and
Belgium on May 10, 1940. With breath-taking speed the defenses of the Low Countries were overrun. In less than a week
of fighting the armies of the Allies were driven toward the
coast, and Nazi tanks were stretching an ominous arm from
Sedan to the Channel. The British and French forces that had
been thrown rather recklessly into Belgium were in acute
danger of being cut off. With a shock of horror the world suddenly realized that the French armies, outnumbered and ill-
equipped, were face to face with disaster. The long cultivation
of a defensive mentality, adhered to by almost all of the French
military leaders, and the dull apathy of the French public were
rudely shaken by the impact of an offensive machine the like
of which had never before been seen.

By the 15th of May the situation had already deteriorated
to the point where it could be described as desperate. Reynaud,
the French Premier and reputedly the strong man of the Republic, was already appealing frantically to the British for
more air support. "It seems probable," he wired, "that German
troops will enter Paris before midnight tonight." Thereupon
the British Prime Minister flew to the French capital. He was
much impressed with the gravity of the situation and promised
to try to send more fighter planes to the Continent. But nothing
came of the project, for an overwhelming majority of the war
cabinet voted it down. The British contention throughout was
that the airfields in France were too exposed to enemy attack
and that, above all, Britain needed such planes as she had for
defense of the home islands. Justified though this stand undoubtedly was, and despite the fact that at least some additional air support was given the retreating French, the Anglo-
phobia that developed rapidly in France after the surrender
was inspired particularly by British failure in this respect.[2]

[2] Department of State: Tels. (May 16, 17) from Bullitt. Notes of Robert

President Roosevelt was one of the relatively few statesmen who were not entirely surprised by the disastrous developments in France. His close personal friend William C. Bullitt was ambassador at Paris and was in intimate contact with most of the French political and military leaders. By telephone and through special codes Bullitt was able to keep the White House immediately informed in a very detailed way.

The ambassador had for a long time been skeptical of France's future if the Germans were to attack in force. He knew that General Gamelin underrated the importance of tanks and aircraft and that he relied far too much on the supposed superiority of the French general staff and its ability to adjust to situations as they might develop. He was also aware of the pathetic state of French war production, and a visit to the Maginot Line in the autumn of 1939 had left him full of dark forebodings as to the possibility of preventing a German break-through. He had therefore urged on Daladier the need for drawing on American industry for planes and guns, and had made arrangements by which French gold was spent to enable the Curtiss-Wright, Pratt and Whitney, and Martin airplane factories to enlarge and get into wartime production.

Beyond this, Bullitt had persuaded the President that France could be saved in the event of attack only if the British put a large army and a formidable air force into the field and if Italy could be kept from attacking France simultaneously with the Germans. The British, to be sure, were more optimistic about the chances that France would hold and were, in addition, very reluctant to accept heavy sacrifices, but every effort was nevertheless made on the American side to bring the British, like the French, to a realization of the dangers and of the need to pool all resources to stem the Nazi onslaught when it came.

Bullitt happened to be with Daladier, the Minister of National Defense, when General Gamelin telephoned the news of the German break-through at Sedan and the threat of the

D. Murphy to me (August 31, 1944). A number of French appeals for planes are reprinted in the German documentary collection mentioned in the preceding note.

destruction of the French army. This news was positively shocking, for no one, even the most pessimistic, had expected the crisis to come so quickly. "It seems obvious," reported the ambassador, "that unless God grants a miracle as at the time of the battle of the Marne, the French army will be crushed utterly." The British, he added, were becoming critical of the French and were not throwing everything they had into the struggle. On the contrary, many of them were already talking in defeatist terms and were unwilling to risk their own future in the common cause.[3]

In this serious crisis the possibility of direct American support was very limited. Public opinion and consequently congressional sentiment was still strongly isolationist, and the action of the government was closely circumscribed by the elaborate neutrality legislation of preceding years. Nevertheless the President did, within the limits of the law, scrape together every available plane for shipment to France and turn over to the French two thousand 75-mm. guns from the stocks of the last war. In addition he used such influence as he had to induce the British to give increased air support to the French armies and left no stone unturned in his efforts to keep Mussolini from joining in the fray.

Viewed from Washington, it was clear that American interests of the most vital character were directly involved in the crisis. Prior to May 1940 the United States still had the armies and navies of France and Britain between it and the Nazi menace. Now suddenly the European front was caving in. France was probably doomed and Britain as well as France might be forced to make peace with Hitler. Not only would the Nazis then command the coasts of Europe; they might even secure control of two of the world's largest navies. In that case (with the major part of our fleet concentrated in the Pacific) they could rule the Atlantic and choose their own time for operations against the Western Hemisphere. Never in our history had we been so directly, so gravely threatened.

[3] Tel. (May 16) from Bullitt. For much of the foregoing I am indebted to information from Bullitt himself.

And therefore the fate of France was of such compelling concern to us. To help France militarily was out of the question. The first and foremost problem was to prevent Hitler's getting control of the French fleet. If he were to secure it, his future operations against Britain would be so much easier. If Britain went under, we ourselves would soon be challenged along our own coasts.

Although Reynaud's fears for the fate of Paris turned out to be somewhat premature, the German advance continued relentlessly and without serious check. Under growing pressure the French Premier therefore undertook a recasting of the government. On May 18 he appointed Marshal Philippe Pétain as Vice-Premier, while Daladier was shifted from the Ministry of National Defense to the Foreign Office, and Mandel took the Ministry of the Interior. Reynaud himself assumed the functions relinquished by Daladier, despite the fact that he had never been concerned with the French forces. On the following day General Gamelin was removed from the supreme command and General Maxime Weygand was appointed to that post.

Since Pétain and Weygand were to play the most prominent roles in the ensuing surrender, a few remarks about them may well be introduced at this point. The marshal, in 1940, was eighty-five years of age, while Weygand was seventy-two. Though both men had emerged from the first World War covered with honor and glory and though both had played an influential part in the formulation of French military policy during the preceding twenty years, they had never been personally close. Pétain and Foch had been notorious rivals, and for that reason, if for no other, Weygand, as Foch's chief aide, was regarded by the marshal as the representative of another camp. None the less, their general conception of French military requirements and policy had been much the same. Both had staked the country's future on defensive plans, and neither had shown much appreciation of the possibilities and implications of mechanized warfare.

During the past five years a veritable library of books and

articles has been published exposing Pétain's past and impugning his loyalty or that of Weygand. It has been pointed out, again and again, that despite his reputation as the defender of Verdun in 1916, Pétain irritated both Clemenceau and Lloyd George, to say nothing of Foch. By his colleagues he was regarded as a pessimist, even as a defeatist in the critical days of March 1918. In the postwar period, according to these critics, he helped to cultivate the defensive mentality and failed to prepare the country to meet the Nazi threat. All told, he has been accused of having had a thoroughly negative temperament and outlook. To Foch has been ascribed the *bon mot*: "If the job requires that nothing be done, Pétain's your man."

The marshal had never taken an active part in French politics, but he was known to be sympathetic to the authoritarian creeds that developed like mushrooms from the spawn of Charles Maurras's royalist movement in the decade before the second World War. His opponents and critics have gone so far as to accuse him of having been a Cagoulard, of having been a friend of Göring, Franco, and other fascists, and indeed of having had commerce with foreigners with a view to plotting the overthrow of the Republic and the establishment of an authoritarian system.

All these charges and other lesser ones were aired at Pétain's trial, but during the proceedings the prosecution voluntarily abandoned the charge of conspiracy. From the welter of conflicting evidence the impartial reader is bound to conclude that there was never any real reason to question Pétain's patriotism, and that the stories of his nefarious subterranean activities rest on little more than hearsay and strained interpretations. On the other hand, there was undoubtedly some fire to explain the clouds of smoke. Pétain was certainly a man of authoritarian proclivities, and it is reasonably clear that many fascist groups idolized him, looked to him as a possible leader, and generally dreamed of him as a new Boulanger. It cannot be shown that the marshal had any direct connection with such groups. On the other hand, there is no evidence either that he discouraged and discountenanced them.[4]

General Weygand was even more conservative than Pétain, in both his military and his political views. In the years before the war he had been one of the leading protagonists of a defensive strategy and had refused to acknowledge the importance even of air power. Politically he was an avowed royalist and clerical, a man much disturbed by the danger of social disorder or radical revolution.

Later writers have marvelled at the fact that Reynaud in the hour of crisis should have appointed to important positions men like Pétain and Weygand. The answer, however, is fairly obvious. It is the one that Reynaud himself has frequently supplied: namely, that the two soldiers were among the most venerated military figures in France and that their advent would inspire public confidence, as indeed it did. Even the parties of the Left hailed the appointment of Pétain. Of course, it was known that both Pétain and Weygand were conservative, not to say authoritarian, in their political views. But the same was notoriously true of most French generals and therefore was not taken into account. On the other hand, little was known of Pétain's pessimistic inclinations. Reynaud claims that he himself learned of these only at a later date. He insists, quite rightly no doubt, that in the hour of despair he believed that the marshal's prestige would be invaluable in maintaining popular morale, and that, as for Weygand, there was no other officer of his stature to whom he could turn. Indeed, it is prob-

[4] By far the most important source is the record of the Pétain trial: *Haute Cour de Justice*: *Procès du Maréchal Pétain* (Paris, 1945). The most detailed biography of the marshal is the fulsome work of his adjutant, General Laure: *Pétain* (Paris, 1941). Among countless critical treatments, see Pertinax (André Géraud): *Les Fossoyeurs* (New York, 1943), which is easily one of the most thorough and enlightening. See further Elie J. Bois: *The Truth about the Tragedy of France* (New York, 1941); Heinz Pol: *Suicide of a Democracy* (New York, 1940); the articles of Henry Bernstein: "Marshal Pétain" (*New York Herald Tribune*, June 9–27, 1941); Michael: *France Still Lives* (London, 1942); Anon.: *Pétain-Laval: the Conspiracy* (London, 1942); Philip Guedalla: *The Two Marshals* (New York, 1943); Francis Martel: *Pétain: Verdun to Vichy* (New York, 1943).

ably safe to say that neither Pétain nor Weygand accepted
their new responsibilities with any gusto or out of any spirit
but that of patriotic devotion. Pétain had been urged upon
Daladier for a cabinet post in March by no less a person than
Herriot and had declined. Weygand and his family are said
to have been bitter over the fact that the general was called
into battle at eleven fifty-five when the situation was already
all but hopeless.[5]

Be all this as it may, so much seems clear: that neither Pétain
nor Weygand had much hope of saving the situation, even on
May 18–19. According to General Laure, the marshal, when
he left his post as ambassador to Madrid, felt that his mission
in Paris would be not so much to make war as to try to effect
a decent peace. A little later Pétain confessed as much to
Bullitt: "It had been obvious to him [Pétain]," reported the
ambassador, "when he returned from his embassy in Spain that
the war was lost." In like manner Weygand is reputed to have
said, as he left his command in Syria, that the military situation
in France was already beyond repair and that in his opinion
a reasonable armistice should be accepted.[6]

There is really nothing very startling in all this. The state
of the French armies was desperate and pessimism was certainly justified. Reynaud himself, though supposedly the
strong man of French politics, had really very little of the
iron determination of a Clemenceau. His mistress, Mme
Hélène de Portes, exercised a great influence over him and
she in turn was the leader of an out-and-out defeatist clique
in Reynaud's entourage. No less a person than Alexis Leger,
at that time secretary-general of the French Foreign Office,
is convinced that as early as May 18 Reynaud had given up
hope and that he wanted Pétain in the cabinet because he be-

[5] *Procès du M. Pétain,* Reynaud's testimony, especially p. 14; Blum's testimony, p. 75; Reynaud's "Memoirs" (*New York Times,* July 21, 1945,ff.);
MS. notes by H. Freeman Matthews and Robert D. Murphy.
[6] Tel. (July 1) from Bullitt. Pertinax: *Les Fossoyeurs,* I, 244, 321; II, 26.
Pierre Tissier: *Le Procès de Riom* (London, 1943), pp. 163ff., quotes books
by Elie J. Bois and Paul Allard to the same effect.

lieved that a surrender would be easier to arrange if men like the marshal would serve as a front.[7]

Such was the general setting. We must return now to the development of the action.

Weygand's plan, when he took over the supreme command, was to attempt to organize a simultaneous attack from north and south in the hope of pinching off the Nazi corridor that ran from Sedan to Abbeville, and thereby to open a passage for the numerous divisions that had been cut off in Belgium. He claimed later that until May 24 he had hopes of success and that the plan failed only because the British, for unexplained reasons, withdrew suddenly from Arras. As a matter of fact, the situation at the front was one of utter confusion. There was no real unity of command or anything like effective co-ordination of operations. The British complained that for days on end they were left without orders, but we need not concern ourselves here with details that had best be left to military critics.[8] The bald fact of the matter is that by May 25 the fate of the Allied armies in Belgium was sealed. The surrender of King Leopold on May 26 was only an episode, though of course it hastened the evacuation from Dunkirk and marked another milestone on the road to disaster.

Added to the inexorable advance of the German armies was the growing danger of Italian intervention and attack on France's Alpine frontier. On May 20 Reynaud was expecting action by Mussolini that very evening and Ambassador Bullitt was urging President Roosevelt to make a last effort to hold the Fascist government back: "My personal opinion," he wired, "is that if Mussolini can be kept from stabbing France in the back, the German drive on Paris will be held." [9] The phrase "stab in the back," incidentally, was so apt that it was soon

[7] Conversation with Leger, July 3, 1944.
[8] The minutes of the Anglo-French conference of May 22, at which Weygand expounded his plan, are reprinted in *Die Geheimakten des französischen Generalstabes*, No. 56. See also the illuminating discussion in Albert Kammerer: *La Vérité sur l'armistice* (Paris, 1944), p. 34.
[9] Tel. (May 20) from Bullitt.

being used by Reynaud on numerous occasions until finally it was sounded to the public in the President's great Charlottesville speech.

The United States government had for a long time been making efforts to deter Mussolini from action against France, but the Italian dictator proved unamenable to argument. Only because of the notorious state of unpreparedness of his army had he reluctantly decided to hold aloof when the Germans invaded Poland. During the entire winter he had chafed under inaction and had spoiled to get into the fray. He was fascinated by Hitler, yet jealous of him. Convinced that Britain and France would be defeated, he was anxious to reap part of the harvest of victory and to intervene as soon as possible.[10]

Under the circumstances there was little hope of holding him back. Even Count Ciano, his son-in-law and Foreign Minister, was unable to exercise effective influence in favor of peace. In February and March Sumner Welles had been sent to the European capitals to explore the possibilities of a peace settlement, without any promising results. At the end of April President Roosevelt appealed personally to Mussolini, but again to no avail. As we now know, the Italian dictator on May 9 made his decision to intervene, without reference to the King or to the grand council or to his political and military advisers. It was a foregone conclusion, therefore, that all last-moment efforts, either of President Roosevelt or of the French government, would prove abortive. Eloquent appeals were made to Mussolini, while the President offered to mediate and Reynaud expressed readiness to discuss Italian territorial claims. But all to no avail. On May 27, some days before the final efforts were made, Count Ciano stated quite frankly to the American ambassador that it was no longer a question of this or that claim: "Even if it were possible for him [Mussolini] to get twice as much as he claims he wants, and get it by peaceful means, he would refuse." To the British ambassador Ciano said quite brutally that Mussolini had decided on May 8

---

[10] Cf. Count Ciano's *Diary*, of which I used the original text before publication.

to go to war and that he was merely awaiting a favorable moment. Even if France were to offer Italy all of North Africa, the proposition would not be accepted. The Duce had remarked that "the efforts of the Allies to buy him off with concessions and the efforts of President Roosevelt he considered indecent and immoral attempts to persuade him to break his pledged word." Considering the fact that the Germans were positively irritated by Mussolini's precipitous intervention, the Fascist dictator's remarks are not without their comic side.[11]

Since from the outset it was highly improbable that anything could be done with Mussolini either by moral suasion or by hard, cold bargaining, the question arose whether actual pressure might be effective. The only way to forestall the catastrophe of an Italian intervention, concluded Ambassador Bullitt and Reynaud, would be for the United States to make an impressive demonstration of naval power by sending the Atlantic fleet into the Mediterranean or at least to Lisbon. Such a move would undoubtedly be advantageous also with reference to the fate of the French fleet in the event of a total collapse. This angle was the one that concerned the President most, and he expounded it cogently and succinctly in a message of May 26 destined for Reynaud and Daladier:

"While we still hope the invasion will be checked, if the worst comes to the worst, we regard retention of the French Fleet as a force in being as vital to the reconstitution of France and of the French colonies and to the ultimate control of the Atlantic and other oceans and as a vital influence towards getting less harsh terms of peace. That means that the French Fleet must not get caught bottled up in the Mediterranean. Those ships in the eastern Mediterranean must be in a position to exit through the Suez

[11] The most important source is Ciano's *Diary*, especially entries for May 1, 10, 13, 27, 31, June 1. See also *Peace and War* (Washington, 1943), Nos. 151–3, 155, 158, 159, 160, 161, 164; Sumner Welles: *The Time for Decision* (New York, 1945), *passim;* and State Department telegrams: (May 20), (May 25), (May 29), (June 3), all from Bullitt. The French side of the problem was thoroughly aired at the Pétain trial: *Procès du M. Pétain*, pp. 30–1 (Reynaud's testimony); 44–5 (Daladier's testimony); 80 (Charles-Roux's testimony).

Canal. Those at Toulon, Tunis, and Algiers must be able to exit
past Gibraltar and be in a position, if the worst comes, to retire
to the West Indies or to safe ports in the West African possessions. . . .

"Finally, if the Germans hold out alluring offers to France
based on surrender of the Fleet, it should be remembered that
these offers are of no ultimate value and that the condition of
France could be no worse, but in fact would be far stronger, if
the Fleet were removed as a whole to safe places." [12]

Bullitt agreed entirely with this argumentation, but insisted
on tying it in with active moves by the American fleet. He
replied to Washington:

"I believe as strongly as I have ever believed anything that you
will be unable to protect the United States from German attack
unless you have the cooperation of the French and British fleets.
I believe that one of the surest ways to obtain such cooperation
would be by sending our Atlantic Fleet to the Mediterranean."
At the same time he urged that a cruiser be sent to Bordeaux to
carry away the entire French and Belgian gold reserves.[13]

Meanwhile French appeals were becoming ever more frequent and insistent. On May 27 the French government
begged the United States for six destroyers and above all for
planes of any description. The British too were clamoring for
some of our old destroyers. But obviously it was impossible to
turn over American warships without a good deal of consideration, and as for planes, they were simply not yet available
in quantity. We had only one hundred and fifty planes that
we could send to France, and these did not leave Halifax until
June 17.[14]

The crucial appeal of the French, however, continued to
be for the mission of the Atlantic fleet. On May 29 Bullitt reported Reynaud's beseeching words:

"It is now or never for the United States. If you can send your
Atlantic Fleet to Tangier and inform Mussolini that you are doing

[12] Tel. (May 26) to Bullitt; Tels. (May 28) from Bullitt for the President.
[13] Tel. (May 28) from Bullitt.
[14] Stettinius: *Lend-Lease*, p. 29 and chap. iv; Tels. (May 27) from Bullitt.

so after the fleet has started, he will not dare to strike. Otherwise, he will strike and in a very few months you will face a joint attack by Germany, Italy and Japan alone." [15]

No doubt kindred thoughts and fears were in the minds of the President and his advisers. But the sad truth of the matter was that we were quite unprepared for such a crisis. The President himself had never envisaged so swift a German victory in the west and, like most other Americans, had relied on the Maginot Line, the French army, and the British navy, backed by American industrial power, to stave off the evil day. On May 16 he had asked Congress to provide for a mechanized army and for fifty thousand planes and had stressed the need for adequate bases in the Atlantic. But of course these were only the first steps in a precautionary program. We were still laboring under the neutrality legislation and had not yet introduced conscription for the army. We had as yet no two-ocean navy and most of our ships were concentrated in the Pacific to meet the growing threat of Japanese action. [16]

So there was really no way of satisfying the French requests, however justified they might be. This was explained to Bullitt by cable on May 30:

"The President desires me to let you know," reported Secretary Hull, "that it is absolutely impossible to consider sending the fleet into the Mediterranean. The presence of the fleet in the Pacific at this time is a very practical contribution to the maintenance of peace in the Pacific. The value of this contribution is fully appreciated by the British Government and, it is assumed, by the French Government as well. What vessels we have in the Atlantic are required under present circumstances either for patrol duty or for special service in South and Central American waters.

"From the strictly practical aspect, the presence of an American fleet at this time in the Mediterranean would result in very

[15] Tel. (May 29) from Bullitt.
[16] See *Report of the Secretary of War to the President* (1941); also Forrest Davis and Ernest K. Lindley: *How War Came* (New York, 1942), pp. 27–8, 45.

serious risks and hazards and it would be impossible, for reasons which are, of course, apparent, for the fleet to base itself on any ports in or near the Mediterranean, should Italy enter the war. Finally, as you will recognize, unless any fleet sent were sufficiently large to be effective, the impression created would be the reverse of that desired." [17]

Consideration of American interests and activities has obliged us to anticipate some features of the French military situation at the end of May and early June. By May 25 Weygand's hopes of cutting off the German salient had been dashed. In a few more days the evacuation of Allied forces from Dunkirk was to begin. At this critical juncture (May 25) the whole problem of the future was considered in an important meeting of the French *Comité de Guerre.* Weygand pointed out the gravity of the situation, but agreed with Reynaud that the French armies must for the sake of honor fight on to the death. The Prime Minister then proceeded to reflect, and from his own lips was first heard the fateful word "armistice":

"It does not follow that our adversary will at once grant us an armistice (i.e., after a fight to the death). Is it not indispensable to avoid the capture of the government if the enemy enters Paris?"

President Lebrun turned to Weygand for the answer to these questions.

In case of defeat "what liberty would the French government have to examine offers of peace, if such were addressed to it? Would the government have greater freedom for examination prior to the destruction of the French armies? To be sure, we have signed agreements which prevent our making a separate peace. Nonetheless, if Germany offers relatively advantageous conditions, we must examine them carefully and weigh them calmly."

Weygand, by way of reply, recognized that the cessation of hostilities was an interallied question. He recognized further

[17] Tel. (May 30) to Bullitt.

that one could not adopt the extreme solution that he had just advanced—namely, the hopeless struggle of the army to save its honor—without examining the consequences in consultation with the British. He agreed with Lebrun that if Germany were to make peace offers, the opinion of the British must be asked. And by way of conclusion Marshal Pétain asked whether each party to the agreement had equal obligations. In his view, "each nation had obligations to the other in proportion to the aid which the other has supplied." Britain, he pointed out, had furnished only ten divisions as against France's eighty.[18]

It will be noted at once how confused and inconclusive the debate was at this meeting. So much, however, is clear: no one suggested asking for an armistice. On the contrary, Reynaud and Weygand were agreed that France must fight to the end. Though Reynaud adumbrated the need for transferring the government from Paris, the discussion hinged upon the possibility that, on the defeat of France, the Germans might offer peace, and indeed might offer peace on relatively favorable terms. Since France was bound by the agreement with Britain of March 28, 1940 not to conclude a separate armistice or peace treaty, it was conceded that London must be consulted. The only discordant note was that introduced by Pétain, who pointed out that perhaps the failure of the British to give more aid might be interpreted as relieving France from at least part of her obligations. No particular attention seems to have been vouchsafed this strange doctrine. On the following day Reynaud went to London, where no doubt the question was discussed. We have no record of the meeting with Churchill, but it seems likely that Reynaud raised the question whether, if the British were unable to furnish greater air support, it might not be in the common interest for France to conclude an armistice before the Germans seized the entire Channel coast area. Churchill evidently rejected this proposi-

---

[18] The minutes of this meeting were published by the Germans in *Die Geheimakten des französischen Generalstabes*, No. 61. They are reprinted in Kammerer: *La Vérité sur l'armistice*, appendix VII. For Weygand's comment on the meeting, see *Procès du M. Pétain*, p. 131.

tion and reiterated Britain's determination to fight to the end.
No doubt he managed to reassure Reynaud to some extent and
to induce him to give up his idea of quitting.[19]

During the ensuing days the Allies effected the evacuation
of their forces from Dunkirk while the German armies were
being marshaled for the assault on the Somme. Although the
military situation was admittedly hopeless, Reynaud appealed
again to President Roosevelt for planes. The President promised that the United States would do its utmost and urged
Churchill to send more planes to France, but neither the President's exhortations nor Reynaud's eleven telegrams and seven
telephone conversations with London brought any substantial result. As a British official explained to Bullitt, the rate of
destruction of planes in battle was so great that if Britain sent
over her remaining planes, none of them would be left in two
weeks. Since there was no longer any hope of saving Paris, or
for that matter of saving the French army, it seemed wiser to
keep the planes in England.[20]

The American ambassador thoroughly disapproved of this
decision, which he thought more reprehensible even than the
defection of King Leopold. The whole business served only
to arouse his suspicions of British policy and intentions. He
feared that the British might be conserving their air force and
fleet in order to use them as bargaining points in negotiations
with Hitler.[21]

Apparently President Roosevelt and Secretary Hull did not
share these fears, for they had already decided to ship to Britain the surplus stocks of American rifles and light artillery that
had been intended originally for France. Actually there was
little danger of defection by the British so long as Churchill
remained in power. The sequel showed that the British decision not to send more planes to France was probably a sound
one. It is most unlikely that more planes could still have
changed the outcome of the battle. On the other hand, had

---

[19] Kammerer: *La Vérité sur l'armistice*, p. 41; statement by Bullitt.
[20] Tel. (June 6) from Bullitt.
[21] Tels. (June 5) from Bullitt.

they been sent and destroyed, the Battle of Britain might have turned out very differently. Still, it was only natural that Frenchmen should have felt abandoned and wronged and that in some circles resentment at the British should have begun to run deep. An early indication of this came during a luncheon conversation that Bullitt had with Marshal Pétain on June 4. The marshal pointed out that the Germans had a threefold superiority in men and an even greater preponderance in planes and tanks. He expected the Germans to cross the Somme (as they did the next day) and to envelop Paris. It was a certainty, he said, that the Italians would join them (as they did on June 10). Since the evacuation of Dunkirk the British were no longer sending any planes. They had left only one division in France and insisted that they could send no more. Pétain therefore felt that the British

"would permit the French to fight without help until the last available drop of French blood should have been shed and that then, with quantities of troops on British soil and plenty of planes and a dominant fleet, the British after a very brief resistance, or even without resistance, would make a peace of compromise with Hitler, which might even involve a British government under a British Fascist leader. . . . He felt that unless the British government should send to France to engage in the battle which was imminent both its airforce and reserve divisions, the French government should do its utmost to come to terms immediately with Germany, whatever might happen to England." [22]

Pétain's remarks to Bullitt sounded the keynote of his policy during the following two weeks. On his own admission, he attempted to persuade Reynaud to ask for an armistice the moment the British refused to send their planes into the Battle of France.[23] The least that can be said is that the marshal's position was direct and simple. He had not approved of the war from the outset. When he took office on May 18 he was already thinking of the need for peace. Since May 25 all were agreed that defeat was inevitable. The British were refusing

[22] Tel. (June 4) from Bullitt.
[23] Tel. (July 1) from Bullitt. Statement to me by Bullitt.

aid and might conceivably be hoarding their potential as a
make-weight in negotiating peace with Hitler. Why, then,
should France play the dupe? Further bloodshed was useless.
France should seek an armistice as soon as possible, the agreements with Britain to the contrary notwithstanding. After all,
what had Britain done for France that the French nation
should now suffer all the losses, only perhaps to be completely
abandoned later? It seems almost as though Pétain thought it
essential to close a deal with the Nazis before "perfidious Al-
bion" should have a chance to do so.

Weygand, too, is reputed to have pressed Reynaud ever
since May 29 to conclude an armistice, but there appears to be
no foundation for this story.[24] The truth of the matter probably is that Weygand looked at the situation primarily from
the military angle and that, like most other leaders in these
hectic days, he despaired at one moment only to hope against
hope during the next. The greatest mistake a historian could
make would be to try to construct a neat, logical pattern when
in actual fact everything was confusion and contradiction.

As an illustration, let us consider the case of Reynaud. There
seems to be no doubt that his inclinations were all in the direction of resistance and that he was much influenced by the
sturdy determination of Churchill. On May 25 he had already
begun to envisage moving the government from Paris. During
the following ten days his mind was busy with the idea of
withdrawing the armies to some redoubt like Brittany, where,
he thought, the forces might hold out for some time, drawing
supplies from England and from the United States. Failing
that, he was already considering the possibility of removing
the government to North Africa and carrying on from there.[25]
At the same time he was being beset by Mme de Portes's plead-
ings and importunities. On June 6 he remade his cabinet, re-

[24] It goes back to Senator Charles Reibel's book: *Pourquoi et comment
fut décidée la demande d'armistice* (Vanves, 1940). Reynaud himself denied
the charge (see Kammerer: *La Vérité sur l'armistice*, pp. 55, 69).

[25] May 29, Weygand's testimony (*Procès du M. Pétain*, p. 132). General
Gamelin thought the establishment of a redoubt altogether feasible at this
time (Gamelin: "Memoirs," Associated Press, July 16, 1945ff.).

lieving Daladier and taking over the Foreign Office himself
and appointing General Charles de Gaulle, who was to be the
very soul of French resistance, as Undersecretary of War. To
counterbalance these moves he named as Undersecretary for
Foreign Affairs Baudoin, a member of Mme de Portes's circle
and a notorious fascist and sympathizer with the Nazis. Along
with Baudoin a number of lesser men of the same stripe moved
into the ministry: Bouthillier, Leca, Devaux, Villelume—all
of them men who later appeared in the front ranks of the collaborators. Mme de Portes boasted of the ministry as her very
own, though how much of an exaggeration this was can be
gauged by anyone who recalls that the cabinet still included
out-and-out diehards like Mandel, Campinchi, and Marin.[26]

Meanwhile it had become imperative for the government
to leave Paris. Papers and records were destroyed pell-mell
and the ministers, parliamentarians, and officials made their
way as best they could to the vicinity of Tours. The roads
were jammed with hysterical refugees, giving the impression
of a terror-stricken population in a state of dissolution. At
Tours the government set itself up as best it could in a number of scattered buildings and residences, with the result that
consultation and co-ordination of action became extremely
difficult. From this time on, both at Tours and later at Bordeaux, confusion became worse confounded, and it is against
this background that the events of the final week before the
surrender must be viewed.

Ambassador Bullitt decided to remain in Paris in order to
use his good offices in effecting the surrender of the capital.
This was in keeping with the American tradition established
by Washburne in 1870 and Herrick in 1914 and, as a matter
of fact, was in accord with the expressed desire of Reynaud.
President Roosevelt agreed to it and requested Bullitt to appoint Anthony Biddle, our ambassador to Poland, as his deputy. Since the President had already asked Bullitt to become

---

[26] On the defeatist clique, see especially the closing chapters of Elie J.
Bois: *The Truth about the Tragedy of France;* Pertinax: *Les Fossoyeurs,*
I, 284.

Secretary of the Navy, the ambassador's continued stay in France was not in question and it was understood that Biddle should be his successor.

Secretary Hull and other American officials felt then and have remained convinced ever since that it would have been better if Bullitt had stayed on the heels of the French government, using all possible influence to keep France in the war and in any event making sure that American interests in the French fleet and colonies were safeguarded. There can be no doubt that Bullitt, had he remained with the French government, might have exercised a real and beneficent influence. He was a man of force and courage as well as of charm, and his knowledge of French affairs was as widely recognized as his profound devotion to the French cause. No doubt he would have been able to give men like Reynaud, Mandel, Daladier, and Herriot substantial support. Whether he or any other individual could have tipped the balance in favor of continuing the war, however, is a very different question. The fact of the matter was that Bullitt at the time was confident that Reynaud would stand firm, as he had promised, and that under the circumstances his own presence would not be essential.[27]

Reynaud left Paris full of determination and brave words. The abandonment of the capital, he told Bullitt, was "not a measure taken with a view to surrender, but a measure taken with a view to prosecuting the war to the bitter end. Neither he nor any Frenchman had the slightest intention of giving up the fight." In the same spirit he sent a message to President Roosevelt apropos of the Italian declaration of war on June 10:

"This very hour another dictatorship has stabbed France in the back. . . . We shall fight in front of Paris; we shall fight behind Paris; we shall close ourselves in one of our provinces to fight, and if we should be driven out of it, we shall establish ourselves in North Africa to continue the fight and if necessary in our American possessions."

[27] Conversations with Secretary Hull and Bullitt. Comments by H. Freeman Matthews and Robert D. Murphy.

To all of which Bullitt commented with confidence: "There is no question whatsoever about Reynaud's determination and the determination of the French army to make the end of France as noble as her past." [28]

On June 11 Churchill, accompanied by Anthony Eden and Sir John Dill, arrived suddenly at Tours, evidently in order to make a last effort to keep France in the war. According to Herriot, Churchill during a private conversation broke down and wept like a child, though at the same time clenching his fists in determination.[29] To Reynaud he said that he almost hoped that the Germans would attack Britain, since that would help to stabilize the situation in France. In any event he promised to try once more to induce the war cabinet to send planes to France, and declared most unequivocally:

"Great Britain refuses to abandon the contest unless utterly crushed. If the French army is obliged to stop fighting, England will carry on in the hope that Hitler will be ruined by his very victories. With its airforce and its fleet, the British Empire can last out for years, and can impose upon Europe the most stringent of blockades." [30]

Apparently Churchill's will to resist made a strong impression on the French leaders. According to Reynaud, even Weygand was not yet ready to give up the game.[31] Only Pétain, steeped in distrust of the British, appears to have been unmoved. That evening at dinner Churchill said to him: "We had some difficult times in 1918, but we came through them. We will come through these, too." To which the marshal replied dryly: "In '18 I gave you forty divisions to save the British army. Where are your forty divisions that we need to save us now?" [32]

Despite Pétain's admiration for Reynaud's pluck, he evidently had decided that an armistice must be asked for at

[28] Tels. (June 9, 10) from Bullitt.
[29] Herriot, reported in the *New York Times*, June 12, 1945.
[30] Reynaud: "Memoirs" (*New York Times*, July 1945).
[31] *Procès du M. Pétain*, p. 15.
[32] De Gaulle's account, published by the A.P. *Washington Post*, June 22, 1945).

once.[33] It is quite possible that he persuaded Weygand of his view, for the next morning the general was thoroughly pessimistic, despite all Churchill's efforts to buck him up. Late in the afternoon the cabinet met at the Château de Cange in order to listen to Weygand's review of the situation, which was presented nervously but objectively and ended with the conclusion that the war was lost and that an armistice should be asked for. To this Reynaud reacted violently, pointing out that France was bound by her agreement of March 28 with the British, and that even if defeated in France itself, the government would still have its colonial empire and its unvanquished fleet. Pétain said nothing, but the great majority of the ministers—Mandel, Campinchi, Marin, Monnet and Chautemps—supported Reynaud's position vigorously. Marin pointed out that where the Germans had so often broken their word, it behooved France particularly to honor her own signature. Furthermore, if France gave up, that would only facilitate the Nazi conquest of Britain and the doom of all civilization. With her navy France together with Britain could still dominate the Mediterranean and North Africa.

Weygand is said to have been somewhat shaken by this formidable opposition, but he stuck to his conclusion. "You want to hold out to the end," he cried; "well, you are at the end." He reiterated his conviction that "the struggle is impossible and futile," and argued against any idea of having the government leave France. And so, after hours of debate, Reynaud agreed to consult with Churchill on the morrow and to inquire what the British attitude would be if "a" French government were to ask for an armistice.[34]

[33] Testimony of Noël, reporting remarks of Pétain on June 11 (*Procès du M. Pétain*, p. 174).

[34] A valuable source is *La Crise de l'armistice*, an unpublished, almost contemporary account by one of the chief participants, a copy of which is in the Department of State. See also Kammerer: *La Vérité sur l'armistice*, pp. 76ff., and especially the testimony in *Le Procès du M. Pétain*: by Reynaud (p. 15), Lebrun (p. 45), Marin (p. 67), and Weygand (p. 134). The contemporary writings of Jean Montigny: *Toute la vérité sur l'armistice* (1940), and Charles Reibel: *Pourquoi et comment fut décidée la demande d'armistice* (1940) also throw some light.

Soon after lunch on June 13 Reynaud, together with Mandel and General de Gaulle, conferred in a meeting of the supreme council at the prefecture of Tours with Churchill, Lord Halifax, Lord Beaverbrook, and General Spears, who had just arrived by plane. There was further discussion of France's desperate need for aid, and the British Prime Minister repeated once more that Britain would give all possible assistance. Unfortunately only a few planes would be available and only three divisions could be sent by October. Reynaud replied quite naturally that this was but slight consolation. He told Churchill of Weygand's demand for an armistice and, having pointed out that he himself would never capitulate, he put the question whether the British government would understand and stick by France if he should find it necessary to step aside in favor of a cabinet that would request an armistice. Before replying, Churchill and his companions walked around the garden for three quarters of an hour and finally reported that they would understand France's position in such an event. The Prime Minister emphasized, however, that anything he might say must not be construed as a decision of the British government, but only as the reactions of three individuals. His own opinion was that in case of disaster Britain would not lose time in bootless recrimination and that in the hour of victory France would be re-established in all her dignity and grandeur. It was agreed that Reynaud should appeal once more to President Roosevelt and that, when the reply had arrived, there should be further consultation.[35]

It must have been at this meeting that Reynaud and de Gaulle arranged with Churchill to have Britain supply shipping for the transport of 500,000 tons of war equipment to North Africa. It is said that the French Premier had instructed Weygand to send all remnants of the army and all available materiel across the Mediterranean, but nothing came of these

[35] Memo. by Biddle on the defeat of France (July 1, 1940) reporting Reynaud in somewhat confused fashion; Churchill speech June 25, 1940; Kammerer: *La Vérité sur l'armistice*, pp. 85ff., with a good deal of unverifiable detail; Jean Montigny: *Toute la vérité sur l'armistice*; and the evidence of Reynaud in *Procès du M. Pétain*, pp. 16, 147.

plans, and so little is known of them that it is impossible to evaluate them properly.[36]

So much is certain, however, that Reynaud was still determined to carry on, either from the Breton redoubt or from North Africa. He met the cabinet for a second time at the Château de Cange late that afternoon and reported his conference with Churchill. Several of the ministers were nettled because they had been kept waiting and had not themselves been given an opportunity to review the situation with their British colleagues. Others objected to Reynaud's commitment of the government against an armistice, arguing that on the previous evening it had been decided to suspend judgment. The discussion became heated but remained desultory. Weygand reported that the army was still fighting but that the military situation was rapidly deteriorating and that he could not guarantee morale for a much longer time. Again he urged that an armistice be requested, and now for the first time Marshal Pétain declared himself. He rose and read a prepared statement as follows:

"We all recognize that today the military situation is very grave. It is such that if the French government does not ask for an armistice, it is to be feared that the troops, no longer heeding the voice of their chiefs, will sink into a state of panic which would render the army incompetent to undertake even the smallest maneuver. . . . It is necessary to examine the consequences which would follow a continuation of the struggle. Assuming that we could resist if we formed a national redoubt, it is clear that the defense of this redoubt could not be organized by routed French troops, but only by fresh British divisions.

"Even if such a redoubt, established in a maritime province (i.e., Brittany) could be organized, it would not, in my opinion, constitute a guarantee of security but would expose the government to the temptation of fleeing such a precarious refuge. Now, it is impossible for the government, without emigrating or deserting, to abandon French territory.

"It is the duty of the government, whatever may happen, to

[36] Pierre Tissier: *Le Procès de Riom,* pp. 163ff.; de Gaulle's account (*Washington Post,* June 22, 1945).

remain in the country, on pain of no longer being recognized as the government. To deprive France of her natural defenders during a period of general confusion means to deliver her to the enemy, means to kill the soul of France, which means further to render her revival impossible.

"The renewal of France must be expected from the soul of the country itself, which we shall preserve by staying where we are, rather than from a reconquest of our territory by Allied guns, under conditions and after a lapse of time which we cannot foresee.

"I am therefore of the opinion that we should not abandon French soil but that we should accept the trials which will come over the country and its sons. The revival of France will be the fruit of this suffering.

"So the question before us at the moment is not whether the French government should or should not ask for an armistice, but rather whether the French government should ask for an armistice or agree to leave Metropolitan France.

"I declare that, so far as I am concerned, even outside the government, if necessary, I shall refuse to leave France. I shall remain among the French people to share its tribulations and misery.

"An armistice is, in my view, the necessary condition for the survival of eternal France." [37]

This declaration widened the scope of the argument, for Pétain struck at the very foundation of Reynaud's plan: namely, to continue the struggle from North Africa. The ensuing debate revealed that most of the ministers were still opposed to an armistice and favored withdrawal to Brittany, which Reynaud described as "a hand extended towards America." But Weygand insisted that Brittany could not be held for more than a few days, whereupon attention turned more and more to North Africa. The general raised objections to this course also, repeating Pétain's queries: would France ever accept such desertion by the government; would France not fall a prey, in her misery and ruin, to complete disintegration and sovietization? Pétain chimed in once more that France

[37] The text is printed in Laure: *Pétain*, pp. 432–3, and is reprinted by Kammerer: *La Vérité sur l'armistice*, appendix XIII.

would never tolerate a government of émigrés. And so the dispute continued until midnight.[38]

The issue was now fully joined, though it had been decided that the government should move next day to Bordeaux and come to a decision there. Reynaud, however, was deeply discouraged and appears to have concluded that he would have to get rid of Pétain and Weygand or else himself give way to a new government "to make peace on the best possible terms and at the same time be able to prevent revolution throughout the country." But decision on this vital matter he also postponed until the following day. In the meanwhile he drafted his message to President Roosevelt, setting forth the desperate plight of France and raising the issue of a possible armistice:

"At the most tragic hour of its history France must choose.

"Will she continue to sacrifice her youth in a hopeless struggle?

"Will her Government leave the national territory so as not to give itself up to the enemy and in order to be able to continue the struggle on the sea and in North Africa? Will the whole country then live abandoned, abating itself under the shadow of Nazi domination with all that that means for its body and its soul?

"Or will France ask Hitler for conditions of an armistice?

"We can choose the first way, that of resistance, only if a chance of victory appears in the distance and if a light shines at the end of the tunnel.

"In the present situation, in spite of the weakening of the enemy's forces due to the sacrifice of the French army, the defeat of England, our loyal ally, left to her own resources, appears possible if not probable.

"From that time on France can continue the struggle only if American intervention reverses the situation by making an Allied victory certain.

"The only chance of saving the French nation, vanguard of democracies, and through her to save England, by whose side France could then remain, with her powerful navy, is to throw into the balance, this very day, the weight of American power.

[38] MS.: *La Crise de l'armistice* and the full account in Reibel: *Pourquoi et comment fût decidée la demande d'armistice;* Kammerer: *La Vérité sur l'armistice,* pp. 85ff.; and the valuable testimony of Reynaud, Lebrun, and Weygand in *Procès du M. Pétain,* pp. 16, 46, 135, 147.

"It is the only chance also of keeping Hitler, after he has destroyed France and then England, from attacking America, thus renewing the fight of the Horatii against the three Curiatii.

"I know that the declaration of war does not depend on you alone.

"But I must tell you at this hour, as grave in our history as in yours, that if you cannot give to France in the hours to come the certainty that the United States will come into the war within a very short time, the fate of the world will change. Then you will see France go under like a drowning man and disappear after having cast a last look towards the land of liberty from which she awaited salvation." [39]

Biddle had an opportunity to speak with Reynaud on the morning of June 14, before the Prime Minister set out for Bordeaux. Reynaud was most depressed and was anxiously awaiting a reply from President Roosevelt. The hope of France, he declared, now depended on the response of America:

"Immediate declaration of war by the United States is only hope for England and for France if she is to continue to fight in North Africa," cabled Biddle. "The French army is cut to pieces and at meeting of Council of Ministers on June 13 Reynaud obtained only with great difficulty the Government's consent to continue the struggle. It was clear to me that in the absence of some positive action by us within the next 48 hours the French Government will feel that there is no course left but surrender." [40]

In this mood of black despair the Prime Minister and the government set out for Bordeaux, picking their way through the unspeakable confusion of the road, jammed as it was with thousands of frantic refugees fleeing from the advancing enemy. One story has it that Reynaud feared that when he was recognized he would be hooted and reviled for his insistence on continuance of the struggle. Actually and to his immense surprise and relief he was cheered as the champion of resistance. It is quite possible that this popular acclaim from

[39] The text is given in *Peace and War*, No. 168; see further the Biddle memo. and the testimony of Reynaud in *Procès du M. Pétain*, pp. 15, 16.

[40] Tel. (June 14) from Biddle.

those who were the chief sufferers may have influenced the Prime Minister to hold out a bit longer.[41]

The government did not arrive at Bordeaux until late in the afternoon of June 14, and on its arrival had to spend some time in getting settled in its scattered lodgings and offices. During the evening and the ensuing morning Reynaud apparently discussed the situation with the British ambassador and with Herriot and Jeanneney. Regarding these conferences, however, we have only the vaguest indications. Our narrative must therefore be advanced to the afternoon of June 15. During the morning President Roosevelt's reply to Reynaud's appeal had come in. It was, of necessity, disappointing, although it was as positive and reassuring as the President, in the circumstances, could make it:

"I wish to reiterate in the most emphatic terms that, making every possible effort under present conditions, the Government of the United States has made it possible for the Allied armies to obtain during the weeks that have just passed airplanes, artillery, and munitions of many kinds and that this Government, so long as the Allied governments continue to resist, will redouble its efforts in this direction. I believe it is possible to say that every week that goes by will see additional materiel on its way to the allied nations.

"In accordance with its policy not to recognize the results of conquest of territory acquired through military aggression, the Government of the United States will not consider as valid any attempts to infringe by force the independence and territorial integrity of France.

"In these hours which are so heart-rending for the French people and yourself, I send you the assurances of my utmost sympathy and I can further assure you that so long as the French people continue in defense of their liberty, which constitutes the cause of popular institutions throughout the world, so long will they rest assured that materiel and supplies will be sent to them from the United States in ever-increasing quantities and kinds.

"I know that you will understand that these statements carry

[41] Alexis Leger, who told me this story, says that he had it from Reynaud's secretary.

with them no implication of military commitments. Only the Congress can make such commitments." [42]

What effect this message may have had on Reynaud we do not know, but on the afternoon of June 15 he submitted to Weygand, who had only just arrived in Bordeaux, an entirely new proposition: the army should simply capitulate, without terms, so that the government could continue to function untrammeled in North Africa or elsewhere. Weygand rejected this suggestion out of hand, as being dishonorable for the army and for France. Reynaud's arguments, that the Norwegians, Dutch, and Belgians had followed this course and that, if necessary, the French government would give the generalissimo instructions to capitulate, all fell flat. Weygand was absolutely adamant on this point, and the two men parted in a huff after a brief discussion.

Immediately after this exchange the cabinet assembled at four p.m. From the welter of fragmentary evidence we can deduce about this much: that Reynaud read the President's message, which was evidently but slight consolation in the hour of doom. Weygand and Darlan were called in and there was renewed discussion of an armistice. Reynaud again declared for observance of France's obligations to Britain and probably in this connection expounded his proposal that the French simply issue a "cease fire" order and at the same time withdraw to North Africa. According to his own account, even Marshal Pétain was won over to this idea and left the room to persuade Weygand, who had in the meanwhile been excused. Reynaud claims that Pétain returned in fifteen minutes, having failed entirely to move the generalissimo. Neither Weygand nor Pétain could in 1945 recall this episode, but it matters little, for, according to Weygand's own statement, neither Pétain nor any human power could have induced him to accede.

The argument therefore reduced itself once more to the alternatives: request an armistice or flee to North Africa,

[42] *Peace and War*, No. 169.

leaving Metropolitan France to its fate. The American ambassador very aptly summed up the arguments on both sides:

"Those that advocate surrender stress the very real likelihood of uprising of an enraged people against the masters, both political and industrial, who have so criminally betrayed and deceived them: the innocent will suffer with the guilty and much blood will flow. They also point to German vengeance which will be wreaked on France for continuance of the struggle from Africa and loss of the uncaptured fleet. They question the morale of a French evacuated army in Africa whose families are left to Nazi rule.

"Those who urge removal of the government to North Africa foresee that only thus can a free and independent France survive; that only thus can the symbol of a living France be maintained; that only thus can the French fleet be kept afloat for the democracies." [43]

Finally Chautemps broke the deadlock with a classic example of political compromise. Not challenging the prevailing sentiment for transfer of the government to North Africa, he pointed out that the French army and people, abandoned to the victorious Nazis, might be massacred like rabbits in their warrens. If this were necessary, the government at least owed it to the country to demonstrate the fact. He therefore proposed that the Germans be asked what the terms of an armistice would be. The terms would undoubtedly be unacceptable—outrageously unacceptable—and the country, roused to indignation and resistance, would understand the heroic flight of the government. Reynaud at once opposed this suggestion, and threatened to resign when a majority of the ministers showed themselves favorable. Evidently a number of them (thirteen out of nineteen, according to Reynaud) saw in the proposal a way of circumventing France's obligation to Britain and at the same time a chance of reconciling the differences between the factions. Reynaud finally agreed to remain and accepted the Chautemps proposal on condition

[43] Tel. (June 16) from Biddle.

that the British be asked to concur in this new move. Therewith the council adjourned at about eight p.m.[44]

It is extremely difficult to evaluate the proposition advanced by Chautemps and to determine Reynaud's attitude toward it. In his testimony at the Pétain trial the former Prime Minister took the line that the whole thing was a cleverly devised subterfuge, intended to prepare the way for surrender. Chautemps denied this charge vigorously and put the blame on Reynaud's weakness:

"I affirm again," he wrote in 1945, "that in view of the unequal clash of wills which was opposing (i.e., bringing into opposition) Reynaud and Weygand, I only tried in good faith to find a way out of the dead end into which Reynaud's weakness had put us." [45]

In consonance with this view, Blum testified at the Pétain trial that most of the ministers welcomed the Chautemps proposal as a possible solution of a hopeless impasse and that they took it at face value. Indeed, Blum maintained that for several days many members of the government continued to believe that Marshal Pétain, on his advent to power, had asked the Germans not for an armistice, but only for the terms of a possible armistice. Blum was convinced that Chautemps was himself under this misapprehension and that he was among those who intended to go to North Africa if the German conditions proved unacceptable[46]

This is an aspect of the problem to which we shall have to revert in the next chapter, though it may be said here and now that at bottom the Chautemps proposal added nothing new. After all, any request for an armistice, in contradistinction to unconditional surrender, implies an inquiry regarding the terms, which may be accepted or rejected. As a matter of

[44] See the detailed account in Kammerer: *La Vérité sur l'armistice*, pp. 109ff., which must, however, be supplemented and corrected in the light of the testimony offered at the Pétain trial. See *Procès du M. Pétain*, pp. 116–18, 147 (Reynaud); 46 (Lebrun); 65–6, 71 (Marin); 76 (Blum); 135–7 (Weygand).

[45] Chautemps's letter to the *New York Times* (August 16, 1945). Conversation with Chautemps (May 1946).

[46] *Procès du M. Pétain*, p. 76 (testimony of Blum).

cold fact, even the so-called "unconditional surrenders" of Italy, Germany, and Japan were based upon conditions, the only real difference being that those powers more or less agreed in advance to accept the conditions laid down by the victor. That was not the case with France in 1940. As we shall see, what Pétain actually did was to follow the Chautemps procedure. The only problem that remains to be answered is whether he was determined from the outset to accept the German terms or whether he kept open the door to some other course.

As for Reynaud, it is almost impossible to say where he stood. In his letters from captivity to Pétain and more recently in his memoirs and in his testimony at the Pétain trial he has been much more vociferous than any of the other participants and has made a strenuous, consistent effort to establish his own particular version. According to this, he was the champion of loyalty to France's treaty obligations, of resistance to the finish, if need be of capitulation of the armies in the field and of transfer of the government to North Africa. The question has often been asked why, when confronted with the demand of Weygand and Pétain for an armistice, he did not drop these men from their commanding positions and remake his cabinet into a truly united government of resistance. His answer is that he considered this seriously but that he concluded that such a move would have been a fatal blow at national morale. Yet instead of rallying his supporters in the cabinet, he threatened to resign himself, which certainly meant leaving the field free for his opponents. The truth is that in these final days he seems to have been unnerved and shaken. He may have half-accepted the Chautemps proposal in the thought that the British would refuse to concur in it. The curious thing is that on leaving the meeting of the council he went up to Weygand and again attempted to insist on simple capitulation of the army. Only a most ingenious and imaginative historian could reconstruct a logical pattern from all this, the more so when one considers that towards midnight of this same exciting day Reynaud spoke to the American ambassador as though he were all in favor of the Chautemps proposal:

"Only by such a move could he show the French people, who have been kept in utter ignorance of the real gravity of the military situation, the severity of the German terms and justify a flight of the government to Africa or England. 'I only hope they won't be too moderate,' he added." [47]

Reynaud at once submitted the Chautemps proposal to the British. Neither Sir Ronald Campbell nor the American representatives were well impressed with this new turn of events. H. Freeman Matthews, the first secretary of the United States Embassy and the most experienced observer on the American side, saw Reynaud three or four times a day at Bordeaux and had grave doubts whether any human being could have succeeded in generating enough courage and energy in the crumbling morale of the French authorities to keep up the fight. It is his considered opinion that Reynaud simply caved in under the strain and under the constant defeatist pressure of his own immediate circle. Mme de Portes was hanging on his coat-tails and begging him to surrender. She even went so far as to look up Matthews and spend an hour in his office weeping bitterly in her efforts to get him to bring pressure on the Prime Minister. Though she knew full well that the United States government was doing its utmost to strengthen the forces of resistance, she was so panic-stricken that she could leave no stone unturned in her efforts to attain her end. [48]

Realizing that the game was almost up, the American ambassador at once reopened the question of the future disposition of the powerful French fleet. He was told at once, though, that the question had been discussed in the cabinet (June 16) and that after a real battle Reynaud had secured the approval of the government not to surrender the fleet at

[47] Tel. (June 16) from Biddle. See further *Procès du M. Pétain*, p. 15 (Reynaud); p. 136 (Weygand).
[48] Comments by Matthews, supported by an interesting manuscript that he wrote in August 1940.

any cost. This statement was confirmed by both Mandel and Campinchi. It seems fairly certain that Admiral Darlan was taking a strong stand on this issue and that, indeed, he was disposed to depart at once with the fleet if an armistice was decided on. Though the evidence is very scanty, it appears that instructions of some sort were sent to the fleet even at this time, the general tenor being that there should be no surrender.[49]

We come now to June 16, the last day of the Reynaud government and the eve of the surrender. Bordeaux was seething with refugees and the government was operating in veritable chaos, scattered about the town and in constant threat of German air attack. The entire atmosphere was one of confusion, hopelessness, and terror, which certainly reacted on those responsible for France's fate. At the Hôtel de Ville Laval was gathering about him a group of politicians who were soon to become the shock troops of the defeatists. On the other hand Herriot and Jeanneney, the presidents respectively of the Chamber of Deputies and of the Senate, were using all their influence to support Reynaud and a policy of resistance from North Africa. These two gentlemen appeared at a session of the cabinet on the morning of June 16 and gave the required authorization for Reynaud's plan. But the only result of the meeting was that Pétain rose and read his resignation in protest against the continued delay in requesting an armistice. He was finally persuaded to withdraw his resignation and await the reply of the British government to Reynaud's inquiry of the preceding night.

The British cabinet was in session during the morning and by noon had worked out a program with respect to the French situation. This was set forth in a telegram that reached Bordeaux in the afternoon:

"On condition, but only on condition that the French fleet shall be directed at once to British ports pending negotiations,

[49] *Procès du M. Pétain*, p. 19 (Reynaud's testimony); p. 115 (Herriot's testimony, account of his conversation with Darlan on June 15); tels. (June 16, 18) from Biddle.

the Government of His Majesty gives its full consent to an inquiry by the French Government with a view to finding out the conditions for an armistice. His Majesty's Government being determined to continue the war, will abstain completely from any part in this inquiry concerning an armistice."

This message was followed a couple of hours later by a second one supplementing the first:

"We expect to be consulted as soon as the conditions for an armistice shall have been received. This is necessary not merely in virtue of the treaty forbidding separate peace or armistice, but also in view of the vital consequence of any armistice to ourselves, having regard specially to the fact that British troops are fighting with the French army.

"You should impress on the French Government that in stipulating for the removal of the French fleet to British ports, we have in mind French interests as well as our own, and are convinced that it will strengthen the hands of the French Government in any armistice discussions if they can show that the French Navy is out of reach of the German forces.

"As regards the French airforce, we assume that every effort will be made to fly it to North Africa, unless indeed the French Government would prefer to send it to this country." [50]

The exact sequence of events is not at all clear at this juncture. Apparently Sir Ronald Campbell did not leave copies of these messages with Reynaud, or if he did, they were withdrawn at once. If Reynaud is to be believed, he communicated the substance of the British reply to the council. No doubt there was some discussion, in the course of which Pétain evidently agreed that the fleet must under no circumstances be allowed to pass into the enemy's hands, but at the same time opposed its being sent to England. Reynaud claims that under the circumstances he was obliged to report negatively to the British ambassador, who thereupon withdrew the con-

[50] The full texts, in French translation, are given in Kammerer: *La Vérité sur l'armistice*, pp. 130-1. A telescoped summary was given by Churchill in his speech of June 25, 1940.

sent of the British to the Chautemps proposal. On the other hand, Sir Ronald Campbell is reported to have stated that these messages were superseded by the famous British offer of an integral union with France.[51]

The British proposal for union was telephoned from London in the afternoon by General de Gaulle, who appears to have inspired Churchill with the idea. It provided for the setting up of a single war cabinet to control all the forces of both nations for the duration of the conflict. We may assume, I think, that the proposal was intended to end, once and for all, talk of British intentions to give in and to strengthen French confidence in British aid. At the same time it involved an oblique arrangement by which French naval forces would be consolidated with the British.

Reynaud at once submitted the British offer to the council of ministers, where, however, it met with a very cool reception. Pétain declared it just another device to postpone or prevent an armistice, while Chautemps opined that it would make France into just another dominion. The matter was not at all carefully considered or analyzed, but was put aside with a few offhand comments. Looking backward, we can see that the moment was hardly opportune for such a far-reaching, long-term arrangement. The fact was that in a matter of hours the French government had to decide whether to sue for an armistice or not.

Ambassador Biddle, who saw Reynaud just after the cabinet meeting of the afternoon, found him very fatigued and despondent. The Premier described the situation as "heart-rending" and reported the pressure for an armistice to be very strong. In view of his pledge to the British, he felt that he could not himself ask for an armistice. It was clear to the Americans that he had made up his mind to resign. "If ever a confident, courageous little man lost his nerve, it was Reynaud," commented one of them later. "He turned literally

[51] *Procès du M. Pétain*, pp. 16, 27 (Reynaud); 46 (Lebrun); 81 (Charles-Roux).

ashen gray in panic and you would never have known him to be the same man of two weeks earlier." [52]

At the evening meeting of the council (eight p.m.) Reynaud did in fact resign and recommended to President Lebrun that Pétain be asked to form a new government. Lebrun tried in vain to persuade him to form a new cabinet of resistance, and Herriot and Jeanneney, when consulted by the President, also urged that Reynaud continue as head of the government. But since Reynaud refused, Lebrun turned to Pétain, who at once produced a ready-made list of his proposed colleagues. This has often been quoted as irrefutable proof of long-cherished designs, but the marshal himself roundly declared later that even though he had a list, it was not a list of the men who actually joined his government. At any rate, before the day was out the new cabinet was in power, with Chautemps as Vice-Premier, Weygand as Minister of National Defense, Darlan as Minister of Marine, and Baudoin as Foreign Minister. Laval was originally slated for the all-important Foreign Office, but his name was withdrawn at the urgent pleading of Charles-Roux, who pointed out that the appointment of Laval to that position would be tantamount to a direct provocation of England. Since Laval refused the Ministry of Justice, he was omitted altogether for the time being. [53]

The resignation of Reynaud is certainly one of the most curious episodes in the entire confused story of these hectic days. It has been asserted over and over again that a majority of the ministers would still have supported him and that if a vote had been taken the sentiment would have been against asking for an armistice and in favor of continuing the fight from North Africa. Efforts have been made to establish the position of the various ministers at that time, and these lead to the conclusion that the vote would have stood at about fifteen against an armistice and eleven in favor of one. If the

[52] Tel. (June 16, nine p.m.) from Biddle.
[53] Kammerer: *La Vérité sur l'armistice*, pp. 136ff.; *Procès du M. Pétain*, p. 19 (Reynaud); pp. 46–7 (Lebrun); p. 51 (Pétain); p. 82 (Charles-Roux); pp. 111, 115 (Herriot); p. 135 (Weygand); pp. 186, 187, 191 (Laval).

President of the Republic, the Presidents of the chambers, and other leading and political figures were reckoned in, the line-up would have been about eighteen to thirteen. As between the eight chief figures in the cabinet, it would have been five to three.[54]

These calculations are probably beside the point, partly because, later on, very few ministers were ready to admit their position on that fateful day, but chiefly because the issue was completely beclouded by the Chautemps proposal. One might easily claim to have been opposed to an armistice but willing to ask what the terms of such an armistice would be, only to reject them when they became known. The real problem for us is to explain Reynaud's decision and to establish his motives. One can argue that he simply caved in and gave up the struggle. But why, then, did he recommend Pétain as his successor, knowing full well that a Pétain government would ask for an armistice? Reynaud himself insists that he was honor-bound to respect France's obligations to Britain and that he could not govern unless it were agreed that the government move at once to North Africa (presumably leaving the army to capitulate, but taking the fleet with it). He explains furthermore that, since Pétain had agreed that the fleet should never be surrendered and since the enemy would undoubtedly demand such a surrender, the marshal would have to reject the German terms and Reynaud would then be called on to form a new government of resistance.

All this is very refined but far from convincing. The explanation of American observers was simpler and more plausible. Biddle saw Reynaud just after his resignation and found that he was calm and entirely himself again. It seemed fairly plain that the Prime Minister had simply suffered a moral collapse and that, unable to carry the burden any longer, he had preferred to shunt the responsibility to his opponents. The situation was hopeless and an armistice was

---

[54] These are the conclusions of Kammerer: *La Vérité sur l'armistice*, p. 154. See also the debates at the Pétain trial on this subject: *Procès du M. Pétain*, p. 47 (Lebrun); p. 69 (Marin); pp. 70-2 (Reynaud).

probably the easiest way out. Pétain would at once request one—that was a foregone conclusion that Reynaud himself recognized. But if the die was to be cast, Pétain was probably the best man to do it:

"It was generally acknowledged among unofficial as well as official circles," wrote the American ambassador a bit later, "that Marshal Pétain had been chosen as chief of the succeeding government, in that he was considered the only man who could lead the people into acceptance of what was expected to be stiff armistice terms and at the same time prevent revolution." [55]

Be all this as it may, the new Pétain government at once decided to ask for the terms of an armistice and in the middle of the night the Spanish ambassador, Señor de Lequerica, was summoned and requested to inquire of the Germans, through Madrid, on what terms they would agree to end hostilities. A bit later the papal nuncio was invited to make similar inquiries of the Italian government.[56]

[55] Tel. (June 16, midnight) from Biddle; memo. by Biddle (July 1, 1940). Reynaud's defense is set forth in *Procès du M. Pétain*, pp. 19, 70, 72.
[56] The details in Kammerer: *La Vérité sur l'armistice*, pp. 169ff.

CHAPTER II

The Armistice

W<small>HEN</small> Pétain and Weygand called in the Spanish ambassador and asked him to ascertain the German conditions
for granting an armistice, they were officially implementing
the Chautemps proposal of June 15. The new Foreign Minister, Baudoin, explained this to Biddle at midnight of June
16. The French army, he said, was "completely smashed"
and it was imperative that an end of the slaughter be sought.
However, if the German terms were to prove "unworthy of
the honor and dignity of France," they would be made public
and their inacceptability would be made manifest to the
French people. This would give them courage to continue
the "moral struggle."

"As to the fleet," reported the ambassador, "he assured me
formally that it would never be surrendered to Germany; as
guarantee Admiral Darlan, whose views he said are well known
on this subject, had been named Minister of Marine."[1]

In a note dated June 17, which was submitted to the Department of State by the French ambassador, the same idea was
expressed in even more positive and forceful terms:

"The French Government is resolved not to yield to any condition contrary to national honor, dignity or independence. If, in
reply to the overtures made to Germany, inacceptable demands
should be returned, it is with fierce resolution that the whole
country, preferring to suffer what it could not accept, would
continue the struggle on bases in the French Empire until the day
when the common effort of all free peoples would lead to its
liberation."[2]

[1] Tel. (June 17, two a.m.) from Biddle. A similar statement was made to
the British ambassador (*Procès du M. Pétain,* p. 82, testimony of Charles-
Roux).

[2] Sumner Welles: memo. of conversation with Count de Saint-Quentin
(June 18, 1940).

Assuming that these statements reflected the understanding of most of the members of the government and of political circles generally, it must be recalled that Pétain and Weygand had at least made it perfectly clear from the outset that they would not leave France under any circumstances. Just what they planned to do if the Germans were to demand surrender of the fleet or were to lay down other terms incompatible with French dignity or honor it is impossible to say. It does seem, however, that they believed that an honorable agreement would be possible as between soldiers and that in any event the effort must be made in view of the hopeless situation at the front. As for France's obligation to Britain and the effect of an armistice on Britain's fate, these matters counted for little with the marshal and the generalissimo. They were convinced that Britain had left France in the lurch and that consequently France owed her ally little if anything. In any case, they were not prepared to sacrifice the national future for the sake of British interests, the more so as they were firmly convinced that in a matter of weeks the British too would be compelled to yield. Weygand later denied with some vehemence that he had ever used the phrase: "In three weeks England will have her head twisted off like a chicken's," but even if he did not use these words, they probably express his opinion accurately enough. Darlan generously gave Britain five weeks more, but in general there was agreement that the Germans would give the British short shrift. No doubt this is one reason, and a very good one, why the French cabinet refused to send the fleet to England. After all, the undefeated fleet was France's best bargaining point with Hitler. Why throw away one's best card so that someone else might play it.[3]

From the standpoint of Britain and the United States, of course, it became a matter of desperate urgency to prevent

---

[3] Tel. (July 1) from Bullitt, reporting his conversations with Pétain and Darlan. Weygand's denial in *Procès du M. Pétain*, p. 139. See also *La Crise de l'armistice;* Pertinax: *Les Fossoyeurs*, I, 325, II, 39; Raymond Brugère: *Veni, Vidi, Vichy* (Paris, 1944), p. 46, reporting statements of Baudoin.

the surrender of the fleet and of the Empire as soon as it
became clear that the French government was determined to
give up the struggle. From the very outset the American representatives at Bordeaux were deeply troubled. Baudoin's assurances regarding the fleet fell far short of the British proposal that the navy seek refuge in British ports, and Darlan's
appointment, too, proved nothing: "His appointment to the
post I feel largely for the purpose of reassuring the British
and ourselves," cabled the United States ambassador. "The
Admiral's new government associates hardly inspire complete
confidence that the French fleet will remain a bulwark against
Nazi aggression." [4]

It would be impossible to overstate the crucial importance
of this issue for the future security of Britain and the United
States. It must be recalled that the French navy was the second
in Europe, that it was unscathed and ready for anything. If
leagued with the British navy, it could play an important role
in the invasion of England, which everyone expected. It
could also help to keep open the sea lanes from the United
States, neutralize the Italian fleet in the Mediterranean, and
protect the French colonies in Africa and elsewhere. Cor-
respondingly disastrous for the British cause and therefore to
the American interest would be the acquisition of French
naval forces by the Germans. [5]

Both the British and the United States governments therefore made hectic efforts to hold the new French government
in line. Churchill renewed his attempts, through the French
ambassador in London, to have the fleet sent to English ports,
and Sir Ronald Campbell did likewise at Bordeaux in conversation first with Baudoin and then with Pétain. The
marshal's reply was that he would prefer to sink the fleet.
Evidently the situation was extremely dangerous, so the British Prime Minister sent off on special mission to Bordeaux
M. A. V. Alexander, the First Lord of the Admiralty, Admiral

[4] Tel. (June 17) from Biddle.
[5] See especially Sumner Welles: *The Time for Decision,* p. 155.

Sir Dudley Pound, the First Sea Lord, and Lord Lloyd, the Secretary for the Colonies.[6]

No less energetic was the American government. On June 17 the Senate passed a stiff resolution refusing to recognize any transfers of territory in the Western Hemisphere from one non-American power to another. Berlin and Rome were at once notified of this policy. On the afternoon of the very same day Secretary Hull sent a message to Ambassador Biddle as follows:

"The President desires that you obtain immediately an interview with Admiral Darlan and subsequently, if possible, with the Minister for Foreign Affairs, and state that the views of this Government with regard to the disposition of the French Fleet have been made very clear to the French Government on previous occasions. The President desires you to say that in the opinion of this Government, should the French Government, before concluding any armistice with the Germans, fail to see that the fleet is kept out of the hands of her opponents, the French Government will be purusing a policy which will fatally impair the preservation of the French Empire and the eventual restoration of French independence and autonomy. Furthermore, should the French Government fail to take these steps and permit the French Fleet to be surrendered to Germany, the French Government will permanently lose the friendship and goodwill of the Government of the United States." [7]

This message, couched in the strongest possible terms, was handed to Darlan as he was on his way to a cabinet meeting on June 18. Furthermore, the American representatives had Baudoin called out of the meeting so that he might be given a copy. The Foreign Minister was much irritated and nettled by the stiffness of the note, but evidently laid it before the council at once. The result was a definite decision by the government that the fleet should under no circumstances be turned over to the Germans and that if surrender were part

---

[6] Pertinax: *Les Fossoyeurs*, II, 149ff.; *Procès du M. Pétain*, pp. 82–3 (Charles-Roux).

[7] Tel. (June 17) to Biddle, reprinted in *Peace and War*, No. 170.

of the German terms, the armistice should be rejected. This decision was at once communicated by Baudoin to Biddle and Sir Ronald Campbell:

"He (Baudoin) wished to assure me," reported the ambassador, "in the name of the Government in the most solemn manner that the French Fleet would never be surrendered to the enemy: 'La question ne se pose pas. . . .' Baudoin added that he could not, however, say that the French Fleet would join the British Fleet; it might be sent overseas or it might be sunk. That question is now before the Council of Ministers. I urged with all possible emphasis that the fleet be moved to safety rather than destroyed." [8]

In amplification of this decision a conference was held on June 19 between Alexander and Admiral Sir Dudley Pound on the one side and Admiral Darlan and Admiral Auphand on the other. On this occasion Darlan gave his oath that the fleet would not be allowed to fall into the hands of the enemy and that an armistice would be rejected if the Germans made such a demand. If later the Germans should attempt to seize any ship of the fleet, that ship would be scuttled by the French. In view of these very positive and solemn assurances, the British negotiators seem to have dropped their demand that the fleet be sent to British ports. They returned home that same day, apparently satisfied that the immediate danger was over. [9]

Before pursuing further the development of affairs at Bordeaux, let us consider the other side of the problem, the aims and objectives of Hitler and his overeager ally, Mussolini. Captured documents and prisoner interrogations now make it possible to speak with some assurance on these matters.

The French request for armistice terms reached Hitler at his headquarters in the vicinity of Sedan. Before arriving at

[8] Tel. (June 18) from Biddle; reprinted in *Peace and War*, No. 171. See also Lebrun's account in *Procès du M. Pétain*, pp. 47, 54.

[9] Biddle memo. (July 1, 1940); Admiral Auphand's account, as reported by Noël Pinelli and Archambaud (*Procès du M. Pétain*, pp. 230, 279, 282). Pertinax: *Les Fossoyeurs*, II, 149ff., evidently relying on some British source, maintains that Darlan promised that in an emergency the fleet would go "to the ports of a friendly power."

any decision, the Führer arranged for a meeting with Mussolini, who was hastily invited to Munich. There the two men, accompanied by their foreign ministers and military advisers, conferred on June 18. It was not until June 19 that the French government was invited to send an armistice commission to receive the terms. The French delegation did not actually set out until June 21, on which day the German conditions were presented in the historic railway car in the forest of Compiègne.

During the years preceding the war Hitler's great objective in foreign policy had been to arrive at an agreement with Britain that would leave him a free hand in the east. In his calculations France had played a very subordinate role. Economic relations between the two countries had been fairly close and quite extensive, and Hitler had a rather high opinion of France's cultural achievement and future cultural mission. But the France of Popular Front days presented a pretty sorry picture on the political side, and Hitler appears to have rated the French army much lower than did many of his generals. None the less, it is fairly certain that the German victory over France came much more quickly than even Hitler expected and that the request for an armistice caught the Führer unprepared. Ribbentrop, who on the whole is an unreliable witness, is probably right in saying that his master rarely had definite, long-range plans and that he relied largely upon intuition and inspirations that came to him in his sleep. So it appears to have been on this occasion. Hitler's interest in France was decidedly limited and his interest in the French colonial possessions was exceedingly slight. His main thought was of Britain and his great hope was to arrive at an agreement with Britain, if possible without further military operations. In general, then, his aim was of necessity not to antagonize the French to the extent of driving them into closer relations and co-operation with Britain.[10]

Mussolini, on the other hand, was quite devoid of all finesse.

[10] State Department: *Special Interrogation Mission*: interrogations of Ribbentrop, Neurath, General Walter Warlimont, and Dr. Paul Schmidt.

Although his troops had gained no glory in the one-week war
against France, the Duce found himself on the winning side
and he proposed to get not only his due but everything he
could lay his hands on. En route to Munich he therefore approved a program that his subordinates had drafted for him.
This provided for the demobilization of France and the surrender of all armaments; Italian occupation of all France east
of the Rhone, and also of Corsica, Tunisia, and French
Somaliland; furthermore, occupation, whenever necessary, of
any strategic points in France, in the French colonies, or in
the French mandates, particularly of naval bases at Algiers,
Oran, and Casablanca; finally, surrender of the French fleet
and the French air force.[11]

These plans were brushed aside by Hitler, who explained
his hopes for an early peace with Britain and his desire not
to antagonize the French too much. If France refused his
terms, he said, the German armies could be at the Pyrenees in
two weeks. But politically it would be unwise to occupy all
France, "in order not to favor the establishment of a French
government in England or elsewhere. It would be better to
permit the existence of a French government *in France*,
which would be the sole responsible one." Germany therefore
proposed to occupy northern France as far as the Loire, as
well as a coastal strip on the Atlantic south as far as Spain and
another strip in the east to the borders of Switzerland:

"With regard to the French fleet the Führer said that the best
thing that could happen would be to have the French sink it.
The worst thing would be to have the fleet unite with the British,
because, in view of the larger number of light French ships, the
united British-French fleets could organize extensive convoys.
That being so, Britain could supply herself without difficulty and
could transport (from the mother country, from Canada, from
India, etc.) large forces to all sorts of places (from Egypt to
Portugal), thus maintaining or creating a series of theaters of

[11] Unpublished *Graziani Papers*, general staff paper, June 18, 1940; see
also *Ciano Diary*, entry for June 17, 1940.

operation. The result would be a long war and the impossibility of striking the enemy decisively ('I prefer for the long run a compact and collected enemy, such as France was, which I can tackle and defeat, rather than enemies who are weaker but are scattered here and there.') That being so, it would not be well to demand purely and simply that the French surrender their fleet. France will not agree to that and, as against the very slight probability that the French may sink the fleet, there would be the much greater probability that they would send it to join the British fleet. It will be better, therefore, to demand that they assemble the fleet in such a way that it cannot be moved or dispersed, either in French ports under control or in neutral ports (preferably Spanish). Furthermore, it seems wise to leave France the hope of regaining her fleet once peace has been made. Once England has been defeated and we come to the making of the peace, we shall see." [12]

Mussolini did not like this approach, but having known in advance that he could not hope for much consideration, he yielded without much argument, the more so as Ribbentrop dangled before the Italians tempting bait for the future: when the peace came Germany would probably take Alsace, the Briey ironfields, part of Belgium, the former German colonies, the Congo, and the principal ports of Norway; Spain should have French Morocco, excepting the Atlantic ports, which would go to Germany; and Italy should have Nice, Corsica, Algeria, Tunisia, Jibuti, and British Somaliland, with a strip to connect Libya with Ethiopia; both sides of the Strait of Gibraltar should be neutralized and Egypt should become an "ally" of Italy. [13]

While Hitler was laying out his program and "conferring" with his Italian colleague, there were several days of painful suspense at Bordeaux. It was not until the morning of June 19 that any message at all came from the Germans, and that message was merely an instruction to name delegates for the

[12] Italian staff report, June 18, 1940 (*Graziani Papers*).
[13] Italian staff paper, June 19, 1940 (*Graziani Papers*); *Ciano Diary*, entries for June 18, 19, 1940.

armistice meeting, the time and place of which were to be notified later.[14] In the meanwhile all was uncertainty, and in the midst of this uncertainty the party of resistance, momentarily stunned by the events of June 16–17, began to take heart again. After all, the "patriot" group comprised many of the most influential men—Daladier, Mandel, Campinchi, Marin, Herriot, and Jeanneney. It must not be forgotten, either, that the consensus of opinion in this group had been that the German terms would be unacceptable. Once that fact had been established, it was generally agreed that the government should move to North Africa and continue the struggle.

On the morning of June 18 Herriot sent a note to President Lebrun in which he protested against the whole idea of an armistice:

> "To make a separate peace is to tear up our solemn agreements with Great Britain and Poland, to compromise our relations with the United States and to dishonor France before the world. . . . Pending controversy, to surrender our fleet or even to sink it is to give material aid and strength to the enemy."[15]

Following this, Herriot and Jeanneney conferred with Lebrun. The President shared entirely their sentiment for immediate departure, but pointed out that Pétain was unalterably opposed. The marshal was then brought into the discussion. He repeated his determination not himself to leave France, but raised no serious objection when Jeanneney suggested that he could delegate his powers. It was agreed with almost no argument that Lebrun and the presidents of the Senate and the Chamber should leave as soon as possible, together with Chautemps, the Vice-President of the Council.[16]

There the matter rested during the day of June 19, during which preparations for departure began to be made. In the evening Biddle reported that he had just talked with Herriot, who had told him:

[14] Tel. (June 19) from Biddle.
[15] Tel. (June 19) from Biddle.
[16] *Procès du M. Pétain*, p. 47 (Lebrun's testimony); p. 58 (Jeanneney); p. 111 (Herriot).

"The French have informed the Germans that negotiations for an armistice must be contingent upon a cessation of the German advance toward the south. If the Germans agree, the negotiations will proceed. If not, the three (Lebrun, Herriot, Jeanneney) will proceed immediately to North Africa, accompanied by a majority of the Government. They will function as the *de jure* French Government and continue the battle from there. This critical move may take place tonight." [17]

As a matter of fact, Admiral Darlan, a few hours earlier, had put the ship *Massilia* at the disposal of the parliamentarians. They were to depart next day from Verdon, below Bordeaux, while the government was to go to Perpignan and then embark at Port-Vendres for Algiers.[18]

On the morning of June 20 the cabinet made up its mind that the government should leave for Perpignan that afternoon. But by the time the appointed hour arrived, Marshal Pétain had changed his mind. Jeanneney, who had already departed, had to be fetched back to Bordeaux by special courier.

There is but one explanation for this sudden *volte-face*, and that was the intervention of Laval, who during these critical days had been gathering about him at the Hôtel de Ville a group of parliamentarians to support Pétain's armistice program. There can be no doubt that the party of resistance intended to set up a legitimate government at Algiers. The legality of the move was in some doubt, but Mandel told Biddle that "the public powers, reduced to their elements, were the President of the Republic, the presidents of the Senate and the Chamber, and a minister." It is altogether likely that Marshal Pétain failed to grasp all the implications of the program of departure, but Laval undoubtedly saw the point at once. In the afternoon he appeared at President Lebrun's lodgings at the head of a delegation of parliamentarians numbering a score. Without ceremony and in a loud and brutal voice he took the President to task, asking him whether he

[17] Tel. (June 19) from Biddle.
[18] Kammerer: *La Vérité sur l'armistice*, pp. 193ff.; Maurice Ribet: *Le Procès de Riom*, pp. 290ff., where Darlan's instructions are given verbatim; see also Pertinax: *Les Fossoyeurs*, II, 149ff.

did not realize that France was defeated and that she would have to pay. If the President were to leave, the government that stayed behind would not have the authority to speak in the name of the country. Furthermore, if the President took with him the seals of the Republic, he would be taking with him the government of the country. This, roared Laval, he had no right to do. If he were unwilling to stand by Pétain and Weygand, let him resign. But he ought to realize that if he and his colleagues departed from France, the people would cry of defection and treason.

Poor old Lebrun put up a very feeble defense. He was clearly intimidated, as were probably others with whom Laval dealt. So much at least can be said for the former Premier and champion of appeasement: He never denied his policy or attempted to apologize for it. At his trial in 1945 he declared roundly:

"Preventing the Government from going to North Africa was probably the best thing that could have happened for France and the Allies. Had we gone there, the Germans would have followed and established themselves there. Russia might not then have entered the war so soon and the Allies would have had trouble landing. . . . All France wanted the armistice at the time. It was only later that some people changed their minds and wanted flight." [19]

Although there had been no final decision on the matter of departure, it had become highly unlikely that the "resisters" could yet win out. On June 21 the American ambassador reported home:

"As the day wears on and while Bordeaux remains in ignorance of Germany's armistice terms, the atmosphere of capitulation grows apace. Such will to resist as still remained is being sapped by the buzzing stories of collapse at the front; by the tales of wholesale disintegration; by the anti-British feeling I have just reported. General Weygand, I am told, has stopped further

[19] *New York Times*, October 5, 1945. On this whole confused business see *Procès du M. Pétain*, p. 48 (Lebrun), p. 111 (Herriot); Jean Montigny: *Toute la vérité*, p. 25; and tels. (June 20) from Biddle.

shipment of materiel to Africa; the sinking rather than escape of the fleet or the major part of it at least seems more probable. I am reluctantly reaching the conclusion that the passing of time has ill served the supporters of a free government in Africa in spite of all valiant efforts. The order to unpack may be expected." [20]

But even though Laval and his friends may have been intent on keeping the government in France, they were probably only too glad to see some of their other opponents leave. Only so can one explain the unimpeded departure of the *Massilia* on June 21, after many delays. By that time most of the parliamentarians had begun to smell trouble and had decided to stay behind. But the most determined—Mandel, Daladier, Delbos, and Campinchi—put to sea. While en route they learned that the armistice terms had been received and that the government was to stay in France. They wanted to turn back, but were unable to do so. Having finally landed at Casablanca (June 24), they did their best to induce General Noguès, the resident-general of Morocco, to declare for resistance and to set up a new government. Noguès was not at all ill-disposed, but eventually yielded to strong pressure from Weygand. Far from scoring a success, the French "patriots" were practically put under arrest and it was only weeks after, when the armistice was already signed and the "national revolution" consummated, that Herriot succeeded in arranging for their return to France. Under the circumstances all efforts made by the British to support a new government in North Africa were bound to fail. Churchill had hastily sent Lord Gort and Duff Cooper to the scene, but they were effectively prevented from establishing proper contact.[21]

Let us turn now to the actual negotiation of the armistice. The French delegation, appointed in great haste, consisted of General Huntziger and Léon Noël, a French diplomat of ex-

[20] Tel. (June 21) from Biddle.
[21] *Procès du M. Pétain*, pp. 36–7 (Daladier's story); p. 112 (Herriot); p. 140; Ribet: *Le Procès de Riom*, pp. 290ff.; Churchill's speech of June 25, 1940; Pertinax: *Les Fossoyeurs*, II, 149ff.; Kammerer: *La Vérité sur l'armistice*, pp. 256ff.

perience. Associated with them were Admiral Le Luc together
with Rochat and Lagarde of the foreign service. The delegation appears to have been given only the broadest general directives: France would accept no dishonorable terms,
neither would she agree to surrender the fleet. According to
Baudoin, the delegation was to insist also that the French
government be permitted to consider the terms in tranquillity
and to emphasize that if the Germans continued their advance
to Bordeaux, the French government would find it necessary
to negotiate from some other point.[22]

After numerous delays the delegation late on June 21
reached Rethondes, where it was received by Hitler and
Keitel in the famous armistice car of 1918. After a brief in-
troductory statement by Hitler the terms were presented by
Keitel and were at once telephoned to Bordeaux, where they
were received about midnight. The French cabinet met from
one A.M. to three A.M. to examine them, and convened again
for discussion on the following day. In general the analysis
of the terms evoked a feeling of relief. It was concluded that
they contained nothing dishonorable, excepting possibly the
demand that German political refugees in France be turned
over to the enemy. For the rest, there was no mention of
Alsace-Lorraine or of any territorial cession. Although three
fifths of French territory was to be occupied, the remainder
was to stay under French control, and the government was
to have "access" to Paris. Finally, as to the fleet, there was
no demand for its surrender, for the reasons already expounded above. Article VIII read as follows:

"The French war fleet is to assemble in ports to be designated
more particularly, and under German and/or Italian control,
there to be demobilized and laid up—with the exception of those
units released to the French Government for protection of French
interests in its colonial empire. The peacetime stations of ships
should control the designation of ports.

"The German Government solemnly declares to the French

[22] Tel. (June 21) from Biddle; *Procès du M. Pétain*, p. 172 (Noël's testimony).

Government that it does not intend to use the French war fleet which is in harbors under German control for its purposes of war, with the exception of units necessary for the purposes of guarding the coast and sweeping mines. It further solemnly and expressly declares that it does not intend to bring up any demands respecting the French war fleet at the conclusion of a peace.

"All warships outside France are to be recalled to France, with the exception of that portion of the French war fleet which shall be designated to represent French interests in the colonial empire." [23]

This article provoked more discussion than any other item of the terms, and at Charles-Roux's suggestion a real effort was made to secure an amendment that would permit of the disarmament of at least some of the ships in North African ports. This the Germans refused, though they agreed that the ships normally based on Brest might report at Toulon instead, and that similar questions might be referred to the armistice commission that would supervise the implementation of the terms. In the end and under considerable pressure from Rethondes the French government acceded, Darlan expressing the thought that the Germans would probably want to preserve the fleet, if only to have a counterweight to Italian sea power in the Mediterranean. In any case, it was generally understood that if the Germans made any move to seize French warships, these would at once be sunk. [24]

The armistice between Germany and France was signed at about six thirty P.M. on June 22, though it did not enter into effect until a similar armistice was concluded between France and Italy on June 24. In the course of the discussions there was no further reference made to the Chautemps plan. Evidently the terms were regarded as much more favorable

[23] Text of the armistice as published by the German government, June 25, conveniently reprinted in Kammerer: *La Vérité sur l'armistice*, appendix XXI. This text appears to be complete and accurate. From testimony offered at the Pétain trial it becomes certain that there were no secret clauses: *Procès du M. Pétain*, pp. 28, 51 (Lebrun); 85 (Charles-Roux); 171 (Noël).

[24] Darlan's statement to Bullitt, June 30, 1940; tels. (June 21, 22) from Biddle; *Procès du M. Pétain*, pp. 48, 54 (Lebrun); 84 (Charles-Roux); 172 (Noël).

than had been generally expected. But even if it had been otherwise, so much time had elapsed and the Germans had advanced so far that calm consideration of the conditions, to say nothing of a flight to North Africa, was no longer feasible. Neither was there any consultation with the British, despite earlier assurances that there would be. Sir Ronald Campbell had a very hard time breaking through Baudoin's evasions, but he managed to learn the substance of Article VIII on the morning of June 22. The provisions of that article struck him with consternation, for it seemed incredible that the Germans would respect their promises, once they had the French ships in their control in French ports. The ambassador went at once to Marshal Pétain to protest, but succeeded only in getting a reiteration of former assurances:

"Your government need have no fear. We hope that the French fleet may be able to reach African ports—Mers-el-Kébir, Casablanca, Dakar. But in any case, the Germans shall not touch it. It would be scuttled first."

The same line was taken by Baudoin in his statements to the British and American ambassadors: most of the French fleet was actually abroad, and in any case the order to scuttle could always be applied. In response to Sir Ronald Campbell's vehement arguments, the Foreign Minister repeated again and again "that the key to the whole situation was scuttling and offered to instruct Admiral Darlan to tell exactly how the scuttling order would work in practice." But Sir Ronald remained unpersuaded. He felt that there had been an organized conspiracy to keep the facts from him and was convinced that Baudoin was "really a crook." [25]

Biddle fared no better than his British colleague and was no less suspicious, despite the misleading assurances that flowed freely from the mouth of Baudoin:

"As to the fleet, I am frankly anxious," reported Biddle. "Baudoin said the Germans had 'agreed' to permit French mainte-

[25] Tel. (June 23) from London; Pertinax: *Les Fossoyeurs*, II, 149ff., evidently based on information from Sir Ronald Campbell.

nance of crews and withdrawal of the fleet to African ports. I
pinned him down, however, to the fact that the fleet is first to
return to ports in Metropolitan France for disarmament under
German control. While he insisted that in case of last minute
German treachery, the ships would be sunk, the value of such a
last minute safeguard seems pitifully small." [26]

Since the armistice had been signed, the British and American governments were obliged to accept the *fait accompli.*
Both governments felt badly let down and neither one of them
was willing to put any stock in Hitler's assurances that the
Germans would not make use of the fleet. In a public statement Churchill spoke of "the grief and amazement" with
which he had read the provisions of the armistice, and in a
great speech on June 25, 1940 he recalled that "the safety of
Great Britain and the British Empire is powerfully, though
not decisively, affected by what happens to the French Fleet."
The "solemn" assurances of the German government carried
no weight whatever with him: "ask half a dozen countries
what is the value of such solemn assurances," he remarked
bitterly. The British government therefore at once recalled
Sir Ronald Campbell from Bordeaux and considered what
further steps should be taken to safeguard British interests.

The American reaction was almost identical. Welles told
the French ambassador very bluntly that the armistice "apparently threw the entire fleet directly into German hands," and
that no store could be put by Hitler's assurances in view of
his past perfidies. A few days later Secretary Hull spoke even
more positively to Count St. Quentin:

"I said I should be frank to say very earnestly and definitely
that this country is greatly interested in France not permitting
Germany to get control and possession of the French Fleet, for
the reason that we have made clear to the world our interest in
and our aid to France in this contest; that if, having incurred the
ill-will of Germany by reason of this fact, France should hand
to Germany a cocked gun to shoot at us, it is naturally a matter
of great importance, especially when the French say that our

[26] Tels. (June 22, 24) from Biddle.

fleet in the Pacific is of real value to French interests in the Far
East, which are very great." [27]

Naturally the interest of the United States, though very
great, was less direct or immediate than that of the British,
who simply could not run the risk of seeing the powerful
French fleet pass into German control. Fortunately a considerable number of French ships were actually abroad. Two
French battleships, two cruisers, and a host of smaller craft
were in British home ports, while at Alexandria lay one battleship and four cruisers. The new and formidable battle-
cruisers *Strasbourg* and *Dunkerque*, together with two battleships and several cruisers, were at Oran in Algeria. The
unfinished *Jean Bart* had been hastily moved from Saint-
Nazaire to Casablanca, and the *Richelieu* likewise had got
away from Brest and had reached Dakar. The British hoped
against hope that men like Mandel and Daladier might yet
win over General Noguès and establish a government of resistance in North Africa, in which case all these ships could
have been used in conjunction with the British fleet. Hence
the mission of Lord Gort and Duff Cooper to Morocco. But
by June 26 or 27 it had become obvious that all British efforts
were to prove abortive—there would be no dissident government in North Africa and that crucial area would remain
loyal to the Pétain government and therefore subject to the
armistice terms.

Under the circumstances the British government felt that
it had no recourse but to the most drastic measures. As the
Prime Minister remarked in his speech of July 4, 1940: "I have
never in my experience seen discussed in a Cabinet so grim and
somber a question as to what we were to do about the French
Fleet." But the decisions arrived at were unanimous. On the
morning of July 3 the British took over such French warships
as lay in British ports. At the same time the French admiral
in command at Alexandria was told that his ships would be
sunk before the British would allow them to return home and

---

[27] Memo. of conversation by Welles (June 24) and by Hull (June 27).

fall under German control. In like fashion Admiral Gensoul
at Mers-el-Kébir, near Oran, was summoned to join the British
or else proceed to British or West Indian ports to be disarmed.
Gensoul rejected all such proposals, whereupon the British
opened fire and destroyed or disabled the larger part of the
French squadron, with a loss of over one thousand French
lives. Thereby a substantial part of the French fleet either
passed into British hands or was immobilized or destroyed.
The threat of a greatly augmented German-Italian sea power
was eliminated and Britain could look forward to the expected invasion of England with somewhat greater assurance.

It stands to reason that the British action called forth a
storm of protest from the Pétain government. The marshal
himself wrote to President Roosevelt denouncing "this odious
aggression," for which, he said, there was no excuse whatever
in view of the assurances that had been given the British government. It is known that several members of the French
government favored an act of war against Britain, but neither
Pétain nor Weygand nor Darlan would agree. It is perhaps
not going too far to assume that, in a sense, the British action
came as a relief, for it solved, at least in a measure, the difficult problem of keeping the French fleet out of German
hands. So the Pétain government broke off relations with the
British, and there the matter rested for the time being.

Before leaving the negotiation of the armistice, some attempt must be made to evaluate this crucial step in the development of the war and of American policy. Subsequent
events have of necessity colored much of the thought on the
subject, and the trial of Pétain has brought out all the venom
that had collected in the minds of the resisters. Those who
believed the French government should go on to North Africa
and continue the fight at Britain's side have stuck to their
view that an armistice was unnecessary and that Pétain's action in signing it was not only cowardly but actually treason-
able. It behooves us, then, to re-examine the pros and cons
and try to arrive at some kind of balanced estimate.

Nothing further need be said of the German policy. It is

reasonably clear that Hitler had nothing resembling a far-
range plan for France. His great and immediate objectives
were to prevent the French government from leaving for England or for North Africa, and to induce the French to keep
the fleet in their own hands. Hence his readiness to leave part
of French territory unoccupied as an inducement to Pétain
and his associates, and hence the general tenor of Article VIII
regarding the fleet. Having thereby deprived Britain of
French support, Hitler undoubtedly hoped to convince the
British of the wisdom of making peace. He could offer
Britain generous terms and in the final settlement recoup himself at the expense of France in the shape of cessions in
Europe and in the colonies.

In the light of later developments it may well be asked
whether Hitler's program was indeed a sound one. It hinged
largely on Britain's readiness to yield, and that proved to be
entirely illusory. No doubt some of his generals saw this at
the time and objected to the Führer's line. General Guderian
has stated that he was violently opposed to leaving part of
France unoccupied. In his opinion the Germans should have
gone right on to the Mediterranean and from the south coast
of France should have gone for North Africa at once. At the
same time pressure should have been brought on the Italians
to undertake an immediate advance on Egypt. With the
Mediterranean completely in Axis control the British would
have been much more disposed to consider a settlement.[28]

The later opinion of men like Weygand and Darlan bears
out this view, though of course it cannot be adduced as evidence of their wisdom in June 1940. Weygand holds it to
have been an irreparable blunder on Hitler's part not to have
seized North Africa, either by an expedition from southern
France or by way of Spain and Spanish Morocco. In like
manner Darlan, just before his death, declared:

"In getting Hitler to sign the armistice, France at least succeeded in making him commit the first and possibly the most

[28] State Department: *Special Interrogation Mission* (interrogation of General Guderian, September 7-8, 1945).

serious of his military blunders. I sincerely believe that but for the armistice the troops of the Axis would immediately have proceeded to occupy North Africa and other French possessions such as Dakar, whence it would have been difficult to dislodge them." [29]

That the Germans made a mistake in leaving North Africa open seems obvious from the sequel of events. Indeed, there is some evidence that they recognized this error almost at once, for on July 16, without special motivation, they approached General Huntziger, who was with the armistice commission at Wiesbaden. According to General Weygand, they admitted that they had committed a *"bêtise"* in not asking for North Africa. In order to rectify their folly, they now asked for bases in the south of France and on the North African coast. They demanded further the use of French tonnage and disposition of the North African railway all the way from Casablanca to Tunis and the right to establish posts, radio stations, and airfields all through that region. Naturally the French government sweated blood over these demands, which had something of the character of an ultimatum. Finally a reply was prepared that pointed out that the German note went far beyond the armistice terms and really constituted a second armistice, which should be discussed at greater length. For days the French government envisaged all kinds of dire consequences to follow upon this evasive refusal, but for unknown reasons the German government dropped the whole matter.[30]

Viewed from the French angle, there were two crucial considerations connected with the whole armistice problem. That France was defeated no one denied. The only questions that were really at issue were, firstly, whether France was obliged, under the terms of the agreement with England of March 28, to continue the struggle somehow if the British government

[29] Darlan: "Message to America" (*Cosmopolitan Magazine*, January 1943). For Weygand's opinion see *Procès du M. Pétain*, p. 138.
[30] All that is known of this dramatic episode came out in the Pétain trial: *Procès du M. Pétain*, p. 86 (account of Charles-Roux); p. 138 (Weygand); p. 172 (Noël).

refused to permit France to conclude an armistice or make a separate peace; secondly, whether in any case France could continue in the war, from North Africa or elsewhere, and, closely related to that problem, whether it would be better for the good of France to strike a bargain with Hitler or to struggle on from abroad.

It should be said at the outset that these considerations were probably never clean-cut in the minds of any of those chiefly concerned. Reynaud's program was relatively straightforward: respect the agreement with Britain, instruct the armies in France to capitulate, move the government to North Africa, and rely on British and American aid to turn the scales ultimately. This was apparently the more heroic course, but it involved leaving the French people to the mercy of Hitler and the Nazis. And it was exactly on this score that Pétain and Weygand differed from Reynaud. The marshal in particular assumed a paternal attitude and declared from the outset his irrevocable determination not to abandon his countrymen in the hour of misfortune. As we shall see presently, there was involved in this decision a dream of remaking France through a national revolution. At any rate, Pétain's primary concern for the French nation and his hope of saving something from the wreckage led him to stake everything on the chance of an "honorable" peace as between soldiers.

In the marshal's calculations, and also in those of men like Weygand and Laval, France's obligations to Britain played no significant role. As we have seen, Pétain took the stand that since Britain had given so little support, she could not expect much consideration and she could not fairly ask that France face complete destruction on her account. There is abundant evidence that with every day anti-British feeling ran higher at Bordeaux and that a goodly number of prominent Frenchmen indulged freely in what the Germans call by the untranslatable word "*Schadenfreude*." They gave British resistance from three weeks to two months, but no longer. The British hope for American aid seemed to them entirely illusory: the United States might ultimately join actively in the struggle, but American supplies and American forces were bound to come too late.[31]

This conviction undoubtedly underlay the attitude of the Pétain government with regard to the French fleet. There can be no shadow of doubt that the marshal and his associates were unanimous in their determination to scuttle the fleet rather than allow it to fall into the hands of the Germans. But they would not allow it to go to British ports because, in the first place, they knew that it was their strongest bargaining point with Hitler and, in the second place, because they feared the use Britain might make of it. A week after the armistice was concluded, Admiral Darlan said to Bullitt that he was convinced that Britain would have to surrender in a matter of weeks:

"Great Britain would die of asphyxiation even without a German invasion. For his part, he did not believe that the British Government or people would have the courage to stand against serious German air bombardments and he expected a surrender after a few heavy air attacks. . . . Under no conditions would he send the [French] fleet to England, since he was certain that the British would never return a single vessel of the fleet to France and that if Great Britain should win the war, the treatment which would be accorded to France by Great Britain would be no more generous than the treatment accorded by Germany."[32]

So the French took a chance with the fleet and were genuinely relieved when Hitler did not ask for its surrender. In order to forestall any possible treachery, Admiral Darlan on June 24 issued explicit instructions that the ships should be scuttled if the Germans tried to seize them.[33]

Marshal Pétain appears to have had no basic objection to the transfer of at least part of the government to Algiers, but it is not at all clear that he took this view originally because

[31] Among countless bits of evidence see tel. (June 23) from Biddle; tel. (July 1) from Bullitt; *Procès du M. Pétain*, p. 85 (testimony of Charles-Roux).

[32] Tel. (July 1) from Bullitt; see also Alec de Montmorency: *The Enigma of Admiral Darlan* (New York, 1943), pp. 87ff.

[33] Kammerer: *La Vérité sur l'armistice*, p. 245; *Procès du M. Pétain*, p. 54 (Lebrun's testimony).

he feared the Germans might overrun the whole of France
and thereby make free deliberation of an armistice impossible,
or whether he did not realize all the implications of such a
move. If the latter was the case, Laval quickly enlightened
him and induced him to reverse himself. In any event, Pétain
did not want to see the French people abandoned, and his
advisers were convinced that anything beyond a very short
resistance in North Africa would be impossible. Troops there
were in considerable number, as well as about one thousand
planes and an admirable fleet. But the troops were ill-
equipped and the planes were obsolete. Whatever may have
been the truth of this much-debated matter, it is clear that
Weygand sent his own emissaries to North Africa and that
he, as well as General George, were satisfied that any long-
term resistance, based on the hope of large-scale aid from
the United States, would be unthinkable.[34]

The main thought, however, was that in the event of the
government's fleeing and attempting to continue the war, all
France would be occupied by the Germans. France would be
put under a "Gauleiter" and would lose all national identity.
Furthermore, Hitler would take his revenge on the French for
their refusal to accept defeat. He would undoubtedly attack
North Africa by way of Italy and probably by way of Spain,
and he would in all probability succeed. Thereby all would
be lost.[35]

This brings us to the essence of the problem: in the long
view, was the conclusion of the armistice in June 1940 the
best thing for France or not? From our present knowledge
the answer, it seems, can only be in the affirmative, and it is
worth recalling that approval of Marshal Pétain's action was
general in France in those sad days. True, it would have been
a great boon to the British to have had the use of the French

[34] *Procès du M. Pétain,* pp. 137–8 (Weygand's testimony); 166–7 (General
George's statement).

[35] In September 1940 Pétain is reported to have told Louis Rougier that
the Spanish government, fearing that Germany would force Spain into the
war, urged him to conclude the armistice. See Louis Rougier: *Les Accords
Pétain-Churchill* (Montreal, 1945), p. 113.

fleet in 1940–1 and indeed throughout the war. On the other hand, through the armistice France was at least enabled to live. There was an unoccupied France, governed and administered by Frenchmen, with an army of a hundred thousand men and at least some measure of independence. Considering the fate of Poland, of Norway, and of almost all Continental states, this is saying more than a little. And when one considers that through the armistice North Africa remained unoccupied and open eventually as a gateway to Europe, the case for the armistice appears to be clinched. At the time, of course, British and American opinion was outraged by the terms as they affected the fleet. But in the end it appeared that British and American fears, however natural they may have been, were unfounded. Later on, Churchill, who indeed had objected on the issue of the fleet rather than on the issue of the armistice generally, confessed to General George that the conclusion of the armistice had actually helped Britain, and that Hitler had made a great mistake in not going on to Africa.[36]

On the evening of June 18 General Charles de Gaulle had initiated in London a rival French government, the mission of which was to continue the war by Britain's side. The British gave this movement financial and other aid and we shall have, in the sequel, to turn our attention again and again to the problems that flowed from the Gaullist movement. Here it need only be remarked that France came out of her defeat much more fortunate than anyone could have expected. Not only were Hitler's terms remarkably lenient, permitting the continued existence of a French nation and a French government, but through de Gaulle France was to have at least some of the advantages of an exile government loyal to Britain and her allies. When, through further developments of the war, Pétain's government became played out, de Gaulle and the Fighting French could take its place. So France was actually able to play both ends against the middle—France had eggs in two baskets.

[36] This was in January 1944: *Procès du M. Pétain*, p. 167 (testimony of General George).

CHAPTER III

Laval and the National Revolution

THE FIRST six months following the collapse of France were for the United States government months of uncertainty and anxiety. The disappearance of France as a great power was in itself an event of tremendous international import, necessitating reconsideration of basic attitudes and calculations. But it must be remembered further that at the time the fall of France was generally regarded as the prelude to greater disasters. Despite the brave and stirring speeches of Churchill, the British cause appeared well-nigh hopeless. It is hard now, even after the passage of only a few years, to recapture the premonition of gloom and even of despair that weighed on everyone. As a matter of fact, we know now that Britain was much nearer the verge of destruction in the summer and autumn of 1940 than she herself could well have realized. In a sense, Hitler's victory in the west came too quickly and too easily for his own good. Had he been able to turn at once on England, he would almost certainly have compassed Britain's downfall.

One need not, therefore, be surprised at the pessimism and defeatism that were rife in France. After all, in many influential circles the war had never been accepted. During the stormy decade of the thirties foreign affairs had been half forgotten in the midst of the social struggle. The Popular Front governments, whatever else might be said of them, had served to accentuate the age-old conflict between the democratic, republican elements and the counter-revolutionary forces. From 1934 onward Hitler and his Nazi doctrines had open and avowed admirers and advocates in France. More

[66]

than a few wealthy industrialists saw in Germany a much-
needed bulwark against communism and, while denouncing
the demands of the working classes, were ready to declare:
"Better Hitler than Blum."

These groups were welcome recruits to the ranks of the
old reactionary movements like the Action Française of
Charles Maurras, which, since the beginning of the century,
had been an inspiration for almost all of the new apostles of
authoritarianism. Maurras had revamped the theories of royal-
ism and clericalism and had first attempted to bolster his
theories with organized action groups. He had gained many
adherents among the aristocratic upper classes, and notably
among the officer caste of the army and the restless younger
intellectuals. It was an easy transition from this initial movement to the Croix de Feu, Cagoule, and similar organizations
of the 1930's that menaced the Republic and aimed at a national revolution that would purge France and pave the way
for her resurrection. These groups and these movements
(though not necessarily pro-German) did not want war with
Germany. Some of their leaders were corrupted by German
gold, but others were probably sincerely and even patriotically
intent on following the German example. In the Germany of
Hitler there was no unemployment, there was no social conflict. Quite the contrary, Nazi Germany was growing in
strength by leaps and bounds and presented an enviable example of well-integrated, well-directed national effort.

The first step in the understanding of the Pétain regime
in France is the realization that the so-called Vichy government reflected the reactionary, authoritarian aspirations of
part of the French upper classes, of at least part of French
big business, and of much of the French officer corps. Pétain
himself had a deep-seated fear of communism and an insur-
mountable distrust of parliamentary democracy. A man of
great personal vanity and self-righteousness, he liked to think
of himself as the savior of France, the man who would lead
his country out of the wilderness of political corruption to
the fair fields of a well-regulated, authoritarian regime, a sort

of *"socialisme de caserne,"* where the common man would
be cared for in a paternalistic way and where he could work,
under discipline and direction from above, for his own and
for the common good. As a military man Pétain yearned for
unity of command and direct, personal responsibility as opposed to the diffuse and obscure obligations of a parliamentary
system.[1] Weygand's ideas are reputed to have been even more
conservative. Though he always took the view that military
men should abstain from political activity, he himself in private criticized the abuses of the French political system and
the corruption of the politicians. Admiral Darlan and numerous others, leaving out of account for the moment men like
Laval, took the same line and supported the authoritarian
policy of which Pétain was the exponent.

These men, for the most part, had disapproved of the war
and had had no faith in victory at any time. They were, as we
have already seen, prepared to throw up the sponge as soon
as their apprehensions began to materialize. As patriots, the
defeat of France was no doubt hard for them to bear, but at
any rate they had a ready explanation for it and they saw at
least some redeeming features in it. In a few words, they
ascribed the national disaster to the parliamentary, democratic regime and more specifically to the mistaken policies,
shortcomings, and corruption of the Popular Front governments. Marshal Pétain himself spoke of

"the sterile struggle of parties and factions, the feverish unleash-
ing of personal ambitions or ideological passions, the permanent
excitation toward division and hate, where a historian could see
the most dangerous epidemic that could befall a nation. . . . The
State, bloated and debilitated, has collapsed more from the weight
of its own weaknesses and its mistakes than under the blows of
the enemy." [2]

[1] See General Hering's statement of Pétain's political views in *Procès du
M. Pétain*, p. 159, and the prosecutor's summation, p. 319.
[2] Article by Marshal Pétain in the *Revue des deux mondes*, September 15,
1940, quoted in Léon Marchal: *Two Years of Deception* (New York, 1943),
p. 13.

There was no use, therefore, in bemoaning fate. France's fall was really the penalty of her own sins, and if France had to suffer, it should be at least to good purpose. It has often been charged and it is altogether likely that Pétain and others were so ready to make peace partly because they feared that the country would lapse into communism if the unequal struggle continued, and partly because they thought that defeat would perhaps be bought not too dearly if France could be saved from herself and remade along more godly lines. Granted the hopelessness of the military situation, their thoughts turned quickly to the opportunity for a national revolution. There was more than a bit of sheer fatalism in their acceptance of defeat.

Bullitt spoke to most of these leaders within a week of the signing of the armistice. His report of July 1 is one of the most remarkable and revealing documents in the entire annals of this great war. Nothing but direct quotation will give anything like the flavor of his comments:

"The impression which emerges from these conversations is the extraordinary one, that the French leaders desire to cut loose from all that France has represented during the past two generations, that their physical and moral defeat has been so absolute that they have accepted completely for France the fate of becoming a province of Nazi Germany. Moreover, in order that they may have as many companions in misery as possible they hope that England will be rapidly and completely defeated by Germany and that the Italians will suffer the same fate. Their hope is that France may become Germany's favorite province—a new "Gau" which will develop into a new Gaul. . . ."

Marshal Pétain told the ambassador in so many words that Germany would attempt to reduce France to the status of a province by securing complete economic control and by enforcing military impotence. He was extremely bitter about the politicians and insisted that the government of France must be radically altered.

"In his opinion one of the chief causes for the collapse of the French army was that the reserve officers who had been educated by school teachers who were Socialists and not patriots had deserted their men and shown no fighting spirit whatsoever. . . ."

Darlan sounded the same note. He too was convinced that Hitler would unite all Europe in a customs union and make France his leading vassal state: "France could do nothing but accept such a position for the moment." The fault had all been with the political regime: "The entire system of parliamentary government in France had been rotten and the high commander of the army (i.e., Gamelin) had proved to be equally rotten." Chautemps, one of the leaders of the Radical Socialist Party, chimed in and remarked quite frankly to Bullitt: "Pétain, Weygand and Laval intend to abolish the present French Constitution and to introduce a semi-dictatorial state in which Parliament would play a small role." Pétain would be the Hindenburg of the new regime, and Laval the Hitler. "Pétain, Weygand and Laval," concluded the ambassador, "all believe that if a dictatorship of this kind should be introduced in France before the peace, France would obtain much better terms than could be obtained under a parliamentary regime." [3]

The concluding remark of Bullitt's report raises a consideration that is absolutely fundamental to an understanding of all that happened in the sequel. It must be remembered that Pétain and his followers looked upon the defeat of France as merely the prelude to the collapse of the entire resistance to Hitler and the Nazis. We know that the Führer at the time shared this view. The armistice terms as we know them betray a hastily drawn document—a document full of provisional arrangements and half-settlements that was intended only to tide over the situation until a definitive peace treaty could be drawn. We need not analyze it in detail to demonstrate the point. What is important here is the thought on the part of the French defeatists that if they at once recognized

[3] Tel. (July 1, 1940) from Bullitt, at La Bourboule.

their failure and dropped out of the struggle, the whole sad
business would be over so much the sooner and they might,
by accepting Hitler, curry favor with him and figure in the
new Nazi Europe as Germany's preferred province. Pétain
and his friends saw in France's misfortune a golden opportunity to effect the national revolution and calculated that if
France could be remade in the Nazi image, the conqueror
would be more lenient in the terms he would finally impose.
Recalling the fact that Britain was given only three weeks or
a month before her day of doom, it is clear that haste was
indicated. Actually the new France emerged less than three
weeks after the signature of the armistice.

Such credit as this achievement may call for belongs not to
Pétain nor to Weygand, whose reforming ideas never seem
to have gone much beyond a nebulous and inchoate state.
The revolution was rather the masterpiece of Pierre Laval,
famed French politician and statesman who had been for
some years in disgrace, but who had emerged in the hour
of crisis and had quickly become the dominant figure on the
scene. We need not stop to review here Laval's political
career, but it is distinctly relevant and important to recall
that throughout the years he had always known what he
wanted, that he had proved himself one of the most adroit of
parliamentary manipulators, and that in a material way he
had made a good thing of serving his country. In 1935 he had
made for himself a malodorous reputation for his dealings with
Mussolini, and later by his systematic delay and obstruction
of the Franco-Russian alliance. Since the advent of the Popular Front government he had been in eclipse. What, during
these years, may have been his relations with the Italian government and whether or not he had any truck with Hitler
and his agents we cannot say. But there is evidence to show
that at an early date he decided where the chances of the
future lay, and that, with reference to French affairs, he soon
came to the conclusion that Pétain was a name and a figure
with which something could be done. By the same token
Pétain is reported to have demanded Laval's inclusion in the

Daladier cabinet of March 1940 and to have retained Laval's name on all the lists of his projected ministry. He may have had no use for Laval personally, but he appears to have considered him a useful go-between in negotiations with the Axis powers.[4]

Laval had arrived at Bordeaux from his château near Vichy during the most critical days of June 1940. He supported the marshal in his demand for the conclusion of an armistice and was taken into the new government on June 24 as a minister of state after he had refused on June 17 to accept any post other than the Ministry of Foreign Affairs. Meanwhile, behind the scenes, and in close collaboration with Marquet, the mayor of Bordeaux, he had built up a large parliamentary following, which he used to ruin the plan of the resisters to transfer the government overseas. Once the armistice had been signed, he devoted himself to the arduous task of persuading the French politicians that the Third Republic must be scrapped and an authoritarian state set up in its place. He is reported to have told the remnants of the French Chamber during these days:

"I have been among you since 1914 and I do not forget that I come from the people. But since parliamentary democracy insisted on taking up the struggle against Nazism and Fascism, and since it has lost the fight, it must disappear. A new regime must follow it, a regime which will be bold, authoritarian, social and national. . . . We have always followed in England's wake. Nothing was more humiliating than the sight of our politicians going to London to ask permission to be French ministers. . . . You can see where all this had led us. . . . We have no other road to follow than that of loyal collaboration with Germany and Italy. I experience no embarrassment in speaking thus, for even in peacetime I favored such collaboration." [5]

[4] See Henry Torrès: *Pierre Laval* (New York, 1941), *passim;* Pertinax: *Les Fossoyeurs,* I, 139, 181; and especially *Procès du M. Pétain,* p. 35 (Daladier's testimony); p. 73 (Gazel); p. 107 (Mlle Petit on Laval's connections with the Italian government); 185–6 (Laval's account of his relations to Pétain).

[5] Torrès, op. cit., p. 262.

Laval had by no means an easy time. Men like Blum, Herriot, Jeanneney, and many others were unmoved and utterly disgusted by his arguments. But the politicians and the statesmen of the Left were momentarily stunned and were laboring under the heavy burden of defeat. Laval had behind him the marshal and the military men, to say nothing of the extremists of the Right and a considerable group representing bigbusiness interests. Many of the latter had developed farreaching economic connections with Germany even before the war and saw in a system of collaboration their only hope for the future. Gradually these forces gained the ascendancy. By July 10 Laval had induced a majority of the members to vote Parliament out of existence in favor of a new constitutional body that was to be summoned later. The utterly ineffectual President Lebrun was deposed and Pétain became chief of state in his place. *Travail, Famille, Patrie* replaced *Liberté, Egalité, Fraternité* as the national slogan, and the authoritarian regime of Pétain's dreams became a reality. Therewith began what has been called "the most shameful page in the history of France." [6] Triumphantly the marshal announced to the National Assembly on July 10:

"We must make a lesson of the lost battles. . . . Having calculated the importance of her defeat, a country such as ours, whatever may be her pains, will not lose herself in vain regrets. . . . It is in military defeat and internal troubles that other countries found strength to discover themselves and transform. . . . The government must have all the power to decide, undertake, negotiate and save what can be saved, destroy what must be destroyed, reconstruct what must be reconstructed. The government consequently ask parliament, meeting in National Assembly, to give its full confidence to Marshal Henri Philippe Pétain,

[6] Pertinax, op. cit., II, 9. It is said that Laval literally dragooned the politicians into acceptance of his program, but this is probably an exaggeration. Stunned by defeat, many of them were no doubt ready to follow any forceful leadership. See the voluminous but inconclusive evidence in *Procès du M. Pétain*, especially the testimony of President Lebrun, of Blum, and of Laval.

President of the Council, to promulgate under his signature the responsibility and fundamental law of a French state." [7]

Article III of the armistice provided:

"The French Government is free to choose its seat in the non-occupied territory and even, if it so desires, to transfer it to Paris. In the latter event the German Government undertakes to grant all the necessary facilities to the Government and its central administrative services, so that it may be enabled to administer both the occupied and non-occupied territories from Paris."

Pétain and his friends at once attempted to secure from the German government permission to return to Paris, which the marshal described as "the heart and brain of the nation, the crucible in which, at all times, the destinies of the country have been forged." But despite Laval's visit to Abetz, the German representative, no settlement was arrived at for "reasons of a technical nature." The new government therefore had to establish itself provisionally at Vichy, from which it had not moved at the time of the Normandy invasion. In a remarkably short time the marshal learned that he was not to rule all of France, but only the poor two fifths that remained unoccupied by the Germans. The vague wording of the armistice terms was soon to be exploited to the full by the conqueror, and one disappointment after another was to await the new French ruler, who in June had been so confident that he could deal with Hitler as with a gentleman.

But we must not stop too long over a discussion of the internal developments in France. Seen in historical perspective, the role played by Pétain and his associates was nothing

[7] One of the most detailed accounts of Laval's efforts and achievements, written by an admirer, is to be found in Jean Montigny: *De l'armistice à l'assemblée nationale: Toute la vérité sur un mois dramatique de notre histoire* (Clermont-Ferrand, 1940). The doctrine and nature of the new regime may be followed in such publications as *Principes de la rénovation nationale* (Paris, n.d.); *Les Messages du Maréchal* (Vichy, n.d.); *La Doctrine du Maréchal* (Vichy, n.d.); and in English in Pierre Tissier: *The Government of Vichy* (London, 1942).

heroic, nothing to inspire confidence either at home or abroad. But it should be remembered that in the summer of 1940 all the facts recounted above were not known, or, if known, not appreciated in their full context. France herself was down and out. Six weeks after the signing of the armistice there were still six million refugees in unoccupied France. Another million and a half able-bodied men were prisoners in Germany. The country was liable to a daily payment of four hundred million francs for the German army of occupation, while the conqueror soon made the line of demarcation between the occupied and unoccupied areas a very real thing. Nothing like free movement or intercourse was possible; consequently there could be no thought of sound economic revival or normal business life. Under the staggering blows of defeat and the tribulations of ordinary existence, the people were completely disillusioned and lost in despair. It was easy to blame the regime that had brought France to such a pass, and it was natural to look to some respected personage for leadership. Under the circumstances Pétain was gladly accepted, and with him the national revolution. After all, the marshal was the hero of Verdun, he was a revered old man, he was the father who stood by his people in adversity and who, it was hoped, would lead the country along the road of liberation to a new era. Charles Vallin, the former vice-president of the Parti Social Français, expressed this very well when he remarked two years later:

"Pétain and Weygand represented in my eyes all the military past and the glory of France; I could not believe that they were not worthy of all my confidence."

When he saw the marshal at Vichy early in July 1940, the latter told him that the resistance of England would be over in two weeks and that he (Pétain) was the only person who could obtain favorable conditions of peace from Hitler. Like countless others, Vallin believed that the old man was playing a canny game of stalling and that he would outdo the Germans when it came to the final accounting.[8]

Ambassador Bullitt brought back similar ideas when he returned home at the end of July. When interviewed by the press on his arrival he said:

"Marshal Pétain is universally respected in France. He is doing his best to bring order out of desperate disorder."

When queried whether he thought that the new France was a fascist state, he refused to express an opinion, but reiterated:

"Marshal Pétain has a tremendous reputation and is thoroughly honest and straightforward. Pétain is absolutely the boss. He is trying to do his best in an extraordinarily difficult situation."

The ambassador no doubt had much to do with the formulation of American policy in these uncertain months. So far as the Vichy government was concerned, it was decided to maintain regular diplomatic relations. At the outset there was some thought of following the British example and at least allowing relations with the new France to lapse, but it was realized almost at once that the fate of the French fleet could be influenced only by representation at Vichy. Furthermore, the only grounds for a rupture of relations could be found in the internal changes in France. But traditionally our policy of recognition had taken no account of foreign governmental forms or ideologies. The test for us had almost invariably been whether another government was willing to live at peace with the United States and was prepared to fulfill the ordinary obligations of international intercourse. We had not broken relations with Fascist Italy nor with Nazi Germany nor with other non-democratic powers like Japan and Russia, and consequently there was no intrinsic reason why the ties to a traditionally friendly power like France should be severed. In the midst of the general uncertainty it seemed, on the con-

[8] Press interview with Vallin, published in *Les Documents*, No. 27 (October 1, 1942). Cf. also Pertinax: *Les Fossoyeurs*, II, 209. A most depressing picture of France was given by Maynard B. Barnes (first secretary of the American Embassy) in his dispatch of July 29, 1940.

trary, to be the part of wisdom to stand by the Vichy government and do whatever might be possible to prevent the new regime from falling completely under the influence of the conqueror. If France itself had broken off relations with Britain after Mers-el-Kébir, that seemed all the more reason why the United States, as a friend of Britain, should keep up contact with Vichy. As a matter of fact, the British government in private recognized the value of the maintenance of French-American relations and itself continued some sort of contact through the Canadian mission at Vichy.[9]

To be sure, General de Gaulle had undertaken to organize a movement of resistance in London and had been recognized by the British government "as leader of all free Frenchmen wherever they may be who rally to him in support of the Allied cause." But this did not constitute recognition of de Gaulle as head of a French government, and the British themselves carefully avoided such recognition. In the summer of 1940 de Gaulle had as yet no following to speak of. No French leader of eminence had joined him and there was no reason to suppose that he had any adherents in France. On the contrary, it is certain that he was merely a name to the overwhelming majority of Frenchmen, both at home and abroad. To have cast off the Vichy government and to have staked the future on de Gaulle would have been a daring move indeed. It would have been surprising if such a policy had been considered at all.[10]

As a matter of fact, what concerned the American government was not the question of ideology, but the question of national interest. The international scene looked extremely black in the summer of 1940. Ambassador Kennedy, in London, made no secret of the fact that he thought Britain

[9] Memo. of conversation between Secretary Hull and Lord Lothian (June 24, 1940); comments by Ray Atherton; Sumner Welles: *The Time for Decision*, p. 156.

[10] Though it has little bearing on this study, it is worth noting that de Gaulle's political ideas were not unlike those of Pétain. For years he had been advocating a national revolution, criticizing democracy, and demanding a stronger executive based on an elite.

doomed, and his opinion was one that was widely shared,
even by thoughtful students of international affairs. The
President, it appears, was never really pessimistic, but he must
certainly have been anxious, not only because we had staked
our hopes on British victory, but because in the Pacific the
Japanese were obviously waiting to take advantage of every
opportunity, and Japan's advance was an ever growing threat
to American interests. At the very moment when France collapsed, the Tokyo government obliged the Pétain cabinet to
close the railroad from Indo-China into China and to permit
Japanese "inspectors" to enforce the closure. Millions of dollars' worth of supplies for China were abandoned to the
Japanese. But all this was merely by way of prelude. Other
and much more far-reaching demands were soon forthcoming
and were supported by Germany after Japan formally joined
the Axis. On September 22 the French government yielded
to an ultimatum: northern Indo-China was occupied militarily by the Japanese, who at once warned all other powers
against interference with this "friendly" arrangement.[11]

We were not sufficiently prepared in the summer of 1940
to accept the challenge thrown down by either Germany or
Japan, even if American public opinion had been favorable
to our doing so. What we saw before us was the prospect of
Britain's collapse, of German domination of Europe and perhaps Africa, and of Japanese hegemony in the Far East and
the Pacific. Secretary Hull was very profoundly disturbed by
the outlook and on October 12 invited officials of the War
and Navy Departments to a conference. In a remarkably discerning and unvarnished survey of the situation he called
attention to all that might happen. We may quote his own
record of the meeting:

[11] General Georges Catroux, at that time Governor-General of Indo-
China, in June 1940 appealed to both the United States and Britain for aid
in resisting the Japanese. Neither government was then prepared to engage
Japan, and said so. See General Catroux's statement in the *New York Times*
August 2, 1945, and the evidence in *Procès du M. Pétain, passim;* tels. (August 9, 1940) from Tokyo, (September 3) from Chungking, (September 19)
from Vichy.

"I opened the conference by saying that we should not overlook possibilities, and that from this viewpoint as well as that of probabilities in fact, I desired to suggest that Hitler recently more than at any time in the past holds the whip hand among his outlaw associates, Japan and others, and that he may at any time order a general advance from London to Tokyo, in the air, on the sea and on the land; that he may announce that the bombardment of Great Britain will continue right through the winter and that there will be no let-up until she is conquered from across the Channel and through the air; that at the same time and during the coming winter every possible effort will be made by the Germans to conquer Egypt, Africa and the Suez Canal, which would mean possession of the Mediterranean; that three avenues might each or all be availed of for this purpose, viz, the avenue across at Gibraltar, the avenue across the Mediterranean near Sicily, and third the route through the Balkans, Turkey and Syria; that Stalin being concerned by the strength of the German army, Hitler by both threats and persuasion might well undertake to keep Russia aloof even from the Turkish and Balkan route contemplated by the Germans; that Hitler might well tell Russia not to bother Japan temporarily, and not to aid Turkey either from a German invasion or from an attack on Greece by the Italians, in case Turkey should come to the aid of Greece; that as a fourth step in the Egyptian campaign Hitler would leave nothing undone to utilize the French forces in the air, on the land and on the sea; that at the same time, having urged Russia not to attack Japan and having required the Vichy government to admit Japan to Indo-China, and Japan in addition being extremely anxious to invade and occupy the South Sea area, might well be prevailed upon by Hitler to take much greater risk in advancing than she otherwise would." [12]

Under the circumstances we gave Britain all the material support we could, and concluded with her (September 3) the famous exchange of World War I destroyers for Atlantic bases. Congress had voted a huge, two-ocean naval program (July 19) and passed a Selective Service Act (September). But we were still a long way from being able to challenge the

[12] *Hull Papers*: Memorandum of October 15, 1940.

aggressors directly, and could not hope for the time being to
do more than "save the pieces." [13]

With regard to France there were three considerations of
paramount importance: (1) To see that the French fleet was
not used against the United States; (2) to see that Germany
and Italy should not get control of French bases in North or
West Africa or in the New World; (3) to see that the Vichy
government did not go beyond the armistice terms in the direction of "abject cooperation and collaboration." [14]

For the time being, the American policy was of necessity
one of watchful waiting. Everything would depend on the
attitude of the Vichy government toward the conquering
Germans, which in turn would no doubt be conditioned by
the fate of Britain. But before we become involved in an
analysis of Vichy policy it will be very helpful to outline
Hitler's plans and hopes, for French policy was in large measure a reaction to German demands. To date, it has been almost
impossible to speak with any assurance of the Nazi program,
but the capture of large numbers of documents and the interrogation of many high German officials have thrown much
light on the problem and have enabled us to give a fairly well-
founded account.

There can be no doubt that the victory over France came
so suddenly and quickly that it caught the Nazis unprepared
for further action. The armistice was concluded on Hitler's
terms, but the question then arose: what next? The career
officials of the German Foreign Office took the view that the
Führer should press his advantage, that he should follow up a
moderate armistice with a generous peace treaty, with few if
any annexations. Such a settlement would convince a majority
of Frenchmen that Germany was not a menace and that it
would be possible to live in amity and collaboration with her.
The first step toward a New Order in Europe would thus be

[13] See *Biennial Report of the Chief of Staff, July 1, 1941–June 30, 1943*,
p. 7; Edward R. Stettinius, Jr.: *Lend-Lease*, chap. iv.
[14] This was the formulation used by Sumner Welles in a background conference with the press on March 26, 1942.

taken and the Führer could consolidate his gains before proceeding to greater victories. Ribbentrop apparently was persuaded to adopt this line and actually submitted a program to Hitler, but without making a favorable impression. The Nazi dictator was not prepared to commit himself and took the stand that when the great conflict was over, someone would have to pay the bill. The questions of France's colonies and fleet should therefore be left open until the final reckoning. France, indeed, was only a very secondary item in Hitler's grandiose conceptions.[15]

Hitler's ultimate objective had always been expansion toward the east and the acquisition of greater *"Lebensraum"* for his people. For years he had attempted to square Britain in order to secure a free hand against Poland and Russia. Since August 1939 he had been in agreement with Russia, but this arrangement had probably never been thought of as more than a stopgap. Göring and others have testified that, despite the opposition of the army, the Führer began thinking and planning an early campaign against Russia just as soon as the victory over France had been won. But once again he was intent on settling with Britain first. It seemed to him altogether incredible that after the collapse of France the British would not realize that they were beaten. No plan for a campaign against England had therefore been drawn. Instead, Hitler staked everything on his speech of July 19, 1940, which was full of general assurances and culminated in an invitation to make peace before it was too late.

It was only after Churchill's failure to react that Hitler, genuinely disappointed, resorted to force. On August 8 began the great air assault on England, which it was hoped would break the resistance of the British in a matter of weeks and make a difficult invasion unnecessary. We need not enter into details here, except to point out that Hitler's calculations might

[15] State Department: *Special Interrogation Mission* (interrogations of Dr. Paul Otto Schmidt, of Dr. Erich Kordt, and of Heinz Trützchler von Falkenstein); War Department: *Historical Interrogation Commission* (interrogation of Dr. Paul O. Schmidt).

have proved correct if the Germans had used their air superiority wisely and if the British had not insisted on fighting and holding on in a most disconcerting way. In any event, it soon became obvious that Britain would not yield until actually invaded and defeated on the ground. But for such an operation the Germans lacked sufficient landing craft as well as naval power. The weather, too, had become unfavorable. By October even Hitler had to acknowledge that his hopes for peace or military victory over Britain had fallen flat.[16]

Under these circumstances Marshal Göring came into his own. Ever since the victory over France Göring had been urging that the next step should be, not a direct assault on England, but an effort to knock Britain out by an indirect attack. The Nazis, he argued, should launch a campaign against Gibraltar, which was notoriously vulnerable. Once Gibraltar had been taken, it would be possible to overrun North Africa, go on to Suez at leisure, and also strike south to Dakar, on the West African coast, whence British trade by the Cape route could be interdicted. If the United States showed any intention of intervening actively, the Germans could at once occupy the Azores.[17]

This plan presupposed the goodwill and collaboration of France and Spain, as well as of Italy, and therefore led to Hitler's conferences with Pétain, Laval, Franco, and Serrano Suñer during the last week of October. But before we turn to those crucial developments, we shall do well to turn back and review the evolution of the French attitude during the few months following the armistice.

Pétain and Weygand and almost everyone at Vichy, it will be recalled, had expected fate to overtake Britain in a matter of weeks. The atmosphere in Vichy circles was quite devoid

---

[16] State Department: a long study of German foreign policy by Erich Kordt (one of Ribbentrop's assistants); interrogations of General Walter Warlimont and Dr. Schmidt; *Biennial Report of the Chief of Staff, July 1, 1943–June 30, 1945*, p. 2 (testimony of General Jodl); *Ciano Diary*, entries for July 7, 16, 19, August 19, 28, September 19, October 4, 1940.

[17] Associated Press dispatch (June 17, 1945); State Department: interrogation of Göring (November 9, 1945).

of any sympathy for France's former ally, and the government was reckoning on getting off easy while Britain paid the price of her ill-advised stubbornness. On the other hand, Pétain and Weygand were determined not to get sucked into the maelstrom again. At considerable risk they rejected German demands that went beyond the armistice and showed no readiness for participation in a war against Britain.

But such was not the view of Laval, who was absolutely convinced of an eventual German victory and of the wisdom of France's collaborating fully and whole-heartedly with the Nazis, even to the extent of hostilities against Britain. He had assumed general charge of French relations with the Germans and spent a good part of his time in Paris, where he conferred with the German representative, Otto Abetz. Abetz, who had long been in ill repute as the leader of the French fifth column, appears to have actually been a fairly innocuous person. An inexperienced diplomat but a friend of Ribbentrop, he seems to have been a sincere though somewhat romantic and decidedly amateurish champion of Franco-German friendship. He had about a billion francs (which were taken from French occupation payments) with which to convert Frenchmen to the new gospel, but Laval was on his side for other than purely pecuniary considerations.

On his return from a visit to Paris late in July 1940, Laval opened his heart to Robert D. Murphy, the counselor of the American Embassy at Vichy. He was convinced, he said, that Germany had no intention of crushing France, but was planning rather "a European federation of states, in which France will play an important role, compatible with her dignity and tradition." He spoke freely of his dislike and distrust of Britain and predicted quite accurately that the air war on England would begin about August 1. "He hoped ardently," reported Murphy, "that the English would be defeated." They had ruined his Italian policy and had concluded the naval agreement with Nazi Germany in 1935. Their whole policy, he concluded, had been stupid.[18]

[18] Tel. (July 29) from Murphy.

But Laval had to contend with the old marshal and with Weygand, who by no means shared his program. The inspired press of Paris, financed by Abetz, was already denouncing the Pétain government as being too uncooperative and was insisting on a new cabinet of recognized pro-Germans, like Flandin, Doriot, and Déat. Such a new government, it was said, would be allowed to return to Paris and would be treated leniently.[19]

It is reasonable to suppose that Laval's exuberant espousal of the Nazi cause must have caused grave suspicion and perhaps acrimonious discussion at Vichy. Weygand, who detested Laval as much as the Germans, is reported to have told him to his face: "You roll in defeat like a dog in filth." [20] But Laval, backed by the Germans, was not to be trifled with. Of the details we know nothing, but on September 9 Weygand resigned as Minister of National Defense and was designated as delegate-general to North Africa with complete authority. If this development was a victory for Laval, it was at best a Pyrrhic victory. Weygand was out of the way and the road to collaboration was consequently much smoother. But in North Africa Weygand was to play a crucial role that was not at all in accord with Laval's plans nor in the interest of the Nazis.

The situation in Africa had developed to the point where it caused great concern to Pétain, even though he knew nothing about the German intentions. It will be recalled that General Noguès, like other French colonial officers and officials, had only reluctantly accepted the armistice and the Pétain government. Had it been otherwise, it is altogether likely that the Germans would have carried the war across the Mediter-

---

[19] Report from Vichy (September 5, 1940). Flandin was not really pro-German and was regarded throughout as a friend of Britain by Churchill (comments by Murphy), but Doriot and Déat each took a cut of 250,000 francs from Abetz's funds (Third Army: interrogation of Rudolf Schleier, who served under Abetz from 1940 to 1944).

[20] Raymond Brugère: *Veni, Vidi, Vichy* (Paris, 1944), p. 60, quoting Weygand. Also Louis Rougier: *Les Accords Pétain-Churchill* (Montreal, 1945), chap. iii.

ranean, for their demands of July 16, discussed above, show
that they very quickly realized the importance of North
Africa. So did the British, who had made heroic efforts to keep
North Africa in the war and who had, in the sequel, recognized General de Gaulle as the leader of all Frenchmen everywhere who were prepared to continue the struggle. It was a
great victory for them, therefore, when some of the more
remote French possessions began to declare themselves against
Vichy and in favor of de Gaulle and the "Free French." The
French stations in India led the way (July 1940), and were
soon followed by French Equatorial Africa (August) and
later by the French Pacific islands.[21]

More important than these territories, however, was French
West Africa and particularly Dakar, from which a hostile
power could interdict British trade and troop movements
around the Cape of Good Hope, to say nothing of menacing
the bulge of Brazil, which was only seventeen hundred miles
away. For these reasons the United States government had
hastily reopened its consulate at Dakar. Thomas Wasson arrived there on September 15 with instructions to watch carefully all German activities.[22] But the British went much further. They equipped and supported a force with which the
Free French undertook, on September 22, to wrest the all-
important base from the control of the Vichy governor,
Pierre Boisson. The attempt failed after some fighting, chiefly
because three French cruisers and three destroyers had been
allowed to slip through the Strait of Gibraltar in time to reach
Dakar and take part in the defense. But even if de Gaulle's
first operation had ended in debacle, his failure, as Churchill
said, "was in no sense due to infirmity of purpose."[23]

The struggle for Africa had thus already begun. At Vichy
it was realized that the outcome was likely to be crucial. The
French government would have to defend this area or permit

---

[21] Details in Barrès: *Charles de Gaulle*, chap. v.
[22] Thomas C. Wasson: "The Mystery of Dakar" (*American Foreign
Service Journal*, XX, No. 4, April 1943).
[23] See Churchill's speech of October 6, 1940.

the Germans to take over, in the interest of their own protection. If that happened, all hope would vanish that North Africa could ever become a springboard for a British or American attack on Europe and the ultimate liberation of France. So Weygand was sent to Algiers as delegate-general, with authority over all North and West Africa and with the assignment to organize and strengthen the whole area for defense. He was to resist all comers—if possible the Germans and Italians and, for the time being, the British also. As the general himself put it: when the British had sufficient forces, France would help the Allied cause from North Africa: "If they come to North Africa with four divisions, I'll fire on them; if they come with twenty divisions, I will welcome them." [24]

Unfortunately this was not Laval's approach. As we have seen, he was fully convinced that France must collaborate with Germany even to the extent of active participation in the war. There is little doubt that his hopes and plans envisaged the use of force and possibly of German help in reconquering the dissident colonies in Equatorial Africa. On October 19 Matthews reported from Vichy that Laval had

"staked his position so openly and definitely on a German victory and cooperation with Germany that he could hardly turn back and retain his prominent place in French political life. Darlan has quoted Laval as having stated literally to him at lunch several days ago 'the only way to save France or what can be saved of France is to do for the Germans what the United States is doing for England.' " [25]

So here was the Vichy government cleanly split, Pétain and Weygand beginning to take new hope and planning to hold the fort until help could come, while Laval was straining at the leash to join the enemy against England. The result was that at the end of October the Vichy government found itself negotiating at one and the same time with both Britain and Germany.

[24] Louis Rougier: *Les Accords Pétain-Churchill*, chap. iii. Pétain took the same line.
[25] Tel. (October 19) from Matthews.

On October 22 Professor Louis Rougier arrived in London, having conferred previously with both Pétain and Weygand and having been given permission to undertake a mission the object of which was, if possible, to remove certain misapprehensions and contribute to better Anglo-French relations. He was received by both Churchill and Lord Halifax, to whom he pointed out that the Vichy regime reflected a variety of views running all the way from extreme collaboration to genuine resistance. There was much discussion of the fleet, regarding which Rougier gave the most explicit assurances. Further items taken up were questions concerning the French colonies and the possibility of allowing food shipments from North Africa to France to pass through the British blockade.

Rougier set down the main heads of these discussions in a memorandum dated October 28, which was amended somewhat by officials of the British Foreign Office. This memorandum stated that British morale continued to be high and that Britain would make no compromise peace. The British were enjoying financial support from the United States and within nine months would have fifteen thousand new planes, which would give them air superiority over the Germans in 1941. The war would last only another year if North Africa were to revolt and if Britain could get bases in Tunisia. On the other hand, if Britain were to lose Egypt and the use of the Mediterranean, the conflict might continue for ten years. A great deal therefore depended on France. Britain would restore the integrity of France if the latter abstained from aiding the Axis and especially if she assisted Britain. If France were to help the Axis powers, Britain would assume no obligation, but on the contrary would do everything possible to strike at France. If, on the other hand, France desisted from any aid to Germany, Britain might allow food shipments from North Africa to France and would agree not to allow de Gaulle to attack French colonies, on the understanding that no effort should be made by Vichy to reconquer the dissident colonies. Britain would also undertake not to attack Marshal Pétain in radio broadcasts, but France was to promise not to cede bases to the Germans and to re-enter the war when Britain gave proof of sufficient power to land and equip colonial forces. France would see to it that the French fleet should be scuttled rather than allow it to fall into German or Italian hands. In a British emendation it was further stated: "If General Weygand will raise the standard in North Africa, he can count on the renewal of the whole-hearted collaboration of the governments and peoples of the British Empire, and on a share of the assistance afforded by the United States." [26]

A tremendous amount of controversy developed later about these negotiations. Rougier claimed that his memorandum, accepted by Pétain, constituted a "gentlemen's agreement" and was so recognized by both governments. On the eve of the Pétain trial the marshal's attorneys took the same line and stated that they proposed to show, through these agreements, that the Vichy government, far from collaborating with the Nazis, was secretly bound to Britain. This prospect provoked the London government to contest Rougier's claim. Churchill roundly denied that any agreement had been arrived at and insisted that although the discussions had taken place, Rougier was not authorized to make any proposals to Pétain or to Vichy. The British, he declared, had envisaged only an approach to Weygand in the hope that he might be induced "to enter of his own initiative into direct and secret negotiations with His Majesty's Government, with the object of bringing North Africa back into the war on the Allied side when the time was ripe." [27]

It would serve no good purpose to examine all the details of these discussions, though the extensive *démentis* of the British government indicate that they must have been of some importance. That there was no formal or regular agreement we

---

[26] The document is reproduced in Rougier: *Les Accords Pétain-Churchill*, pp. 131ff., 416ff.

[27] Churchill: statement in Parliament (June 12, 1945) and the later Foreign Office statement (*New York Times*, June 13, July 17, 1945), together with Rougier's reply (*New York Times*, July 21, 1945). On this whole episode see also the testimony in *Procès du M. Pétain*, p. 145 (Weygand); pp. 247–8 (Admiral Fernet).

may take as certain, but that does not detract from the fact that Pétain was prepared to sound out the British terrain and that Churchill made efforts to organize French resistance in North Africa. On this last point there was no chance of action at the time. Weygand was in West Africa when Rougier passed through Algiers on his way home, but the British proposals were put before him in a letter. According to Rougier, the general held that premature action would compromise everything: "Only in the distant future, when the British are in force, can we open our arms to them," he is reported to have said. As for Pétain, he too was unable to follow through. Laval, in the interval, had replaced Baudoin as Foreign Minister, and it was impossible to let Laval into the secret. Probably for that reason the reply from Vichy was regarded by Churchill as inadequate. None the less, relations were distinctly improved. The British radio did indeed moderate its remarks on Pétain, and food shipments between North Africa and France were more or less ignored by the British navy. There were no further attacks on French colonial territories and indeed negotiations of one kind or another were carried on for some time at either Lisbon or Madrid.[28]

Now, this entire episode took place at the very time that Laval was scoring his great triumph at the Montoire conferences with Hitler. The German Führer, as indicated above, had taken up Göring's Gibraltar scheme and had decided to develop closer relations and possibly collaboration with France and Spain. Thus Laval was given his golden opportunity. Captured German documents, added to French testimony, enable us to give a pretty complete and accurate account of what occurred.

According to Laval's own rather dramatized story, the German ambassador had told him that Ribbentrop was coming to France and that an interview could be arranged. Laval had informed Pétain and had set out with Abetz from Paris for an unknown destination. It was not until the Loire had

[28] Rougier: *Les Accords Pétain-Churchill*, chap. v; letter of A. de Montmorency in the *New York Times*, August 1, 1945.

been crossed and the party was approaching Montoire that Laval learned that he was to see Hitler. The German record, kept by Dr. Paul Schmidt, reproduces the conversation of October 22, 1940. Laval expressed his gratitude for a chance to talk with Hitler. He recalled that even before the war he had favored Franco-German collaboration and an organization of Europe. This he regarded as the only possible policy for defeated France and he was trying to persuade Pétain of it. He hoped Germany would not abuse her victory.

Hitler replied by blaming France for bringing on war, but stressed the fact that the outcome of the conflict was certain. Those Frenchmen who still hoped that the situation would change for the better were utterly deluded. As for himself, he preferred collaboration with France, if suitable conditions existed.

Laval agreed that Germany would surely win: "England will be defeated, and as a Frenchman he could only add that he desired the defeat of Britain with all his heart." Britain had rushed France into war and had then given very little support. Since the armistice British policy had been abominable. He was sure that many Frenchmen favored collaboration and would be willing to pay their share of the costs of war if only the Führer would agree to a fair settlement.

To this Hitler pointed out that a final settlement would be possible only after the end of the war, and then the Germans would have to approach not only the problem of Europe, but of Africa. He thought it likely that French interests could be safeguarded, and suggested that if Pétain agreed to collaboration in principle, he (Hitler) would be ready to meet the marshal for a discussion—an invitation that Laval accepted in Pétain's name. The meeting ended with some reflections on how Britain rather than France might be made to pay for German, Italian, and Spanish aspirations in Africa.[29]

While Laval returned to Vichy to arrange for Pétain's visit

[29] State Department: Captured German Documents. Laval's account (*Procès du M. Pétain*, p. 194) does not differ materially from the German record.

to Hitler, the Führer himself went on to Hendaye, where he was to meet with General Franco and the newly appointed Spanish Foreign Minister, Señor Serrano Suñer, chief of the fanatically fascist Falange. Franco had long since revealed his appetite for territorial expansion. After the collapse of France he had unceremoniously taken over control of the international Tangier territory. At the same time he had offered to enter the war on Germany's side, provided that Hitler could supply Spain with munitions and food and provided further that Spain should receive Gibraltar, French Morocco, the Oran Province of Algeria, and an enlargement of the Río de Oro colony. The Germans were slow to react, fearing that any move might precipitate a coup by the British. Thereupon the Caudillo had sent Serrano to Berlin to press his claims to French Morocco. Conversations were carried on envisaging an exchange of French territory for submarine bases in Río de Oro or Fernando Po, and all aspects of an attack on Gibraltar were analyzed. The Spanish emissary was burning with eagerness for action, but, as we now know from the record of Hitler's discussions with the Italians, it was felt in Berlin that the Spaniards did not have "the same intensity of will for giving as for taking." They were asking a great deal, and Hitler was concerned lest assignment of French Morocco to Spain should lead to a French revolt in Africa and alliance of the dissidents with Britain.[30]

Such was the situation when the two "friends" met. Hitler expounded the military situation as it was and as it would be after Britain's defeat, which was not far distant. If Spain would cooperate, Africa could be shut off against England and, once Gibraltar had been taken, the Mediterranean too would be closed. He therefore proposed an immediate alliance between Germany and Spain and the latter's entry into the war early in 1941. In January German forces, with Spanish support, would

[30] The earlier phases of the Spanish question are very well reflected in the captured German documents published by the Department of State under the title: *The Spanish Government and the Axis* (Washington, 1946); also tels. (September 23, 26, 1940) from Madrid.

attack and take Gibraltar, which would then be given to Spain
along with certain African territories. The Führer made no
bones, however, about pointing out the difficulty presented by
Spanish claims. It was of great importance to Germany to
avoid a French revolt in North Africa that might enable the
British to establish a foothold there. Once Britain was conquered, it would be easier to disregard French interests. But
for the moment French susceptibilities must be considered.

Now, this was not at all to Franco's liking. It seems likely,
as the American ambassador believed, that Franco hoped to
realize Spain's national aspirations without actually fighting,
and that Serrano Suñer had dragged him further in the Axis
direction than he or the army felt prepared to go. At any rate,
he began to hedge and evade, while even Serrano constantly
broke in with other considerations: the food situation in Spain
was desperately bad, and Spain lacked modern armaments. In
a war with Britain the Spanish coasts and the Canary Islands
would be extremely exposed. Hitler tried to reassure him:
Germany could send air squadrons to the Canaries and two
modern divisions to Spanish Morocco. The attack on Gibraltar would be carried out by special troops.

But Franco remained dubious. He pointed out that Spain
should be in a position to defend herself and to conquer Gibraltar by her own efforts. No doubt the Germans would
conquer England, but he feared the government would flee
to Canada and from there, with American aid, would occupy
the Azores and the Canaries. Under the circumstances he
could agree to an alliance only if Spain were promised all of
French Morocco and part of Algeria. Even then Spain could
enter the war only when she had sufficient food and adequate
armament.

Hitler was furious at meeting such resistance, but he needed
Spanish help and finally agreed that Spain "would receive territorial compensation out of French North African possessions to the extent to which it would be possible to cover
France's losses from British colonies." This in turn was but
slight consolation for the Spaniards, and the meeting broke up

with no firm engagements. Details were to be worked out later, and in actual fact led to a good deal of friction and ill feeling. Hitler never forgave Franco for his unwillingness to be persuaded and is said to have remarked frequently that he would not name such a fellow even as a *Kreisleiter* in his government.[31]

In the meanwhile Pétain had been persuaded to pay Hitler the visit at Montoire that Laval had arranged for. Apparently the old soldier was very averse to taking this step, but it was pointed out to him that he simply could not decline without giving offense. In that case the French people would be made to pay. Besides, how was he ever to secure concessions—for example, in the matter of the French prisoners in Germany— if he were unwilling to discuss these questions with Hitler. Under the pressure of these considerations he finally agreed to accompany Laval. On the appointed day, October 24, Pétain and Hitler met at Montoire.

Here again we can draw upon the very careful German record of the discussions. Hitler greeted the marshal cordially and expressed regret that the meeting had to take place under circumstances so painful to a Frenchman. Pétain remarked that he, personally, had always been opposed to the war and had done his utmost to prevent such folly on the part of the government. Then, coming down to the problem, he referred to Laval's report regarding possible collaboration and regretted that close relations had not been developed before the war. Perhaps it was not yet too late, especially in view of Britain's attitude toward France.

Hitler recognized the fact that Pétain had always been an opponent of the war, but pointed out that France had none the less provoked the conflict and had been defeated. If Ger-

[31] By far the most detailed account is in the unpublished memorandum on German foreign policy by Erich Kordt, who was present. But see also the State Department interrogations of Erich Kordt, Paul Schmidt, and General Warlimont, and Carlton J. H. Hayes: *Wartime Mission in Spain* (New York, 1945), pp. 64–5, referring to a confidential report of Serrano Suñer. The record of the Hendaye meeting in *The Spanish Government and the Axis*, No. 8, is very incomplete. Tels. (October 24, 31, 1940) from Madrid tend to bear out the German version.

many had been the loser, no doubt France would have treated
her more harshly than in 1918. But he was determined to
adopt another approach. His objective was to crush England.
Only the weather was holding him back, but in the meanwhile he would continue the attack by air and by submarine.
Britain's position was already untenable and the United States
would be able to do little before 1942. By that time Britain
would be occupied or else reduced to a heap of ruins. "The
thought of an American landing on the Continent is militarily
speaking a pure illusion." Furthermore, Russia was bound to
Germany by treaty, and Germany's own potential was enormous. Germany and her allies constituted a military power
that no combination in the world could attack or conquer.
But the point was to end the war as quickly as possible, for
there was no business less profitable than war. All Europe
would have to pay the costs and so all Europe had the same
interest. To what extent would France help?

Pétain replied that he could not define the limits, but was
ready to accept the principle of collaboration. He promised
to consult his government on his return. At this point Laval
interjected to stress the importance of Pétain's assent and to
beg Hitler not to press France to make war against Britain.
It would be necessary to prepare French opinion. Therewith
the conference ended, the upshot of the discussions being recorded as follows in German, French and Italian:

"The German Reich and its ally, Italy, did not want the war
against France and England. Contrary to the sincere desires of
the German Government to live in peace with England and
France, these two powers declared war on Germany. The further
efforts of the German Government, aimed at putting an end to
this futile struggle, broke against the resistance of the former
French Government and of the present British Government.

"Once this struggle is ended, it will be evident that either
France or England will have to bear the territorial and material
costs of the conflict.

"Inspired by the superior, continental interests of the pre-
ponderantly European powers, Germany, Italy and France, re-

ferring to the discussions which took place on 24 October 1940 between the head of the French State and the Führer of the German Reich, have agreed in the present Procès-Verbal, upon the following:

1) In accord with the Duce, the Führer manifested his determination to see France occupy, in the New Europe, the place to which she is entitled, and to have the French people participate in the cooperation of European peoples which will prove indispensable in the future.

2) The Axis Powers and France have an identical interest in seeing the defeat of England accomplished as soon as possible. Consequently, the French Government will support, within the limits of its ability, the measures which the Axis Powers may take to this end. The details of this practical cooperation will be dealt with in a special agreement between Germany and Italy on the one hand and France on the other.

3) Under this condition and in order to permit France equally to take military measures in Africa, Germany and Italy are prepared to authorize France to employ certain contingents beyond the stipulations of the armistice convention and the agreements for its implementation. Questions of detail will be settled by the armistice commissions in concert with the French delegations.

4) The Führer declared to the head of the French State that, after the defeat of England and the retrocession of the German colonies, there will be an opportunity, within the framework of a general peace settlement, for a repartition of colonial possessions in Africa, a repartition which, while assuring a harmonization of reciprocal interests, would take account of political necessities and economic needs of the interested European states. This concerns above all the four powers: Germany, Italy, France and Spain. To the extent that this new order in Africa will involve necessary territorial modifications in the existing French colonial domain, the Axis powers will undertake to see that, at the conclusion of peace with England, France obtains territorial compensations and that, in the final accounting, she retains in Africa a colonial domain essentially equivalent to what she possesses today.

5) The two parties are agreed that this Procès-Verbal be kept absolutely secret.

6) The Government of the Reich undertakes to secure im-

mediately the assent of the Italian Government to the above points, and to request the Italian Government to subscribe to this Procès-Verbal." [32]

It is hard, even at this time, to arrive at a just evaluation of the Montoire meeting. Hitler, having just come from a disappointing and irritating debate with Franco, was evidently not in an exuberant mood and did not press Pétain for any specific engagement. According to Dr. Schmidt, the Führer was distinctly disillusioned. He had hoped for a specific French commitment to take part in the war against Britain, and he had found even Laval evasive, stressing general co-operation.[33] To be sure, Pétain had agreed that the defeat of Britain at an early date was most desirable, and he had accepted a program involving colonial readjustments at Britain's expense. But all this was in very general terms. All the details were to be worked out later and so the door was left wide open. Pétain is reported to have remarked to one of his friends: "It will take six months to discuss this program and another six months to forget it." [34]

So Montoire settled nothing. The Germans would have to defeat Britain as best they could and the French would give only such aid as they could. But despite all this vagueness in the agreements themselves, it must be remembered that at the time nothing specific was known in the world at large and there was therefore a free field for all sorts of rumors.[35] It was commonly supposed that Hitler had promised France a definitive peace in return for use of the fleet, for the cession of bases, and for a repartition of colonies. In general, the confabulations at Montoire seemed so ominous that both the British and the American governments were genuinely alarmed and at once

[32] The text, in French and German, is among the captured German documents. Schmidt's account of the Montoire conference likewise. On the French side see *Procès du M. Pétain*, pp. 176–7 (Trochu's account, based on information from Du Moulin de la Barthète); 194–7 (Laval's account).

[33] Interrogation of Dr. Paul Schmidt.

[34] *Procès du M. Pétain*, p. 313 (Estèbe's testimony).

[35] State Department interrogation of Erich Kordt; Kordt believes that one of Hitler's chief objectives in arranging the Montoire and Hendaye meetings was to demonstrate to Britain how completely the Continent was under Nazi control.

went into action. King George transmitted, through American channels, a personal appeal to Marshal Pétain on October 25. His Majesty assured the marshal of Britain's continued goodwill toward France and begged him not to harm a former ally by making concessions beyond the armistice or by taking sides against her.[36]

At the same time President Roosevelt addressed the marshal in much sterner terms::

"In the opinion of the United States Government, the fact that the French Government alleges that it is under duress and consequently cannot act except to a very limited degree as a free agent is in no sense to be considered as justifying any course on the part of the French Government which would provide assistance to Germany and her allies in the war against the British Empire. The fact that a Government is a prisoner of war of another power does not justify such a prisoner in serving its conqueror in operations against a former ally.

"The Government of the United States received from the Pétain Government during the first days it held office the most solemn assurances that the French Fleet would not be surrendered. If the French Government now permits the Germans to use the French Fleet in hostile operations against the British Fleet, such action would constitute a flagrant and deliberate breach of faith with the United States Government.

"Any agreement entered into between France and Germany which partook of the character above mentioned would most definitely wreck the traditional friendship between the French and American peoples, would permanently remove any chance that this Government would be disposed to give any assistance to the French people in their distress, and would create a wave of bitter indignation against France on the part of American public opinion.

"If France pursued such a policy as that above outlined, the United States could make no effort when the appropriate time came to exercise its influence to insure to France the retention of her overseas possessions." [37]

[36] The full text of the letter is given in *Procès du M. Pétain*, 327.
[37] Tel. (October 25, 1940) Hull to Matthews.

A diplomatic warning could hardly be couched in more outspoken terms. In Vichy it seems to have created some consternation, and there was complaint of its "painfully curt" wording. The officials of the French Foreign Office, many of whom were devoted to friendship with the United States, were deeply dejected. Yet they admitted to Matthews that "Laval and Hitler have sold the marshal on a policy of straight-out cooperation with Germany, a policy which most of the foreign office officials have actively or passively tried to resist." [38]

In his reply to President Roosevelt, on November 1, Pétain questioned the fairness of the American government's insinuations:

"To answer the anxiety of President Roosevelt, he (Pétain) desires to state that the French Government had always preserved its liberty of action and that I knew that he might be surprised at an appraisement as inaccurate as it is unjust. The French Government has declared that the French Fleet would never be surrendered and nothing can justify questioning today that solemn undertaking."

The marshal then went on to remind the President that it was the British who had taken action against the French fleet, and not vice versa; that, in fact, the British government was supporting French rebels who were endangering the unity of the French Empire. Nevertheless, France would not engage in any unjustified attack.[39]

Secretary Hull declined to take this reply at face value. A few days later he had a long conversation with the newly arrived Vichy ambassador, Gaston Henry-Haye—a conversation in which no words were minced. The Secretary pointed out that the Vichy government, like the governments of Berlin, Rome, and Tokyo, showed no disposition to be frank and friendly. The American government was in no way taken into its confidence and had to depend on rumors and reports in order to form any idea of what French policy was:

[38] Tels. (October 26, 1940) from Matthews.
[39] Tel. (November 1, 1940) from Matthews.

"I said that the chief trouble seems to be that high-ranking officials in the French government seem disposed to keep entirely away from this Government in most everything that relates to normal relations, and at the same time to keep extremely close to Hitler and to show every sympathetic interest in his plans and purposes, revealing all the while the utmost antipathy toward Great Britain and the cause for which she is fighting."

The ambassador, though not outstanding in point of intelligence, at once divined that Hull was referring to Laval, which the Secretary admitted:

"I added that we propose to be on our guard with respect to acts of the Vichy Government, inspired by M. Laval, that are intended to aid, by French connivance, the military activities of Hitler, such as supplying of naval and air bases, or other help given by the land, sea or air forces of France."

The American government, he continued, still retained its high regard for Marshal Pétain and its understanding of the difficulties of France as a captive nation, in honor bound to live up to the terms of the armistice. But it could not recognize the right of the Vichy government to go beyond those terms, to the detriment of other nations:

"I said that M. Laval may think he can appease Mr. Hitler just as others heretofore have imagined that they could appease him; that that was his affair; that this Government, however, recognizing the great misfortune of the French Government in not pursuing the long-view objectives within sufficient time for its safety, does not propose to trust Hitler for one split second to fall in with any government on a course of appeasement; that the French Government, therefore, should understand the position of this Government and its determination to take no chances." [40]

These are only a few excerpts from a long document, but since that document has been published by the Department of State, there is no point in reproducing it in full. It is well worth reading, however, for anyone who still has any doubts

[40] Memo. of conversation between Secretary Hull and the French ambassador, November 4, 1940.

about the American official policy toward the Vichy system
and particularly toward the policy of Laval. There was no
thought whatever of indulgence toward the new regime. The
Secretary, like the President, reiterated American sympathy
for the plight of France, but left no shadow of doubt that he
did not consider France's misfortune any excuse for her collaboration with her former enemy to the detriment of the
Allied and therefore the American cause.

The Vichy government showed no inclination to continue
the debate. Laval had spoken quite unreservedly to the Paris
press on October 31 and had made no bones about his intentions:

"In every domain, and especially in the economic sphere and in
the colonial sphere, we have envisaged and will continue to
examine in what practical forms our collaboration may serve the
interests of France, of Germany and of Europe."

Knowing the man, there is no reason to suppose that he would
change his course. On the contrary, there was every reason
to anticipate the worst. It therefore behooved the American
government to keep a weather eye open and to take such
measures as the situation might seem to call for.

Hard on the heels of the Montoire conference and the exchange of views outlined above, came a letter from Churchill
to President Roosevelt. This referred to reports that had come
to the British that the French government would bring the
battleships *Jean Bart* and *Richelieu* from African ports to
French Mediterranean bases for completion. "It is difficult,"
wrote the Prime Minister, "to exaggerate the potential danger
if this were to happen, and so open the way for these ships to
fall under German control. We should feel bound to do our
best to prevent it." The British, he added, had already warned
Vichy on this score, and begged the President to do likewise.[41]

Steps were immediately taken to this end, and renewed
warnings sent to Vichy: "For your personal information

[41] Tel. (November 10, 1940) from London.

only," wrote the President to Churchill, "I am letting the French government know that this government would be prepared to buy these two ships if they will dispose of them to us." We were ready to promise that in such an event the ships would not be used in the course of the war.[42]

In this connection Matthews, the American chargé d'affaires, sought and obtained a personal interview with Marshal Pétain on November 16 and received from him a renewal of earlier assurances:

"I have given the most solemn assurances that the French Fleet, including these two ships, shall never fall into Germany's hands. I have given those assurances to your Government; I have given them to the British Government and even to Churchill personally. I reiterate them now. They will be used to defend French territory and possessions. They will never be used against the British unless we are attacked by them. I cannot sell those ships even if I wanted to. The terms of the armistice prevent it, and even if they did not, the Germans would never permit it. We are under their heel and are powerless." [43]

Although this answer was probably expected in Washington, nothing was left untried. Matthews was instructed to tell the marshal that the President's offer to buy or lease these ships, or for that matter any part of the French navy, remained open if France wished to take advantage of it.[44] So much at least had been gained, that Pétain had renewed his earlier assurances and that, indeed, he had declared himself on the larger issues of French policy. In the same audience of November 16 he told Matthews that he thought the policy of collaboration was much misunderstood in the United States. By it he meant "only economic collaboration and in no sense military aid to Germany in her war against Britain, nor cession of bases." With regard to Britain he remained very critical: the

[42] Tel. (November 13, 1940) to London; tel. (November 13, 1940) to Vichy.
[43] Tel. (November 16, 1940) from Matthews.
[44] Tel. (November 18, 1940) Welles to Vichy.

British had pushed the French into the war and then had given
them very little help. Even now they were supporting "the
traitor De Gaulle." But, he added, he bore them no hatred and
he realized that France must hope for a British victory:

"They are fighting a good fight now and he does not believe
that they will ever yield. On the other hand, they cannot land on
the Continent and invade Germany. He therefore sees after much
tragic destruction a drawn peace. The sooner that could come,
the better, for France will pay the price." [45]

These remarks are of the utmost interest for anyone attempting to unravel the tangled skein of French policy during
this period. They leave but little doubt that Pétain had changed
his views radically during the autumn months. The collapse
of Britain had not come and there could be no thought of invasion before spring. And with the successful defense of Britain had vanished Pétain's hopes of an early and favorable peace
with Germany. As a matter of fact, the German attitude had
proved to be hard and ruthless, as witness among other items
the events in Alsace and Lorraine. The marshal's dreams were
dissipated and he now saw hope only in the victory of Britain.
However, he did not see how Britain could win, and he therefore thought that a compromise peace, the sooner the better,
would be the most desirable solution. It will be important, in
the sequel, to follow further the evolution of the marshal's
thought. For the moment, though, it is essential to remember
that Laval was in the saddle. As we know, he was filled with
hatred of the British and was absolutely confident of a German victory.[46] He was not only willing but eager to embark
upon a policy of collaboration with Hitler. According to him,
France should be fitted as snugly as possible into the new Nazi
order in Europe.

Pétain's assurances and hopes, then, were of only slight practical value. The part of wisdom would be to leave nothing to

[45] Tel. (November 16, 1940) from Matthews.
[46] At the Pétain trial he reiterated his stand and asked quite uncompro-
misingly: "Do you think that in 1940 any man of sense could imagine anything but a German victory?" (*Procès du M. Pétain*, p. 195).

chance, and with that thought in mind the United States government proceeded to take some necessary precautions.

One of the danger spots, as seen from this side of the Atlantic, was the French foothold in the West Indies—that is, the islands of Martinique and Guadeloupe. We had declared against the transfer of such New World territory from one non-American power to another, and the Havana Convention of July 30 had aligned all the American governments behind this defensive policy. But Martinique presented a special problem that had nothing directly to do with the possibility of its cession. At Martinique lay several French warships, including the aircraft-carrier *Béarn*. There were also at Martinique 106 American airplanes that had been en route to France in June 1940. Finally, there was gold bullion to the value of twelve billion francs ($245,000,000) which had been moved from Canada during the crisis. Rear Admiral John W. Greenslade had been sent to Martinique in August 1940 to make sure that neither ships nor planes nor gold would be moved and that the islands would not be made a base for German submarine activity. The French governor of the islands, Admiral Robert, proved to be an out-and-out supporter of Marshal Pétain, though the sentiments of the inhabitants were divided. Many wished the French government to return the planes to the United States in exchange for much-needed food and supplies, but Admiral Robert gave only very general assurances. In the course of the summer he suppressed the general council and instituted a military regime that gave him complete control. The situation was in every way unsatisfactory, and after the Montoire conference and Laval's open avowal of the policy of collaboration it became downright dangerous. As Secretary Hull said to the French ambasador on November 4, if the French government was in earnest about its earlier assurances to maintain the *status quo* on Martinique, it should be willing to implement these assurances, as, for instance, by removing some of the parts of the ships, or by removing the naval personnel, or by permitting American ships to make periodic inspections. For fear that these suggestions would meet with no real response, Admiral Greenslade was sent on a second mission to the islands.[47] He told Admiral Robert that the United States government had decided "to send an airplane carrier and patrol planes to St. Lucia in order to observe day and night the movements of French naval vessels." [48] Since not even the hard-bitten old admiral could take this news lightly, he accepted a gentleman's agreement by which he promised to give the American government ninety-six hours' notice before any intended ship movements. The United States was to be allowed to station a naval observer at Port de France and to have the right to maintain a naval and air patrol. In return the Americn government agreed to supply the French islands with food, which was to be paid for from blocked French funds.[49]

Of equal or even greater importance, however, was the potential danger presented by the French colonies in West and North Africa. In the autumn of 1940 the first steps were taken toward the development of a policy that was to become the crux of our entire relationship with Vichy France.

It will be recalled that early in October General Weygand had arrived in Algiers as delegate-general of the Vichy government, with power to invoke and if need be to take any measures required for the security of North and West Africa. He was to reorganize the forces and to resist any attack from whatever quarter. In this way the Vichy government hoped to frustrate any spread of dissidence or any assault by the Free French. At the same time it was hoped that North Africa could be strengthened to the point of discouraging any German or Italian plans of aggression. Weygand at once undertook a tour of the entire area, going as far as Dakar. On November 2 he made a public address in which he voiced the

[47] On the earlier developments in Martinique I rely on the dispatch of V. Harwood Blocker, August 21, 1940, and the memorandum on the whole problem by J. D. Hickerson, October 1, 1940 (both in the Department of State).
[48] Tel. (November 6, 1940) Hull to Vichy.
[49] See Forrest Davis and E. K. Lindley: *How War Came* (New York, 1942), p. 147.

determination of North Africa to resist any attack. There were numerous conferences of high French officials and very possibly some united protest against Laval's aims and intentions. We now know from German documents that Laval was planning a campaign to reconquer Equatorial Africa, despite his realization that such an operation would probably involve hostilities with Britain. When Pétain took him to task for this policy later, Laval pointed out that in any event Britain would then be the aggressor. He had, he said, no hate for the English people, but would hail the day when Churchill, Eden, Duff Cooper and Hore-Belisha would be lynched. This being Laval's aim and attitude, it is not surprising that Matthews should have reported him distinctly annoyed by Weygand's stand and perhaps determined to have the general recalled.[50]

One real possibility existed for action by either Britain or the United States, so far as North Africa was concerned, and this lay in the economic field. Cut off from normal imports, the entire region had become desperately short of sugar, tea, gasoline, and clothing. The British were prepared to take advantage of this situation, and before the end of September informed the American government that they proposed to make a clearing arrangement with Morocco, exchanging sugar and tea for phosphates. This scheme might be extended to Spain and Portugal also, and the British were willing to relax the blockade even to the extent of permitting American-Moroccan trade, provided it were limited to goods that were to be consumed in Morocco.[51]

[50] Captured German documents: telegram from Abetz to Ribbentrop (January 19, 1941), reporting Laval's account of his talk with Pétain; also record of the meeting of Hitler, Ciano, and Laval at Munich (November 10, 1942); testimony of Peyrouton (*Procès du M. Pétain*, pp. 243–4). Further, State Department memorandum: *The Political Implications of American-Moroccan Trade* (November 12, 1940); British White Paper, summarized in *New York Times* (August 2, 1945); and Pétain's statement at the Peyrouton trial (*Washington Post*, July 22, 1945).

[51] *The Political Implications*, etc.; also the memorandum prepared (1944) by the Division of Research and Publication of the Department of State entitled *The Role of the Department of State in the North African Economic and Political Program from Its Inception to the Invasion* (pp. 4–5).

Several members of the Near Eastern Division of the Department—notably Wallace Murray, Paul Alling, Henry Villard, and the desk officer for Morocco, Rives Childs—had already been speculating on the possibility that Weygand's North African appointment might be a reflection of Vichy's efforts to keep that important region from falling under Axis control. On August 26 Matthews had reported from Vichy a conversation with Monick, the newly appointed secretary-general of the French protectorate, who had spoken urgently of the desirability of closer economic ties between the United States and Morocco. It was evidently Monick who had initiated negotiations with the British in the hope of maintaining at least some measure of economic independence for the protectorate. It was he, too, who commissioned A. G. Reed, the manager of the Socony-Vacuum Oil Company in Morocco, to go to Washington and explore possibilities with both British and American authorities.

When Reed reached the capital on October 25, a certain amount of discussion had already taken place in the Department, more particularly between the Near Eastern Division, the Trade Agreements Division, and the Office of the Economic Adviser. The soil had therefore been prepared and Reed was sympathetically listened to when he suggested the shipment of a small amount of petroleum from Aruba to Morocco in return for minerals like manganese and cobalt. He pointed out further that such an exchange would have a larger political significance inasmuch as it would tend to keep Morocco from dependence on Metropolitan France and indirectly on the Axis. It was his impression that this thought was in the minds of General Noguès and Monick, and that the purpose of Weygand's appointment was to protect North Africa against absorption by the Germans.

As a result of these preliminary discussions a memorandum was prepared which recommended that Reed be permitted to use American diplomatic cables, on the plea that "from our larger defense interests it is important that French Morocco should not fall into hostile hands, and anything done to bol-

ster the morale of the authorities and people of that area and
to avoid the collapse, whether economic or political, of French
Morocco is all to the good." Thus the political side of the
question was first illuminated.

Unfortunately the economic adviser of the Department
was unfavorably disposed toward a trade agreement. The
Near Eastern Division therefore had to reckon largely on securing its end through the British. This procedure on the
other hand did not appeal to Adolph Berle, who gave the
American plan his full backing. Early in November it was decided to instruct Consul-General Cole at Algiers to open discussions with Weygand, while John Campbell White at Tangier was to pursue the subject farther with Monick. It was
just at this time that Matthews reported another conversation
with Monick at Vichy. The Frenchman now proposed to
make available a store of cobalt at Casablanca that he was intent on keeping from the Axis. He said that he had heard nothing from Reed and that the matter was pressing, since both
Weygand and Noguès were determined not to permit establishment of an Axis foothold in Morocco.[52]

The Department at once instructed Matthews to inform
Monick of our interest and on November 13 sent a message
to Cole at Algiers. At the same time a long memorandum on
The Political Implications of American-Moroccan Trade was
completed by the Near Eastern Division for transmission to
White at Tangier. This paper, dated November 12, argued
eloquently that everything should be done to bolster the
morale of the French and the natives in North Africa, and to
prevent economic collapse. It led to a heated debate with the
economic adviser, who was unalterably opposed to the whole
scheme but was finally overruled by Berle. It was only on December 3 that the document was finally sent off to Tangier.
In the meanwhile, however, Bullitt's attention had been called
to Matthews's reports of his talks with Monick. Bullitt was
much impressed with the possibilities and called the President's attention to them. This was probably the origin of the

[52] Tel. (November 6) from Matthews.

mission of Robert Murphy to North Africa in December.[53]

Murphy, who for ten years had been in Paris as American consul-general and then as counselor of embassy, was instructed to visit French North and West Africa and to report on the general conditions in that area. He spent almost a month there, from mid-December to mid-January, and his findings served to introduce a new phase in American policy, the first fruits of which were the Murphy-Weygand agreement of February 1941. But this new departure had better be considered in connection with later developments.

The present chapter may be brought to a convenient close with the dismissal of Laval from the government on December 13, for this important event brought new hope to Britain and the United States and introduced a new phase in American-French relations. Although it cannot be said even now that the circumstances surrounding Laval's fall are perfectly clear, we have detailed accounts both from Laval and from his opponents and we know at least something of the international implications of this event, which after all are our chief concern.

We may, I believe, begin with the proposition that Pétain had for some time been disgusted with Laval's collaborationist policy and with his high-handed, intriguing methods. Laval was spending more and more of his time in Paris with Abetz and evidently did not bother to give the marshal or his colleagues anything like a complete account of his activities. According to Laval's own story, Abetz was arranging a meeting with Ribbentrop for December 22, at which time it was said France would receive certain concessions, such as reduction of occupation costs, relaxation of the demarcation line, return of prisoners, and so on. What was to be demanded by the Germans in return was not stated, neither do we know whether Pétain had any wind of a new collaborationist deal. It seems,

[53] This account of the genesis of the Economic Accord is based largely on a memorandum prepared for me by J. Rives Childs entitled *The Birth of the North African Economic Accord*. On the French side see Weygand's account in *Procès du M. Pétain*, p. 145.

however, that the marshal was sick and tired of his subordinate, that he suspected him of intrigue with the Germans, and that he feared plans for the reconquest of the African colonies, with an ensuing break with Britain.[54] At any rate, on December 9 he sent to his Paris representative, General de La Laurencie, a letter for Hitler explaining that he could no longer work with Laval and was therefore obliged to dismiss him. For obscure reasons, this letter was recalled before its delivery.

Then on December 13 Laval arrived at Vichy with the glad tidings that Hitler had magnanimously decided to return to France the ashes of Napoleon's son, the Duke of Reichstadt. It would be necessary for the marshal to be present at the ceremonies, which were only two days off. Pétain objected, but once more was persuaded that he could not afford to offend Hitler. There matters stood at four in the afternoon. At eight the marshal suddenly called a council of ministers and unceremoniously demanded that all members resign. After they had done so, Pétain announced that only the resignation of Laval and of Ripert would be accepted. He accused Laval of not keeping him informed, of having obstructed the return of the government to Versailles, of having inspired vicious newspaper attacks on the Vichy regime by Déat, and so forth. That same evening Laval was arrested and taken to his estate at Chateldon. But Abetz, as soon as he learned of these dramatic happenings, went straight to Vichy and secured Laval's liberation. There followed a hot argument between Pétain and Laval, but the old marshal stuck to his guns and refused to entertain the suggestion that Laval should be taken back into the cabinet.

The story most current at Vichy, which is not implausible, was that, in addition to other grievances, Pétain had been led to believe that Laval and the Germans had hatched a scheme by which they could reduce the marshal to the status of a

---

[54] According to Erich Kordt (State Department interrogation) the Germans, in the hope of embroiling France with Britain, were constantly urging Laval to show his sincerity by getting on with this project.

mere figurehead, while Laval would become the actual ruler of France. The men involved in the overthrow of Laval seem to have been first Peyrouton, the Minister of the Interior, and then Darlan and Bouthillier, who supported him. Peyrouton led the attack because he was convinced that Laval was pursuing a policy of extreme collaboration of his own, and planning an expedition to Equatorial Africa. He felt so vehement on the subject that he even tried to persuade Pétain to have Laval shot as a traitor. This, however, was going further than the marshal dared go.[55]

Flandin was appointed to succeed Laval as Foreign Minister, and every effort was made to convince the Germans that the change in ministers did not portend a change of policy. Indeed, Pétain had drafted a letter to Hitler in which he declared roundly: "I remain more than ever a partisan of the policy of collaboration, the only policy which can assure France of the definitive peace which Your Excellency and I so strongly desire to bring about." [56] This letter was not actually sent, but a similar message was dispatched. None the less the downfall of Laval was hailed in France with general satisfaction. It was taken not only as a demonstration of the old marshal's firmness and determination, but also as "recognition of the unpopularity of Laval's enthusiastic and determined march down the path of collaboration with the Nazis and of the bad name which that policy was giving France abroad." [57]

[55] Tels. (December 14, 16) from Murphy, reporting statements of Rochat and of Baudoin. Also tel. (January 23, 1941) from Admiral Leahy, reporting Flandin's account, and later comments by Murphy. More recent material is the testimony in *Procès du M. Pétain*, pp. 195–9 (Laval's story); 243–4 (Peyrouton); 267 (Berthelot); and the story told the Germans by Darlan (Captured German Documents: report of Darlan interview with Hitler, December 24, 1940).

[56] *Rapport du Général de La Laurencie*, May 3, 1941, published in *Les Documents*, No. 36, February 15, 1943. La Laurencie was a close friend of Pétain's and acted as French representative in Paris.

[57] "It was his [Laval's] persuasive powers," Matthews reported from Vichy, "that engineered the death of the Third Republic and organized the new regime, and it was he who hoped behind the dignified and patriotic façade of a tired and aged Marshal to go the whole way in aid to Germany." Tel. (December 18, 1940) from Vichy.

It is more than likely that, despite all asseverations to the contrary, the dismissal of Laval was due largely to Pétain's objection to a policy of all-out collaboration. In any event, the Germans refused to be misled by sugared declarations that the whole episode was merely an internal row and had nothing to do with foreign policy. Abetz told one of his friends that the whole business was very deplorable, for Laval was the man who had created the climate for good Franco-German relations. For that reason the German ambassador did his utmost to get Laval reinstated. He failed, as we have seen, thereby giving rise to further suspicions on the part of Hitler. When Darlan came to the Führer on Christmas Eve with elaborate explanations, Hitler told him to his face that he put no stock in French excuses and that he was appalled by the motives that had been attributed to him. He had had real hopes of Pétain as a level-headed soldier, but it was clear now that France was reverting to the policy that had brought on her defeat.[58]

[58] Captured German Documents: report on the Hitler-Darlan meeting of December 24, 1940. Also the interrogation of Dr. Paul Schmidt with reference to the near break in Franco-German relations.

CHAPTER IV

Alarums and Excursions

FOREIGN POLICY, in time of a great war, is directly conditioned by the ebb and flow of military events. The relations between powers at such a time are necessarily fluid. Each state must be on the alert to readjust to sudden and often unexpected fluctuations, and for those states that are directly concerned it may be a matter of life and death whether or not the adaptations are made correctly and in time. Diplomacy, after all, is as much a weapon as are guns or tanks or planes.

It therefore behooves us, before continuing our chronicle of Franco-American relations, to take stock, at least briefly, of the course of events in the first half of 1941. The period, on the whole, was one of the blackest of the entire conflict so far as the Allied cause was concerned. It is true that Hitler's armadas of the air were defeated in the first great assault on Britain, and that the anticipated invasion of the embattled island did not take place. None the less the situation remained extremely precarious. On the sea the Germans were sinking valuable ships and cargoes faster than British and American industry together could replace them, and there was no reason to suppose that in the spring the much dreaded assault on Britain would not be undertaken in earnest. No one could know, in the early months of 1941, where the Nazi lightning would strike next.

As a matter of fact, England was still to be spared, for, as we now know from German sources, Hitler's inspirations were not proof against the unforeseen and least of all against the selfish calculations of his allies. While the Führer was busily attempting to inveigle Pétain into a policy of collaboration, he learned to his amazement that Mussolini, his "tattered lackey," in the words of Churchill, was about to attack

Greece, evidently in the hope of securing for himself dominion over the eastern Mediterranean while the Nazis were preparing to advance in the west. Hitler hurried off at once to
Florence and tried to dissuade his colleague from an adventure
so rash that all the Italian generals opposed it. But the·Duce
would have his way. On October 28, 1940 the attack on
Greece was begun, only to bog down very quickly in a series
of severe setbacks for the aggressor. In the end the Nazis had
to come to the aid of their ambitious but luckless friends, until
in April and May 1941 the German legions were on a new
march of victory, which led them as far as Crete.

These developments, outwardly spectacular, were to prove
fatal to Nazi hopes of ultimate victory. Hitler, it will be recalled, had yielded to Göring's importunities and had decided
on a grand assault upon Gibraltar. Franco's hardly concealed
opposition had introduced a sour note into the Nazi program,
but a far more serious problem emerged when on November 12 Molotov arrived in Berlin and set forth a Russian program so extensive and so ominous that Hitler was driven to the
conclusion that war against Russia could not long be delayed.
In December orders were given to plan for an attack on Russia
in May 1941.

It is well known that the Italian debacle in Greece diverted
the Germans and that the unexpected resistance of the Yugoslavs in April 1941 threw the entire Nazi war machine off
schedule. But beyond that, the hapless situation of the Italians
in the Balkans was matched by an equally awkward development on the southern side of the Mediterranean. In September
1940 Marshal Graziani had been ordered, despite all his misgivings, to launch an assault on Egypt. The British fell back,
but only in order the better to prepare a counteroffensive.
In December General Wavell turned on Graziani at Mersa
Matruh and drove the Italians out of Cyrenaica. By February
1941 the British had occupied El Agheila and might well have
gone farther had they not thought it expedient to rush some
of their forces to the support of the Greeks.

In order to cope with this new situation the Germans

planned a vast pincers operation. Three army groups were to
be employed. One was to move through Spain, take Gibraltar, and move on into Morocco, whence it was to overrun
North Africa as far as Tripolitania. A second was to advance
from Italy into Tripolitania, and a third was to overrun the
Balkans, capture the Dardanelles, and push on through Turkey to Suez. The Mediterranean having fallen completely
under Nazi control, the British were to be offered peace on
condition that they ally themselves with Germany against
Russia.

The first part of this program was given up, for in December, when Franco was informed that the Germans proposed
to march on Gibraltar on January 10, the Spanish generalissimo declared flatly that Spain could not enter the war for
some time. Even if Gibraltar were taken, the British would
seize the Canaries, and the Americans might occupy the
Azores, Madeira, and the Cape Verdes. Under the circumstances Hitler had to abandon this part of his plan. But the
Germans did carry through the Balkan campaign and did ship
General Rommel and the motorized Afrika Korps from Sicily
to Tripolitania. Rommel struck on March 24 and took the
British by surprise. They were obliged to fall back from their
previous conquests and by mid-May only Tobruk still held
out. Had Rommel been decently reinforced he might have
gone clear to Alexandria and Suez. But on June 22 Hitler
turned on Russia and therewith began a new phase in the epic
struggle for Europe.[1]

The upshot of it all was that by June 1941 the Germans
had brought the entire Balkan area under their control and
that they dominated all of North Africa from Tunisia to the
borders of Egypt. Although we now know that Hitler felt

---

[1] On Axis plans and activities see the *Ciano Diary*, entries for August 8,
11, 19, September 14, October 17, 1940, and especially the following German sources: *The Spanish Government and the Axis*, No. 11 (report of
the conference between Franco and Admiral Canaris, December 12, 1940);
Ninth Air Force: *Intelligence Summary*, pp. 135-6, (June 11, 1945), interrogation of Göring; State Department: *Special Interrogation Mission*, interrogations of Göring, Jodl, Guderian, Warlimont, Paul Schmidt, Erich Kordt.

constrained to abandon his plans for a west Mediterranean campaign and concentrate his might against Russia, the British and American governments could not at the time know this decision. It was generally feared that the Führer had Franco in his pocket and that a combined German and Spanish assault on Gibraltar and North Africa was inescapable. We shall see that both London and Washington were constantly on tenterhooks in anticipation of such a move and that every possible attempt was made to induce France to obstruct the Nazi scheme.

But to concentrate attention exclusively on the Mediterranean problem would be to produce only a partial picture. On the other side of the globe developments were less spectacular, but none the less inexorable. Already established in Indo-China, the Japanese were beginning to take Thailand also under their "protection." In March they "mediated" successfully the border dispute between Thailand and Indo-China, robbing one of their "allies" (France) in favor of the other (Thailand). At the same time they began to bring ever increasing pressure to bear on the Dutch East Indies, which were already marked down as part of the "Greater East Asia Co-Prosperity Sphere." The five-year non-aggression pact concluded between Japan and Russia on April 13, 1941 was another and, for the United States, a disconcerting item. How much it might mean, no one could say at the time, but in any event it dispelled for a while all thought that Russia might call a halt to the Japanese advance in China.

In the face of all this the United States could as yet do very little. The country as a whole was certainly not yet ready to take a firm stand. It was enough for the moment that it followed the government lead to the extent of declaring itself on the side of Britain and other opponents of the Nazis— enough that it was willing to implement its expressions of sympathy to the extent of accepting the lend-lease bill and appropriating some seven billion dollars to the support of those who were fighting aggression. For the rest, we could look only to the speeding up of our productive capacity and to the progress of our two-ocean navy, and hope against hope that our diplomacy might succeed in staving off the evil day.

How were these conditions reflected in our relationship to France? Let it be remembered that we had maintained the ordinary diplomatic ties to Vichy without enthusiasm. Liberal and especially radical circles might criticize the Department of State for having truck with a fascist regime and might even suggest that we ought to throw all our support behind de Gaulle; but there was as yet no very strong feeling on one side or the other. Felix Morley, for example, held that collaboration between France and Germany was inevitable and that France, in her desperate plight, should not be blamed for it. If the Vichy government was becoming a puppet of Hitler, he argued, it was largely because we, in our cold hostility, were making it so: "If spokesmen of the American people insist upon hanging swastikas around the necks of the French leaders, there the swastikas will eventually be found." [2]

So we followed a policy of watchful waiting, exercising such influence as we could to hold France within the limits of the armistice agreements and block real collaboration with Germany. The Montoire conference and the publicly announced Laval policy of collaboration were not at all to our liking and had evoked very plain speaking on the part of our leaders. By the same token, Laval's fall was hailed as at least a slight break in the right direction. But such hope as there might be for the future was centered almost entirely on Marshal Pétain himself, on the hero of Verdun, the man who could not conceivably sell out to the traditional enemy of France. Certainly nothing much could be expected of Flandin, nor of Admiral Darlan, who was to succeed Laval as vice-president of the council. Already on December 14, 1940 Matthews reported a long conversation with Darlan, which was anything but encouraging. The admiral's opinion was that the Germans would probably win the war, despite their failure to do so in the summer or autumn of 1940:

[2] Felix Morley: "U. S. Responsibilities to France" (*Philadelphia Evening Bulletin*, October 25, 1940).

"He is completely convinced that the British can never win on the Continent, though he does not anticipate their collapse. In any event the British Empire is finished."

Canada and probably Australia and New Zealand would draw closer to the United States, while India and South Africa would become independent:

"This being the case, the future of Europe will be governed by collaboration between the United States and France; for even if Germany wins the present war, France will, given the strength and character of her people and German weaknesses, eventually be the dominating continental force. . . . A German victory is really better for France . . . than a British victory."

Britain would ask too much: probably Madagascar and Dakar; while Germany would probably take only Alsace and Lorraine, "which are lost anyway," together with the Cameroons and British Nigeria.

Thereupon Darlan launched on a tirade against the British. His family, he maintained, had been five times ruined by the British, and never by the Germans. The British high command, he argued, had shown itself unutterably imbecile and he had no words strong enough to denounce "the drunkard Churchill, who had crawled to him on his knees during ten months, only to turn on him at Mers-el-Kébir." The only bright spot in all this ranting was Darlan's obvious effort to hold the goodwill of the United States. He renewed his assurances as to the French fleet and the French bases, though he warned that if the British insisted on the complete blockade of France, "we may attack Gibraltar and with Spanish and German help the Rock wouldn't hold out long." In closing he urged the American government to supply the French African colonies, if only in her own interest, for if trouble should start there, the Germans would get there first.[3]

[3] Tel. (December 14, 1940) from Vichy. The hope that in a new Europe the French would, by sheer force of intelligence and *savoir-faire*, be able to take over leadership from the Germans was by no means unique with Darlan, but was expressed again and again by many French officials (notes by Murphy).

This report, discouraging as it was in many respects, did
not deter the Washington government from pursuing a plan
that had already been decided upon. In view of Pétain's demonstration of authority, it had been thought wise to send a
prominent and influential figure as ambassador to France in
succession to Bullitt. General Pershing was first considered
for this post and he would, of course, have been an ideal
choice. But because of his serious ill health the idea had to be
given up. In his place the President named Admiral William
D. Leahy, whose long naval career and varied experience in
special assignments were guarantees of his qualifications. As an
admiral he would, in addition, be able to talk with Darlan as
one sailor to another.

The instructions to Admiral Leahy constituted a long and
important document, well reflecting the views of the American government with respect to France. Dated December 20,
1940, they began with emphasis on the "unique position" of
Marshal Pétain and pointed out that under the existing constitution his word was law:

"Accordingly, I desire that you endeavor to cultivate as close
relations with Marshal Pétain as may be possible. You should
outline to him the position of the United States in the present
conflict and you should stress our firm conviction that only by
defeat of the powers now controlling the destiny of Germany
and Italy can the world live in liberty, peace and prosperity; that
civilization cannot progress with a return to totalitarianism."

Since there was reason to believe that Pétain had not always
been informed of the acts of Laval and in view of the fact
that the same situation might exist under the new vice-president, Leahy was instructed to call the marshal's attention to
such acts of the French government as might be inimical to
the United States. The policy of this government was to support those nations that were defending themselves against
aggression, and this meant all possible assistance to Britain
short of war. As for Franco-German relations, the President
expressed his concern lest the French government should co-

operate with Germany beyond what was required by the armistice terms. Leahy was to persuade Pétain and his government of "the conviction of this government that a German victory would inevitably result in the dismemberment of the French Empire and the maintenance at most of France as a vassal state." Furthermore, with reference to the future of the French fleet, the instructions read:

"I believe that the maintenance of the French fleet free of German control is not only of prime importance to the defense of this hemisphere, but is also vital to the preservation of the French Empire and the eventual restoration of French independence and autonomy. Accordingly, from the moment we were confronted with the imminent collapse of French resistance, it has been a cardinal principle of this administration to assure that the French fleet did not fall into German hands and was not used in the furtherance of German aims."

The President then rehearsed the various assurances that had been given on this point, most recently by Marshal Pétain on December 12. Leahy was to keep warning the French government on this score:

"You will undoubtedly associate with high officers of the French navy. I desire, therefore, that, in your relations with such officers, as well as in your conversations with French officials, you endeavor to convince them that to permit the use of the French fleet or naval bases by Germany or to attain German aims, would most certainly forfeit the friendship and good will of the United States, and result in the destruction of the French fleet to the irreparable injury to France."

The instructions ended with assurances that the United States, through the Red Cross, would send food to France in so far as such relief would not prejudice British victory. With regard to the French West Indies and French Guiana, all the United States desired was maintenance of the *status quo*, but for this reason it was essential that French ships in those possessions should be immobilized. Finally the President noted his "sympathetic interest" in the efforts of France to maintain

her authority in North Africa and to improve the economic
status of that region: "In your discussions you may say that
your Government is prepared to assist in this regard in any
appropriate way." [4]

While Admiral Leahy was en route to his new post, the
British government was renewing its efforts to improve relations with Vichy France and if possible to strengthen French
resistance. In view of the frequent criticism of United States
policy by the British, the story of the secret official contacts
is of some importance. The original negotiations through
Rougier were taken up again in December through Chevalier,
a member of the Vichy government and a school-day friend
of Lord Halifax. The British Foreign Minister suggested that
while a state of "artificial tension" be maintained to deceive
the Germans, the French and British should agree on certain
important particulars: France should not allow the Germans
to acquire the fleet or bases of any kind; neither should France
attempt to reconquer the dissident colonies. On the other
hand, the British would permit shipments of food, oil, rubber,
and other commodities to pass through the blockade. Pétain
agreed to these points in principle and, as noted above, they
served as a working arrangement. But throughout the marshal
insisted that, though he preferred collaboration with the British, he had the Nazis in his country and was therefore obliged
to observe the armistice terms, including Article IX, by which
France engaged to do nothing to aid Germany's enemies.

The ultimate objective of the British was, if humanly possible, to bring Pétain and the new regime over to the Allied
side. They indicated that if the French government would
move to North Africa or enter the war against the Axis, they
would send a strong expeditionary force to support it and
that in such an event the combined British and French fleets
could control the Mediterranean and frustrate a Nazi advance
through Spain to Gibraltar. [5]

As a matter of fact, there was never the slightest chance

---

[4] Printed in full in *Peace and War* (Washington, 1943), pp. 596ff.
[5] See Chevalier's account in *Procès du M. Pétain*, pp. 254–5.

that Pétain or the government would move to North Africa and it is very surprising that the British government persisted in ignoring that fact. On January 13, 1941 Secretary Hull cabled to Admiral Leahy saying that Churchill was concerned lest Pétain had not realized that the British proposals involved more than a suggestion of aid in the event that the French government decided to cross to North Africa.[6] Ten days later he relayed another message to Vichy: Pétain should know that Britain would give every facility for mobilization and departure of the French fleet from Alexandria if the French government decided to cross to North Africa and resume her place in the war.[7] This was later modified to say: "in the event of the resumption by the French North African Empire of hostilities against Germany and Italy."[8]

It is not the purpose of this paper to attempt an analysis of British policy with regard to Vichy France or to North Africa, an analysis that would in any event be impossible for lack of adequate documentation. But the British advances mentioned above are of interest as a reflection of the Prime Minister's hope that Pétain might yet be induced to re-enter the war on Britain's side. This entire episode, in order to be understood, must be viewed against the background of events during January 1941. It was the time of Wavell's spectacular march across Cyrenaica to El Agheila—a British success that might well provoke German intervention in Africa to save the Italians. In the military sphere there was real danger that the Germans might oblige the Vichy government to grant rights to the naval base at Bizerte, or that Nazi forces, even without the consent of Vichy, might simply occupy Tunisia and perhaps all of North Africa. Early in January an American representative at Rome reported that it had been learned

[6] Tel. (January 13, 1941).
[7] Tel. (January 22, 1941) Hull to Leahy.
[8] Tel. (January 29, 1941) Hull to Leahy. The mission of Colonel Groussard to London at this time to inquire about possible British aid to the French in North Africa was probably part of this entire negotiation, but nothing is known of it beyond what was stated by General Lacaille at the Pétain trial (*Procès du M. Pétain*, p. 225).

from a "party in ministerial circles" that Germany and Italy would denounce the armistice with France and would attack Corsica and Tunis:

"The German General Staff is said to be making preparations and plans to send more than 50,000 motorized Italian and German troops to North Africa. A combined air and naval attack is planned at Bizerte and other ports in Tunis by German aviation from Sicily and the Italian fleet from Sardinia. Troops will be landed following the establishment of bridgeheads." [9]

The date for the attack was reputedly January 20 or 23.

The crucial question in this whole business was whether the Vichy government would yield to pressure from Berlin. When Admiral Leahy arrived at his Vichy post early in the new year, he found himself in a tangle of uncertainty and rumor. Since the Germans had refused to reconcile themselves to the dismissal of Laval, Admiral Darlan had been sent to Hitler at Beauvais. The admiral brought Hitler Pétain's Christmas greetings along with letters thanking the Führer for his thoughtfulness in transmitting the ashes of the Duke of Reichstadt and explaining in detail the reasons for Laval's dismissal. Darlan reinforced the letter and tried to convince Hitler that the Laval affair was a purely personal row; "The policy of the new French government would be true to the principle of collaboration with Germany." But the Führer remained skeptical and voiced his indignation in no uncertain terms. In his view the whole episode indicated that France was slipping back into her old disastrous policy. Darlan did his utmost to dispel these ideas. He argued that the lenient armistice had proved to him that Hitler intended to accord France an appropriate position in the new Europe. Darlan could have run off with the entire fleet, but he had convinced himself that the only hope of France was in co-operation with Germany in a new Europe. He had always favored collaboration and begged Hitler to continue the Montoire policy.

[9] Tel. (January 22, 1941) Hull to Leahy. Actually, of course, the Afrika Korps was dispatched, but directly to Tripolitania, without need of a base in Tunisia.

But the Führer remained evasive and noncommittal. According to German sources, the Montoire policy was already dead. Hitler had never thought it through in concrete terms and had not even settled in his own mind what territorial claims he would make on France. Ribbentrop, Abetz and the Foreign Office might talk of a "New Order," but Hitler had little use for it. More and more he listened to the extremists in his entourage who preached a policy of getting as much as possible out of France and forcing France, if necessary, to contribute to Germany's war. Laval appeared the most likely candidate to help implement this policy, and that explains why more and more the Germans insisted on his reinstatement.[10]

Admiral Leahy had a long talk with Darlan after the latter's return from his pilgrimage, but the Frenchman "spent most of the time telling how hopelessly inefficient and unreliable the British naval staff was during the time France was engaged in the war against Germany." All the old recriminations were warmed up, to the annoyance of the American ambassador, who was doubtless more interested in the present than in the past:

"Admiral Darlan impressed me as a well-informed, aggressive, and courageous naval officer, incurably anti-British, who believes that the Nazi regime cannot long survive after the passing of Hitler, and that the French people will then attain a position of great influence or control in a new Europe that will emerge from this war. While he does not believe a successful invasion of the British islands can be accomplished, even under the existing condition of British inefficiency, he is confident that the Germans will win the war and establish a new order in Europe."

All that was left for the Germans to do, he concluded, was to attack Russia, "and the moment Germany starts that, it means her downfall." [11]

---

[10] Captured German Documents: report of the meeting of Hitler with Darlan, December 24, 1940. Also the State Department and War Department interrogations of Dr. Paul Schmidt and the manuscript study of German foreign policy by Erich Kordt.

[11] Leahy File, p. 7, supplemented by tel. (January 21, 1941) from Leahy.

From all this nothing much was to be learned of what was going on behind the scenes. But other ministers were a little more enlightening. Flandin, the Foreign Minister, was quite frank with the ambassador, who noted:

"I learned . . . that the Germans are applying annoying pressure on the French government to reinstate M. Laval as a member of the cabinet of Marshal Pétain, and that M. Laval wishes to make the Marshal only a figurehead ruler without authority over his ministers, and that Marshal Pétain has as yet not reached a decision as to the necessity of appointing M. Laval to a membership in the cabinet." [12]

As for the marshal himself, Admiral Leahy reported to the President:

"Marshal Pétain is remarkably capable for a man of his age, but the burden of work which he has assumed is beyond his physical capacity. He does not appear to have complete confidence in any of his cabinet. He has an intense dislike for M. Laval, who is trying to displace him as actual head of the government and relegate him to the position of a symbol. He is very sensitive to German pressure, particularly when it is applied to the war prisoners, to the food supply, and to the authority of his Vichy government. He will make every effort to live up to the terms of the armistice and not to go beyond those terms. He will not under any conditions abandon continental France and move his government to Africa. He and his cabinet are so impressed by the failure of France to even delay the German army, that they believe that an English victory is impossible." The people desire a British victory and many officials hope for it, without expecting it. "They are, therefore, in a frame of mind to make almost any

[12] Leahy File, p. 9. The accuracy of Flandin's account is borne out by Abetz's telegrams to Ribbentrop of January 9, 10, February 4, 1941 (Captured German Documents). These telegrams reveal that Laval wanted Pétain restricted to the office of chief of state, with Darlan as his deputy. Laval was to be prime minister and also hold the portfolios of the interior and foreign affairs. Abetz did his utmost to induce his government to intervene in Laval's favor and racked his brain to find proposals that would be palatable to Pétain, but Hitler evidently made no reply and Pétain remained stubborn.

compromise with Berlin." Pétain, under pressure, would probably take back Laval, despite the fact that he considered him dishonest and unpatriotic . . . "a bad Frenchman."[13]

It all made a dreary outlook, which threatened with every day to become darker. The American representatives could not know the real state of French and German relations and it was in the French interest to leave a corona of uncertainty around the problem. The externals, at least, seemed to indicate that Darlan was eager to sell out. In February the admiral set out for Paris again, where he conferred with Abetz and with Laval. Since Laval refused to accept Darlan's proposal of a directory (Darlan, Laval, Huntziger) to run the government under the marshal's supervision, and since Hitler had failed to express himself, Pétain took the bit in his teeth and remade the cabinet. Flandin was dropped as Foreign Minister, to be succeeded by Darlan, who shortly after was named also as vice-president of the council and Minister of the Interior, in addition to the post of Minister of Marine, which he had held since June 1940. About the only consolation that the British and Americans could derive from the whole sorry crisis was that the marshal had stood firm and had refused to take Laval back on the latter's terms. Darlan, to be sure, was bitterly hostile to the British and openly proclaimed his determination to collaborate with the Germans, but even so the pro-British elements in Vichy considered him "definitely a lesser evil and a lesser danger than Laval."[14]

In the meanwhile it was anyone's guess whether the Germans would attack North Africa. Admiral Leahy found, on inquiry, that French army and navy officials doubted it, but Peyrouton, the Minister of the Interior, remarked in resignation: "If they [the Germans] should ask for Bizerte, we are helpless. What could we do?"[15] At the same time the issue

---

[13] Leahy File, p. 11 (letter to the President of January 25, 1941).
[14] Tels. (January 29, February 3, 7, 8, 10, 1941), all from Leahy. See also Laval's testimony at the Pétain trial, and Abetz's telegram of February 4, 1941.
[15] Tel. (January 24, 1941) from Leahy.

was being fought out, more or less, in the open. On January 23 General de Gaulle in an address charged that the Germans were planning to land at Bizerte to march to the aid of the Italians. A little later (January 31) he appealed to General Weygand to join Free French forces in the conquest of Libya. Weygand, in turn, rejected this suggestion on February 1 and urged his troops to remain faithful to Vichy. On February 7 he declared that the French would never agree to the occupation of Bizerte or any other part of North Africa.[16]

But there was yet another possibility, another danger. Spain to all appearances was teetering on the verge of war, and the air was full of rumors that, having allied herself with Germany and Italy, Spain would open to the Nazis the road to Gibraltar and Morocco. There was great apprehension, therefore, about what might have been hatched out when General Franco and Serrano Suñer visited Mussolini at Bordighera on February 10–12. Actually there was no need for anxiety on the score of Spain. We now have the texts of the correspondence between Hitler and Franco of February 1941. These reveal the situation in all its nakedness. The Führer, in rather blistering terms, called the Caudillo to account for his repeated evasions and warned him that Spain would get no food until she entered the war. "The attack on Gibraltar," in the words of the Führer, "and the closing of the Straits would have changed the Mediterranean situation in one stroke." Months had been lost and it behooved Franco to declare himself. But in reply to this outburst the Caudillo gave tit for tat, going so far as to point out that "in order that the closing of Gibraltar may have a decisive value it is also necessary that the Suez Canal be closed at the same time." For the time being at least, the break was almost complete. There can be no doubt that Franco's unyielding opposition obliged Hitler to

[16] Newspaper reports, listed in a study by the Office of the Coordinator of Information, dated December 3, 1941 and entitled *The Problem of German Occupation of Northwest Africa.*

shelve his western Mediterranean plans till some more favorable moment.[17]

But the crisis was only postponed, for by the middle of February the British campaign in Libya had come to a halt and therewith the immediate occasion for action had passed by. How seriously it was regarded for a time in London, however, is shown by the British naval attack on Genoa on February 9. Referring to this bombardment, Churchill described Genoa as "the naval base from which perhaps a Nazi-German expedition might soon have sailed to attack General Weygand in Algeria or Tunis." [18] But let us return to the evolution of American policy toward Vichy France during the ambassadorship of Admiral Leahy.

From the very moment of his arrival in France, the new ambassador urged upon his government the dispatch of food and clothing to unoccupied France, so that the Germans might not weaken the Pétain government by capitalizing the general misery of the population.[19] But such a policy could be put into effect only within very narrow limits, because of British refusal to relax the blockade. During the summer and autumn of 1940 Herbert Hoover had led an active campaign in favor of relief to France and had marshaled a good deal of sentiment for such a course. But on December 10, 1940 the British government had officially declined to countenance any such scheme, on the theory that relief would serve only to aid the German war effort and postpone the liberation of the very populations that were to be relieved. The American government felt obliged to accept the British view, so that nothing could be done beyond the sending of medical supplies and food for children through the Red Cross. A number of such shipments were made and were very gratefully received as a token of American sympathy. It is impossible to document

---

[17] *The Spanish Government and the Axis,* Nos. 12, 13; also Franco's appeal to Pétain for support (*Procès du M. Pétain,* p. 174).

[18] Churchill speech of February 9, 1941.

[19] Tel. (January 29, 1941) from Leahy.

the importance of such a contribution, but American aid did keep French children supplied with milk and demonstrated to the French that they were not entirely forgotten or deserted. As a result, American prestige remained high and the French as a people continued to look across the Atlantic for final salvation.[20]

Much more important, however, and of much greater long-run effect was the gradual development of the economic accord with French North Africa. It will be recalled that the Department of State had decided, toward the close of 1940, to send Robert D. Murphy to North Africa to report on conditions and prospects. Murphy arrived at Algiers on December 18 and stayed in North Africa just about a month. His report is a masterly document, full of keen observations and of interesting sidelights on personalities and conditions.

On his arrival Murphy found that General Weygand had gone to Dakar on a visit of inspection, but the American emissary had a long talk with Yves Chatel, Weygand's chief civilian adviser. "Chatel," he reported, "is forward-looking, clever, and eager for American assistance. He is a confidant of Weygand and loyal to Pétain." Chatel denied any subversive action by the Germans in North Africa and thought Italian influence on the decline. The population generally was apathetic, but its faith in France might well be weakened if the economic crisis became acute.

There followed a conversation with Count de Rose, Weygand's adjutant and the man who, more than any other, served as a go-between, conveying the thoughts of the commander. De Rose told Murphy what he probably already knew, that the British had made great efforts to induce Weygand to break away from Vichy, and that they had promised all aid.

[20] Statement of the British ambassador (Lord Lothian) of December 10, 1940; statement of Secretary Hull at his press conference on December 11, 1940; statement of the British Embassy at Washington, March 10, 1941; and statement of Acting Secretary Sumner Welles, March 22, 1941. (All of these statements are printed in *Documents on American Foreign Relations,* III, 505ff.)

Weygand, however, had been but little impressed with these advances and had referred them to Pétain. Both de Rose and Chatel were positive that Weygand would never attempt to lead a dissident movement in North Africa. He would take military action only if Pétain ordered him to do so, or if the Germans occupied all of France or attempted to invade North Africa, or if the United States were to enter the war. "As much as they wish to see Britain win, and there is no doubt that these men desire a British victory, they feel that French Africa is their sole remaining trump, and that it must be played only on a well-timed, carefully planned basis." In the interval Murphy found that the army, as reorganized by Weygand, comprised about 120,000 effectives, in addition to over 100,000 demobilized officers and men.

From Algiers, Murphy went on to Dakar, where he was received by the Governor-General, Pierre Boisson, and by Weygand himself. Both were very friendly, and both "declared repeatedly that of course they hoped and prayed for a British victory, but, British victory or not, their determination is to oppose any German effort to dominate French Africa." At the same time they made no secret of their loyalty to Pétain.

The great issue, of course, was economic aid. When the conversations were resumed somewhat later in Algiers, Weygand and Chatel supplied Murphy with a whole stack of memoranda, setting forth North African needs. They said quite frankly that the United States alone could bring salvation. The sooner it could come, the better, for it was believed that the Germans would force the issue in the spring and it was therefore important that the country should be strong enough to offer effective resistance.[21]

While Murphy was investigating the needs and possibilities on the spot, discussions were proceeding in a desultory way in Washington. Early in December Paul Guérin, the assistant director of the Moroccan Railways, arrived in the capital on

---

[21] Murphy Memorandum; *Visit to North Africa,* dated from Lisbon, January 17, 1941. See also Weygand's account in *Procès du M. Pétain,* p. 145.

a special mission. He made an eloquent plea for economic
help and underlined the American interest by suggesting that
"he thought Spain would endeavor to bite off as much of
Morocco as possible, profiting by developing circumstances."
The Germans, too, he thought, had their eyes on Moroccan
bases.[22]

Whether as a result of these representations or not, agreement seems to have been reached in the Department that
something should be done to prevent Morocco at least from
falling into crisis. But it was perfectly obvious from the outset
that nothing could be done without previous clearance with
the British. Officially the entire area was subject to the British blockade, though this, to be sure, was at that time anything
but tight. In accordance with their own interests and with
their understanding with Vichy, the British were allowing
ships to pass freely between North African ports on the
Mediterranean and the harbors of Metropolitan France, and
apparently there was traffic even between the Atlantic coasts
of Morocco and Axis ports of western Europe. Furthermore,
the British themselves were in almost constant negotiation
with the Spanish and French Moroccan authorities and were
arranging to supply Morocco with much-needed green tea
and sugar for the native population in return (for both
Britain and Spain) for a supply of Moroccan phosphates.
There was some reason to suppose, therefore, that the necessary arrangements could be made for trade between the
United States and Morocco.

On December 18, 1940 there was held a conference in the
Department between Berle, Murray, Alling, and Villard on
the American side, and A. K. Helm and A. D. Marris on the
British. Berle pointed out the incongruities in the British
blockade policy and inquired about the triangular British-
Spanish-Moroccan trade. After all, it was strange, he re-
marked, that while Britain was carrying on barter with
Morocco it was refusing navicerts for American trade. To

---

[22] *North African Economic Memoranda,* I, No. 31 (December 9, 1940).
These memoranda form a special file in the State Department archives.

this the British representatives said that they had no adequate information, but would refer the question to London.[23]

The British reply was inordinately late in arriving, in all probability because the matter was referred to the Ministry of Economic Warfare, which was not at all well disposed toward any relaxation of the blockade, however slight it might be. In the meanwhile Murphy had completed his inquiry and had reported home. The Department was anxious to settle on some definite policy, so on January 27, 1941 Helm was invited to a second discussion of the matter. The argument this time was based more squarely on political considerations. Ray Atherton stressed particularly that in the preceding weeks there had evolved an American policy toward Morocco that would entail a resumption of a considerable volume of trade. It was to the interest of the United States and, it was hoped, also to that of Great Britain to prevent a disintegration of the situation in Morocco. The following considerations conditioned our approach to the problem:

(1) "That the resumption of trade along these lines is desirable in itself and that a failure to arrange it might lead to a disintegration of the internal political situation.

(2) "There is always the possibility, given the uncertain situation in Metropolitan France, that a French Government may move from unoccupied France to Morocco, and a trade policy along the lines which have been mentioned above would not close the door to such a move, should it later prove to be advantageous to France.

(3) "There have been recurring rumors in the last few days of the possibility of the Germans launching an effort to occupy Tunis. From what we have learned from General Weygand, the attitude of French North Africa, at the minimum would be 'uncooperative' toward such a move on Germany's part, with a strong probability that active resistance might be forthcoming. In our view it is important to make it possible for General Weygand to maintain his position along these lines in North Africa." [24]

[23] Ibid., No. 36 (December 18, 1940).
[24] Ibid., No. 54 (January 27, 1941).

The British diplomat turned a sympathetic ear, but his remarks once again were quite noncommittal. Finally, on January 30, 1941, the British Embassy handed in a reply, dated January 24, which was followed by a more formal document on February 7. Since this is a basic document it will be well to quote verbatim some of the salient passages:

"The British Government would welcome United States interest in Morocco. Although they are not as confident as the United States Government appear to be that General Weygand will enter the war, they are ready to support the United States policy based on this assumption, provided that no serious breach in the blockade is thereby involved. They would consequently agree to the supply of essential requirements to Morocco by the United States, provided that excessive stocks are not built up and that steps are taken to see there is no risk of the goods reaching the enemy. For this purpose His Majesty's Government regard it as essential that United States officials be appointed at ports and on the railways, and they understand that the French authorities in Morocco would accept their supervision. If desired by the United States Government, His Majesty's Government would be willing to include Algeria and Tunisia in the agreement, provided that guarantees against re-export could be really effective; they cannot themselves hope to control shipments across the Mediterranean in present circumstances. His Majesty's Government are of opinion that it is important to exclude West Africa for the time being, in view of their relations with the free French colonies, though they would in any event have to consult General de Gaulle on this point."

The British memorandum then went on to say that in British negotiations with Morocco it had been the aim to secure the release of British and neutral shipping in Moroccan harbors, and that it was hoped that the United States government would press this important point. Finally:

"His Majesty's Government are also anxious to get some undertakings in writing from General Weygand as to his future attitude before acquiescing or collaborating in economic assistance to North Africa, and they are instructing their representative to endeavor to obtain such undertaking if he is able to go to Algeria to see General Weygand." [25]

The British note was received without enthusiasm at the Department. Coming after weeks of waiting, it struck a somewhat patronizing tone and at the same time by implication accused the United States government of having gone ahead with its arrangements without taking the British into its confidence. As a matter of fact, Murphy, who had been sent back to Tangier, had reported from there on the discussions that were being carried on between the British and the French Moroccan officials. The British, according to his message, had arranged for French Morocco to supply Spanish Morocco and Spain with foodstuffs, while Britain would furnish to French Morocco automotive parts, agricultural machinery, coal, and so forth. David Eccles, the British negotiator, remarked to Murphy on this occasion that he knew the Spaniards would not be able to pay, but he felt "that the British have succeeded at a very small cost in dissuading the Spaniards from plunging into a military adventure with the Germans." [26]

Since the very crux of the American policy was to fortify Morocco and North Africa generally in the same way, it was hard to understand the British attitude. Secretary Hull therefore told the new British ambassador, Lord Halifax, on February 10, that

"This Government is going forward with its arrangements to send gasolene, sugar and certain other staple commodities to French Africa, in accord with the agreement with General Weygand."

The ambassador expressed the hope that such shipments would be made contingent on the turning over of British vessels in Moroccan harbors. To this Secretary Hull replied:

"I believed we could be of more help to the British in this matter by pursuing our course of conciliation and offering relief

[25] Ibid., No. 58 (February 7, 1941).
[26] Tel. Murphy to Hull (Lisbon, January 29, 1941).

of food and goods than we could by making the turning over of the ships a condition precedent. I added that, of course, the British could pursue their own policy in this respect." [27]

There were some further notes and explanations, but these we need not follow in detail. In a final memorandum to the British Embassy the Department stated:

"It is the considered opinion of the Department of State that it is urgently necessary to resume trade relations on a restricted basis with French North Africa, if there is to be prevented an economic breakdown in that area which may have far-reaching and perhaps disastrous consequences. It has therefore been decided to authorize at once the unblocking of the necessary funds to permit the shipment of a tanker of petroleum products to Casablanca. This is the first step in a program which this Government proposes to pursue with a view to furnishing minimum and urgently needed supplies to French North Africa." [28]

The note of urgency in these statements was, of course, an echo of the critical days of late January and early February, when it seemed as though Pétain would have to take back Laval and as though Vichy France would become a party to German aggression in North Africa. It was necessary, therefore, to get on with the business. For that reason Murphy was instructed to work out an agreement with General Weygand or his representatives. He was directed to tell General Weygand:

"that, given suitable guarantees that goods imported from the United States would be entirely for local consumption, the Department would be willing to permit the shipment to any designated port in North Africa of additional quantities of petroleum, sugar, tea, and coal and other products deemed urgently necessary to prevent a breakdown of the economic system in French North Africa, permitting meanwhile the unblocking of sufficient French funds."

[27] *North African Economic Memoranda*, No. 59 (February 10, 1941).
[28] Ibid., No. 62 (February 13, 1941).

Murphy arrived at Algiers on or about February 18, but, finding General Weygand abroad, proceeded to Tangier. There he conferred with the French officials, notably Marchal and Monick, with whom he had already discussed the situation during his visit in January. The French had already worked out a draft agreement that followed closely the lines required by Washington, including the provision of control of shipments by American officers, which the French welcomed rather than opposed. Murphy returned to Algiers and secured the approval of General Weygand (February 26, 1941), who initialed the draft memorandum, though he proposed that a final agreement should be concluded between Vichy and Washington. This Murphy declined to consider, but the memorandum was nevertheless forwarded to Vichy and thence to Washington on March 1, immediately after Murphy's return from Algiers. It reached Washington on March 4 and met with no objections. On March 10 the Vichy government, through Admiral Darlan, officially sanctioned the arrangements that had been made: These later came to be known as the *Murphy-Weygand Agreement*. The main points of accord were that the United States would supply North Africa with needed American products, provided that shipments should not be allowed to accumulate in North Africa and that the consumption of all products so imported should be exclusively in North Africa. American officials were to control the handling of the shipments in North African ports and on the railways. Payment for goods should be made through French funds in the United States, which the American government would unblock as required.[29]

The final negotiation of the economic accord had no doubt been hastened in some measure by reports received by the

---

[29] The Murphy negotiations are conveniently summarized in a State Department memorandum dated February 28, with a supplement, entitled *Trade with North Africa* (*North African Economic Memoranda*, I, No. 75). The Darlan note, March 10, is in the same collection (No. 78a). The text of these documents is given in full in Appendix I of the present study. See also Weygand's account in *Procès du M. Pétain*, p. 145.

British from Tangier of an ever increasing infiltration of German officials and agents into North Africa. The German armistice commission was rapidly replacing the Italian commission, and threatened in a short time to take over control of all activity in the region, to say nothing of fifth-column work among the French and Arab populations. On February 17 it was reported that the German commission numbered already eighty persons, including specialists in aero-construction and engineers whose mission was to prepare some of the Atlantic ports for use as submarine bases.[30]

This was only the first of a number of alarming reports that began to flow into London and Washington. On March 14 Felix Cole, our consul-general at Algiers, cabled that he had heard that a "massive" German infiltration was in progress that would total 6,000, with 800 officers and men in Casablanca alone. Every effort was made to substantiate these reports, which in the end proved to be quite unfounded. None the less, it was established that the Germans had about sixty officials and agents in North Africa, and it seemed all too likely that more would follow. Everywhere rumors were rife that in the early summer the Germans would take over the entire area.[31] Added to this was the unconcealed policy of the Darlan government to collaborate with the Germans, and Darlan's publicly announced determination to use French warships to convoy food and supplies to France if the British insisted on enforcement of the blockade.[32] During March the situation remained extremely uncertain and appeared fraught with danger. It was not until Rommel counterattacked against the British in Libya that fears of German action against North Africa were somewhat allayed.

It was in connection with the possibilities of such action that General Weygand visited Vichy from March 5 to 10.

[30] Memorandum of conversation, February 19, 1941 (*North African Economic Memoranda*, I, No. 72).

[31] Memorandum of conversation between Lord Halifax and Sumner Welles, March 21, 1941 (*North African Economic Memoranda*, I, No. 87a); memorandum signed by Wallace Murray (March 24, 1941).

[32] Leahy File (February 24, 1941).

On that occasion he assured Ambassador Leahy that he was "determined to oppose with all force at his command an attack on French Africa by anybody."[33] But at the same time the general's adjutant, Count de Rose, made it clear that Weygand had little to resist with. He therefore urged that the anti-Axis powers should prepare to supply promptly whatever might be needed later for successful war in North Africa.[34]

Even more interesting, in this same connection, was a personal appeal made by Churchill to the President on March 13. Referring to Darlan's threat to break the British blockade, the Prime Minister raised the question whether the President might not intervene as the friend of both sides and attempt to arrive at a working agreement:

"We fear very much prolongation of the war and its miseries which would result from breakdown of blockade of Germany from profiting directly or indirectly from anything imported into unoccupied France. Dealing with Darlan is dealing with Germany, for he will not be allowed to agree to anything they know about which does not suit their book. . . .

"You might be able to procure Vichy assent to a scheme allowing a ration of wheat to go through, month by month, to unoccupied France and something for French Africa as long as other things were satisfactory. These other things might form the subject of a secret arrangement of which the Germans will not know, by which German infiltration into Morocco and French African ports would be limited to the bare armistice terms, and by which an increasing number of French warships would gradually be moving from Toulon to Casablanca or Dakar."

Along with this came a British memorandum that Lord Halifax was to take up with the President or with the Department of State. This document was closely reasoned and quite specific:

"His Majesty's Government feel that the most immediate danger is the penetration by German experts of French North

[33] Leahy File (March 9, 1941).
[34] Dispatch, Leahy to Hull (March 12, 1941).

Africa, which they know is being actively pursued and which, they fear, will pave the way either for the entry of German troops into French North Africa from Tripoli or for the collapse of Spanish resistance to Germany. His Majesty's Government think that the latter would certainly occur if Spain felt that Germany had succeeded in taking her in the rear, and there are already signs that Spanish resistance to German pressure is likely to weaken if German infiltration into the Mediterranean area is permitted to continue."

The memorandum then proceeded to analyze what the British thought was involved in the projected American shipments to North Africa. These, the British felt, would not be sufficient to warrant French acceptance of conditions that were deemed necessary. It was therefore suggested that the United States government offer Vichy an assurance of "reasonable supplies of principal commodities, with guarantees against re-export and of navicert facilities for 5/8,000,000 bushels of wheat for unoccupied France." In return Vichy should accept the following conditions:

(a) That Marshal Pétain should prevent further Axis infiltration into French North Africa, and in particular the entry of uniformed or armed Germans or Italians.

(b) That an adequate number of American observers should be sent to unoccupied France and to French North Africa, and that a British observer or observers should be allowed to accompany the Americans sent to North Africa, or alternatively that British consular officers should be readmitted to their former posts in French North Africa.

The British government desired also that French warships in the ports of Metropolitan France should gradually be sent to African Atlantic ports and remain there. Lord Halifax was to stress the British view that

"verbal assurances from Marshal Pétain and General Weygand about German infiltration into French Africa would not be sufficient to remove the deadly menace to the common interest involved in a collapse of our present policy towards Spain and the occupation by the enemy of French African ports. . . . His Majesty's Government hope that the United States Government would arrange to send the greatest possible number of American observers to French North Africa and that some of these officials would be of sufficient standing to counteract German infiltration and to discuss with the French the possibility of armed resistance." [35]

What the British were now proposing, in effect, was really two different things: that the existing arrangements were inadequate for securing from the Vichy government far-reaching guarantees that would probably have led to a rupture between France and Germany, and that presumably the agreement should therefore be given up; or, secondly, that the Murphy-Weygand Agreement be greatly extended, to include unoccupied France and to ensure much larger supplies, always in return for the above-mentioned guarantees. But despite the eloquence of the appeal, the Washington government evaded a detailed reply. The British proposal was hardly practicable and there was no chance of Pétain's exposing himself to such an extent to German wrath. The Murphy-Weygand Agreement went as far as we thought we could or should go at the time, so we contented ourselves with its implementation.

One of the crucial points in the whole arrangement with Weygand was the establishment of American control officers. The French, from the outset, had raised no objection to the plan, but had, indeed, welcomed it. [36] The Department, on its side, had at once recognized the possibilities of the scheme—possibilities that extended far beyond the economic accord into the military and naval sphere. Representatives of the War and Navy Departments were therefore consulted and the suggestion was made that the services contribute personnel "who could, in addition to their control duties, prepare

---

[35] These documents are in *North African Economic Memoranda*, I, No. 82.
[36] *North African Economic Memoranda*, I, No. 67 (February 17).

such reports on their observations as might be of interest to the War and Navy Departments." [37] Both services took up the idea with alacrity and in the sequel several civilians, all highly qualified in the French language and in French affairs, were sent out to serve as "technical assistants" to the various American consulates. They were, however, appointees of the Department and acted under its direction as non-career vice-consuls. Over them all Robert Murphy, while officially still counselor of embassy at Vichy, was sent to Algiers to serve as a kind of high commissioner. He was to direct the American control organization and to maintain contact with the French authorities. At the same time he was to supervise all American consulates and report on all matters of political, economic, or military interest.[38]

It would be both tedious and unnecessary to pursue in all detail the working-out of the plans for relief of the French. The road was anything but easy. Within the Department there were some who were peculiarly sensitive to any British objections, as they were to the clamor of those Americans who objected to all aid to Vichy France and her colonies. The British themselves came to accept the North African accord and indeed to cheer us along on this course.[39] On the other hand, they declined to view the arrangements as part of the larger American policy toward Vichy France, and made difficulties about the projected shipments of Red Cross supplies to the unoccupied zone. Secretary Hull therefore took the matter up himself with Lord Halifax, asking once more just what the British policy might be. In the American view the North African problem and the Vichy problem were closely related:

[37] Memorandum by Wallace Murray, March 13, 1941 (*North African Economic Memoranda*, I, No. 80).
[38] The details are well summarized in the memorandum of the Division of Research and Publication entitled *The Role of the Department of State in the North African Economic and Political Program.* Also a statement dated November 29, 1944 by Wallace Phillips, who was at that time special assistant to the Director of Naval Intelligence and had much to do with the selection of the control officers.
[39] *North African Economic Memoranda*, II, No. 104 (April 4, 1941).

"If Pétain should be over-ridden by the Darlan-Hitler forces, the whole structure of British-American plans for North Africa would crash to the ground; that Weygand takes orders from Pétain; that these and other conditions render it entirely necessary to hold up the hands of the Pétain branch of the French Government at Vichy; that we have been struggling almost daily since the French Government left Paris to uphold that element in the French Government which opposed Hitlerism and Hitler; that it was very tedious and delicate work, especially when many of the leading Britishers seemed to have no comprehension of its nature and importance to them." [40]

Lord Halifax had no real answer to the Secretary's remonstrance. Looking backward after several years, however, it is not hard to see why the British were anxious and uncertain. Early in April the Germans had begun their victorious march through the Balkans, while in Libya Rommel was pressing steadily on to the frontiers of Egypt. Logic seemed to dictate that at any moment the Germans might advance through Spain, or from Libya, to take over North and West Africa. Had not the Nazi writers for years been pointing out the importance of Spain and the significance of French Africa? Dakar is "an Atlantic Gibraltar—a good U-boat base," wrote one of the geopoliticians at this very time. "If Germany stops traffic on this route, Britain's fate is sealed." Germany must forestall occupation of West Africa by the United States, wrote another, for "the projecting corner of West Africa is the natural eastern end of a blockade line which enables an extra-European power dominating the Atlantic to make German use of African territory questionable." [41]

Things might have been different if there had been reason to suppose that Marshal Pétain would be able to offer real

[40] Memorandum of conversation, April 8, 1941 (*North African Economic Memoranda*, II, No. 114).

[41] Hermann Rockel: *"Dakar das Zentrum der seestrategischen Stellung Frankreichs am mittleren Atlantik"* (*Zeitschrift für Politik*, XVII [1940], pp. 419–26); Konteradmiral Donner: *"Geographie und Seemacht"* (*Wissen und Wehr*, May 1941, pp. 153ff.). On the importance of Spain see Ewald Banse: *Germany Prepares for War* (New York, 1934, p. 316); Heinz Barth: *"Spaniens historische Mission"* (*Volk und Reich*, 1941, pp. 77–93).

resistance to German designs or demands. But the situation in Vichy was thoroughly discouraging. Hardly had Admiral Leahy arrived before the German-controlled Paris press was denouncing him as a Freemason, a representative of Jewish bankers, and a British agent.[42] Pétain, of whose patriotism and good intentions the ambassador was fairly convinced, appeared as a pretty weak reed to lean upon. He spoke at length and with much bitterness of the group of traitors led by de Gaulle and evidently feared that Free French forces might attack North Africa and thus bring Weygand's forces into conflict with the British.[43] Admiral Leahy suspected, and probably with justice, that de Gaulle had a larger following in France than Vichy officials were ready to admit, but none the less Pétain seemed resigned to Darlan's policy of collaboration. It was reasonably clear that Darlan was doing his utmost to make character with the Germans and to help them forget the allurements of Laval. Yet Pétain defended his minister and remarked only that "his trouble is his habit of telling anecdotes about the British." Furthermore, the marshal confessed that he had no power to resist the increasing German demands:

"He has told me that when the German demands appear to him to be outside the Armistice Agreement, and when he objects on that ground, the Germans claim the right to make the final interpretation, and when he disagrees, they carry out their intention without regard to his attitude in the matter."

The old soldier's one consolation lay in the shrewd guess that sooner or later, when the Germans had dispersed their forces, they would face trouble in all the occupied countries. "He believes also that Germany cannot avoid a clash with Russia." [44]

In the meanwhile, reports of German infiltration into North Africa kept multiplying and the fear in London of a Nazi advance through Spain became almost pathological. Secre-

[42] Leahy File (February 23, 1941).
[43] Ibid. (March 18, 1941).
[44] Ibid. (March 19, April 1, 21, 1941); tel. (April 22, 1941) from Leahy.

tary Hull spoke with Lord Halifax of the situation again on April 19:

"I said that if Pétain should yield to the pro-Hitler influences in his Government there might be left three courses for this and the British Government to pursue: 1) Either we or the British protest strongly; 2) We or the British take definite action with the use of force to establish ourselves at Dakar or Casablanca, to which he added a supposition that neither of us was in a position to do that; 3) An attempt be made to get General Weygand to invite the British or some other force to come in and aid him against the German invasion. I remarked that General Weygand has softened considerably towards the British-American viewpoint, and that Mr. Eccles of the British Government and Mr. Murphy for my Government have had full and more or less effective personal conferences with General Weygand on this question of resistance against outside attack; that he has repeatedly said that he would fight Germany if she came in. . . ." [45]

Actually, for the moment neither the British nor the American government could do much more than worry and warn. Weygand himself was probably determined to resist to the limit, but he had only men, not equipment sufficient for successful action. The British, driven back in Libya, had nothing to spare, and the United States was not even in the war as yet. All we had to work with was the new economic accord, and that was little enough. Eccles, who was in Washington at the time, remarked bitterly in this connection that "it was about 11:55 in respect of economic cooperation with both Spain and French Africa, but he felt that straw and carrots should be held out for what they were worth." [46]

And so we continued on tenterhooks, while the horizon steadily darkened. Speaking in New York on April 24, Secretary of the Navy Knox recalled to his audience the grave menace that confronted us:

[45] Memorandum of conversation, April 19, 1941 (*North African Economic Memoranda*, II, No. 128).

[46] Memo. of April 24, 1941 (*North African Economic Memoranda*, II, No. 138).

"Too few of us realize, and still fewer acknowledge, the size of the disaster to American hemispheric safety if Germany, already the conqueror of France, should establish herself in Dakar, a French colonial possession. From there, with her surface ships, submarines and long-range bombers, a victorious Germany could substantially cut us off from all commerce with South America and make of the Monroe Doctrine a scrap of paper."

At this very time Admiral Leahy was hearing even from French officials in Vichy that France's colonies would probably be lost: "Definite fear is expressed by many observers that a move of German troops through Spain and unoccupied France will begin in the near future. Neither in France or in Spain can any effective opposition be expected." Reports began to come in of large German troop concentrations in the west, near the Spanish border, and to top it all, it became known that Darlan had left for Paris to confer with the German representatives:

"The Marshal expects an early advance of German troops through Spain with the purpose of either taking Gibraltar or occupying some place on the coast from which the Straits can be controlled by gunfire and from which troops can be sent to Spanish Morocco."

He understood the danger, noted the ambassador, but saw no way of preventing it.[47]

There is some evidence that Pétain's ominous remarks, and by derivation the fears of the British and Americans, were far from being unfounded. The transit of Spain and the attack on Gibraltar were once more being envisaged as part of the larger German strategy in the Mediterranean. According to Noël, Marshal Pétain told him at this time (April 21) that the situation was very grave and that even Darlan was worried. Hitler had asked that German forces be permitted to cross unoccupied France to Spain so that they could attack Gibraltar and then occupy Spanish Morocco. He had demanded further that France agree to the transport of German

[47] Leahy File (April 29, May 1, 2, 3); tel. (May 4, 1941) from Leahy.

forces across Algeria and Tunisia. Pétain added that he proposed to resist to the utmost of his ability.[48] It was at this time
too that Churchill struck a most pessimistic note. He warned
President Roosevelt that he regarded the situation of Spain
as hopeless and that he feared Gibraltar would be lost or at
least immobilized. Furthermore, he could not see how Britain
could hold out beyond August 1941 unless the United States
entered the war in full force.[49]

It is true that Darlan, through the French ambassador at
Washington, had once again renewed his assurances that the
French government, so long as he was minister, "would not
agree under any circumstances to undertake any actions in
the interest or benefit of Germany other than those which
were specifically called for by the terms of the Armistice, and
that nothing beyond this would be agreed to." [50] But aside
from the fact that Darlan's statements were not trusted by
the Department, there was nothing in what he said to prevent
the French from simply yielding to German demands. The
worst was therefore to be expected when Darlan set out for
Berchtesgaden early in May.

It was at this crucial moment that the British government
once again proposed to warn Marshal Pétain, pointing out
that the destinies of Syria and North Africa were at stake. If
the French were to allow the Germans to cross to Spain and
use North Africa for operations against the British, France
would be maneuvered into war, and Britain could then no
longer distinguish between occupied and unoccupied France
in the conduct of operations. On the other hand, if France
were to resist, Britain would give all possible aid. The British
and French fleets could probably prevent any enemy crossing
of the Mediterranean.[51]

[48] *Procès du M. Pétain,* p. 174.
[49] Memorandum of Sumner Welles, submitted to the Pearl Harbor Inquiry (*New York Herald Tribune,* December 19, 1945); statement of William C. Bullitt to me (December 1945).
[50] Memorandum of conversation, April 25, 1941 (*North African Economic
Memoranda,* II, No. 141).
[51] *North African Economic Memoranda,* II, No. 151 (April 29, 1941).

In an aide-mémoire to the United States government the British pointed out that they could do no more, but hoped that the American government, which could speak with authority at Vichy, and which had a special interest in North and West Africa, would be prepared to go further than it had in the past: "Indeed, His Majesty's Government hope that the United States Government will feel able to arrange for some units of the United States Fleet to visit Dakar and Casablanca."

But the British government's proposals met with vigorous objection on the part of Welles. Such a message to Vichy, he argued, would become known to the Germans within fifteen minutes of its delivery and might precipitate on the part of the Germans exactly such action as Britain wished to avoid:

> "I said it seemed to me that from the standpoint of the interests of both our Governments what was desirable was to try and persuade the Marshal to play for time and to resist at every point with the hope that eventually the situation, in North Africa at least, could be stabilized and strengthened to our common advantage."

Furthermore, Pétain was not really in control of the French fleet. He would of necessity have to consult with Darlan and other pro-German elements. Welles thought it far wiser to have Admiral Leahy see Pétain and express in the strongest terms the hope of his government that the marshal would resist and refuse to go beyond the armistice terms. To this Lord Halifax assented.[52]

After discussion with Secretary Hull, Welles informed the British ambassador that the Department had decided to negotiate with Vichy for the delivery of two shiploads of wheat to unoccupied France, as requested by the French government. Lord Halifax saw great objection to this, but found the Department firm in its decision:

[52] Memorandum of conversation, April 29, 1941 (*North African Economic Memoranda*, II, No. 151).

"It seemed to us wise and desirable to do what we could to demonstrate in a practical way that we desired to assist the Marshal in relieving distress in unoccupied France, and we believed that thereby we would make it easier for him to maintain his own prestige and position and to resist German pressure because of the support the population would give him. I said that what the British Government in essence proposed was merely for us to continue delivering sharp and frequently menacing messages from the British Government to Marshal Pétain, and that it did not seem to us that our policy would be advanced by limiting ourselves to the transmission of messages of this character."

A cable was therefore dispatched to Admiral Leahy asking him to see Pétain at once, and by all means alone. He was to say that the United States wished to help France by relieving distress and was therefore arranging to send two ships. But this could not be done if France yielded to German pressure or went beyond the terms of the armistice.[53]

The ambassador was unable to see Pétain at once, and in the interval affairs at Vichy had entered a most dangerous phase. The entire month of May was a period of prolonged crisis, which we must now examine. Some aspects of the problem are still confused, but we have available a good deal of material—enough at least to provide a consistent account.

Darlan, it will be recalled, had been wooing the Nazis ever since December, but only to get the cold shoulder. The Germans were still pining for Laval and refused to collaborate with any other French government. This meant that both Pétain and Darlan had hanging over them the threat of Laval's return to power. As the situation shaped up in May 1941, the Germans were in a position to advance on Suez by way of the Levant States or by way of Spain, or both. French aid would be of great value to them and consequently nothing was more natural than that they should attempt to engineer the reinstatement of Laval, with whom they knew they could do business. In a letter to Weygand (April 26) Marshal Pétain forecast a difficult period and expressed his fears of Laval's

[53] Tel. (April 30, 1941) to Leahy.

return. Under the circumstances he and Darlan seem to have been agreed that they must be amenable to German demands.[54]

Because of the delicacy of the situation, Darlan operated in great secrecy. He claimed to have the full support of the marshal, but it is impossible to say how completely Pétain was informed. In a number of instances Darlan seems to have acted first and reported afterward. For the most part even high officials at Vichy, both in the Ministry of Foreign Affairs and in the Ministry of War, were kept completely in the dark, and it may be said at once that many of them were as much concerned and alarmed by Darlan's negotiations as were the members of the American mission, whom they alerted at all crucial moments.

Darlan's procedure in general was to make concessions to the Germans out of hand, in the hope of attaining later some larger and more definitive arrangement. Thus he agreed at the outset to make available to Rommel a number of French trucks that had been stocked in North Africa. Weygand and Esteva were furious, but were confronted with a *fait accompli.*[55]

After these preliminaries Darlan was invited to Paris to confer with Abetz (May 3). Evidently delighted to be received into the good graces of the victors, and on assurance that Laval would be left out of account, he promised everything. To enable the Germans to support the uprising against the British that had conveniently broken out in Iraq, he agreed that France should make available to the rebels stores of munitions (including planes) that were stocked in Syria, and furthermore that France would aid in the transport of further supplies across the mandated territory. The French would aid in refueling and repairing German planes in transit and would put at their disposal an airfield in northeastern Syria. Objectionable French officials were to be recalled from both

---

[54] Unpublished diary of a French diplomat who was very close to developments. This diary covers the period April 26 to June 6 in great detail and is one of the most valuable sources.

[55] Diary of a French Diplomat, April 26.

Syria and North Africa, and the trucks that were to go to Rommel were to be loaded with German supplies shipped from Marseille or Toulon to Bizerte. In return the Germans were to permit the rearmament of six French destroyers and seven torpedo boats, to relax the stringent travel and traffic regulations between the zones of France, and to arrange for a substantial reduction of the costs of occupation. There was also some talk of a campaign against the Gaullists in Equatorial Africa and of the policy of reinforcing Weygand and Boisson for this purpose.[56]

There is every indication that Pétain, probably greatly relieved to know that the danger of Laval had been exorcised, approved of these dealings. However, the marshal had departed on May 5 for a week's rest in southern France and was therefore inaccessible to Admiral Leahy. The American Embassy had got wind of the supply of trucks to Rommel and was deeply disturbed. Admiral Leahy had in hand a personal message from the President to Pétain, dated May 8, urging the marshal to defend the French colonies from attack, especially from the Axis powers. But on the very day this was written, Darlan had instructed the French commander in Syria, General Dentz, in a special secret navy code, to give the Germans all facilities but to oppose any retaliatory action by the British. Not only that. The Germans, pleasantly surprised by Darlan's readiness to comply, had invited him to Berchtesgaden, where on May 11-12 he conferred with Hitler himself.

The Führer's attitude toward France had undergone a remarkable change. He could still not refrain from harping on France's responsibility for the war, but insisted that he had no military ambitions and that he was convinced that the gains of war never equaled the costs. He had, he said, no desire to tyrannize over France and was interested only in the protection of German interests. At the same time he yearned for European unity, which gave Darlan an opportunity to urge

[56] Captured German Documents: telegrams of Abetz to Ribbentrop, May 5, 6, 7, 8; also Diary of a French Diplomat.

that the Germans organize the Continent for defense. It was
obvious, he pointed out, that Britain must be disposed of.
France, he declared, was willing to work with Germany to
that end. A modest beginning had been made in the economic
sphere and in the recent collaboration in Syria. France would
go farther along this road, but would of course require concessions that would make collaboration palatable to the
French people.

Hitler replied that he was no fanatic for territory (*"kein
Raumfanatiker"*). If France would defend her colonies, she
might keep them. On the other hand, if the Germans had to
defend them, they would take them over completely. In any
event France would have to show goodwill and readiness to
do something decisive. If England were not completely defeated and if the Führer could not count on France, he would
have to keep the Departments of Nord and Pas-de-Calais.
Unofficially it was indicated to Darlan that if France were
really co-operative, she could expect favorable territorial
readjustments in both Europe and Africa. In return for Alsace
and Lorraine, she might be given Wallonia and French
Switzerland. In Africa, Tunisia would perhaps become a con-
dominium of France and Italy, and Morocco of France, Germany, and Spain, but France would receive compensation in
the form of a cut of the British colonial spoils.[57]

There can be no doubt that Darlan was proceeding according to a carefully thought-out program. He detested the
British and was certain of their defeat. Even if the war ended
in compromise, he argued, Britain would no longer play an
important role, but would be merely a satellite of the United
States. The thing to do, therefore, was to make the best arrangements possible with the power that was sure to dominate Europe. France would, to be sure, have to make concessions, but then, France had lost the war and would fare no

---

[57] Captured German Documents: meeting of Hitler and Darlan, May 12.
Unfortunately this document is so light-struck as to be in large part illegible.
Further information on the discussions is to be derived from the record of
a confidential address of Darlan to the students of the Leaders' School at
Uriage (June 2, 1941) and from the Diary of a French Diplomat.

better even if the British won. They would demand bases everywhere—Calais, Dakar, Bizerte—and who knows how much more? It was therefore in the best interests of France to pitch in, help Germany to liquidate the war, and strike as good a bargain with the victors as possible.[58]

Before Darlan got back to Vichy (May 13) Pétain had already returned, only to be confronted by an insistent demand for an audience from Admiral Leahy. The old marshal feared greatly that the Americans would present something like an ultimatum, and the ambassador found him nervous and worried. He was therefore greatly relieved when the admiral was calm and cordial. He presented the President's message and called attention to his government's uneasiness. Pétain said that he did not yet know what Darlan had accomplished, but he promised in no case to give "any voluntary active military aid to Germany." This was at best an equivocal assurance and did not relieve the ambassador of his fear that the French government was moving rapidly toward collaboration with the Nazis. He therefore warned Pétain "that any military assistance to Germany beyond the strict requirements of the armistice will bring about a permanent loss of friendship and good will of the American people toward France."[59]

How justified Admiral Leahy's apprehensions were appeared from a message broadcast by the marshal on May 15, after Darlan's return to Vichy:

"You have heard that Admiral Darlan recently conferred with Chancellor Hitler. I had approved this meeting in principle. The new interview permits us to light up the road into the future and to continue the conversations that had been begun with the German Government.

"It is no longer a question today of public opinion, often uneasy and badly informed, being able to estimate the chances we are taking or to measure the risks we take, or to judge our acts.

[58] Diary of a French Diplomat, reporting Darlan's remarks to him on May 17, 1941.
[59] Tel. (May 13) from Leahy; Diary of a French Diplomat, entries for May 12, 13, 14.

"For you, the French people, it is simply a question of following me without mental reservation along the path of honor and national interest.

"If through our close discipline and our public spirit we can conduct the negotiations in progress, France will surmount her defeat and preserve in the world her rank as a European and colonial power."

It seems reasonably clear that Pétain at this time was prepared to support Darlan's policy, if only to avoid the chance of more adverse developments. He urged an emissary of Weygand to tell the latter not to pay any attention to gossip and twaddle, but to realize that the Vichy government could follow no other course and that in any case Pétain had German assurances with regard to North Africa.[60]

Sensing the dangers inherent in the situation, President Roosevelt, after conferring at length with Hull and Welles, issued a public statement on May 15 in which he recalled past assurances given by Pétain and then appealed directly to the French people to stick by the ideals of liberty that they had always cherished:

"It is inconceivable they [that is, the French people] will willingly accept any agreement for so-called 'collaboration,' which in reality will imply their alliance with a military power whose central and fundamental policy calls for the utter destruction of liberty, freedom and popular institutions everywhere.

"The people of the United States can hardly believe that the present Government of France could be brought to lend itself to a plan of voluntary alliance implied or otherwise which would apparently deliver up France and its colonial Empire, including French African colonies and their Atlantic coasts with the menace which that involves to the peace and safety of the Western Hemisphere."

But Pétain and Darlan continued on their course unmoved. Even the marshal's closest friends were unable to argue the policy with him. Negotiations with the Germans were at once

[60] Diary of a French Diplomat, May 17, 18.

opened at Paris and were carried out on the French side by Darlan himself and by General Huntziger, on the German side by Abetz and General Warlimont, the representative of Field Marshal Keitel. They progressed unruffled, to the accompaniment of ever stronger American warnings and protests. Discussing the situation with Henry-Haye on May 20, Secretary Hull said bluntly:

"that the definite belief was created in every nation of the world that the French Government at Vichy had gone straight into the arms of the German Government presided over by Hitler, with all the implications of such a step; that the well-known pro-Hitler officials of the French Government have finally taken over control and, having done so, their first thoughts were to deliver France body and soul to Hitler.

"I added that this country is thoroughly dedicated to the success of the British, who are fighting for this great cause of popular institutions and life and liberty, and that any military aid rendered to Germany beyond the strict terms of the armistice is an attempt to slit the throat of the United States indirectly, and hence the deep feeling this country has in the reported new plan of 'collaboration' between the Vichy Government and Germany." [61]

Admiral Leahy too was in despair and began to speculate on the possibility of saving North Africa by reinforcing Weygand:

"If an army of 250,000, thoroughly equipped with modern weapons, including aircraft, should reinforce General Weygand's small, badly equipped force before the Germans arrive in North Africa, it would, in my opinion, insure control of the Mediterranean Sea and shorten the duration of the war by half.

To be sure, noted the admiral, there was no indication whatever that Vichy would ask for such aid and it was not at all certain what Weygand would do. But part of his army at least might side with us, and most Frenchmen would approve: "It makes one very unhappy to think how easy it would be to

[61] Memorandum of conversation (May 20, 1941) in *North African Economic Memoranda*, II, No. 167.

put the Germans back on their heels with so small an army if it were available and free to move." [62]

That was the fly in the ointment: we did not then have the army. All we could do was to take such precautions as were feasible. In view of persistent reports of Nazi designs on Africa and on the Spanish or Portuguese islands, the President on May 22 ordered the chief of naval operations to have ready in thirty days an expedition of twenty-five thousand men to take the Azores.[63] A few days later the President warned the country in a radio address (May 27):

"They [the Nazis] also have the armed power at any moment to occupy Spain and Portugal; and that threat extends not only to French North Africa and the western end of the Mediterranean, but also to the Atlantic fortress of Dakar, and to the island outposts of the New World—the Azores and Cape Verde Islands. The Cape Verde Islands are only seven hours distant from Brazil by bomber or troop-carrying planes. They dominate shipping routes to and from the South Atlantic. The war is approaching the brink of the Western Hemisphere itself. It is coming very close to home."

One other instrument of action was at our disposal: namely, economic support of North Africa. Murphy had in the meanwhile arrived at Algiers and had had an opportunity to discuss with Weygand the implications of recent events in Vichy. He found the general unchanged in his attitude:

"He personally reiterated the assurances previously given that he would do his best to defend North Africa against any aggression; the supplies which we had agreed to make available under the terms of the North African Agreement were more urgently needed than ever." [64]

Under the circumstances, as Welles told the British ambassador, the Department decided that it had nothing to lose in proceeding with the Murphy-Weygand Accord:

[62] Leahy File (May 22, 1941).
[63] Tel. (May 21) from Leahy; statement of Admiral Stark at the Pearl Harbor Inquiry (*Washington Post*, January 1, 1946).
[64] Memorandum of conversation between Welles and Halifax, May 23 (*North African Economic Memoranda*, II, No. 170).

"If this assistance to General Weygand were now withheld, it would be obvious that General Weygand would consider that no kind of assistance could possibly be forthcoming from the United States, no matter what might happen, and it would be logical to suppose that in the event he would materially change his present attitude." [65]

Lord Halifax received this decision with something of a wry face. The British were clearly disappointed that we continued to humor Vichy and that we were even prepared to go on with support of North Africa. David Eccles, the representative in Washington of the British Ministry of Economic Warfare, a man who could not be accused of mincing words, made no secret whatever of the attitude of his government: "Our situation is now so difficult and dangerous that I cannot see the value of a few shiploads of supplies except as a curtain-raiser to a military drama." Speaking to a member of the Department, he stated that

"the fact may as well be realized that, unless something tangible in the form of American military assistance could be expected, the British Government was not interested in permitting economic supplies to reach General Weygand from the United States; unless there were prospects of staff talks with American participation, as well as some definite evidence that we intended to follow up the present plan with the use of American armed forces or war materials, the continuance of the economic plan was so much waste of time." [66]

The British were frankly disgruntled with our French policy, and they continued to be so for some time. And yet it soon appeared that they were wrong and that the American policy was not only sound but far-sighted. All through May the British and Americans had lived in dire apprehension, expecting the Nazi storm to break on North Africa at any time. What actually happened was enough to justify our worst forebodings.

In the midst of the Paris negotiations Darlan had announced

[65] Ibid.
[66] Memorandum by Wallace Murray of June 4, 1941 (*North African Economic Memoranda*, II, No. 178).

publicly that the policy of collaboration was to be a reality. Speaking on the radio (May 23) he said:

"The Chancellor did not ask me to hand over the fleet to him. Every one knows—the British better than anyone—that I will never hand it over.

"The Chancellor did not ask me for any colonial territory. He did not ask me to declare war on England.

"Why has he acted so?

"Germany began the war alone and judges herself able to end it alone against no matter what coalition.

"At no moment in the conversations was there any question of France abandoning in any way her sovereignty.

"France is freely choosing the road she is taking. On her depends her present and her future. She will have the peace which she makes for herself. She will have the place in the organization of Europe which she will have made for herself."

He therefore pursued his objective quite undaunted by protests and admonitions. On May 28 he signed the three so-called *Paris Protocols*, by which, in return for vague promises of concessions in political and economic matters, France agreed to make available to the Iraq rebels three quarters of the munitions and stocks in Syria; to facilitate the staging and supply of German planes passing over Syria; to provide the Germans with an air base at Aleppo; and to permit the use of ports, roads, and railroads for transport of supplies across Syria. With respect to Africa, the French agreed to the use of the port of Bizerte by the Germans, and also of the railroad from Bizerte to Gabès; French trucks and guns were to be sold to the Germans; French ships were to be made available for carrying supplies across the Mediterranean, and French warships were to serve as convoys; finally, Dakar was to be made available to the Germans as a supply base for submarines, warships, and planes.[67]

[67] The terms were produced in some detail by Prosecutor Mornet at the Pétain trial (*Procès du M. Pétain*, p. 332). They were communicated in detail to the Italians by the Germans (Captured German Documents: telegram of May 24, to Rome). The complete text is given for the first time in the Appendix of the present study.

At the present time it is still impossible to say whether Pétain was informed in detail of these negotiations. That he had initially approved Darlan's policy, at least "in principle," seems certain. But when members of his entourage alerted him and broke the alarming news that Darlan was proposing to make Bizerte and Dakar available to the Germans, he acted as though he knew nothing. When it was pointed out to him that such concessions would mean a rupture of relations with the United States and probably war with Britain, he agreed at once to have Weygand and Boisson summoned to Vichy for discussions.[68]

Weygand arrived on June 2. Having been forewarned, he came equipped with a lengthy memorandum, in which he set forth the strength of anti-German feeling in North Africa and the danger of disturbances if any concessions were made to the enemy. The increasing number of German officials in the area was already causing unrest, and if France's empire was to be preserved, it would be necessary to adhere strictly to the principles of not granting any bases to the Germans or Italians, of defending Africa with French forces against all comers, and of not deliberately entering the war against England. If any other course were followed, it would be impossible to answer for the consequences. In any event, it was almost certain that the British would resist by force any effort by the Germans to secure a foothold.

On June 3 a *"petit conseil"* of the chief ministers was held in the marshal's presence. Darlan gave the substance of the protocols and indicated that if the French rejected them, the Germans would solve the North African problem by advancing through Spain. Thereupon Weygand read his memorandum and made a scathing attack on Darlan's whole policy. Having refused to be associated with any scheme to turn over bases to the enemy or indeed with any policy of collaboration, he stalked out, leaving the council to make up its mind.

The ministers, with the exception of General Bergeret, decided for Darlan on the theory that the French government

[68] Diary of a French Diplomat.

was too far committed to turn back. In the afternoon, however, Pétain called in Weygand, Huntziger, Laure, and Platon to consider the matter further. The old man begged Weygand not to desert him, but to stand by in his hour of trial. The general, after hours of "mental torture," decided that he must obey, but restated his objections and emphasized to the marshal that the country would accept the policy of collaboration only if it were publicly told that the armistice regime had been replaced by a system of military solidarity with Germany and that the Nazis had undertaken in writing to respect the integrity of France and her colonies, return the prisoners of war, renounce an indemnity, and abolish the line of demarcation.

No decision was taken, pending the arrival of Boisson and Esteva. Darlan, however, was unmoved. Speaking to Admiral Leahy on June 4, he made no bones about stating his views:

"If Germany needs food, she will get it in Russia, and if Russia is not willing to give it, she will take it. An attack against Russia, he added, would last no longer than the Greek and Yugoslav affairs. There is thus no likelihood of starving Germany and as for manpower, he himself had seen the large numbers of soldiers in the center of Germany itself. He did not see therefore how the British can possibly win.

"If the war continued, he went on, communism would prevail in Europe. And as for France:

"France is like a prostrate man with a great stone on his chest which he must seek to push off by all means in his power in order to live." [69]

But in the meanwhile Boisson arrived and at once threw all his weight into the scales on Weygand's side. Esteva did the same, though he discreetly avoided antagonizing his superior, Darlan. During two heavily charged days the text of the protocols was subjected to detailed analysis, from which it emerged that the concessions to be made by the Germans were much vaguer and less significant than Darlan had made them out to be. Weygand and his friends, including many

[69] Tel. (June 4, 1941) from Leahy.

officials of the French Foreign Ministry, were simply appalled. Darlan, they concluded, after a good breakfast with the Führer, was prepared to give the Germans the moon if they asked for it. Unfortunately, they were asking only for Africa, which was something more tangible and profitable. These men at once informed officials of the American Embassy of the state of affairs, and indirectly, at least, all the influence of Admiral Leahy and his staff was brought to bear. Pétain was confronted with the possibility of a rupture of relations. This, together with Weygand's prediction of a popular uprising in both France and North Africa and Weygand's and Boisson's refusal to allow the Germans to take over Bizerte or Dakar, finally decided the marshal.

At a council of ministers on the afternoon of June 6 the opposition to Darlan closed ranks and the admiral was obliged to yield. He agreed that the protocols should be reconsidered and that he himself should inform the Germans. He would propose a complete re-examination of Franco-German relations, though he doubted if the Germans would accept such a solution. Therewith this whole crucial episode was disposed of. On leaving Vichy, Weygand wrote Pétain his understanding of the decisions of the government: nothing was to be changed in the existing regime of North Africa; that is to say, no land, naval, or air base was to be conceded to the Germans or Italians in the territories that comprised French Africa; Weygand's mission to defend French Africa against all comers was to remain unchanged.[70]

How Darlan made his peace with the Germans we do not know. The Germans, however, were on the eve of the great attack upon Russia, and this entailed, for the time being at least, abandonment of the grandiose plans that had been

[70] Diary of a French Diplomat. This is far and away the best source, but a great deal of evidence was also presented at the Pétain trial; see *Procès du M. Pétain*, p. 138 (Weygand); p. 256 (Chevalier); p. 260 (General Bergeret); p. 268 (Berthelot); p. 299 (letter of General Juin); and pp. 332, 363 (summations by the prosecution and the defense). The American telegrams were also very well informed: tel. (June 4) reporting Monick's statement; tels. (June 6, 7) from Vichy; tel. (July 10) from Murphy at Algiers; tel. (August 10) from Murphy.

elaborated for the Mediterranean. At any rate, France suffered no dire consequences, excepting for the loss of Syria, which could be taken as eloquent proof of the costliness of Darlan's policy. His concessions to the Germans in Syria had raised a storm of indignation and an outbreak of dissidence. On June 8 the British, aided by the Free French, began the invasion of the country. The Vichy government naturally denounced this "aggression" and declared its determination to fight to the end. But secretly many of the men of Vichy were glad to see the British take over so as to keep the Germans out. Had the British not committed the inexcusable blunder of employing Frenchmen to fight other Frenchmen, there would certainly have been less bitterness in France, and the Vichy forces would probably have offered only a token resistance. In any event, the outcome was a foregone conclusion. On July 12 the French commander was obliged to sign an armistice, which put an end to Vichy rule in the Levant and established the British athwart the German route to Suez. But by this time Hitler's armies were already in full career across the Russian plains. The most acute phase of the Mediterranean crisis was over, and therewith this chapter may be brought to a close.[71]

The spring of 1941, culminating in the dramatic episode of the Paris Protocols, was undoubtedly the most crucial period in the history of our relations with Vichy. The Germans were in full career toward victory, and there seemed to be almost no possibility of forestalling a great onslaught on North Africa and the Near East. The British all but lost their nerve in their frantic efforts to deal with the situation and blew now hot, now cold toward our attempts to keep France in line. But throughout the crisis the American policy remained steadfast and consistent. The President and the State Department resisted the tide of emotionalism in favor of de Gaulle, which

[71] On the Syrian crisis see the statements of Secretary Hull on June 6 and 13, and those of Ambassador Henry-Haye on June 6 and 13. These are conveniently reprinted in *Documents on American Foreign Relations*, III, 402ff. See further tels. (May 17, June 12) from Leahy.

rose rapidly after the Montoire policy of collaboration had been announced. We were not yet in the war and we were not in a position to act militarily. Our one hope was to serve as a brake, to operate as a deterrent on the men of Vichy.

Admiral Leahy's original optimism about Pétain and Darlan soon evaporated. Darlan, at least, had made up his mind to collaborate, even in a military sense. Luckily, we had undertaken to support Weygand in every way possible, and Weygand was just as intent as we were on excluding the Germans from North Africa and blocking any program of collaboration. To the general undoubtedly belongs the chief credit for frustrating the Darlan policy, but there can be no question that Admiral Leahy's influence was also of great importance. Weygand's great argument was one which the ambassador himself was constantly using: namely, that military collaboration would mean not only hostilities with Britain but a rupture of relations with the United States. That was one eventuality that Pétain, always intent on his personal popularity, could not bring himself to face, for he knew that the country would not understand it.[72] But at best we came through the crisis nip and tuck, and this chapter may be appropriately concluded with a quotation from President Roosevelt's letter to Admiral Leahy of June 26, which revives all the tension and anxiety of the foregoing months and at the same time sounds the keynote of new developments:

"You have certainly been going through a life that has aspects akin to punching-bags, roller coasters, mules, pirates and general hell during these past months. I think that both you and I have given up making prophecies as to what will happen in and to France tomorrow or the next day.

"Now comes this Russian diversion. If it is more than just that, it will mean the liberation of Europe from Nazi domination . . . and at the same time I do not think we need worry about any possibility of Russian domination." [73]

[72] See Sumner Welles: *The Time for Decision*, p. 159, for an estimate of Leahy's influence. I am indebted also to comments by H. Freeman Matthews, who was on the spot.
[73] Leahy File (June 26, 1941).

CHAPTER V

Calm before the Storm

THE GERMAN ATTACK on Russia in June 1941 marked, in the words of Winston Churchill, "one of the great climacterics of the war." For more than five months, until the great offensive bogged down, the world lived in anxious suspense while the Nazi machine rolled over the great steppes toward the Soviet capital. Hitler himself confessed that, once this last formidable opponent on the Continent had been eliminated, the way would be clear for the final and decisive assault upon Britain. In the interval, to be sure, the British were bound to enjoy something of a respite. In the Near East they had managed to hold Rommel at the very gates of Egypt. By July they had suppressed the hostile insurrection in Iraq and, with the aid of the Free French forces, had conquered Syria from its Vichy rulers. It was more than unlikely that Hitler, deeply engaged with Soviet forces more powerful and determined than he had expected, would be able either to resume his offensive in the Near East or to pay much attention to North Africa. Only the Battle of the Atlantic continued without a break. But even in that theater there was a gradual turn for the better. The United States sent troops to Iceland, and in September President Roosevelt, following a submarine attack on an American vessel, proclaimed the beginning of a shooting war.[1] Before the dark day of December 7 the United States government had revised its neutrality legislation, had begun to arm its merchant ships, and had made possible the shipment of arms and munitions to friendly ports in American bottoms. More yet, the Washington government

[1] According to Admiral Stark's testimony at the Pearl Harbor Inquiry, the President in October issued orders for American ships in the Atlantic to fire on any German or Italian forces. This was tantamount to entering the war against the Axis powers of Europe (*Washington Post*, January 4, 1946).

[162]

had followed the British lead in accepting Soviet Russia as a full-fledged member of the anti-Nazi front and had joined in giving all possible material support to the Russian cause. Everything depended, then, upon the outcome of the stupendous struggle in the east until the treacherous attack of the Japanese made further decisions easy. With the story of the Russian campaign we have no concern, but against the background of that story we must examine the further development of affairs in France and North Africa before resuming our narrative and analysis of American policy.

There was no major change in the composition of the French government during the second half of 1941. Pétain officially and Darlan actually were in complete control of the situation. What Pétain's attitude toward the Nazi attack on Russia may have been we do not really know. Hating communism, he may well have looked with relief upon the diversion of German power to the east, which might mean at one and the same time a relaxation of pressure on France and the liquidation of the greatest ideological menace. The marshal, reported Admiral Leahy on June 27, "expects Germany to succeed in occupying those provinces of Russia near the German border and to set up therein independent buffer states which will cause the downfall of Stalin and remove the menace of Communism." [2]

Darlan, who shared Pétain's hatred of the Bolsheviks, was even more positive in forecasting a Nazi victory. Even before the German attack he had predicted it, adding that it would not take longer to succeed than had the offensives against Greece and Yugoslavia.[3] In other words, there was no doubt in Darlan's mind that Hitler would soon be supreme on the entire continent. He therefore concluded that it behooved him to be on the right side. If there was one point on which all sources were agreed from the outset, it was that Darlan

[2] Leahy File (June 27, 1941).

[3] Tel. (June 4, 1941) from Leahy. The Germans, as we know, were confident of easy victory. Even Göring, opposed though he was to the attack on Russia, was convinced that the Soviet armies would be rolled up in no time (State Department interrogation of Göring).

was an opportunist of the first water, to which might be added
the further observation that he was a really strong man, quite
prepared to face unpopularity and opposition if necessary to
gain his end.

Conditions in France were very bad, and growing rapidly
worse. To analyze them in detail would take us too far afield.
Suffice it to say that the situation created by the armistice,
which, it must be remembered, was thought of as a purely
temporary arrangement, was bound to become progressively
less bearable. There were still some million and a half young
men prisoners in Germany, a sad state of affairs, which was a
prime factor in the rapid drop in French industrial and agricultural production. Furthermore, the artificial division of
the country into zones and the suspension of normal trade
with the outside world necessarily aggravated conditions.

It was natural, therefore, that discontent should have become more widespread and more articulate. The mass of the
nation, to be sure, was still lost in the slough of hopelessness
and defeatism.

"Morale has collapsed completely," reported an observer after
several weeks in Vichy, "and it is still at a low ebb. I heard it said
often that France was a second class nation and asked nothing
better than to remain one; that she was a tired nation, having lost
too heavily in the last war; that she has suffered too much; that
she did not want this war, was not prepared to wage it, and was
led into it by England; that the Germans could perhaps run
Europe better than anyone else." [4]

And yet such reliable reports as we have all agree that the
country had no use for collaboration with Germany. On the
contrary, these reports state that the lower classes in particular
were overwhelmingly in favor of the British and looked to
them for salvation. Furthermore, these people did not blame
Pétain for the turn that French policy had taken. The American quoted above confirmed that the marshal was the only

[4] Observations of an American, a copy of which is in the Office of
Strategic Services, Central Information Division.

person who commanded general respect: "Almost everyone is of the opinion that he is only playing for time." "The hero of Verdun is said to be all that the French now have," reported another observer. His extreme Rightist views offended some, but for the most part they were overlooked or ignored in the interests of the larger national good.[5]

On the other hand, no one seems ever to have met anyone among the French populace who would say a good word for Darlan and his followers in the government. They were universally detested as rank opportunists and crooks. So strong, indeed, was the feeling that resistance groups were already springing into being, especially in the occupied zone. We need not stop to distinguish and describe them, for in 1941 they were still fairly insignificant, though they were numerous enough. It is worth noting, however, that they were by no means directed against the marshal, but rather against the Germans and against those Frenchmen who collaborated with them. Staff officers of the French army and members of the Deuxième Bureau supported resistance movements from the start. One of the most promising groups was that headed by General de La Laurencie, a close friend of Pétain, albeit an opponent of collaboration and a pronounced Anglophile. La Laurencie's efforts were directed toward co-ordinating the patriot groups to form an army of "Friends of the Marshal." It was said that Pétain knew of the movement and tacitly approved it. Its aim was to set up a complete government organization in skeleton and to prepare military units to aid British landing parties.[6]

A question that is bound to arise in this connection, and one that has a real bearing on American policy, is the question whether at this or at any later time before the invasion

[5] Report from Madrid, March 8, 1941; observations of Commander R. H. Hillenkoetter, at Vichy, October 7, 1941.

[6] OSS Report mentioned above. A detailed history and analysis of the French underground movements in *Survey of French Underground Movements* (Office of Strategic Services, Research and Analysis Branch, January 28, 1944), and in an OSS report of June 1945 entitled *Lessons from the Resistance to the German Occupation of France.*

of North Africa popular sentiment in France was strongly in favor of General de Gaulle and the Free French organization in London. On this point the evidence is utterly conflicting. Admiral Leahy, who earlier in the year had suspected that Gaullist sympathies were more widespread than was generally supposed, took the view in the summer that de Gaulle had no great following.[7] In the same way Commander Hillenkoetter reported in October 1941: "For every ten Frenchmen who are pro-British, one cannot find more than one who may be called pro-De Gaulle." This he thought was due to the fact that the general was not at all well known and that he spent too much of his time in London instead of fighting. On the other hand, the American observer mentioned above thought the lower classes were "almost solidly De Gaulle." "De Gaulle has become a hero of the lower classes and most of the youth. The efforts of the Government to portray him as a traitor and the execution of anyone found working for his interests in France, have simply fanned the flame." In like fashion, a prominent American correspondent, who, however, was at times more imaginative than thorough, stated quite unequivocally in a letter:

"De Gaulle by his continued opposition to Germany has the moral support of 90% of the French. Obviously their support is only moral, but he is a heroic figure to many millions, and once peace is re-established and the inevitable amnesty follows, De Gaulle may come back as a great leader."[8]

What the truth may have been, in view of these contradictory reports, is almost anyone's guess. Certainly de Gaulle could not have been more than a name to most Frenchmen, but the population at large was unquestionably hostile to the Germans, and many no doubt looked upon de Gaulle as a symbol of national resistance to the traditional enemy. Just as the upper classes were largely Pétainist, the lower classes tended to look to de Gaulle, knowing nothing, of course, of

[7] Leahy File (July 28, 1941).
[8] OSS Files (May 10, 1941).

his semi-fascist political and social views. It would certainly be a mistake to attempt in this matter any categorical statements or sweeping generalizations. The development of the de Gaulle organization was a long and arduous process. The whole movement was still amorphous and became important only as it became better constituted and as the German policy in France became so harsh as to evoke a strong and widespread reaction.

In any event, popular feeling had not yet turned against the marshal, and Darlan, as the Vice-Premier chosen by the marshal, had nothing much to fear. Pétain was an old man, vain and authoritarian, but no longer able to keep control over details. There can be no doubt that much was done without his knowledge and that he reigned rather than governed. Actually he was almost as helpless in the hands of Darlan as he would have been in the hands of Laval. For Darlan was an aggressive character and had the French fleet behind him, and the fleet was perhaps the biggest single stake in the whole business. Darlan had managed to induce the Germans to release all naval prisoners, and he now had under him a force of some sixty-six thousand. The rank and file of the crews are reported to have been anti-German and anti-collaborationist even in 1941, but the officers were loyal to Darlan, almost to a man. They were prepared to follow his orders unquestioningly, and he rewarded many of them with high and influential government posts. After Weygand's dismissal (November 1941) all the French colonies, for example, were under the command of French admirals.[9]

But Darlan's henchmen were not confined to the fleet. His policy of collaboration with Germany could count on more than enough eager supporters among French industrial and banking interests—in short, among those who even before the war had turned to Nazi Germany and had looked

[9] Commander Hillenkoetter's report, October 7, 1941. The question of Pétain's personal control and responsibility was raised and thrashed out again and again at his trial. See particularly the remarks of General Trochu (*Procès du M. Pétain*, p. 181).

to Hitler as the savior of Europe from Communism. These were the elements which had originally backed Pétain and Weygand—elements that stuck to the program after both these men had begun to back away from it. These people were as good fascists as any in Europe. They dreaded the Popular Front like the plague and were convinced that they could prosper even under Hitler's iron rod. Many of them had long had extensive and intimate business relations with German interests and were still dreaming of a new system of "synarchy," which meant government of Europe on fascist principles by an international brotherhood of financiers and industrialists. Laval had long been associated with this group. Darlan, though not one of the "boys," was clever enough to take them into camp. If they worshipped Laval, they served Darlan, as they would have served anyone who played the game.

"This group," wrote Ambassador Biddle from London early in 1942, "should be regarded not as Frenchmen, any more than their corresponding members in Germany should be regarded as Germans, for the interests of both groups are so intermingled as to be indistinguishable; their whole interest is focussed upon furtherance of their industrial and financial stakes." [10]

Many important banking groups must be included in this category: the Banque Nationale pour le Commerce et l'Industrie (which was Laval's group *par excellence*), the Banque de l'Indochine (of which Baudoin was the chief), the Banque de Paris et des Pays Bas, and others. But peculiarly identified with the Darlan regime was the Banque Worms et Cie, headed by Hippolyte Worms, with Gabriel Leroy-Ladurie and Jacques Barnaud as the dominant figures. To realize the extent to which members of the Banque Worms group had been taken into the government by the autumn of 1941 a brief survey of the council and of the Secretaries of State will be most profitable. Of the ministers, Joseph Barthélemy (Justice), Pierre Caziot (Agriculture), Lucien

[10] Dispatch (January 7, 1942).

Romier (State), and Henri Moysset (State) might be described as Pétain men—that is, men who were not necessarily collaborationist, but who favored the authoritarian program of the marshal. On the other hand, Pierre Pucheu (Interior), and Yves Bouthillier (National Economy) were members of the Worms clique. General Bergeret (Secretary of State for Aviation) was included by some among Pétain's personal following, by others among the Worms group. Excluding Bergeret, the Secretaries of State were almost to a man associates of the same clique. They were Jacques Barnaud (Delegate-General for Franco-German Economic Relations), Jerome Carpopino (Education), Serge Huard (Family and Health), Admiral Platon (Colonies), René Belin (Labor), François Lehideux (Industrial Production), Jean Berthelot (Communications), and Paul Charbin (Food Supply). Jacques Benoist-Mechin (in charge of Franco-German relations) was a journalist long associated with Otto Abetz and, according to all reports, a mere stooge of the Germans. Among the Worms group should be mentioned further a large number of somewhat subordinate officials (chiefly secretaries-general) like Lamirand, Borotra, Ravalland, Bichelonne, Lafond, Million, Deroy, Filippi, Schwartz, and Billiet.[11]

From this list it appears at once that practically every ministry or secretaryship touching economic affairs was in the hands of one or another of the Worms clique. Many of them, like Pucheu, Bouthillier, Barnaud, and Lehideux were able men—as able as they were self-interested and unscrupulous. Pucheu, of whom quite a bit became known through his trial for treason, was an excellent organizer and a man who, in point of ambition, was hardly second to Darlan himself. He

---

[11] Dispatch (January 7, 1942) from Biddle. The most detailed information on the Worms group may be found in *Worms et Cie* (Coordinator of Information, Research and Analysis Branch, Report, March 3, 1942), and *Activities of Banque Worms et Cie* (Office of Strategic Services, Research and Analysis Branch, Report, November 15, 1943). See also Louis R. Franck: "The Forces of Collaboration" (*Foreign Affairs*, October 1942), and Raymond Brugère: *Veni, Vidi, Vichy* (Paris, 1944), pp. 133ff.

had been closely associated with the Cagoulard and other prewar fascist movements. As an agent of the Cartel Sidérurgique he had sought to promote co-operation between French and German heavy industry. In other words, he, like several of the others, had a collaborationist past and was not only willing but eager to join up with the enemy. Darlan could count on these men, who not only arranged for the shipment of goods and manufactured products to Germany, but also served as go-betweens in arranging the transfer of French manufacturing establishments to German ownership or control. Needless to say, they turned a pretty penny in the process and furthered their own affairs at the same time. This economic collaboration, which was a very real thing from the outset, was not affected by the vicissitudes of political collaboration. It was well established before the war and served well the purposes of both German and French interests.[12]

All of the collaborationist banks had considerable interests in North Africa and the other French colonies, and maintained branches there. The Banque Worms, for example, owned extensive mines, shipping lines, and commercial companies in North Africa. It and others like it rapidly drained North Africa of such resources as could be made available to the Germans. It has been estimated that during 1941 alone some five million tons of goods were landed at French Mediterranean ports, mostly from North Africa. Included were such strategic materials as cobalt, molybdenum, manganese, and high-grade iron ore, to say nothing of foodstuffs. Probably sixty to eighty per cent of all these imports went to the Germans.[13] Fortunately for them, the great banking and industrial interests, always intent on playing safe, were permitted by the Germans to transfer their huge profits to their North African branches. Calculations have shown that prior

[12] See especially the State Department interrogation of Dr. Paul Schmidt.
[13] *The Economic Contribution of French North Africa to the Axis* (Board of Economic Warfare, Blockade and Supply Branch, Report, September 12, 1942).

to the invasion of North Africa the French banks taken together transferred no less than twenty-five billion francs in this way.[14]

It stands to reason that this merciless exploitation of France in the interests of the traditional enemy was bound to arouse ever greater popular resentment and unrest. Hence the rapid growth of opposition and resistance groups during the autumn of 1941, to which must be added the revived activity of the Communists, whose consciences were eased by the German attack on Bolshevik Russia. Assassination and sabotage became the order of the day as the year wore on. The Germans shot hostages by tens and dozens in reprisal, until the whole world was horrified and scandalized. Marshal Pétain protested and besought mercy. But Darlan and his associates took the whole thing as part of the business. Pucheu, who was later to pose as an opponent of collaboration and a secret protector of resistance groups, distinguished himself at the time by building up an efficient French Gestapo and by ferreting out all those who refused to conform.[15]

Considering the character and policy of the Darlan regime, it may seem to have been utterly futile for us to maintain relations with Vichy France. But there were at least some extenuating circumstances, some rays of hope. For one thing, it was fairly clear that Pétain himself was not in sympathy with the Darlan policy. He had dismissed Laval not only for personal reasons but for his policy of collaboration. In like fashion he might get rid of Darlan at an opportune moment. At any rate, with encouragement and support he might at least be trusted to hold collaboration to a minimum—to restrict it to the economic sphere. And, apart from the marshal himself, there were not a few officials in Vichy who were strongly anti-German in their sentiments and who looked to the United States as well as to Britain for ultimate deliverance. It is rather important to remember, in this connection, that

[14] *Activities of Banque Worms et Cie*, cited above.
[15] For Pucheu's apology see his letter to Admiral Auboyneau of April 14, 1943 (OSS Files) and the record of his trial in March 1944.

the entourage of the marshal was a most heterogeneous group.
On the one hand there were numerous representatives of the
extreme Rightist groups, men of the Action Française and the
Cagoule, to say nothing of the Banque Worms circle. Many
of these men were simon-pure collaborationists, but others
were ardent nationalists, despite their authoritarian proclivities. Some of the latter had done their best to withhold stores
of arms from the Germans. They continued to operate a
Deuxième Bureau and to build up an army staff in secret.
They laid plans for the organization of new divisions for the
day when British or American forces might land in France,
and they encouraged resistance groups not only in training,
but in the clandestine manufacture of weapons. Most of this
activity was carried on with the knowledge of Pétain and
with his blessing. General Revers, the chief of staff of the
small armistice army, was the secret chief of the Ordre de
Résistance de l'Armée.[16]

But in addition to these men there were many members of
the army and of the civil service (notably the Foreign Ministry) who were so strongly anti-German and pro-American
that they went out of their way to supply the American representatives with information or to transmit timely warnings.
For example, the Deuxième Bureau in the spring of 1941 made
secret arrangements with the United States army to send
important intelligence to Washington through the French
Embassy. The ambassador, Gaston Henry-Haye, knew nothing of this, though he undoubtedly suspected something ir-
regular.[17]

Among the civil servants there were a number who were no
less obliging, and some who later paid for their patriotism in
the prisons and concentration camps of the Gestapo. Some
of them might well be mentioned here by name, but since
they were so numerous that it would be impossible to include

[16] *Procès du M. Pétain*, p. 42 (Daladier); pp. 228–9 (General Picquendar);
pp. 234–5 (General Lafargue); and further the OSS report on *Lessons from
the Resistance to the German Occupation of France*, pp. 22ff.
[17] Conversation with Colonel Preston Goodfellow, August 14, 1943.

them all, a partial list would of necessity be discriminatory. All told, we had strong adherents in the army, and many of the key men in the Foreign Ministry were actively collaborationist—on our side. Under the circumstances the Vichy picture was not entirely devoid of bright spots. For intelligence purposes, if for no others, it was eminently worth while to maintain the connection.[18]

Yet this course became ever more difficult as time wore on. The alarming developments of May 1941 had called forth a number of unvarnished statements by Secretary Hull and other American officials, all of which condemned the Vichy government for its collaboration with the enemy. To these declarations large parts of the American population shouted amen, expecting that momentarily relations with Vichy would be severed. Unhappily the line taken in public discussion was an almost exclusively ideological one, demanding a break with fascism and unqualified support of de Gaulle and the Free French. Why, asked Samuel Grafton in his popular column, do we recognize fascism when it is called Hitler but not when it is called Pétain? "Why does a simple change of names that would not fool a hotel clerk bewilder our State Department and throw it off its track and make it seem virginal, ignorant and naive?" "We try at one and the same time," he continued, "to chuck Fascism under the chin and to scold our people for not rising in higher anger against it; we want the people to roar while Leahy coos and lifts his glass in a toast to the ferrets who rule France." [19]

In like manner many aggressively patriotic organizations, like the Committee to Defend America, the Fight for Freedom, and the Union for Democratic Action, called upon the

[18] The survey of French Foreign Office officials was made in a memorandum prepared in the Department of State, probably based on information from H. F. Matthews, and dated October 1941. Matthews tells me that in his opinion eighty-five per cent of French officialdom was on the American side. See also the testimony of Lavagne (*Procès du M. Pétain*, p. 305).

[19] Samuel Grafton: "I'd Rather Be Right" (*New York Post*, May 20, 21, 1941). These passages are of course not quoted for their intrinsic value, but only as illustrations of a large volume of uncritical, sensational writing.

Department to break with Vichy and "deal only with the
leaders of Free France." [20] But all this was not nearly so simple
as it sounded. If there was one thing that should have been
clear, it was that to break with Vichy would have been tantamount to leaving the field to the collaborationists. On the
other hand, it was by no means clear that anything much
would be gained by recognizing de Gaulle as the representative of the real France. A very large part of the French people
as well as of French officialdom was deeply imbued with the
doctrine of national unity under the marshal. He was the legal
head of the government, and the French as a people had a
well-known *"complexe de légalité."* The British themselves,
though they were de Gaulle's sponsors and backers, carefully
abstained from going all the way to recognition. Furthermore,
de Gaulle had not succeeded in rallying many prominent
Frenchmen to his cause. The movement, in the summer of
1941, could hardly be described as impressive or even promising. In its ranks were representatives of every shade of opinion, from extreme Right to the far Left. Not a few of de
Gaulle's followers had previously been in the service of Vichy.
These men could not unite on any coherent program for the
new France; neither did they trust each other or, for that matter, General de Gaulle. The Free French delegation in Washington was anything but inspiring. One representative of de
Gaulle arrived after another. None of them was a man of
prominence or standing, and no two of them seemed to be
pulling in the same direction. Some of them spoke openly and
in a most disparaging way of their leader and at times different
members of the delegation took entirely different lines. Intrigue and personal bickerings were all too common. In a
word, the Free French organization was not one easy to deal
with and secrecy in negotiation was out of the question. [21]

To recognize de Gaulle would unquestionably have meant

[20] See the protests of these organizations in the *New York Times*, July
14, 27, 1941.
[21] *De Gaulle, the Free French, and the French Underground* (OSS:
Foreign Nationalities Branch, report, July 9, 1942).

the end of relations with Vichy, for if there was one matter on which Pétain felt strongly, it was the activity of the "traitor" de Gaulle. Not wanting to break with Vichy, we therefore had to move with the utmost caution and circumspection. In so far as the Free French were actually fighting the enemy, we agreed to support them in a discreet way. In July 1941, arrangements were made for the purchase by the Free French of non-military goods required by the French colonies. Even military supplies were made available, but only through lend-lease channels by way of the British until on November 11, 1941 President Roosevelt proclaimed: "I hereby find that the defense of any French territory under control of the French Volunteer Forces is vital to the defense of the United States." In other words, American support in materiel, if it was not assured to the Free French movement as such, was at least assured to the colonial territories under Free French control. Farther, at the time, the government was not prepared to go.

And now to turn from what Churchill called "the sad and sorry and squalid tale of what is going on at Vichy" to at least a cursory examination of the chronological development of our policy during the second half of 1941. As aforesaid, the invasion of Russia made less likely for the time being any German advance in the Mediterranean area. Still, memories of the scare of May and June 1941 were still recent, and the preoccupation of the Nazis in the east might prove to be of short duration. Furthermore, there arose the obvious question whether we should not exploit the opportunity supplied by the diversion of the enemy's main effort.

So long as Darlan remained at the helm, there could be no abatement of our anxiety. This was clearly revealed when, early in July, the President announced to Congress that American troops were being sent to Iceland. Part of the message to Congress is so pertinent that it may well be quoted verbatim:

"The United States cannot permit the occupation by Germany of strategic outposts in the Atlantic to be used as air or naval bases for eventual attack against the Western Hemisphere. We have no desire to see any change in the present sovereignty of those regions. Assurance that such outposts in our defense-frontier remain in friendly hands is the very foundation of our national security and of the national security of every one of the independent nations of the New World."

The President then went on to state that American forces had already been sent to the bases leased from Britain in the West Indies, in order "to forestall any pincers movement undertaken by Germany against the Western Hemisphere." [22]

On that very day Robert Murphy reported from Algiers a conversation that he had had with Monick, one of the important French officials in Morocco and one of those most eager to prod the United States into action. Monick said that he had talked with a number of Frenchmen who had been recently in Berlin. They had described to him a Nazi Eurafrican scheme, which in all probability had been discussed between Hitler and Darlan during the latter's visit to Berchtesgaden in May. The main thought was that the Germans would advance in Russia only far enough to surround the Black Sea. Thereafter they would turn through the Near East and sweep over North Africa. Spain would be drawn into the war, and the Germans would establish themselves in Casablanca and Dakar. [23]

To add color to such reports, Weygand arrived in Vichy on July 11 for renewed conferences. Though Murphy reported him as having left Algiers "determined not to yield and in a fighting mood," there was every reason to suppose that the Germans had revived their demands on the French government and that Weygand's opposition might be overridden. Presumably the whole problem was thrashed out again and the decision to evade or if necessary resist the German demands was renewed. But for us simply to wait and see was too dangerous. President Roosevelt therefore at once sent to Admiral Leahy a message for Pétain admonishing him against any concessions. To this Admiral Leahy replied on July 16 that he had seen Pétain and Darlan, without very assuring results:

[22] Message to Congress, July 7, 1941 (printed in *Peace and War*, No. 216).
[23] Tel. July 7, 1941 (from Algiers).

"Admiral Darlan stated very clearly that he could not say that Germany has not asked for use of the bases. He did say that as long as the present political arrangement with Germany based on the Armistice continued, no foreign Power would be permitted to use the bases. He repeated 'for so long as the present political arrangement with Germany lasts,' indicating and leaving with me an impression that there may soon be a change in the existing Armistice Agreement. I was told in this interview that Japan will in the immediate future occupy bases in Indo-China with the purpose of projecting military operations to the southward." [24]

Here was bad news heaped upon evil tidings. On the other side of the globe the Japanese were keeping step with their Nazi friends. Having already established themselves in northern Indo-China, they were now about to make themselves masters of the south, whence they could menace Thailand, Malaya, and, above all, the rich Dutch Indies. Whatever the pretext for the move, its results were almost certain. Another message was therefore sent to Vichy without delay, but once again Admiral Leahy could report no hope:

"Admiral Darlan suggested that Germany probably does not look with much favor on the acquisition of the Dutch islands by Japan and that a consultation between French and German authorities might be used to delay a decision. He expressed a fear that Japan may move against Indo-China within a week, whether the French Government agrees or not." [25]

The fear expressed by Darlan was to prove justified only too soon. On July 21 he informed Leahy that the Vichy govern-

[24] Leahy File (July 16, 1941). I have not seen the text of the President's message. Among the Captured German Documents is a letter from Pétain to Hitler dated July 22 in which the marshal says he is pained by the German demand for air bases in North Africa, that this demand goes far beyond the armistice terms and is incompatible with French honor. To comply would mean abandoning parts of North Africa to the mercy of the German military authorities. He hoped, concluded the marshal, that the question could be settled by agreement and as between equals, not by a *Diktat*. This letter makes it fairly clear that the Germans had renewed their demands, though we know nothing further of the details.

[25] Leahy File (July 19, 1941).

ment had had to yield. On July 29 the Japanese published the glad news of an agreement with Vichy for "common defense" of Indo-China against alleged designs of British and Gaullists. As usual, Tokyo affirmed that the agreement had been concluded in all friendliness and announced that no other power had any right to take umbrage or interfere. First Welles and then President Roosevelt himself gave the Japanese ambassador, Nomura, an unvarnished evaluation of Japanese action and intent and stated roundly that any agreement between Tokyo and Vichy could be only the result of pressure by Berlin on the Vichy government. Obviously, then, Japan was aiding Hitler and obviously, too, this step would be the last before an attempt to conquer the South Seas.[26] In a public statement on August 2 Welles said in part:

"For reasons which are beyond the scope of any known agreement, France has now decided to permit foreign troops to enter an integral part of its Empire, to occupy bases therein, and to prepare operations within French territory which may be directed against other peoples friendly to the people of France.

"Under these circumstances, this Government is impelled to question whether the French Government at Vichy in fact proposes to maintain its declared policy to preserve for the French people the territory both at home and abroad which has been under French sovereignty.

"This Government, mindful of its traditional friendship for France, has deeply sympathized with the desire of the French people to maintain their territories and to preserve them intact. In its relations with the French Government at Vichy and with the local French authorities in French territories, the United States will be governed by the manifest effectiveness with which those authorities endeavor to protect these territories from domination and control by those powers which are seeking to extend their rule by force and conquest, or by threat thereof."

It stands to reason that this latest move on the Far Eastern checkerboard raised a howl of indignation in the United States, indignation that was directed almost more against

[26] *Peace and War*, Nos. 218, 220.

Vichy than against Tokyo. First in Syria, now in Indo-China, the Darlan regime, despite all its protestations, was yielding without even a show of resistance. With ever increasing emphasis came the cry of public opinion that relations with France should be severed, that we should frankly and openly espouse the cause of the Free French, and that we should at once safeguard our own interests by seizing Martinique and Dakar.[27]

And why, it may be asked, did we not proceed thus neatly and logically? Partly, no doubt, because we still lacked the necessary military power to oppose either Japan or Germany, and it could hardly be supposed that the Germans would accept the seizure of Dakar without reacting. But partly, too, because there was good reason to suppose that Weygand would hold North Africa, despite Darlan and even in the event of a German assault. Murphy, in particular, was confident that Weygand could be counted on and that, through him, the United States could ensure itself against a German occupation of North and West Africa. After all, Weygand had been willing to negotiate the Economic Accord of February 1941, the objective of which was to maintain some kind of economic sufficiency in North Africa and prevent an outbreak of unrest which might have provoked German intervention. What if he was loyal to Pétain? That in itself did not mean that he did not hate the Germans or that he was not prepared to work with the United States toward a common objective. Quite on the contrary, he had shown by his strong attitude in June 1941 that he opposed French collaboration with Germany, with particular reference to the cession of North African bases. Whatever his past sins or his current political views, he had demonstrated his determination to keep the French imperial possessions out of German hands, and that was the most important consideration from the standpoint of American policy.

[27] See, for example, the protests of various organizations printed in the *New York Times* (August 10), in the *Christian Science Monitor* (August 11), and in the *New York Post* (August 27).

It must be confessed that prior to July 1941 the Economic Accord had been a pretty one-sided affair. We had lost no time in sending over the vice-consuls who were to supervise the distribution of goods. These men, chosen chiefly from the army and navy, had taken their posts at the key ports and railroad centers. They had been instructed to report frequently and in detail not only on the fate of American imports into North Africa, but on the general movement of trade and on all significant military and political developments.[28] With Weygand's permission the American agents were able to have diplomatic-pouch service and to use a secret cipher in their communications with Washington. By July and August their reports were already beginning to come into Washington. For example, Vice-Consuls Knight and Rounds, after two weeks at Oran, sent back detailed information on the battleship *Dunkerque* and on all other ships in the harbor; on the Germans they had observed there; on the German propaganda among the Arabs; on the attitude of Admiral Jarry and of General Charbonnes, both of whom were friendly.[29] In similar fashion Vice-Consul King at Casablanca reported at length on the German infiltration and activity in Morocco.[30] The intelligence thus collected became more and more voluminous as time went on. Its value is so obvious as not to require particular comment. As Secretary Hull once remarked, our vice-consuls watched events like a thousand hawks. Whatever might happen in North Africa, we were bound to know something about it and to be forewarned.[31]

As against this very important gain we managed to do but little in return. By July 1 only two tankers with petroleum products had been sent to North Africa. By October another tanker had been dispatched and four cargo ships with general merchandise, chiefly sugar, tea, coal, cotton goods, and to-

---

[28] Memorandum by Wallace Murray, June 11, 1941 (*North African Economic Memoranda*, II, No. 181).
[29] Dispatch (July 6, 1941) from Murphy.
[30] Dispatch (August 5, 1941) from Murphy.
[31] Kenneth Pendar: *Adventure in Diplomacy* (New York, 1945) gives a vivid personal account of these activities.

bacco.[32] For one reason or another it seemed almost impossible to implement the program or to live up to the shipping schedules that were drawn up religiously every three months. In the Department of State itself there were some who had never been enthusiastic about the scheme and who were constantly finding technical obstacles to put in its way. There were difficulties about priorities and licenses, and the British, who blew now hot, now cold, but mostly cold, added to the confusion by their control over navicerts, and so on. At any rate, the plan made haste exceedingly slowly, and one could hardly have blamed any Frenchman for feeling bitter about it. If North Africa had been really dependent on our help to prevent collapse, it might have gone under at almost any time.[33]

Yet Weygand appears to have abstained from criticism. He stood his course without flinching and in a sense became our one great hope. As Murphy had reported, he went off to Vichy on July 10 in a fighting mood, and Welles therefore seized the occasion to bolster his morale by sending him, through Murphy, the President's views on the situation, as they had already been sent to Admiral Leahy for communication to Pétain. The President, Murphy was to say, was much exercised by reports that France and Germany had completed the framework of a peace treaty that would give Germany the use of North and West African bases. The United States was concerned solely that these bases should remain in friendly hands:

"So long as effective control over such ports as Casablanca and Dakar remain actually in French hands under the control of General Weygand, and no German infiltration into those ports is permitted, and no direct or indirect German authority is there exercised, this Government will consider those ports as remaining in 'friendly hands.' What would be essential, however, from the standpoint of the United States, would be to prevent the utilization by the Germans and other unfriendly powers of those ports

[32] *Exports from the United States to North Africa*: memo dated November 3, 1941 (*North African Economic Memoranda*, II, No. 255).

[33] State Department Memorandum of 1943 on *The Role of the Department of State in the North African Economic and Political Program*.

as military, naval, or air bases. This does not imply occupation by the United States of such outposts, but it does imply the prevention of their occupation by Germany."

The President, added Welles, had spoken in the highest terms of General Weygand and was sure that he would not permit German domination of North or West Africa. He recognized the general's difficulties in getting military supplies, but suggested that the new ferry route across Africa, which was then being developed, might have possibilities in an emergency.[34]

In a sense this message was nothing more than a repetition of a pious wish. There was no mention of economic aid to North Africa and only the merest indication that at some time we might be prepared to give military support. At Vichy Weygand had probably learned of recent German importunity and pressure and he undoubtedly heard of Japan's extensive demands. It is no wonder, then, that Murphy found him low in spirit on his return to Algiers. Weygand expressed himself as not very favorably impressed with the reports of the American defense effort. In Murphy's own words:

"General Weygand believes that he may be faced with a crisis in September or October next, on the theory that the Germans will turn their attention to this area, especially the Atlantic bases, by then. Several of his advisers believe that the German Eurafrican Plan will function in North Africa by that time. . . . His close associates suggest that if the United States is interested in military support of Weygand, it is important that I tell him what military aid the United States could give him for the purpose of resisting Axis aggression, and *when* this could be done. . . . If I could inform the General that there is under study at Washington a program of *substantial* military aid,—that factor alone would have an important effect." [35]

The same overtone occurred again in Murphy's report of his talk with Weygand following the transmittal of Welles's message: the general expressed himself as pleased and interested, but said bluntly "that he would not enter into a commit-

[34] Tel. (July 17, 1941) from Welles to Murphy.
[35] Letter (July 15, 1941) from Murphy to Hull.

ment regarding the general policy of his government without authorization, neither had he any intention of taking independent military action." To the best of his knowledge, there had been no recent action changing the status of French African ports or conceding their use to the Germans. As before, he was determined to resist aggression. According to Murphy, the general seemed a bit disappointed that the President's message "did not go further to the extent of a preliminary outline of what volume of supplies might be forthcoming and what the possible time lag might be in the event of an emergency." [36]

These reports from Murphy are of considerable interest and real importance, for they mark the beginning of an intermittent attempt on his part to secure for Weygand concrete promises of American military support. Looking backward, we can see that Murphy was perhaps too sanguine about Weygand. No doubt the general was determined to resist German encroachment at all costs and as best he could. In all likelihood he would have accepted military supplies if they had been offered him and if he had thought it possible to accept such aid without provoking German action. But he made it very clear to Murphy that he would not take *independent* military steps. Our representative tended to overlook these reservations and relied rather too heavily on the suggestions and pronouncements of Weygand's entourage, in which no doubt there were many men more adventurous than the general himself.

In any event, the United States government was not yet prepared to lend military support in North Africa and, indeed, the situation in the summer of 1941 did not seem to call for such drastic action. As Murphy himself admitted: "It is clear that we have a far greater time margin than we dared hope some months ago." [37] That, at least, was an undiluted blessing, though of course the threat was still there, for at bottom the situation was unchanged. From both Vichy and Al-

[36] Tel. (July 21, 1941) from Murphy; also letter of Murphy to Wallace Murray (July 30, 1941).
[37] Letter to Murray (July 30, 1941).

giers gloomy prognostications continued to arrive in Washington. On July 28 Admiral Leahy wrote to the President:

"Indications here point to a German move against the Mediterranean upon the completion of the Russian campaign regardless of the outcome. It is practically certain that Germany some time ago demanded the use of French African bases, and that Darlan was unable to deliver them because of the resistance offered by General Weygand. It is generally believed here that the demand will be renewed and that Weygand will at that time not succeed in preventing use of the bases by Germany."

Now that Indo-China had been abandoned to the Japanese, added the admiral, it would be particularly hard for the French to resist German demands. It was entirely possible that Pétain was not informed of that deal until the negotiations were practically completed:

"It seems to me," concluded the ambassador, "that he [Pétain] is surely if slowly being manoeuvred into a position where his only purpose will be to hold the loyalty of the French people and make speeches to school children and veterans." [38]

From Algiers Murphy continued to report in the same tenor: Weygand's staff was convinced that great changes were on the way at Vichy and that the French government "will go all out in support of the German program." One of the general's aides had remarked "that Weygand is developing the conviction that Vichy now simply operates under German domination and controls; that in reality the marshal has no freedom of action." And thereupon followed the usual tempting suggestion from Weygand's associate: "If the general can be brought to believe that the African trump, which is the last France has, can be played with a chance of winning, he will feel justified in taking responsibility." [39]

By this time the alarms had become almost chronic. On August 8 General Weygand again visited Vichy, and once more the air was full of rumors that the Bizerte concession was un-

[38] Leahy to the President (July 28, 1941).
[39] Tel. (August 2, 1941) from Murphy.

der discussion.[40] Whether there was anything in these rumors it is impossible to say. On his return to Algiers, Weygand told Murphy: "There is no change in our situation in Africa and no concessions have been made to the Germans." In all likelihood the discussions at Vichy were concerned rather with Pétain's radio address of August 12, which marked the death-knell of whatever was left of democratic government in France. It was a pathetic picture that the old man drew of his country as a prelude to his new assertion of authority:

"For the last several weeks I have felt an ill wind rising in many regions of France. Disquiet is overtaking minds; doubt is gaining control of spirits. The authority of my government is made the subject of discussion; orders are often being ill-executed.

"In an atmosphere of false rumors and intrigues, the forces of reconstruction are growing discouraged. Others are trying to take their place without their nobility or disinterestedness. My sponsorship is too often invoked, even against the government, to justify self-styled undertakings of salvation which, in fact, amount to nothing more than appeals for indiscipline.

"The National Revolution, which I outlined in my message last October 11, has not yet taken its place among accomplished facts.

"It has not yet forced its way through because between the people and me—who understand one another so well—there has arisen a double screen of partisans of the old regime and those serving the trusts."

Following this sad recital of failure, the marshal announced that "authority no longer emanates from below. The only authority is that which I entrust or delegate." Activity of political parties was to be suspended and new powers of repression were to be set up: "I will double the means of police action, whose discipline and loyalty should guarantee public order," and so forth and so on.

All that Matthews could say for this speech was that it contained nothing about further collaboration with the Germans.

[40] Leahy File (August 3, 11, and 12, 1941); tel. (August 10, 1941) from Murphy.

For the rest, it made the Vichy regime appear as a full-blown
fascist state, headed by a pathetic old man:

"The Marshal," wrote Matthews, "partly due to his great age,
has come to regard himself more and more as the patriarchal ruler
of France, an uncrowned king without the elaborate settings of
royalty. His purpose is to save France from repeating 'the errors
of the past'—and he longs for a peaceful world in which to build.
To him and to those who surround him, those errors are at-
tributable to 'Jews, Free Masons, Communists, and Demagogy,'
and under the heading of the last named the indicating swing of
the pendulum includes basic representative government. He reasons the 'rebuilding of France in the spirit of the national revolution' demands loyalty and a blind trust in him and his wisdom by
his people; those who are not inspired to trust him must be enemies of France."

But to all this the American diplomat added shrewdly:

"To Darlan and the ambitious, energetic Pucheu the reorganization of the Government means something else: the concentration of power in their hands with emphasis on the police and their
spies, so reminiscent of their Gestapo tutors. Behind the slogans
of loyalty to their country and to chief, they intend to cover
arrests of their enemies and freer use of the rubber hose." [41]

For American policy the practical significance of Pétain's
speech was simply that it made it more difficult for the Department of State to stick by the Vichy connection. A few
weeks later, on September 24, the Free French National Committee was organized in London and was given a considerable
measure of recognition by the British government, in practice
if not in theory.[42] This was the signal for renewed demands in
the American press for a definite break with the Fascist regime of Pétain and a frank commitment to de Gaulle. Yet
from the standpoint of national interest, the position had not
changed. We never had and we never could have based our
policy on purely ideological considerations, and the link to
Vichy, however tenuous, still promised greater advantages

[41] Tel. (August 21, 1941) from Matthews.
[42] Dispatch (October 6, 1941) from Johnson at London.

than a new tie with the Free French. As the weeks wore on, it became more and more likely that the Germans would not be able to dispose of the Russians in one campaign. In all probability they would then attempt to stabilize the eastern front and renew their efforts to get control of Bizerte, so that they could the more easily reinforce and supply Rommel's army on the frontier of Egypt. Or, again, they might make an advance through Spain and down the West African coast in order to cut the South Atlantic route to Britain and threaten American security by way of Brazil. On August 15 Secretary Stimson in a radio address once more stated our paramount interest in Dakar and West Africa:

"Germany has been pushing into North Africa and we have reason to believe that a major advance will be made by her into that continent. At Dakar, which is held by Vichy forces, now friendly with Germany, the great western bulge of the African coast narrows the South Atlantic Ocean until the distance from Dakar to the easternmost point of Brazil can be easily traversed either by air or sea. The German controlled press of Paris today is openly urging that Germany be invited by Vichy to come into Dakar."

Actually we know that there was no serious German infiltration in North or West Africa at this time. Murphy's reports indicated that there were about two hundred Germans connected with the armistice commission in Morocco. As for Dakar, there were, excepting for a few Jewish refugees, no Germans there at all, according to the testimony of our consul, Thomas C. Wasson.[43] The curious thing, however, was the very inactivity of the Germans. Various explanations of it have been advanced. It has been suggested, for instance, that Darlan's well-known hatred of the British lulled the Germans into a false security. But this version seems hardly plausible, in view of the fact that the Germans seem at no time to have trusted Darlan completely or to have been taken in by his

[43] See Thomas C. Wasson: "The Mystery of Dakar: an Enigma Resolved" (*American Foreign Service Journal*, April 1943, p. 169). Also tel. (October 29, 1941) from Wasson.

protestations. It is more likely that the Germans, or at least
Hitler, underestimated the possibilities of North Africa. Theo-
dor Auer, the German consul-general in Casablanca, once told
Murphy that he spent half his waking hours trying to convince Berlin of the strategic importance of the area. Besides,
the Germans had so low an opinion of British and American
capabilities that they were probably not seriously worried by
thoughts of hostile action.[44]

Nevertheless, it is fairly clear that the Germans, deeply involved in Russia, were not entirely happy about the African
situation. The constant references to Dakar in the United
States and the growing demand in the American press that
we should simply seize that important base before the Germans
had a chance to act were all bound to arouse suspicion. The
same was true of the Economic Accord, the first fruits of
which were beginning to manifest themselves. Murphy reverted again and again to the anxiety of local Germans, and
the permission given the Vichy government to strengthen the
fortifications of Dakar (September) was probably not un-
connected with this anxiety.[45]

In the prevalent uncertainty there was little to do but continue on the appointed course and hope to gain time. On
September 12 Admiral Leahy handed to Pétain yet another
personal letter from the President, urging the necessity for
preserving French sovereignty in the African colonies. The
marshal's reply was that he had no intention of ceding to the
Germans any bases in Africa, but that France was a conquered
country and he could never know "when the Diktat may
come." Darlan, on his part, admitted that the Germans might
attack Africa through Bizerte or through Spain, but he
doubted whether it would be in their interest to move at the

[44] Comment by Murphy.
[45] Dispatch (August 27, 1941) from Murphy at Algiers; Memo. to the
President (September 17, 1941), in *North African Economic Memoranda*,
II, No. 238. At the Pearl Harbor Inquiry it was revealed that at the Atlantic
Charter meeting in August Churchill communicated to the President a
British plan to invade the Canary Islands in September. The President agreed
that, upon request of the Portuguese government, American forces should
occupy the Azores (*New York Herald Tribune*, December 19, 1945).

moment. Slyly he suggested that American activities in North
Africa were arousing German suspicious. In a written reply
Pétain assured the President that it was France's intention to
defend her Empire against all comers, but reminded him that
thus far the only attacks had come from the British, who were
constantly trying to sow discord. "Please tell the President,"
he remarked to Leahy, "that so long as the British tolerate De
Gaulle and his activities, there can be no better understanding
between them and ourselves." De Gaulle he described as "a
viper that he had warmed in his bosom." [46]

All this, of course, got us nowhere. It is important only for
the record, as showing our constant preoccupation with the
African problem and our repeated efforts to stave off hostile
action by Vichy. The only other course would have been to
plan systematic aid to Weygand and come to an agreement
with him regarding future contingencies. As a matter of fact
it is more than doubtful whether the general would ever have
entered upon such a bargain. Assuming that he hated the Germans and that he detested de Gaulle, it could hardly be said
that he had any use for the British or any exaggerated hope of
the Americans. Besides, on his own testimony, he would never
have led a dissident movement in North Africa. Pétain was
his superior and he would take his orders from Vichy. His
orders, as we know, were to defend North Africa against all
comers. If the Germans were to attack, he would fight back,
however hopeless his chances might be. [47]

Nevertheless, the plan of promising Weygand American
aid was reverted to again and again by Murphy, inspired no
doubt by some of the more patriotic and ambitious members
of the general's entourage and stimulated by the hope that
the general might persuade Vichy that the United States could
really give substantial and timely support. It was put forward

[46] Tels. (September 12, 18, 1941) from Leahy.
[47] Such was the general conclusion of Lieutenant Colonel Solborg's report
to American Military Intelligence after a prolonged visit to North Africa,
which ended in September 1941. On Weygand see further Raymond
Brugère: *Veni, Vidi, Vichy*, pp. 90–2, and Renée Gosset: *Le Coup d'Alger*
(Montreal, 1944), pp. 27ff.

also by Paul Guérin, the French representative in Washington
dealing with supplies under the Economic Accord. But this
was a problem for the army and navy rather than for the Department of State. The question seems to have been submitted
to the services, only to meet with a negative response. At a
time when war with Japan was becoming more than a possibility, we could not afford to commit ourselves elsewhere.
"Both the Army and Navy, however, stated that it was a
policy agreed upon with the British that as soon as possible a
reserve staff should be constituted for emergency use in whatever area would be of benefit to the Anglo-American bloc.[48]

So we continued our policy of watching and encouraging,
plodding along with the Economic Accord, which still lagged
far behind any agreed program and which continued to be
the butt of all kinds of picayune attacks by American and British economic agencies.[49] In the meantime the situation at Vichy
was gradually deteriorating. The wholesale shooting of hostages by the Germans in October not only outraged the whole
civilized world, but put the Pétain government in a most pathetic light. It also cooled what ardor there may have been for
collaboration and stimulated the hatred for Darlan and his
system.[50] This, taken together with the stalling of the German
advance in Russia, appears to have shaken even Darlan to a
degree:

"The unexpected difficulties encountered by Germany in Russia have caused French officials, including Darlan and other collaborationists, to lean over toward our side of the question and
their final attitude is dependent upon the outcome of the campaign in Russia." [51]

[48] Memorandum of Atherton to Welles (August 21, 1941); see Guérin's
proposals of October 9, 1941 (*North African Economic Memoranda*, II, No.
346A), and the Department's memorandum: *The Role of the Department
of State in the North African Economic and Political Program*, pp. 25–7.

[49] Murray's Memorandum of October 14, 1941, in *North African Economic Memoranda*, II, No. 247. Also further memoranda in the same collection, Nos. 257, 258.

[50] OSS Files (October 8, 1941).

[51] Leahy File (October 15, 1941).

The same development was noted by one of Darlan's own associates, Capitaine Bachy, who reported the growing strength of the anti-collaborationists and asserted that Pétain was more opposed than ever to any agreement that would definitely bring France to the side of Germany. "The most unpopular, or rather the most detested man in France is Admiral Darlan," he admitted. The admiral, he thought, took this very much to heart. "However strongly anti-British he may be, he is just as much if not more strongly anti-German and clearly realizes that the Allies have a great chance of final victory." In any event, neither Vichy nor Darlan would ever hand over the fleet to Germany: "Those vessels which are stationed at Toulon have orders to sail to North Africa if the Free Zone should be occupied, and, if that should prove impossible, to scuttle themselves." [52]

Whether Darlan was gradually turning from the policy of collaboration or not, the time had certainly not yet come when he could throw down the gauntlet to France's oppressors. At best, he could beat a cautious and hesitating retreat, evading when feasible and giving way when necessary. It is quite impossible to speak of these matters with any degree of assurance, since information on affairs inside Vichy is scrappy and all the historian can do is to piece together bits of evidence that are often contradictory. What appears to have been happening in Vichy in the autumn of 1941 was something like this: Darlan, having taken the Banque Worms group into his fold, was beginning to discover that his friends were heading for a goal that they were determined to attain even in spite of himself. A number of reports touch on the fact that the ambitious and vigorous Pucheu had his eye on Darlan's job and that he was supported by the rest of the Worms clique. As Minister of the Interior Pucheu was primarily responsible for the ruthless repression of all opposition, which did more than anything else to discredit the collaborationist

[52] Letter from Lisbon, reporting Capitaine Bachy's remarks, October 17, 1941 (OSS Files).

regime. He is said to have been opposed to territorial concessions to the Germans, but he and his friends were evidently
prepared to go to any other length to win the favor of the conqueror. In other words, he threatened to out-Darlan Darlan
himself.

On one point, however, the two men seem to have held the
same view: namely, the need for getting rid of Weygand.
With Darlan this was probably due to the fact that the general was constantly obstructing any concessions to the Germans in North Africa. Furthermore, Weygand's position in
North Africa was almost an autonomous one. He was building up there a military force and a personal prestige that put
him beyond the control of Darlan. The admiral's thirst for
power was such that he could not help being jealous of the
general. As for Pucheu, he no doubt realized that Weygand
and the policy of the Murphy-Weygand Agreement were
arousing the suspicions of the Germans and that only the general's dismissal would make possible whole-hearted collaboration. Be this as it may, Pétain was later to tell Admiral Leahy
that ever since December 1940 the Germans had been pressing
for Weygand's removal and that they had suspected him of secret negotiations with the United States for military aid.[53] For
weeks before the general's final dismissal on November 18,
Vichy was full of rumors of German insistence that he be got
rid of, and of the fact that Darlan and Pucheu were united in
their determination to oblige.[54]

We now know more of the actual details. In September
Abetz had submitted a written demand for the general's removal, on the grounds that his very appointment had been an
act of hostility and that the Germans had no confidence in
him. Pétain evaded and temporized for several weeks, but in
November Abetz reappeared and became insistent. The marshal gave the ambassador a piece of his mind, but summoned
Weygand to Vichy for consultation. "I shall work only in
agreement with Weygand," the old man assured Matthews.

[53] Leahy File (November 19, 1941).
[54] Leahy File (October 30, 1941).

"He will return to Africa. As I have done all along with the Germans, I am trying to gain time." [55]

Weygand knew perfectly well what was in the wind, but he tried desperately to hold his position. In a memorandum he argued that the armistice had left France a trump card in the shape of the French Empire. This protected her against excessive German demands. Since the failure of the Nazi attack on England and since Hitler's setback in Russia the French Empire in North Africa had taken on ever greater value, especially in view of the fact that the Germans were now obliged to turn their attention once more to the Mediterranean and to the Battle of the Atlantic. [56]

Whether the general was ever given an opportunity to advance and defend his thesis it is impossible to say. By the time he arrived in Vichy, his fall was already a foregone conclusion, for Benoist-Mechin had brought from Paris "a sort of ultimatum" from the Germans demanding that he go, as promised by Darlan. The marshal felt that he had to comply. In a note to Admiral Leahy announcing Weygand's dismissal, he stated unequivocally:

"As a result of German pressure which has been exerted for several months and which this morning took an imperative form, the Marshal has taken the decision to suppress the Délégation Générale in Africa, which involves the recall of General Weygand.

"If the Marshal had not made this decision, there is every indication to believe that German troop penetration into Africa would have been inevitable and would undoubtedly have occurred very soon." [57]

---

[55] Tel. (November 11) from Leahy.
[56] Dispatch (November 18) from Murphy.
[57] Tel. (November 18, 1941) from Leahy. On Weygand's dismissal see his own testimony and that of Lavagne (*Procès du M. Pétain*, pp. 142, 306). At the Nürnberg war-crimes trials it was revealed that Field Marshal Keitel had ordered the assassination of Weygand for fear that he might rally around him the French forces in North Africa and thereby endanger Germany's southern flank. Though the orders were not executed, they throw an interesting light on German evaluation of the situation (*New York Times*, December 1, 1945).

The very next day the marshal amplified his account somewhat, assuring Leahy that the decision had caused him great pain, but that he was helpless. "I am a prisoner," he repeated twice. The Germans, he reiterated, had long pressed for Weygand's dismissal and had then sent a "brutal ultimatum" threatening to occupy France and quarter a large army there, so that the French would starve.[58]

Robert Murphy, whose information was generally reliable, got another slant from his French friends in Algiers. There it was said that Weygand's fall was due to the charge brought by his enemies that he was hopelessly compromised because of his dealings with the United States:

"My conversation with these officials," reported Murphy, "convince me that there was no German ultimatum demanding Weygand's dismissal. That decision I am told results from a combination of German pressure and the eagerness of the cabal consisting of Darlan, Benoist-Mechin, Pucheu, Lehideux and Marion to eliminate Weygand. . . . The group undoubtedly convinced the Marshal that dire consequences would follow if he retained Weygand." [59]

In any event, the episode left the marshal in none too favorable a light. Admiral Leahy, who had always respected the old soldier, felt more than bitter about his "abject surrender." Writing to President Roosevelt after his interview with Pétain, he described the government of France as one "headed by a feeble, frightened old man, surrounded by self-seeking conspirators," and controlled by a group that was devoted to the Nazi philosophy, probably for its own safety. The admiral saw no reason to suppose that in future Pétain, under pressure, would not concede the use of the African bases, or of the French fleet. He despaired of exercising any further influence and gave up hope of giving "some semblance of backbone to a jellyfish." [60]

The question then was what attitude the United States

[58] Tel. (November 19, 1941) from Leahy.
[59] Tel. (November 19, 1941) from Murphy.
[60] Leahy to the President (November 22, 1941).

should adopt. We could take a strong line and go as far as we wished, but would that serve any good purpose? The ambassador, foreseeing Weygand's fall, had originally come to the conclusion that we should not make an issue of it. He noted on November 15, 1941:

"At the present time, and until England or America is prepared to occupy North Africa with a sufficient military force to join with the natives in a successful resistance to an Axis invasion, it would appear the part of wisdom to surrender the initiative and not interrupt our present delaying tactics of continuing to provide facilities through which the native population may obtain necessities from overseas."

But then the event itself made him waver: "This abject surrender to a Nazi threat at a time when Germany is completely occupied in Russia is the kind of jellyfish reaction that justifies the stoppage of all assistance to France." [61] Still, he could not bring himself to advise a break. He suggested to Washington the possibility of suspending economic aid to North Africa and recalling the ambassador for consultation, but he did not recommend any positive action. [62]

Murphy, on the other hand, urged at once that no change be made in our policy, at least until the full facts were known. [63] A couple of days later he received a message from Weygand himself, begging that the existing policy should be maintained:

"Continue, I beg of you, to favor the supply program. As the Marshal told Admiral Leahy nothing is changed in French policy by my departure. Just suppose that I have passed to the other world. French Africa would continue notwithstanding that unimportant normal accident. Major Gasser, who will give you this letter, will tell you how much I count on the maintenance between our two countries of the union necessary for the near future of the world." [64]

[61] Leahy File (November 18, 1941).
[62] Tel. (November 19, 1941) from Leahy.
[63] Tel. (November 19, 1941) from Murphy.
[64] Tel. (November 21, 1941).

But the Department did not wait for guidance from abroad. On the day after Weygand's fall Welles called in the French ambassador, Henry-Haye, and told him what had happened

"made necessary a complete change in the policy which this Government had hitherto carried out vis-à-vis France. I said that the American Government had made every effort to strengthen the resistance of the French Government to increased pressure from Germany, in the hope that the French Government would agree to no terms or provisions on the part of Germany which exceeded, in the slightest degree, the terms of the armistice agreement in 1940. I said that this new step agreed upon by France implied that Germany would now rapidly increase its practical and effective control throughout North Africa, and that a situation of this kind was regarded by the United States as a direct threat to the security and national defense requirements of the United States." [65]

On the following day a press release announced that the whole American policy toward Vichy was being reviewed, and that all plans for economic assistance to North Africa were suspended.

No doubt this step was taken too hastily, for on further consideration the Department reversed itself. A careful memorandum, prepared by the Division of European Affairs and dated November 28, argued that since the German operations in Russia were bogged down for the winter, the Nazis might well shift operations to the western Mediterranean, as a counterweight to the British advance in Libya, which had begun on November 17 and was making good progress. The Germans might go through Italy and Tunisia or through Spain. They might get the French to make North African bases available or to grant the use of their fleet. To prevent such developments, the United States had played along with Vichy:

"Any severance of these relations, unless it follows upon an overt act on the part of Vichy, nullifying its assurances, would so affect the already discouraged French public, whose sole hope

[65] Memorandum of conversation (November 19, 1941).

for the future lies in the United States, as to leave it no alternative but complete collaboration with the Axis."

Furthermore, it was argued, the Economic Accord had been of great intelligence value to Britain and the United States. In conclusion it was recommended that no recognition should be given the Free French movement, since this would be contrary to the feelings of the French people.

These were the weeks just before the attack on Pearl Harbor, a time when American attention was focused on the last desperate discussions between Secretary Hull on the one hand and Kurusu and Nomura on the other. But despite the gravity of the Pacific crisis, we could not afford to neglect, even for a day or a week, the danger that might face us from French Africa. After all, it was impossible to explain Weygand's fall as anything but an attempt to remove the chief obstacle to full collaboration between Vichy and the Nazis, which in this case meant almost certainly the concession of bases in North Africa, if not an agreement about the future of the French fleet.[66]

It must be remembered that for the first time in the war the military position of the Germans was bad. They had suffered a severe setback in Russia, and in Egypt the new British Eighth Army, under General Montgomery, opened an offensive against Rommel on November 17. For a time the fighting was indecisive and Rommel made excellent use of the troops and tanks that he had. But by mid-December he was beginning to fall back, not stopping till he had reached El Agheila.

Under the circumstances the use of Tunisian ports for the supply of Rommel was bound to become a burning question once more. Reports began to arrive in Washington from Spanish sources that the Nazis had asked Vichy for facilities in Bizerte, Mers-el-Kébir, and even Dakar. According to British intelligence, the Germans had offered to return 850,000 French prisoners if the Vichy government would permit use of the ports of Toulon and Marseille, as well as freedom of

[66] Tel. (November 20, 1941) from Murphy, quoting the opinion of Count de Rose, Weygand's diplomatic adviser.

passage through unoccupied France for German troops and munitions. France and Spain were to sign a pact for mutual defense of North Africa against any British attack, while Germany herself would take over all naval and air bases in North Africa.[67]

It was at this juncture that Marshal Pétain, with Darlan and General Juin, had an interview with Marshal Göring at Saint-Florentin (December 1). After some preliminary courtesies Pétain took the offensive, claiming that the Germans had failed to live up to the promises made at the time of the Montoire meeting. He had always understood that collaboration meant a bargain as between equals. If this were to be a case of dealings between victor and vanquished, there could be no question of collaboration, but only of what the Germans called a *Diktat*. France, he admitted, had made the mistake in 1919 of not concluding a peace of collaboration, with the result that she had won the war but lost the peace. Germany was now running the risk of making the same blunder. She could win the war alone, but not the peace. No real peace would be possible without France.

The marshal then read Göring a memorandum addressed to Hitler. This rehearsed the earlier German promises to return prisoners, to abolish the line between occupied and unoccupied France, to reduce economic demands, and to permit some rearmament of France, especially of North Africa. None of all this had materialized and consequently it was impossible for the Vichy government to persuade the French people of the value of collaboration. What exactly was the German government prepared do in the way of concessions?

Göring's reply was that this memorandum was not fit to be shown to the Führer, for its tone suggested that France, not Germany, was the victor. The Germans could not be expected

[67] Tels. (November 26, 28) from Weddell; report of a neutral ambassador at Vichy (December 15); report of Weygand's former liaison officer at Vichy (December 6); memorandum of Colonel William J. Donovan to the President (January 22, 1942). These reports are in the OSS Files.

to give up real advantages in return for vague promises, and besides, Germany must keep a strong position in the west in view of the war with Britain. After all, what had the Vichy government done to convince the French people of the advantages of collaboration? So far as Göring could make out, the atmosphere of Vichy was hostile to the Germans.

There ensued a rather heated debate. Pétain said France could not fit into the new Europe unless she knew what her place would be, to which Göring replied that Germany must first know in detail in what ways and to what extent France would collaborate. After all, Germany was defending all Europe against Bolshevism. What was France doing? Why did not the French fleet at least proceed against England? The trouble was that the French intellectuals were still hoping for a British victory and deluding themselves with the "fantastic idea" that the United States would play a decisive role.

The discussions between Göring and Darlan were even more acrimonious. Darlan tried to point out that, after all, the French had made airfields available to the Germans in Syria and as a result had lost that valuable territory. In view of so sad an experience, it might be well for the Germans to permit further rearmament of North Africa. But Göring would not listen to such a suggestion. Hitler, he pointed out, felt that he could not trust all the French generals. He had proof, for example, that "Weygand was eager for a strengthening of the North African forces only so that he might build up a relatively strong army and put it at the disposal of the British when an opportune moment arrived." Germany therefore had to be careful, and incidentally wanted to know about the possibility of making use of Bizerte and other Tunisian ports to supply Rommel. To this Darlan and Juin replied at once that if France were to make Bizerte available, the result would surely be conflict with England and probably an attack by the Americans on Dakar, Martinique, and Guadeloupe.

The Saint-Florentin meeting ended on a very unpleasant note. The French complained and then they evaded, until

Göring, losing patience, exclaimed: "Well, Monsieur le Maréchal, who are the victors, you or we?" To this Pétain remarked that he had never been made to feel more keenly that
France had been defeated. Actually, however, the marshal had
come off very well. He had turned the tables on Göring and
had escaped any commitments. The Nazi leader went away
deeply dissatisfied and told Mussolini a short time afterward
that he was decidedly skeptical of French goodwill and of the
prospects of collaboration. We now know from German
sources that Hitler was profoundly disappointed in the French.
Their reaction to German advances was decidedly reserved
and they were forever asking what France's ultimate fate was
to be. At no time did they show any readiness to join in the
war against England. Since this was what Hitler wanted most,
he was bound to be disillusioned. His one hope was still of
Laval, who could be expected to force collaboration down the
throats of his countrymen.[68]

It stands to reason that the American government was not
on the inside of Franco-German discussion and could not
know of the latent tension. But the State Department was
fully aware of the dangers that beset North Africa as Rommel
fell back, and it was probably in view of these dangers that
the premature decision to suspend the Economic Accord was
so quickly rescinded. On December 6 a telegram was sent to
Vichy asking Admiral Leahy to tell Pétain that if he would
renew his assurances with respect to the fleet and the colonies,
and if he would state that Weygand's dismissal meant no
change in Vichy's North African policy, the United States
government would consider the renewal of the economic relief program. This message was delivered to Pétain and Darlan on December 11, and the desired assurances were given

[68] Captured German Documents: report of the Saint-Florentin meeting
(December 1, 1941). The accuracy of this report is borne out by the French
record (*Procès du M. Pétain*, pp. 372) and by Göring's account to Mussolini (Captured German Documents: report of the meeting of Göring
and Mussolini at Palazzo Venezia, January 28, 1942). On the German dis-
illusionment about collaboration see State Department interrogation of Dr.
Paul Schmidt.

on the following day. Thereupon American policy was restored to its previous course.[69]

By this time we were already in the throes of war, not only with Japan, but also with Germany and Italy. Promise of the renewal of the Economic Accord was made in part conditional on France's declaring her neutrality and restating the assurances already so frequently given in the past. What these assurances might be worth in the long run no one could say. Only this much was clear: that thus far they had not been violated. Perhaps it might still be possible to hold France in line. No one could say, for it was often impossible to separate truth from falsehood in the cloud of rumor that hung over Vichy and Paris. It was true that Darlan and Pucheu had forced the ouster of Weygand. On the other hand, there were fairly convincing reports that Darlan had begun to doubt the ultimate victory of Hitler and was becoming cooler toward the program of collaboration. In fact, some indications went even farther and suggested that Darlan was beginning to support Pétain in resisting German demands. Pucheu was commonly described as a formidable rival to Darlan, and was reputed to be hatching a plot with Jacques Doriot and Marcel Déat by which the whole Vichy government would be upset and replaced by one at Paris under direct German auspices.[70]

If true, these stories meant, in sum and substance, that as Darlan was beginning to shy away from the implications of collaboration, so the real dyed-in-the-wool collaborationists of the Banque Worms type were drifting away from Darlan and attempting to strike a new bargain with the Germans, a process that was finally to result in the return of Laval. But of course much of this is speculation. Even if it seems plausible and reasonable now, it was all very obscure at the time. In December 1941 neither the Department of State nor anyone on this side of the Atlantic had information sound enough to

[69] Tel. (December 6, 1941) to Leahy; tel. (December 19, 1941) from Vichy.

[70] An interesting report from a French intellectual, brought out of France in December 1941 and sent to the President by Colonel William J. Donovan (in OSS Files).

warrant a prediction. We were operating pretty much in the dark. All we knew was that Vichy was a Pandora's box and that we must be ready for anything. Under the circumstances it seemed wisest to keep the box well in view at least. So long as we maintained an embassy in Vichy, we were at least in a position to hear and see many things, and we at least had close contact with those Frenchmen who, though members of the Vichy government, were nevertheless opposed to collaboration and pinned their hopes on an Allied victory. In the same way our Economic Accord with North Africa gave us the opportunity to observe on the spot and report on Axis activity, as well as to maintain relations with a growing resistance group in that area.[71]

And all this we had for a ridiculously low price: prior to Weygand's dismissal we had shipped to North Africa three tankers and four cargo vessels. The distribution of the goods had been carefully supervised by our vice-consuls, so that there was no chance of transshipment to France or Germany. But even had it been otherwise, the game would have been well worth the candle. As Murray remarked in a memorandum: "Even if an entire shipment of American goods fell into the hands of the Axis, it would have no real effect on the course of the war and might actually call favorable attention to the efforts of the United States."[72] So it was certainly the part of wisdom to keep alive the arrangements with North Africa, for with our entry into the war the threat from that region became immeasurably greater. The first hectic months of our belligerency were soon to prove that.

[71] Memorandum: *Activities of American Control Officers in French North Africa* (November 7, 1941), in *North African Economic Memoranda*, II, No. 256.
[72] Memorandum of October 14, 1941 (*North African Economic Memoranda*, II, No. 247).

CHAPTER VI

On the Razor's Edge

THE OPENING months of America's participation in the great war were about as depressing and discouraging as any period in the nation's history. The disaster at Pearl Harbor robbed us for the time being of any hope of stemming the Japanese advance, for our naval supremacy in the Pacific was smashed that Sunday morning in December, and the best we could hope for was sufficient time to reconstruct our forces. The British, deeply involved in Europe, had been quite unable to offer effective opposition to Japanese aggression and could hardly be looked to for aid, the more so as the loss of the *Prince of Wales* and of the *Repulse* dashed all expectation of co-operation in the Eastern seas. So the Japanese had things pretty much their own way until they reached and threatened Australia. Thailand and Malaya were overrun in a matter of weeks, and Singapore was taken on February 15, 1942. By the end of March the Dutch Indies were securely in enemy hands and Burma also had fallen a victim. The Americans fought an epic battle on Bataan, but it was a losing fight from the outset. The peninsula had to be abandoned on April 9.

So spectacular was the success of the Japanese that our attention was of necessity focused on developments in the Pacific. But this did not mean that the European scene could be neglected. Indeed, it was never lost from sight, but continued to be a primary preoccupation of the United States government.

In the early autumn of 1941 it had seemed that Russia was doomed. Hitler was already announcing triumphantly the imminent liquidation of yet another great power and was already gloating over his forthcoming victory over Britain. However valiant the resistance of the Russians, there appeared to be but slight chance that they would be able to turn the tide. Thoroughly alarmed, the British were anticipating an unbroken German march to the Caucasus and were making preparations to build up an army to meet the victor when he broke through to the Near East. Truly, the outlook could not have been much blacker.

But the Russians did not go down in defeat. They held at Leningrad and at Moscow and, to the intense surprise of even the most hopeful, they counterattacked before the year was over and drove the enemy out of Rostov. The menace to the Middle East from the north was obviated for the time being, while General Auchinleck, attacking Rommel in Libya, simultaneously drove back the Germans and Italians, capturing a large part of the opposing forces and taking El Agheila in January 1942.

But the British victory had its seamy side, for it raised the question at once whether the Nazis, temporarily frustrated in Russia and hard pressed in North Africa, might not shift their ground and essay an attack on Tunisia or Morocco. To be sure, the Vichy government had declared its neutrality, but no one believed for even a moment that if the Germans brought sufficient pressure, Pétain and Darlan could resist. Indeed, Weygand's dismissal made France's submission all the more likely. Nor was anything much expected from Spain, whose Foreign Minister, Serrano Suñer, was notorious for his pro-Nazi disposition. Spain was suffering from an acute economic crisis, with much of the population on the brink of starvation. Even though Franco was anxious to avoid involvement in the war and though the army might object to a German incursion, there was little likelihood that Spain could stop the Germans once they had decided to come on. During the first hectic weeks after our entry into the war one report after another came into Washington announcing that Spain was on the point of joining in the fray and that the Germans were massing troops in southwestern France, either by way of exerting pressure on the Madrid government or by way of preparing for occupation of the country. Alexander Weddell, our ambassador to Spain, was unable to verify any of the reports or rumors and thought it not impossible that all the alarms were part of the German war of nerves. Nevertheless, he recognized that if the Germans were bringing pressure on Franco, they were doing so in greatest secrecy, and he by no means excluded the possibility that the Germans might move on Spain at some later time. In view of the constantly recurring reports that the French were about to concede to the Germans the use of Tunisian bases, there was little comfort to be found in the midst of the confusing uncertainty.[1]

The general apprehension felt in Washington and London at Christmastide 1941 is very well reflected in some documents prepared outside the Department of State. Early in December the Office of the Coordinator of Information (later Office of Strategic Services) completed a pretty detailed study of the *Problem of a German Occupation of North Africa.* It was there pointed out that the 80,000 troops that the French had in North Africa, as well as the 50,000 to 70,000 that were in West Africa, had only small arms and light artillery, without mechanized equipment or anti-tank or anti-aircraft guns. Quoting a *Survey of Northwest Africa,* prepared by Military Intelligence in August 1941, it pointed out that the supply of munitions would be sufficient for only about ten days' operations by the entire force. There appeared to be no real obstacle to a German pincer movement through Spain and through Sicily to Morocco and Tunisia. The British advance in Libya might soon make Tunisian ports essential for the Germans. By and large, the military and political advantages of occupying North Africa seemed to outweigh the probable or even the maximum costs of such an operation to Germany.[2]

Much the same line was taken in studies prepared in London at approximately the same date. One such paper envisaged continued Nazi pressure on France and Spain and conjectured

[1] Messages of Colonel William J. Donovan to the President, December 11, 12, 13, 1941; tels. (December 13, 14, 17, 24) from Weddell.
[2] COI, Research and Analysis Branch: *The Problem of a German Occupation of North Africa* (December 3, 1941).

that recent negotiations between Pétain and Göring had dealt
with the passage of German troops to North Africa and with
the cession of French North African bases.[3] Even more explicit was a more extended analysis of *The Possibilities of Axis
Action in French North Africa*. The opinion was there expressed that the Nazis would aim at all strategic points from
Tunisia (whence they could succor their troops in Libya) to
the Atlantic (where they could attack British shipping). It
was thought that the Germans would continue their pressure
on Vichy, in the hope of getting what they wanted without
the use of coercion. But if Vichy resisted, the Germans might
withdraw forces from Russia and occupy all of France. Far
easier, however, would be an advance through Spain. It was
not thought that Spain would resist. The Germans could be
on the frontiers of French Morocco within six weeks after
crossing the Pyrenees. All told, the Nazis would require only
four or five divisions to occupy North Africa if Spain collaborated and contributed the seven divisions in Spanish Morocco. If Spain offered resistance, the job could still be done
with some fourteen German divisions.[4]

One more item may be added in this connection. On December 13, 1941 Colonel (later General) Donovan reported
to the President that Dr. Hans Thomsen, the former German
chargé d'affaires in Washington, had remarked to a friend:

"The next war move of the German armies may well be the
attack of Great Britain, or it may be the occupation of Spain and
Portugal with the consent of those countries and the passage to
Africa of large forces that will make impossible the sending of
anything more than a token army by the United States to
Africa."

The question quite naturally arises: why did not the Germans take advantage of a situation so obviously favorable to
them? Their suspicion of American aid to North Africa and

[3] OSS Files.
[4] OSS Files.

their insistence on the dismissal of Weygand leave no doubt that they appreciated the possibilities of the North African situation, especially in view of the British advance in Libya. Why, then, did Hitler hesitate?

The answer must be a twofold one. We have since learned from German sources that the Nazi setback in Russia was even more disastrous than could be known at the time. It shook the Wehrmacht to its very foundations and rocked the Nazi dictatorship itself. That being so, Hitler could hardly venture to become deeply involved on another front. If he had been able to enlist the aid of France and Spain the situation would, of course, have been different. But so far as we know, the Caudillo was as much opposed as ever to being drafted into a war against Britain, and the Vichy government was no more accommodating. It was pointed out in the preceding chapter that in December 1941 the Germans had renewed their efforts to obtain the use of French ports and shipping. Of the details we know next to nothing, but there are two entries in the *Ciano Diary* that throw a faint light on the subject. On December 29 the Italian Foreign Minister noted: "Mussolini says that he is writing to Hitler on the question of Tunisian ports; either France agrees to cede them or we must take them by force." And on January 20, 1942 he noted: "The Führer refuses to think of accepting the conditions stipulated by Vichy for our use of the Tunisian ports. He is right; they are cut-throat conditions."

These were strong words. We are not in the habit of thinking of Pétain or Darlan as laying down "cut-throat conditions" to the Nazis. And yet they did so, and even if Hitler rejected them, he had to scale down his demands before he got through. As we shall see, the French were obliged before long to permit German supplies to go from North Africa and even from France to Rommel's army, but the fact remains that neither Bizerte nor any other North African base was turned over to them.

Since for the most part we began to prepare for war only

after we were already involved in it, there could be no thought in December 1941 or January 1942 of any large-scale operation anywhere. Consequently we were driven back on diplomatic sparring and on any other means that might be at hand. With regard to Spain, even before Pearl Harbor we had laid plans to relieve the economic crisis by supplying petroleum, foodstuffs, fertilizers, and some machine tools, our aim being substantially the same political aim that we were following in North Africa. But the Spanish plan had been suspended when rumors of a German invasion of Spain became rife, and was taken up again only at the end of December at the instigation of Lord Halifax, who pointed out to Secretary Hull that the "chief purpose of this sort of cooperation as viewed by the British and ourselves is as it has begun, to encourage the Spanish influences which are opposed to Hitler marching an army through Spain on its way to the French possessions in Africa." [5]

For the rest, all sorts of remedial proposals were put forward. General Donovan, for example, pointed out to the President that it was probably only a question of time before the French fleet would be turned over to the Germans. He therefore suggested the desirability of a combined Anglo-American surprise attack against such elements of the French fleet as would constitute advantageous targets. The same idea was urged on the President by a member of the British purchasing mission in these words: "We must complete the task we essayed at Oran, in order to remove the risk of these units falling into German hands, and leave ourselves free to recreate an effective Line of Battle in the Far East." [6] As a matter of fact, General Donovan inclined to the view that even with our very limited forces we should attempt a daring coup before it was too late: "Immediate reinforcements of North African army by American air and ground troops seems the only possible move which could retrieve the situation," he wrote to

[5] Tel. (November 26, 1941) Hull to Weddell; Memo. of conversation between Hull and Halifax, December 29, 1941.
[6] Donovan to the President, December 14, 1941.

the President; "Double thrust at Africa under present circumstances would almost surely succeed." [7]

The possibility of action in North Africa was certainly in the President's mind and was one of the topics of discussion between him and Churchill during the latter's visit to Washington at Christmas 1941. It was decided by the two statesmen to approach Weygand to see whether he would return secretly to North Africa and throw in his lot with an Anglo-American expeditionary force that it was hoped could be sent. Freeman Matthews, who was on leave in this country prior to his reassignment to London, was hastily summoned to Washington and was informed of the plan. He pointed out that Weygand would probably not agree to act independently and that he would in all likelihood inform Pétain, from whose entourage the scheme might easily leak to the Germans. To this Churchill replied that he did not care whether the Nazis learned of it or not. He and the President finally concluded that Weygand's prestige was such and that his aid would be so valuable that the risk of sending him a message would be justified. In any event, plans for a military expedition would go forward with or without the general's aid. Thereby France would be brought back into the war whether Pétain liked it or not.

Matthews was therefore sent off post-haste to Europe. Unfortunately, bad weather delayed him all the way across the Atlantic and he did not reach Lisbon until January 7. Since he could not himself return to Vichy without attracting attention, he passed his instructions on to Henry P. Leverich, one of the secretaries of the American Legation at Lisbon, who set out at once for Vichy. [8]

Leverich arrived at the French capital on January 12 with oral instructions, the upshot of which was that an emissary should be sent to Weygand to inquire "if, in the event of possible contingencies, he will assume leadership of the French

[7] Donovan to the President, December 27, 1941.
[8] Notes by Matthews.

colonies." The contingencies envisaged were four: (1) the death or elimination of Pétain as head of the French state; (2) indication or evidence of a German move towards North Africa through Spain or elsewhere; (3) evidence that the French fleet was to be used for German purposes; (4) use of French African bases by Germany, directly or indirectly.

A short time afterward Admiral Leahy received further instructions to convey a special message from the President to either Pétain or Weygand or both. This message recalled that the President was about the best friend the French had, and that one of his most cherished wishes was to see France restored to the splendid position she had enjoyed throughout history. This meant also the French Empire. But any concession that France might make to the Axis would hurt the United States:

"Now that the United States is in the war, it should be perfectly clear to the French Government and the French people that if Germany or Italy attacked unoccupied France or any of the French colonies, in any way, the President could not regard acquiescence to such an attack as anything else than playing the German game.

"On the other hand, resistance by the French against German or Italian attack either in France itself or in any part of the Colonial Empire would be regarded by the President as a normal and natural reaction. Such resistance would have not only the moral support of the United States, but it would also have the physical support of the United States by every possible military and naval assistance we could bring to bear."

On January 20 Douglas MacArthur 2nd, of the American Embassy at Vichy, conferred secretly with Weygand in a hotel near Nice. He delivered the President's oral and written messages, but elicited nothing but a discouraging reply:

"The General was courteous and agreeable, but declined to give any consideration to the possibility of his taking any action in the African problem. He said that he is now a private citizen with no political status, that he is completely loyal to the Marshal, and that if France should be so unfortunate as to lose the services of the Marshal, he would under the legally designated successor have no opportunity to render service to the country."

In fact, he insisted that he would have to inform Pétain of the American advances, though he would keep the *démarche* secret from all others.

The categorical refusal of Weygand to act excepting under instructions from Vichy served at last to explode the idea that he could be made into another de Gaulle. While he was still in North Africa he had been enigmatic, but had left open the door of hope. Now that he had been recalled, he spoke specifically and definitely, and his answer was an unqualified rejection of all proposals. Therewith he passed out of the picture. Even the most optimistic were obliged to write him off.

As for Pétain, he contented himself with monotonous repetition of a well-worn theme. Admiral Leahy communicated the President's message to both the marshal and Darlan on January 27, and thereupon reported as follows:

"Reading from a pencil memorandum he [Pétain] said that he had made it very clear that his Government will resist invasion by British, Gaullists, Germans or *Americans*."

Use of the French fleet by the Germans, he asserted, was no longer a question. Neither was German use of bases in North Africa. He did not consider invasion of North Africa from either Spain or elsewhere at all imminent. In the event of such an invasion he would accept American aid only if he himself had requested it.

"My general impression as a result of this interview," reported Admiral Leahy, "is that America cannot expect any co-operation whatever by Vichy in an effort to exclude the Axis from French Africa when and if Germany desires to move in that direction." [9]

Considering the hopelessness of leaning on either Weygand or Pétain, let alone Darlan, the question might be asked whether perhaps we would not have done better to stake our

[9] Tel. (January 20, 1942) Hull to Leahy; tel. (January 27) from Leahy. The most important source for the mission to Weygand is the Leahy File (January 12, 15, 18, 22, 25, 27, 1942).

money on the Free French. This idea had already been put forward in a message from General Donovan to the President, sent on the eve of Churchill's arrival in Washington. The Coordinator of Information suggested the desirability of taking up with the British Prime Minister "the deplorable condition of the whole Free French movement in this country and inquire into the advisability or possibility of getting out of France some leader, perhaps like Herriot." [10]

This suggestion revealed the feeling long prevalent in American government circles that de Gaulle himself was unable to rally or organize an effective French resistance movement. At the same time it insinuated the possibility of finding a more acceptable leader and then giving the movement real backing. But once again events outran the planners and nipped a fruitful idea in the bud. On December 24, while the President and Churchill were celebrating Christmas Eve, Free French forces, under Admiral Émile Muselier, occupied the islands of St. Pierre and Miquelon, off the coast of Newfoundland. This episode was of really crucial significance in determining our further attitude toward both de Gaulle and the Free French. Even though this aspect of American policy is not the chief concern of this paper, it must be perfectly obvious that our policy toward Vichy France was conditioned in part by our hope or lack of hope in the Free French, and therefore at least a brief examination of the circumstances is in order.

The French islands in the Western Hemisphere—those in the Caribbean as well as St. Pierre and Miquelon—were still under the authority of Vichy. The supreme commander of these possessions was Admiral Robert at Martinique. Both the admiral and his subordinate at St. Pierre, Baron de Bournat, ruled with an iron hand according to the Vichy gospel. Popular unrest was ruthlessly suppressed and all stirrings of Free French sentiment were systematically stamped out. [11] So far as

[10] OSS Files: Donovan to the President, December 23, 1941.
[11] Cf. Ira Wolfert: "The Seizure of St. Pierre" (*Washington Star*, January 13, 1942).

the United States government was concerned, all this was an internal affair of the French. Our one interest was to maintain the *status quo* in these islands and prevent their being used by the enemy as submarine or air or communications bases. Various missions had been sent to Admiral Robert and agreements had been concluded that safeguarded American interests. These agreements had been renewed early in December, following our entry into the war. Had the hard-bitten old admiral proved too recalcitrant, we should have been obliged to take over control of the islands, a procedure that had been often and eloquently advocated in the American press.

St. Pierre, however, presented a special problem, for there was on that island a powerful wireless transmitting station that might well have served as a guide to enemy submarines operating on the northern sea-lanes. Early in November 1941 the Canadian government had informed Washington that it was considering dispatching Canadian personnel to exercise control over all messages transmitted by this station. The Department of State raised no objection to this policy and indeed agreed, in the common interest, to join Canada in economic pressure if Baron Bournat rejected the Canadian suggestion.[12]

But before any concrete steps were taken, the Free French came into the picture. It was the natural desire of de Gaulle and his supporters to get control of the islands. Consequently the Free French Minister of Marine, Admiral Muselier, was sent in late November to inspect the Free French corvettes that were on anti-submarine patrol with the British off Newfoundland and "if circumstances permitted to undertake rallying the Miquelon Islands to Free France." Muselier did not have orders to take action, but he was given carte blanche by de Gaulle, who in turn appears to have had Britain's blessing. On December 4 the Canadian government informed Washington that London had suggested occupation by the Free

---

[12] Much of this paragraph is drawn from a memorandum sent by Secretary Hull to the President on January 11, 1942.

French, a suggestion that did not appeal to the Canadians.[13]

Muselier, recognizing the new situation created by America's entry into the war, cabled back to de Gaulle on December 9, saying that he could carry out the operation about December 14, but stating that he would go to Ottawa to secure the consent of the Canadian and American governments. He requested that de Gaulle at the same time secure formal British approval. The reply which he received from London (December 13) was that the British considered Canada and the United States as the powers chiefly concerned. There was no time for negotiations, added de Gaulle: "I leave it to you to obtain a result if possible with the means at your disposal. Anyhow, I assume the responsibility of any initiative that you may consider possible in this matter." [14]

These messages make it perfectly clear that de Gaulle, though he may have been encouraged by the British attitude and may have counted on the London government to back him up in case of trouble, did not have anything like formal approval for his plan. As a matter of fact, it would appear from these documents that the Ottawa government had warned London of its opposition and that thereupon there had been a modification of the British attitude.

Be that as it may, Muselier adhered to his plan of consulting the Canadian and American governments. The outcome was not encouraging, for though the Canadian admiralty was not unsympathetic, the External Affairs Department was distinctly hesitant, in consideration of the probable American stand. In Washington the situation had to be viewed, of course, in the light not only of our relations with Vichy and with Admiral Robert, but also of our agreements with the Latin-American governments. The position of the State Department was that

[13] *Concerning the Crisis Which Occurred between General de Gaulle and Admiral Muselier after the Liberation of the Miquelon Islands,* an important unpublished account from a French source, sent to the Department in a letter from Matthews to Atherton, April 3, 1943; also Hull to the President, January 11, 1942, and Whitney to Donovan, from London, December 10, 1942.
[14] The French account, as above.

occupation of the islands by Canada would be the best solution of all. Muselier discovered all this from his conversations with J. Pierrepont Moffat, the United States minister at Ottawa. Thereupon the admiral "expressed bitter disappointment and said that he felt that the American government was making a mistake but that he would 'of course not proceed to the occupation.' " [15]

The outcome of all these discussions was duly reported to de Gaulle, but the general by this time had decided to take the bit in his teeth. On December 17 he cabled Muselier urging but not ordering action without reference to the attitude of the powers: "I repeat that I assume full responsibility on your behalf in this matter." And on December 18:

"We know for certain that the Canadians intend to [destroy] radio station at St. Pierre. Therefore, I order you to carry out rallying of Miquelon Islands with means at your disposal and without saying anything to the foreigners. I assume complete responsibility for this operation, which has become indispensable in order to keep for France her possessions." [16]

In the interval the Canadian government reported to the Department of State that the British were unwilling to go along with the Canadian plan of control and that therefore the Ottawa government would not proceed. [17] Where this might have ended, it is difficult to say, and it does not matter. For Muselier, despite his misgivings, had made up his mind to obey orders, after which he intended to resign. On December 24 he landed with a small force and took control of the islands, without previous warning to the Canadian or any other government. But the admiral acted against his better judgment, and bitterness took the edge off his joy in achievement. The American consul at St. Pierre reported him as much wrought up against de Gaulle and declaring that he himself was not a gangster:

[15] French account, supplemented by Hull's memo. to the President of January 11, 1942.
[16] French account, as above.
[17] Memorandum of Hull to the President, January 11, 1942.

"He is convinced that General de Gaulle's order was that of a dictator and that he is certain that the General did not even consult the National Committee of the Free French at London, of which he is president, but issued the occupation order under his own responsibility."

He openly proclaimed his intention of resigning,

"as a protest against the unilateral order given to him by the General without the prior approval of the United States and Canada. The reason for his planned resignation is that Free France is on the side of and fighting for democracy to crush totalitarianism and he thinks the General's action was not democratic enough to fit his ideal of France." [18]

The whole incident was clearly one that required explanation all around. From Ottawa Moffat reported the Canadian government as "shocked and embarrassed" and feeling that the whole business was "so close to a breach of faith that it cannot fail to embarrass their future relations with the Free French." [19] The British government, on its side, disclaimed all responsibility and maintained that Muselier had acted against the instructions and orders of the Foreign Office. Indeed, the Foreign Office reported that on December 17 de Gaulle had given assurances that no occupation would be attempted. His argument now was that he had learned that the Canadians were planning action with American approval and that such a development would have deprived the Free French of all *raison d'être*. Therefore he felt obliged to act.[20]

The whole incident left the Department of State and the American government in an almost impossible situation. On December 13, following Vichy France's proclamation of neutrality, President Roosevelt had said in a message to Pétain:

"You may rest assured that the Government of the United States under present circumstances and in view of the instructions which you have issued to Admiral Robert will continue to give full recognition to the agreement reached by our two Gov-

[18] Dispatch (December 26, 1941) from Maurice Pasquet.
[19] State Department memorandum, December 26, 1941.
[20] Tel. (December 25, 1941) from London.

ernments involving the maintenance of the status quo of the
French possessions in the Western Hemisphere."

Added to this were the obligations entered into by the United
States government at the Havana Conference of 1940, outlaw-
ing the use of force to effect the transfer of sovereignty, possession, or control of any territory in the Americas held by
belligerent nations.

Under the circumstances the Department of State could
do nothing less than condemn the high-handed action of the
Free French. But this public announcement was bound to be
the signal for a violent explosion of American public opinion.
Rarely had the Department been exposed to more abusive criticism. The Union for Democratic Action demanded reconsideration of the American condemnation and declared, in a protest sent to Secretary Hull: "Surely appeasement of Vichy
need not go so far as to guarantee Vichy's rule in parts of the
Western Hemisphere like the island of St. Pierre." [21] Groups
of prominent citizens, probably more well intentioned than
well informed, adopted the same argumentation and demanded
that the President reorganize the Department's personnel so
as to bring it "into line with the anti-Axis war effort to which
the rest of the Government and the country itself are dedicated." [22]

What motivated all this excitement was certainly hatred of
Vichy rather than devotion to de Gaulle and the Free French,
at least among the great majority of Americans. As it happens, a public-opinion poll had been taken in December 1941.
This revealed that about 75 per cent of those polled believed
that Vichy did not represent the real attitude of France and
that Pétain's government took its orders more or less directly
from Berlin. It is particularly interesting to note that fully
65 per cent of those questioned believed that sooner or later
Vichy would turn over the French fleet and the North African
bases to the Axis. The long and the short of it is that the majority of Americans looked with great suspicion on the Vichy

[21] *New York Herald Tribune*, December 28, 1941.
[22] *New York Times*, January 2, 12, 1942.

policy of collaboration and, after the fall of Weygand, feared that Pétain and Darlan would make concessions to the arch-enemy of the United States and Britain.[23]

But this same poll revealed a curious ignorance of de Gaulle and the French resistance movement. Of those polled only 34 per cent could state correctly who de Gaulle was; 3 per cent gave a mistaken answer and 63 per cent were unable to reply. A few more, but only a few, could say something intelligent about the Free French: 42 per cent knew what the movement was; 8 per cent gave the wrong answer; and 50 per cent gave no answer at all. Of those who were instructed, 76 per cent held that de Gaulle and the Free French represented the de-sires of the French people, while only 13 per cent believed that Pétain did so.

From the viewpoint of the Department, however, these dis-tinctions had little practical value. The fact was that Ameri-can policy was under fire and that there was a terrific outcry against any intention or plan of returning the two islands to Vichy rule. On the other hand, there were real dangers in-herent in any other course. Admiral Robert made no secret of his view that the United States was "obligated to obtain the reestablishment of French sovereignty over St.Pierre-Mique-lon."[24] In the meanwhile Admiral Leahy had cabled from Vichy:

"Darlan referred to the St.Pierre-Miquelon incident and said that Germany has already used the seizure of those islands by De Gaulle as an argument for the entry of Axis troops into Africa, in order that it may be protected against similar invasion."

It is altogether likely that this was mere camouflage, but of course one could not tell. Secretary Hull himself foresaw "ominous and serious developments," and wrote to the Presi-dent: "it is a mess beyond question, and one for which this government was in no remote sense responsible."[25]

[23] Results of the poll may be found in *Pour la Victoire* (February 28, 1942).
[24] Hull to the President, January 8, 1942.
[25] Hull to the President, December 31, 1941.

Things might have been a bit easier if our British allies had given anything like effective support. But Churchill, who happened to be in Washington at the time, appears to have been none too sympathetic. It took a lot of persuading by Secretary Hull and Mackenzie King, the Canadian Prime Minister, to make him see the light.[26] Even then it was impossible to induce him to condemn the Free French or to call de Gaulle to order. Instead of that he indulged in vituperation against Vichy. Speaking at Ottawa, he gave his eloquence free rein:

"The men of Bordeaux, the men of Vichy—they lie prostrate at the foot of the conqueror. They fawn upon him. And what have they got out of it? The fragment of France which was left to them is just as powerless, just as hungry as, and even more miserable because divided than the occupied regions themselves. Hitler plays from day to day a cat and mouse game with these tormented men. One day he will let out a few thousand broken prisoners of war from the million and a half or million and three quarters he has collected. Or again, he will shoot a hundred French hostages to give them a taste of the lash. On these blows and favors the Vichy Government have been content to live from day to day. But even this will not go on indefinitely. At any moment it may suit Hitler's plans to brush them away. Their only guarantee is Hitler's good faith, which, as everyone knows, biteth like the adder and stingeth like the asp. Some Frenchmen there were who would not bow their knees and who under General de Gaulle have continued to fight at the side of the Allies. They have been condemned to death by the men of Vichy, but their names will be held, and are being held, in increasing respect by nine Frenchmen out of every ten throughout the once happy, smiling land of France."

This sounded very much like approval of de Gaulle and his doings, and so it was interpreted at the time. No wonder that Secretary Hull complained to the President:

"Our British friends seem to believe that the body of the entire people of France is strongly behind De Gaulle, whereas according to all my information and that of my associates, some

[26] Memorandum of conversation with King, January 9, 1942.

95% of the entire French people are anti-Hitler, whereas more than 95% of this latter number are not De Gaullists and would not follow him. This fact leads straight to our plans about North Africa and our omission of De Gaulle's cooperation in that connection." [27]

Yet finally Secretary Hull managed to work out what seemed like a reasonable compromise—one that would or should be acceptable to the United States, Canada, and Britain on the one side and Vichy on the other, and that therefore should make the withdrawal of the Free French perfectly logical. The islands were to be placed under what was really an American-Canadian-British trusteeship, though the phrase had to be avoided in view of the Havana agreements. The important wireless station was to be under the control of observers appointed by the United States and Canada. The islands were to be neutralized and demilitarized. The administrator was to be withdrawn for the duration of the war and a consultative council was to serve as the governing body. All the armed forces were to be recalled and the United States and Canada were to furnish economic assistance.

To this proposal the Vichy government was prepared to assent, though it wanted the administrator to stay on at least for a while, presumably for the sake of appearances. But Churchill accepted this solution only subject to the approval of de Gaulle, who lost no time in rejecting it. Thereupon the British Prime Minister cabled London from Ottawa stating that if de Gaulle remained recalcitrant, the United States would send armed ships to expel the Free French. This in turn caused consternation among the Canadians, though it was evidently only intended to enable the British government "to thump de Gaulle over the head." [28] However, British action against de Gaulle hardly went beyond a light slap on the wrist. Secretary Hull soon realized that no support could be

[27] Hull to the President, December 31, 1941.
[28] Tel. to Vichy (January 8, 1942); memo: *Suggested United States Proposal for Settlement of the St. Pierre-Miquelon Situation;* memo. of telephone conversation between Moffat and Atherton (January 15, 1942).

expected from our allies, once de Gaulle had achieved a *fait accompli*. As the public clamor died down in the United States, Hull reluctantly concluded that the best thing would be to let the matter rest until the end of the war.[29]

Ostensibly de Gaulle had scored a resounding success, but he had forgotten the old diplomatic adage that it is dangerous to play little tricks on great powers. Prior to the St.Pierre-Miquelon affair our government had had little to do with de Gaulle and the Free French movement and had shown little interest in it. After all, in 1941 the movement still comprised only a handful of Frenchmen, most of them living abroad. Patriotic and courageous many of them no doubt were, but it was nevertheless true that the group was torn by dissension and had little beyond what the British government was willing to provide. There was no convincing evidence that de Gaulle and his followers had many adherents in France, and even if there had been, we were bound to regulate our attitude toward the Free French in accordance with our policy toward Vichy. This government was convinced that the national interest would be best served by maintaining good relations with Pétain's government. Once that is recognized, it is easy enough to understand that we could not cultivate de Gaulle. After the St.Pierre-Miquelon affair relations naturally became worse. It was perfectly obvious that de Gaulle personally had been chiefly responsible for what looked like a cheap parlor trick. He had put the United States in a most embarrassing position and had thereby built up a resentment in official circles that it was almost impossible to overcome.

Summing up the entire St. Pierre crisis in a note to the President, Secretary Hull reiterated that his great preoccupation throughout had been not to outrage Vichy, because he still hoped to hold that government to its assurances regarding the French fleet, colonies, and bases.[30] Everything depended on the degree of faith one might have in Vichy and in Vichy's desire or ability to resist Germany. The British, of

[29] Hull to the President, February 2, 1942.
[30] Hull to the President, February 2, 1942.

course, had none, and for that reason backed de Gaulle for
all they were worth. It was therefore natural that they should
have attempted to turn away from the Free French leader
the wrath of the American government. John G. Winant's
report of a conversation with Anthony Eden is very revealing in this connection:

> "He told me that he realizes the Free French had gotten off base
> and had made a mistake, but he hoped that in considering the in-
> cident we would relate it to the total war situation and he felt it
> would be a mistake to humiliate De Gaulle or to build up the
> Vichy Government at this time. He told me that he had informa-
> tion which made him feel that the Germans would use such a
> position to do damage to supporting elements in France." [31]

In much the same spirit Lord Halifax attempted to intercede
in Washington. He suggested to Welles that Free French
observers should be invited to attend the meeting of the
President and the Prime Minister with representatives of the
refugee governments. This Welles rejected out of hand, taking the opportunity to explain once more how this government viewed the French problem:

> "I said that, as the British Ambassador well knew, this Govern-
> ment had been moving heaven and earth to keep on close terms
> with the Vichy Government, in the hope that through such in-
> fluence as we could exercise in Vichy and in North Africa, the
> French Fleet would not get into German hands, and North Africa
> would not be used as a base for military operations by the Ger-
> mans."

If the President were to invite the Free French, especially
after the St. Pierre episode, the Vichy government would
suspect us of playing both ends against the middle, and the
Germans would at once exploit the situation to our detriment.
None the less, Lord Halifax hoped that we would not "harden
our hearts against the Free French," on which Welles commented as follows:

[31] Tel. (December 31, 1941) from Winant.

"I was unable to see that the Free French movement at the present moment had anything very much to commend it from the practical standpoint. I said unfortunately there were no outstanding men with qualities of leadership and of initiative directing the Free French movement and providing that kind of inspiration to free men, both in France and in other parts of the world, to join in a movement against their German oppressors. I said I felt that if some man like Herriot could get out of France and lead the movement, the situation would undoubtedly be very different, but that I could not see that either General de Gaulle or his associates provided any rallying point for French patriotism. For all these reasons I felt it was wiser and in the best interest of both Governments for the two Governments for the present to pursue their respective courses until and unless existing conditions changed." [32]

Much the same view was clearly presented by Anne O'Hare McCormick in the *New York Times* (January 7, 1942). While applauding de Gaulle's action, the well-known columnist questioned his acumen in proceeding without the consent of Washington:

"Whether our policy toward France has been wise will be proved by events. It is a considered policy, however, patiently followed in the face of opposition, and fully understood by the Free French as well as the British. It may be argued that our entry into the war changes our relation to the 'United Nations' fighting Hitler, but our belligerency does not diminish the necessity of waging diplomatic battles as successfully as we can until we are ready for military battles. . . .

"The St. Pierre affair cannot be considered apart from our policy toward France as a whole, and to criticize it as State Department policy is absurd to anyone who knows the facts. . . . The fact is that Washington has been fighting a delaying action in France as truly as General MacArthur has been playing for time in the Philippines. And every week gained in the campaign against French collaboration with Germany is as important as any action in the field."

[32] Memorandum of conversation (December 27, 1941).

Well-balanced and understanding analyses of this sort unfortunately continued to be rare. The dust stirred up by the St. Pierre incident was exceedingly slow in settling and criticism of the Department was repeatedly voiced in the press as well as in official circles. The argument of the critics was almost a stock argument: that nothing was to be gained by appeasing Vichy. The danger of Pétain's turning over the fleet to the Germans was a purely imaginary danger, for the French public would never stand for it and the crews would scuttle their ships rather than surrender them to the enemy. Pétain, it was argued further, was leading the United States by a string simply in order to freeze out de Gaulle.[33]

Others again argued that the Germans could take anything they liked when the moment seemed to them opportune. There was therefore no sense in contaminating our high resolve to win the war by playing the Vichy game.[34] Naturally this same point was made again and again by de Gaulle's own associates. For instance, early in February de Jean, who acted as de Gaulle's Foreign Minister, submitted the following thoughts on American policy:

"The French people's spirit of resistance, not Vichy, has prevented the French Fleet from falling into the hands of the Germans. Therefore, the main purpose of the United Nations' policy should be to build up the spirit of the French people, not to support Vichy. This spirit is symbolized by the Free French. Therefore, the French people are disheartened by our distrust of and failure to support the Free French.

"The fact that Hitler 'tolerates' the presence of the American Embassy in Vichy proves that he finds its existence useful.

"Pétain would prevent and sabotage any effort towards resuming the struggle against Germany in North Africa." [35]

At the very same time Colonel Billotte, the Free French Minister of War and chief of the military intelligence service,

[33] Waverley L. Root: "Vichy Bait for Washington" (the *Nation*, January 17, 1942).

[34] Memo. of Lieutenant Colonel Solborg to General Donovan, January 27, 1942.

[35] Donovan to the President (February 8, 1942).

warned an American official in London "that the Russians are urging De Gaulle to accept Russian recognition as the 'head of the French Government.'" Furthermore, he remarked, he was constantly hearing from his secret agents in France that "the State Department's attitude is bewildering Frenchmen everywhere and discouraging their resistance to the Germans." [36]

And so the debate continued, without even a chance of reconciliation of opposing viewpoints. In all likelihood we shall not know for a very long time—perhaps never—what the merits of the conflicting arguments were. For even now no one can say how the French people felt at that time. The only point on which all the evidence is in agreement is that the overwhelming majority of Frenchmen (ninety-five per cent is a figure frequently named) were hostile to the Germans and opposed to collaboration. What percentage of them favored de Gaulle we do not know. Neither can we say to what extent our Vichy policy may have estranged French sentiment. In any event, it would be a grave mistake to suppose that hostility to the Germans and to collaboration was the same thing as condemnation and opposition to Vichy. To many Frenchmen, Pétain was still the grand old man who was doing his best to save what he could from the wreckage and who, if he made concessions to the enemy, was doing so only in order to gain time.

But when all is said and done, the St. Pierre episode was of significance for the development of our policy toward de Gaulle and the Free French and had very little to do with our policy toward Pétain and the Vichy regime. That policy had been formulated long before and was adhered to unswervingly until the time of the invasion of North Africa. It never was and never became a policy that we thought we could rely on. Quite the contrary, it was a day-by-day, hand-to-mouth policy all the way through. No one in the Department liked the Vichy regime or had any desire to appease it. We kept up the connection with Vichy simply because it

[36] Donovan to the President (February 9, 1942).

provided us with valuable intelligence sources and because it was felt that American influence might prevail to the extent of deterring Darlan and his associates from selling out completely to the Germans. Darlan had already provided the enemy with facilities in Syria and had knuckled under to the Japanese in Indo-China. But as yet the French fleet was in French hands and North Africa was untouched. These were the two all-important issues, the ones on which our national safety depended. About the fleet we could do little beyond the use of persuasion and warnings and even threats. But North Africa held possibilities, and to these we must now turn.

In the earlier part of this chapter attention was called to the highly precarious state of affairs after our entry into the war. Weygand had been dismissed and there was every reason to fear that the Germans, driven back in Cyrenaica, might turn their energies to French North Africa. The great question was how such a disaster could be forestalled. The problem was discussed between the President and Churchill during the latter's Christmas visit to Washington, and plans were outlined for a joint expedition against North Africa, with or without the aid of a French rising. We have seen that Weygand refused to co-operate in such a venture. Ultimately the whole idea had to be abandoned because of the bad turn of events in the Far East and the reversal of fortune in the Libyan campaign. For the time being, we could only fall back on our policy of trying to keep Vichy in line and at the same time making such secret preparations as might be feasible. There were various possibilities and a host of difficulties. Some of these we must try to analyze.[37]

In the first place we must disabuse ourselves of any idea that there was unity of feeling or aim in Morocco, Algeria,

[37] On the early North African plans see *Biennial Report of the Chief of Staff, July 1, 1941—June 30, 1943*, p. 18. Comments by Matthews. Bullitt tells me that in December 1941, when he was in Cairo as ambassador-at-large, he and a British representative induced General Georges Catroux to draft a plan for an operation against North Africa, and that this was cabled jointly to Roosevelt and Churchill at Washington.

and Tunisia. To all appearances the entire area was under effective Vichy control. In the course of eighteen months hundreds and even thousands of suspect officials had been removed and replaced by reliable men of the collaborationist stamp. Even before the year 1940 was out the elite of the Vichy henchmen had been organized in the Service d'Ordre Légionnaire (S.O.L.), only to be reinforced a little later by the formation of Jacques Doriot's Parti Populaire Français (P.P.F.), roughly the equivalent of Hitler's brown-shirts. These were the shock troops of French fascism, the rowdies who initiated the anti-Semitic terror in North Africa and worked in conjunction with Nazi agents and spies. Finally, mention must be made of the *Comités d'Organisation* or *Groupements*, which exercised complete control of the economic life of the country. These graft-ridden bodies were the tools of the Vichy collaborationists, the chief financial support of the S.O.L. and the P.P.F., and the willing helpers of the German armistice commission in its systematic looting of the country.[38]

The harsh political and economic regimen that was gradually introduced in North Africa permitted of no open opposition, but it did make for much latent discontent and unrest. Among the natives of Morocco, for example, anti-French feeling was strong and dangerous. There was every reason to suppose that leading native chieftains, like El Glaoui, might be enlisted against the French and almost certainly against the Germans if the latter were to attempt an invasion. In Algeria, on the other hand, things were quite different. There the Vichy system enjoyed considerable popularity among the numerous French *colons*, who exercised much more effective control over the native population. But in Tunisia, again, there was little sympathy with the policies of Vichy. Pro-British feeling seems to have run strong there, just as pro-American sentiment did in Morocco.

The aim of our Economic Agreement had been primarily

[38] OSS Files: anonymous memorandum on *The Situation in North Africa from 1940 to 1943*, dated July 18, 1943.

to save North Africa from economic ruin and from the
disturbances that were bound to follow collapse. Bad conditions would have given the Germans an excellent excuse to
interfere. But the story of our feeble efforts during 1941 had
shown that there were much more promising lines that could
be followed in that region. Weygand, to be sure, scrupulously
avoided committing himself to any anti-Vichy policy and
confined himself to declaring that he would defend North
Africa against invasion. But Robert Murphy and his vice-
consular associates had soon discovered that many officers and
officials on Weygand's staff, to say nothing of less important
officials throughout the area, were not wedded to Vichy.
They were, in fact, extremely patriotic Frenchmen who
looked forward to the day when France might again take
part in the war by the side of Britain and the United States.
Outwardly they were, for the most part, loyal to Pétain.
Inwardly a good many of them were decidedly conservative
in their views, royalist in fact, but, for all that, intensely opposed to the Nazis and to any collaboration with them. "It
will never be fully known until after the war," wrote the
American consul-general at Algiers, "what mulish passive resistance was exercised day in and day out by multitudes of
French officials dealing with the Germans." [39]

Murphy, when he took over his North African assignment
early in 1941, soon discovered that these men had already
managed to construct at least the skeleton of a resistance
movement, or, perhaps better stated, that various nuclei of
resistance were already in process of development. To follow
the evolution of these secret groups is, of course, extremely
difficult and fortunately not really necessary. Nevertheless,
the main lines of organization are not only interesting but
important.

According to Free French sources, the resistance movement
in North Africa dates back to August 1940, when a certain
André Achiary organized groups in Algiers, Oran, and
Cherchell. This movement was soon joined by men like

[39] Felix Cole: *Memorandum on North Africa*, January 26, 1943.

Roger Carcassonne (an Algerian industrialist) and Henri d'Astier de la Vigerie (a member of the Deuxième Bureau and a former Cagoulard). It operated under a directorate which met frequently and arranged for the penetration of the police system, the army, and especially the general staff. Shock troops were organized and regular watch was kept over all ship movements. Much of the information gathered was then turned over to the American vice-consuls. Toward the end of 1941 an important recruit was secured in the person of José Aboulker, who became the chief organizer at Algiers.[40]

At first there were undoubtedly several different groups, operating without knowledge of each other. Thus we hear of a movement, started in November 1940 by a Captain Beaufre, of Admiral Abrial's staff. This group appears to have been primarily a military one. Under the able guidance of Lieutenant-Colonel Jousse, it attempted to plan for the re-entry of North Africa into the war on the side of the Allies. One of the most active and one of the most interesting of its members was Jacques Lemaigre-Dubreuil, who long before the war had been prominent in French fascist movements and might be regarded as a typical example of the French banker and big-business man who was not only ready but eager to play the Nazi game. After the fall of France he acted as intermediary for the Franco-German economic commission at Wiesbaden and is said to have served as a purchasing agent for the Germans in North and West Africa. He became a partner of the Banque Worms and was a close associate of men like Pucheu, Leroy-Ladurie, and Barnaud. These excellent connections made it possible and in fact easy for him to travel to and fro without arousing suspicion, and he therefore served frequently as the intermediary between important personages.[41]

[40] *Les Cahiers français*, No. 47 (August 1943). This is a special number devoted to the history of the French resistance in North Africa. See also Renée Gosset: *Le Coup d'Alger*, chap. iii, and Kenneth Pendar: *Adventure in Diplomacy* (New York, 1945), for a good deal of detail.

[41] OSS Files: report entitled *Portrait of a Two-Way Collaborationist* (July 23, 1943); Gosset, chap. iii.

It is almost impossible to assess with any degree of assurance
the role played by men like Lemaigre-Dubreuil. Was he an
agent of the Germans, or was he simply an opportunist—a
representative of great industrial and banking interests, ready
to play both sides and secure his future no matter what turn
the wheel of fortune might take? Or, again, was he a sincere
and patriotic Frenchman, who was double-crossing the Germans and his Vichy connections only in order to prepare the
way for France's revival? Robert Murphy, who had a great
many dealings with Lemaigre, has maintained stoutly that
Lemaigre was loyal and devoted. In a letter written after the
invasion, when some attention was being given to Lemaigre's
peculiar activities, Murphy wrote:

"For the past two years Lemaigre-Dubreuil has cooperated
with me. He established, with my knowledge and approval, a de-
ceptive police record in France. This record showed that he was
a collaborationist, and through months he cultivated Laval, Abetz,
Dubrinon (Auer and Company) and obtained useful information
from them which I included in my State Department reports.
Also he functioned as a liaison between myself and General Giraud. Lemaigre-Dubreuil is known to me as a courageous, patriotic Frenchman who hates the Germans and Italians with an intelligent implacability and favors the Allies." [42]

In a word, Lemaigre and the group with which he was associated contributed heavily to the American cause in North
Africa. These were the men with whom Murphy was primarily connected and who constantly urged upon him the
need for military supplies if North Africa was to be defended.[43]

Although Weygand's fall was a great blow to this group,
the belligerency of the United States opened up new and
grander possibilities. Apparently there was some consolida-

[42] Murphy to Colonel Donovan (January 11, 1943).

[43] Lemaigre-Dubreuil has written a detailed statement of the history of
this group, without in any way minimizing his own part. A copy of the
English translation of this is in the Department of State, entitled *France's
Re-entry into the War on the Side of the Allies,* and will be referred to
frequently in the sequel.

tion of the various movements, men like Achiary, Aboulker
and d'Astier de la Vigerie joining with Jousse and Lemaigre.
The objective now came to be internal preparation and action
to aid an American or Allied debarkation in North Africa.
Already in December 1941 the group presented Murphy with
a detailed memorandum on requirements, worked out by
Colonel Jousse, the principal military expert of the movement. No formal reply was made to this communication, or
to another note of the same kind that was presented in February 1942. The reason given by Murphy was that the United
States government was still hoping to enlist the aid of Weygand, which we know to have been true.[44]

We may leave the story of this North African resistance
movement for the moment, summing up its ideas and aims in
the words of Murphy himself:

"In essence, their purpose is the establishment in French Africa
of a provisional government operating independently of Metropolitan France. They are searching and hope to find shortly a
military leader (General Delattre de Tassigny, commanding in
Tunisia, is the man they have in view now). They feel that he is
sufficiently ambitious, ruthless and able to lead such a movement.
They also have in mind that Yves Chatel, who succeeded Weygand as Governor-General of Algeria, will fill the top civilian role
in such a provisional set-up. The control would be in the hands
of four or five men at the most. Their immediate action would
consist of cutting off all communications with Metropolitan
France, at which time they will require both economic and military support from the United States. By military support they
mean materiel and munitions.

"Another phase of their current study is a formula under which
a bridge could be constructed between themselves and the De
Gaulle organization. Their conviction is that a large number of
desirable military and civilian officials otherwise available, because of an undoubted antipathy which exists among them,
would shrink from the idea of forming part of the De Gaulle organization."[45]

[44] Cf. Lemaigre account, as cited above.
[45] Letter of Murphy to Welles, November 27, 1941.

Here, then, was what we had to operate with in North Africa: a good deal of local distress and discontent, especially among the natives of Morocco; a fairly numerous and well-organized group prepared to resist German penetration or aggression and only too ready to work with the Allies against the common enemy; and finally a considerable staff of American officials and observers, who could gather important intelligence and at the same time serve as advisers and supporters of the resistance groups. There were, at this time, twelve members of Murphy's staff in North Africa, in addition to nine members of the regular consulates (Casablanca, Dakar, Algiers, Tunis), and four more members of the Tangier consulate.[46]

Whatever secret or subversive activity was to be carried on in North Africa was primarily the responsibility of the Office of the Coordinator of Information (later the Office of Strategic Services) under Colonel (later General) William J. Donovan. This agency had been set up in July 1941 and had been entrusted not only with the establishment of a secret intelligence service, but also with the organization of special operations. In October General Donovan had appointed as chief of special operations (SO) Lieutenant Colonel Solborg, who had just returned from an extended tour of North and West Africa and had been in active contact with the leaders of the French resistance. The plan as worked out by General Donovan and Colonel Solborg, in conjunction with the Department of State, was to establish connections with the native chieftains, especially in Morocco, and at the same time to foster, encourage, and support the resistance groups.

In December 1941 it was arranged with the Department of State and with the Navy Department that Lieutenant Colonel William A. Eddy (USMC) should be sent to Tangier as naval attaché. Colonel Eddy was at the time naval attaché at Cairo. He had had long experience in the Near

---

[46] State Department memorandum by J. D. Jernegan, dated February 5, 1942.

East and spoke Arabic fluently. Since he was well known to the State Department and fully trusted, he was the ideal person to co-ordinate military and naval intelligence in the Moroccan area. His first assignment was, if necessary, to aid J. Rives Childs, our chargé d'affaires at Tangier, who was to discuss with General Luis Orgaz, the high commissioner of Spanish Morocco, an economic plan similar to that concluded by Murphy and General Weygand. Our objective was to establish control officers in the Spanish zone as in the French. But Colonel Eddy's mission had further objectives. He was to establish contact with Murphy and work closely with him. Henry S. Villard, the assistant chief of the Near East Division of the State Department, conferred with Colonel Eddy at Bermuda in January 1942 and asked him "to instruct Mr. Murphy on behalf of the Department that the proposals of the French for military and fifth-column aid to the Allies were of great interest to the Department. Mr. Murphy was authorized to encourage the French to perfect these plans for assistance to the Allies." [47]

But before any subversive activities could be launched in North Africa, relations with Vichy once more approached the breaking-point. Ever since the Germans had begun to operate against the British in Libya, they had been drawing supplies for their forces from North Africa. During 1941 these supplies consisted chiefly of fruit, vegetables, and live-stock, but surreptitiously Darlan had also furnished in April some trucks and munitions. [48] Then, at the end of December, Darlan admitted to Admiral Leahy that a certain amount of gasoline was being sent to Rommel's retreating army. His excuse for thus aiding the Nazis was that Hitler had threat-

[47] Conversation with Colonel Eddy (December 8, 1943); State Department Memo. on *The Role of the Department of State in the North African Economic and Political Program*, p. 34, notes. Villard tells me that in view of the army's inability to promise supplies it was necessary to bolster the morale of the French with general assurances and promises.
[48] Captured German Documents: report of the Hitler-Darlan meeting of May 12, 1941; *Procès du M. Pétain*, p. 95 (testimony of General Doyen).

ened to occupy Morocco if the delivery of gasoline was refused.[49] Details of this traffic have never become known, but on January 30, 1942 Admiral Leahy cabled that it was rumored in Vichy that the Germans would soon reopen the whole question of Franco-German relations, involving "complete collaboration in Metropolitan France and North Africa." Abetz had made several trips to Berlin, and Benoist-Mechin and de Brinon had been flitting to and fro between Paris and Vichy. Rumor had it that Bizerte and the right of German transit through Tunisia were under discussion.[50] At this very time Darlan paid a visit to Italy and conferred with Count Ciano. Reliable reports stated that the French admiral had made an oral agreement to permit shipments to Rommel's troops in French bottoms, by way of Tunisia. On his return to Vichy, Darlan admitted to Admiral Leahy that in an effort to prevent the forcible seizure of Bizerte, he had agreed to ship two hundred tons of food each week and a total of five hundred Italian trucks via Tunis to the Axis forces in Libya. . . . "He stated that no military material has been or will be shipped to Libya via Tunis."[51]

Darlan's concluding statement was nothing less than a lie, even if one allows for difference of opinion as to what constitutes "military material." Actually the French allowed about four thousand tons of gasoline (half of it aviation fuel), as well as food, trucks, and guns to pass through Tunisia into Tripoli.[52] French patriots at Gabès did what they could to render the gasoline useless by adding chemicals and even substituted gasoline drums filled with water, but that had nothing to do with the principle or with the general practice.[53] In Washington the whole business was regarded as a matter

[49] Leahy File (December 30, 1941). Also the memorandum of B.E.W., Blockade and Supply Branch: *The Economic Contribution of French North Africa to the Axis* (September 12, 1942), chap. ii.
[50] Tel. (January 30, 1942) from Leahy.
[51] Leahy File (February 7, 9, 1942).
[52] OSS Files: memo. of February 20, 1942, by David W. King.
[53] OSS Files: Letter of Colonel Eddy to General Donovan (February 15, 1942), reporting information from Doolittle, the American consul-general at Tunis.

of real gravity, the more so as it violated innumerable promises previously made by Darlan. The President himself took alarm and sent a message to Churchill referring to increasing signs of German activity in the Mediterranean:

"The situation has become so menacing, particularly in the face of certain definite information which has come to us, that we have informed our military and naval people that it is more than likely that we shall not be able to remain much longer in North Africa." [54]

At the same time the President cabled to Admiral Leahy a strong warning to Marshal Pétain. In this he called attention to French collaboration in supplying Rommel and stated:

"There can be no justification under the terms of the armistice for the shipment of war materials or other direct aid to the Axis powers, and without official assurances from the Vichy Government that no military aid will go forward to the Axis in any theater of war and that French ships will not be used in the furtherance of their aggression, Admiral Leahy will be instructed to return immediately to the United States for consultation as to our future policy." [55]

In the meantime Welles spoke to the French ambassador in Washington in very plain English, recorded as follows:

"I said that I regarded the situation which had arisen as the most serious one which had developed in the relations between the Vichy Government and the Government of the United States. . . . I said that it was inconceivable that the Ambassador could assume for a moment, or that his Government could assume for a moment that, if this was not immediately and completely checked, the present policy of the United States towards France could continue." [56]

Yet, despite this unequivocal language, Admiral Leahy found it extremely difficult to bring Darlan into line. A

[54] Draft message (February 5, 1942).
[55] President to Churchill (February 11, 1942), in Roosevelt Records.
[56] Memorandum of conversation, February 10, 1942.

French note of February 16 was simply an exercise in eva-
sion and as such was thoroughly unsatisfactory. And before
the debate could be carried much farther, the situation was
complicated even more by the discovery that a German submarine had taken refuge at Martinique. Thereupon Leahy
was instructed to obtain categorical assurances that Axis ships
and planes would not be permitted to enter French ports in
the Western Hemisphere. In the event of a refusal of such
assurances, the United States government threatened to take
the necessary measures to prevent such enemy action.[57]

A veritable barrage of notes now set in. Admiral Leahy
was utterly disgusted with this eternal bickering and urged
that he be recalled. No one, he cabled the President, expected
the United States government ever to take positive action.
The time had come when we must show that we were not
bluffing. But the President replied that precipitate action at
the time would be most inadvisable.[58] As a matter of fact,
Darlan was finally brought to the point of giving at least partial assurances: namely, that the French government "would
not lend any military aid to one of the belligerents in any
place in the theater of operations, particularly the use of
French vessels for the purposes of war, nor all the more,
adopt a policy of assistance to the Axis powers beyond the
terms of the armistice agreements." [59] Even this statement he
made as gracelessly as possible, complaining to Admiral
Leahy about the tone of the American notes and saying that
the French government accepted them only in order to avoid
giving a pretext for a rupture of relations with a government
that for some weeks appeared to be seeking a quarrel. Reporting the entire debate to Henry-Haye, Darlan cabled that
he had promised once more that the French fleet would not
be surrendered to Germany or any other power: "Never
since the armistice has Germany made the slightest attempt
to get control of the French fleet, for Germany knows too

[57] Leahy File (February 16, 21, 1942).
[58] Leahy File (February 20, 22, 1942).
[59] Statement of Welles to the press, February 27, 1942.

well that such an attempt would not have even the least chance of success." [60] Actually it was not until March 23 that the United States government agreed to close the argument and to resume shipments to North Africa under the Economic Accord.[61] Under the circumstances it can well be imagined that the last shreds of confidence had gone out of our relations with Vichy. We expected no good from Darlan and were only hoping to gain time.

Since the time available to us was likely to be very short, we had to move as expeditiously as possible in North Africa. The plan of General Donovan, the Coordinator of Information, was roughly as follows: Lisbon was to be the center for intelligence and operations, which were to be conducted under cover of the military attaché. The attaché was to coordinate his activities with those of the British. He was to recruit agents, establish a secret chain of communications with Tangier, Casablanca, Algiers, Bizerte, and Tunis, and through agents there he was to get in contact with friendly elements in the North African army, navy, and administration and in native circles:

"The plan involves organization of groups to receive and hide material, which will be supplied them directly by ship from us or by road and train from Tangier to Casablanca. A group of operatives will be supplied by the British together with equipment to organize and direct the subversive parties I shall put at their disposal in Morocco." [62]

It has already been pointed out that these plans were laid and implemented with the co-operation of the Department of State. The Department agreed, through Villard, to recall

[60] OSS Files (March 3, 1942); sent to the President by General Donovan.

[61] President to Churchill (March 22, 1942): "At a time when the United Nations are preparing to meet the enemy by force before it can occupy various areas, it seems to me important that we should take advantage of the possibility that we can hold the Axis off from other areas by using such psychological and economic weapons as are available." Churchill agreed (March 27) and added: "We value your contacts with Vichy and it is well worth paying a certain price." (Roosevelt Records).

[62] OSS Files: memorandum by Colonel Solborg for General Donovan (February 6, 1942).

any vice-consuls who proved ineffectual and to have the
others instructed in the special work that was before them.
The supervisors of the Economic Accord were to be used for
the organization of cells of local sympathizers "for active
militant work from Morocco to Bizerte." Murphy was informed that the Department had a serious interest in the military possibilities of North Africa and that he should continue
his conversations with various leaders and groups to determine
their capacity and ability to collaborate with us when the
time came.[63] He was to work in closest touch with Colonel
Eddy at Tangier.

In the meanwhile Colonel Eddy had arrived at his post. He
found that the British were already in contact with a group
in Morocco and that plans were under way to land supplies
for this group near Agadir and Fedala.[64] Eddy thereupon paid
a visit to Gibraltar, where he conferred with Viscount Gort
and with the representatives of the British secret intelligence
service and the British special operations executive. Apparently the British decided, in view of the American plans, to
give up their own scheme, though arrangements were made
for full co-operation in developing the necessary network of
communications.[65] It was arranged further that the center of
operations should be Tangier, where Eddy could keep in constant touch with his British colleagues not only for the exchange of intelligence but for the preparation of operations.[66]

Two quite different propositions were before us at this
time, the one a bit fantastic, the other extremely serious.
Doolittle, our consul at Tunis, had hatched out a scheme for
replacing the pro-Vichy Tunisian Prime Minister by an official better disposed to the Americans and British. It was
suggested that, through the use of bribery, a number of members of the old Bey's family could be mobilized to effect a

[63] Tel. (April 2, 1942) Hull to Murphy.
[64] Conversation with Colonel Eddy (December 8, 1943); OSS Files: memo.
of February 21, 1942.
[65] OSS Files: letters from Eddy to Donovan (February 15, 25, 1942).
[66] OSS Files: *Memorandum on the Political Situation, S.I.S.-S.O.E. Operation Set-up* (March 10, 1942).

a palace revolution. The trick could be turned, it was thought, for a few million francs (twenty thousand to thirty thousand dollars). General Donovan at once made fifty thousand dollars available for this plot, but in the end the whole business was laid aside at the instance of Murphy, who felt it would be unwise, to say the least.[67]

Less in the line of light opera was the plan that had, in the meanwhile, been elaborated by the leaders of the French resistance in Algeria and Morocco. These men had made up their minds to resist German action in North Africa at all costs, and if possible to bring about a revolution in the army that would enable them to re-enter the war on the side of the United States and Britain. One of the ablest and most active of the leaders, Colonel Van Hecke, had drawn up in February a careful schedule of requirements, but this schedule had to be revised in the light of the situation in Libya and because of the fact that the British no longer enjoyed air and naval supremacy in the Mediterranean. In their new form the French requirements were formidable indeed. Nevertheless, Colonel Eddy sent them on to Washington after discussing them at length with the French leaders.[68]

Even General Donovan found it hard to accept the French estimates, for military supplies were not easy to come by in the opening months of 1942. He therefore cabled Eddy: "The supplies requested appear to be enormous and quite out of proportion to the projected operations." But Eddy insisted that the figures had been carefully worked out. He urged that the French organization offered the only chance to assure effective resistance to Axis aggression, and that the operations contemplated were independent of any projected American expedition. In a letter to General Donovan, Eddy expressed his fears that the whole movement would come to naught if supplies were not forthcoming:

[67] OSS Files: Doolittle to Eddy (February 25, 1942); tel. Donovan to Eddy (March 16, 1942); Eddy to Donovan (March 25, 1942).
[68] OSS Files: Eddy to Donovan (March 19, 1942), transmitting the French war plan, dated March 13.

"It is my conviction that failure on our part to give this support will be fatal to our plans to keep Morocco and North Africa strong enough to resist enemy aggression. We will not find such leaders elsewhere and we dare not lose them now. . . . I have just talked with Mr. Murphy, who is in full accord with the plans and who has complete confidence in the leaders. Please note that these requisitions are being made quite independently of any possible American expedition. The supplies are needed, and will be used, no matter who invades North Africa. The organization will resist with or without our supplies; their plans are complete for action against Axis attack through Algeria or Spanish Morocco, or from any other direction. They only ask for our material help immediately to make resistance effective. They are taking all the risk, they will receive, distribute and use the supplies, every step being taken with the threat of execution as traitors if they are uncovered. The least we can do is to help supply them on their own terms, which are generous and gallant." [69]

It was an eloquent plea, but one that could not, at the time, be answered favorably. Eddy went to Lisbon to consult with Colonel Solborg, who had meanwhile arrived there as assistant military attaché. Solborg pointed out that plans for an expedition to North Africa had had to be shelved in view of the requirements in the Pacific. All that could be done for the French was to give them financial assistance, which was done, and to collect at Gibraltar such supplies as could be obtained. [70]

All through April the situation continued to be tense, coming gradually to a crisis. All arrangements had been made for the landing of supplies on the Moroccan coast. They were to be consigned to the Office of Posts, Telegraphs, and Telephones, the officials of which were in the plot. The Berger brothers, industrialists in Casablanca (code names *Tweedledum* and *Tweedledee*), were the managers of the scheme. [71]

[69] OSS Files: Eddy to Donovan (March 11, 1942).
[70] OSS Files: tel. (March 19, 1942), Eddy to Donovan; tel. Murphy to Eddy (March 21, 1942); tel. Eddy to Murphy (March 24, 1942); tel. Murphy to Eddy (April 9, 1942).
[71] OSS Files: Eddy to Donovan (April 1, 1942); memo of David W. King to Eddy and Murphy (March 2, 1942); letter of Eddy to Donovan, transmitting the plans (April 8, 1942).

In short, everything was prepared and only the goods were outstanding. Murphy urged the need for action and begged for the mission of a regular army officer to carry on discussions with the French leaders. The French, he cabled, "consider it of great importance to gain an idea of approximately when we may be able and ready to extend our cooperation to them. Naturally, in the development of their organization the essence is the timing." [72]

Things were moving entirely too slowly for our representatives on the spot. To them the situation appeared to be well-nigh desperate, and they feared that our failure to act would discourage the French patriots and result in the loss of their valuable aid. No doubt both Eddy and Murphy were sucked into the excitement and impatience that had overcome the patriots. This becomes perfectly clear from the cables that were exchanged in rapid succession toward the middle of April. On the 10th of the month Eddy reported to Washington:

"German breakthrough Tunisia with possible simultaneous attack through Spanish Morocco expected by French command. French are now determined to resist and asked today how soon we can deliver twenty thousand anti-tank mines 15 kilos. each at Port Lyautey. They will want eight thousand similar mines elsewhere later. Utmost secrecy and speed requested by French." [73]

This was followed almost at once by another urgent appeal:

"There is rapidly approaching crisis in military events and French ability to resist. Cannot wait for delayed answers regarding authority to finance resistance and exchange rates. Subject only to the approval of Murphy and Childs, I propose now to use the fifty thousand dollars now credited to me here. This I will use at my discretion to finance Arab and French resistance. I also request immediate credit for a half million dollars for me to use on similar terms as above in an emergency." [74]

[72] Tel. (April 2, 1942) Murphy to Hull.
[73] OSS Files: tel. (April 10, 1942) from Eddy.
[74] Tel. (April 12, 1942) from Eddy.

A third cable was sent off on the next day, to this effect:

"We are also asked by our French partners how soon we would
be able to furnish heavy material to Bathurst, Freetown or Liberia
and kept there by Americans, secret from knowledge of agents
of the Axis and ready for French vessels to pick it up and transport to Morocco or Tunis at H Hour." [75]

What this heavy material was to be may be learned from yet
another urgent cable, which listed one thousand motorcycles,
five hundred motorcycles with side-cars, fifty 105-mm
howitzers with trucks and tractors, one hundred and fifty
105-mm anti-aircraft guns, three hundred 37-mm anti-aircraft
guns, four hundred and fifty M2A4 tanks, three hundred
M–3GRT–6 tanks, one hundred and fifty scout cars, and one
hundred and fifty jeeps.[76]

   This was a substantial program, which obviously raised a
real issue of allocation and supply. General Donovan replied
at once, pointing out that Washington had not received the
alarming intelligence mentioned by Eddy and asking for a
full report. At the same time Eddy's cables were referred to
the Joint Chiefs of Staff, who in turn asked the Joint Intelligence Committee for an opinion. Eddy replied at once in a
rather despairing cable:

"Other departments naturally have no evidence corroborating
secret intelligence of well-organized French military organization determined to resist Axis. Only Murphy can confirm and he
is urgently requesting me to finance and supply on the modest
scale requested in my recent despatches. French leaders would
be arrested on slightest suspicion and shot if exposed. They have
now news in advance of Laval Government and fear Vichy surrender of North Africa soon. If Malta falls, Germans plan to enter
Tunisia with or without Spanish zone attack on Morocco. . . .
Robinhood [i.e., Colonel Van Hecke] speaks for Etat Major of
General Juin, high officers in Morocco and thousands of disci-
plined troops. . . . The British SI sources confirm my own with
regard to approaching crisis. We have days before us, not weeks.

[75] Tel. (April 13, 1942) from Eddy.
[76] Tel. (no date) from Eddy.

The Axis grip on North Africa, Tangier included, is growing tighter by the hour." [77]

Meanwhile the Joint Intelligence Committee had examined the problem and had submitted to the Joint Chiefs a not unfavorable report. In this it was pointed out that as yet there was no specific evidence of German intention to break through Tunisia or attack through Spanish Morocco. Indeed, the Axis forces in Libya and Spanish Morocco were inadequate for such an operation. On the other hand the Axis had sufficient troops in Italy that could be transported to Algeria and Tunisia. The British forces in the western Mediterranean were not adequate to prevent such a move. Furthermore, "the reinstatement of Laval indicates a possible turn-over in North Africa in connection with the development of collaboration." The conclusions, therefore, were these:

a). "It is impossible to prevent Axis occupation of North Africa in the event that the Axis is prepared or intends to use military force in the near future.

b). "It is probable that, unless some support is given to disaffected elements, a peaceful turn-over will take place.

c). "Assuming that Vichy collaboration means eventual Axis control, civil or military, it is possible that a useful strategic and political end would be served by aiding disaffected elements to initiate and maintain a continuing guerilla opposition, by taking at this time action to force a military rather than a peaceful occupation." [78]

In other words, military opinion held that an Axis occupation, if attempted, could not be prevented, but that it might be well to support the patriots in order to make the occupation militarily more difficult. None the less the Joint Chiefs insisted on further information regarding the size of possible Arab and French opposition and demanded assurances that any material sent would reach the proper persons. To this, Eddy replied that "the extent of opposition is limited only

[77] Tel. (April 15, 1942) from Eddy.
[78] J.I.C. (April 14, 1942).

by cash to ensure native leaders, whose potential is several hundred thousand, and by equipment for French." [79] While awaiting further developments, Eddy paid a visit to Gibraltar, whence he reported:

"Lord Gort sent for me to ask how Gibraltar can help groups resist in North Africa. He offers to assemble reserves of arms for emergency shipment. We are desperately hoping and waiting." [80]

As it turned out, Eddy's hopes were to be blasted. On April 20 the Joint Chiefs of Staff examined the cables that had come to General Donovan. The verdict was as follows:

"After careful consideration of these dispatches and other pertinent information on the subject, the United States Joint Chiefs of Staff viewed unfavorably the proposal to furnish war materials to French Morocco at this time. They are, however, in accord with the policy of expending funds judiciously for the purpose of initiating and maintaining guerilla opposition in that area."

This was a severe blow to Donovan as well as to Eddy and Murphy, but none of them were men to give up hope. In communicating the decision to Eddy, General Donovan urged him not to be discouraged. "If we are right, it will work out right," he cabled in characteristic fashion.[81]

And so for the time being, at least, the whole matter lapsed. In the meanwhile all attention was focused on the dramatic events in Vichy, which brought Pierre Laval back into power on April 15, 1942. This sensational affair was one of the important developments of these crowded months, and with a short consideration of the circumstances this chapter may appropriately come to a close.

The Germans, it will be recalled, had taken Laval's dismissal in December 1940 very hard. They had, in fact, never become reconciled to it and apparently continued to doubt

[79] OSS Files: tel. (April 15, 1942) Donovan to Eddy; and tel. (April 16, 1942) from Eddy.

[80] OSS Files: tel. (April 19, 1942) from Eddy.

[81] OSS Files: memorandum of the Joint Chiefs to General Donovan (April 21, 1942); letter of Donovan to Eddy (April 23, 1942).

Darlan's sincerity as a collaborationist. And so, though Laval
was, for a year or so, in eclipse, he continued to be a threat
to Pétain and Darlan. Time and again it was rumored that
the Germans would insist on his return to power, and there
was no reason to suppose that at some opportune moment
they would not raise the issue in earnest.

The time for action seemed to have arrived in March 1942
in connection with the ill-fated Riom trials, which had been
carefully rigged to convict Blum, Daladier, and others of
responsibility for the unpreparedness of France in the period
after the advent of the Popular Front government in 1936.
The trials were a farce from the outset and deceived no one,
least of all the French. Both Blum and Daladier spoke out
bravely and effectively, with the result that they indirectly
illuminated the responsibility of others, like Pétain and
Gamelin, and at the same time cast at least a faint halo around
the much-maligned Third Republic. "The Third Republic
never looked so good as it has under fire from its successor,"
wrote an American correspondent who followed the ses-
sions. So completely, indeed, was the Vichy government
exposed that the Germans themselves ordered the proceedings
stopped. Pétain and his national revolution were thoroughly
discredited, while the people of France were aroused as they
had not been during the two years of their captivity. "There
are very few fence-sitters," wrote the same correspondent,
"or middle-of-the-roaders with no opinion. Marshal Pétain
no longer wields much influence on the great mass of
patriots." After the raids of the R.A.F. on Paris, he reported,
the population scribbled on the walls: *"Pétain au dodo, Darlan au poteau, De Gaulle au boulet"* (Pétain to bed, Darlan
to the firing squad, de Gaulle on the job). Collaboration, he
concluded, was definitely through as a political instrument;
"It has never been officially disowned, but no one talks of it
any more." [82]

It was only natural, therefore, that the Germans should
have decided on a change—a change which came so sud-

[82] OSS Files (March 23, 1942).

denly that Laval himself appears to have been surprised by it.
In March he had had the honor of an interview with Marshal
Göring, from whose own lips he had heard that relations between Germany and France had become very bad—Hitler
now knew what the real sentiments of the French were and
would act accordingly. Göring advised Laval not to re-enter
the French government, but to wait until peace had been made
and real collaboration became possible. Laval, perhaps somewhat gleefully, insisted that he must inform Pétain of this
sad state of affairs and thereupon sent his son-in-law, Count
René de Chambrun, to Vichy. Chambrun evidently did his
job well and painted so frightening a picture that the old
marshal decided he must see Laval in person.

The two men met in Pétain's automobile on March 25,
deep in the forest of Randan. After some recriminations the
marshal complained that Darlan's foreign policy had proved
a complete failure and that he would like Laval to return
and save the day. But Laval refused all offers short of full
powers, arguing that unless France were given a strong government the country would soon be flooded by communism.
But his demands were too much for Pétain, who would brook
no rival. Nothing came of the negotiations, of which Darlan
and Pucheu learned only after they were over with. Both
men were dispatched to the forest of Randan themselves, but
this was only a piquant detail, since their efforts appear to
have been of no avail.[83]

Commenting on these operatic maneuverings, an American correspondent at Vichy wrote to his New York chief:

"Laval is hated, vomited by France. It is easy to predict that if
he does go through with this and does form a cabinet, he will be
an early target for an assassin. His policy of collaboration, which
he is trying to revive for the benefit of Germany, after it has
been buried for months, is detested by 99% of Frenchmen."

[83] *Procès du M. Pétain*, pp. 200–1 (Laval's account); 288 (de Brinon); 307
(Lavagne). Also tels. (March 26, 27, 31, 1942) from Leahy, which are obviously based on information from Ralph E. Heinzen, who had his story
from Laval himself.

Laval, he went on, had assured him that his return to power would not involve any change in French-American relations. On the contrary, the Germans would permit him more than they had allowed Darlan:

"On the other hand, he ardently wants a German victory over Russia and over England; he believes in them. If he had a chance, he said, he would send a million French volunteers to fight alongside of Germany against the Bolshevists. But he would never mobilize the French army or furnish a single soldier or sailor to Germany for use against America. He would give any guarantee that America wants that no French island or no part of the French Empire would ever be used as an Axis sub or airplane base against the Allies. But he would not tolerate any Allied interference if he began to fight to win back from De Gaulle the dissident colonies. An aggressive military campaign against De Gaulle, particularly in Africa, would be one of his principal policies."

Even without this ominous statement of policy and intention the very name of Laval was enough to arouse uneasiness and apprehension in American circles. For that reason the President had already cabled a message to Admiral Leahy, asking him to tell Pétain that "the appointment of M. Laval to an important post in the Vichy government would make it impossible for America to continue its present attitude of helpfulness to France." [84]

But warnings of this sort were not likely to have much effect. If the Germans insisted, there was little if anything that Pétain could do. For a moment it seemed as though the Laval project might fail, for the reports that he had been to Paris to confer with the Germans were followed almost at once by rumors that he had not succeeded in extracting any concessions and that therefore the marshal would not appoint him. As a matter of fact, Pétain received his rival on the morning of April 2 and conferred with him for an hour. Nothing happened immediately, and it was thought that Laval's demand for full powers or nothing had been rejected. [85]

[84] Leahy File (March 28, 1942).
[85] Tel. (April 2, 1942) from Leahy.

But hopes based on these rumors were soon to be blasted, and all efforts made by the President to forestall a Laval government were to prove vain. On April 9 the President received the French ambassador, Henry-Haye, and spoke in a most sympathetic vein, if the report of the ambassador to his government is to be believed. "Never," the President is said to have remarked, "have our two countries understood each other better than during the past few weeks." He was very much annoyed, he added, by the St.Pierre-Miquelon incident and expressed the hope that the Vichy government would allow the matter to rest. He was much irritated with the Free French and with the scorn that they showed for American criticism.[86]

This approach to the problem had no more effect than a strong American note sent to Vichy on April 13, which was promptly rejected as an insult. By that time the appointment of Laval had already been decided upon. Admiral Leahy learned a day or two later that Darlan, in order to foil Laval, had reported to the Germans the various American efforts to prevent the appointment, and that thereupon Hitler had decided to make the matter a test of strength between Germany and the United States.[87] Be that as it may, Laval's advent to power was announced on April 15, and two days later the entire Darlan cabinet resigned. Darlan, however, remained commander-in-chief of all land, sea, and air forces, responsible directly to Pétain.

It was inevitable that the return of the champion of collaboration should create a storm of indignation in the United States. Major George Fielding Eliot at once announced that it signified "the bankruptcy of a political line of action which never made sense from the strategical viewpoint, and which was insisted upon by officials who were not accustomed to giving weight to military considerations." He urged that the Allies seize the Vichy bases at once and thereby save them-

---

[86] Tel. from Henry-Haye to Darlan (April 9, 1942).
[87] Tels. (April 14, 15, 1942) from Leahy; *Procès du M. Pétain*, p. 307 (Lavagne's account).

selves much greater efforts and losses later.[88] The Union for Democratic Action and kindred organizations took much the same line, demanding severance of relations or even war with Vichy France, recognition of the Free French movement, and seizure of French possessions, at least in the Western Hemisphere.[89]

Actually the Department of State needed no prodding. The time had at last come for taking some positive action. After conferring with the President, Sumner Welles on April 16 had a frank discussion with Henry-Haye. He stated unequivocally that the United States would not maintain relations with a Laval government. We did not believe, he pointed out, that Pétain would be in a position to resist if Laval began to go beyond the assurances that had been given theretofore. To implement this decision Admiral Leahy was instructed at once to return home "for consultation." "The Department is of the opinion," he was informed, "that no room for doubt must exist in the American mind and, above all, in the French mind, that the focal point of the future of American-French relations is German control over any French government dominated by Laval." [90]

But the admiral's return was delayed for some weeks by the illness and death of his wife. Outwardly, then, nothing was changed for the time being. In the interval various attempts were made on the French side to reassure Leahy about Laval's intentions. Count de Chambrun, Laval's son-in-law, tried to convince the ambassador that the new Vice-Premier was no longer convinced of a German victory, but that he was a firm believer in a negotiated peace, which would put France in a strong position.[91] In much the same vein Marshal Pétain protested that "while M. Laval is much closer to the Germans than he is, neither of them will agree to give any armed assistance to an enemy of the United States. He indi-

---

[88] *New York Herald Tribune*, April 16, 1942.

[89] *New York Times*, April 22, 1942; *Christian Science Monitor*, April 24, 1942.

[90] Tel. (April 16, 1942) Welles to Leahy.

[91] Tel. (April 21, 1942) from Leahy.

cated that France will be required by force of arms to give
economic assistance to Germany." [92]

Most important, of course, were Laval's own statements
regarding his position and intentions. He called on Admiral
Leahy on April 27 and tried to convey the impression of "being fanatically devoted to the interests of France, with a conviction that they are bound together irrevocably with the
interests of Germany." He denied that he was either fascist
or pro-Nazi and asserted that he was interested only in the
welfare of France:

"He felt that the United States had committed a serious error
in entering the war, and that in the event of a victory over Germany by Soviet Russia and England, Bolshevism in Europe would
follow inevitably. Under such circumstances, he would prefer
to see Germany win the war.

"He was prepared to defend France and her Empire against all
comers and he stated specifically that if the British or the Americans were to attempt to effect a landing either on the soil of
Metropolitan France or on French North African territory, he
would resist them to the best of his ability. His Government, he
maintained, would take no step to provide military assistance to
the Germans."

In this connection he expressed himself in the most vehement
terms against Britain and de Gaulle: "It is true that if I could,
I would take De Gaulle and his followers by the throat." But
unfortunately he lacked the military power to do anything
about Syria, Equatorial Africa or New Caledonia.

"My policy," he continued, "is based on reconciliation with
Germany, and without such reconciliation I see no possibility of
peace, either for Europe or for France or for the world. I am
certain that Germany will be victorious. But even if she were defeated, my policy toward Germany would be the same, for it is
the only one that is in the interest of definitive peace."

In any event, at the end of the struggle, he was convinced,
"France will be the intermediary between the United States

[92] Leahy File (April 27, 1942).

and Europe." Summing it all up, Admiral Leahy felt that "M. Laval is fully committed and may be expected to go as far as he can in an effort to collaborate with Germany and assist in the defeat of what he termed Soviet-British Bolshevism." [93]

[93] Tel. (April 27, 1942) from Leahy; tel. (May 18, 1942) from Tuck.

CHAPTER VII

North African Plans

THE SIX MONTHS that intervened between the reappearance of Laval and the American invasion of North Africa brought no fundamental change in the European or the world situation. The second German campaign in Russia began late—really not until July 1942. The fighting was stiff, but the Nazi machine advanced with seemingly inexorable might, rolling on from the Black Sea toward the oilfields of the Caucasus. Not until the invaders reached Stalingrad on the Volga were they brought to a stop (in September), and even then it appeared all too likely that they would still be able to push on southward to Baku. In this emergency every effort was made by Britain and the United States to keep the Russians supplied, but German air and submarine power made the famous convoy route to Murmansk a hazardous one, which took a large toll of warships as well as cargo vessels. In the Atlantic, too, the Nazi submarines continued to raise havoc. Many thousands of tons of shipping were lost every month, and only in the autumn did the figures for new construction finally catch up with the statistics of losses.

In the Mediterranean and North Africa Allied affairs did not prosper either. Before the army of Egypt had been adequately reinforced to complete the expulsion of Rommel from Libya, at the end of May the combined German-Italian forces, greatly strengthened from Sicily by sea and air, launched an attack. Within a month Rommel had taken Tobruk and was sweeping on not only to the frontier of Egypt but almost to the edge of the Nile delta. The invaders were at last stopped at El Alamein, though for a time it seemed very doubtful if Alexandria and Egypt could be held. Reinforcements by the tens of thousands were rushed from

Britain, and supplies from the United States, but the Mediterranean was almost completely under the control of the enemy. Only Malta held out, despite terrific air bombardment. Meanwhile all shipments to Egypt had to be taken round the Cape of Good Hope, an arduous and time-consuming route.

During all these months the United States was still girding for action. In the Pacific the brilliant defensive Battle of Midway was fought on June 3, but it was not until August 7 that we were prepared to take the offensive at Guadalcanal. Our chief objective during the spring and summer had to be to hold off the enemy and gain time. And so it was with our French policy. In the words of Sumner Welles: "American diplomacy has been forced to undertake what is not a very gratifying role, not a very agreeable role, and not a very sympathetic role, that is, to fight a rear-guard action." [1]

It will be recalled that Laval's advent to power had resulted in the instructions to Admiral Leahy to return home for consultation. Relations with Vichy France had not been broken off, but to all intents and purposes we refused to have much more to do with the Pétain-Laval-Darlan consortium, and we made no secret of our attitude toward it. The great question was what Laval's response would be. For the moment the chances of his taking an outright hostile stand appeared to be fairly slight. Anthony Eden, the British Foreign Minister, for example, believed that, if anything, Laval's return to power was a revelation of German weakness: "Probably the Nazis feared increasing influence of Leahy and did not like the way things were going in unoccupied France. Surely they wanted to protect their rear before launching a spring campaign." Eden's prognostications were something like this:

"Laval will lie low for a while in order to quiet apprehensions in America as well as in France, and to dig in politically. Laval no doubt still hopes to mediate between Washington and Berlin and to acquire enough prestige in the New Order to feather his own nest and that of France. . . . Laval will do nothing about the Vichy warships for a time and neither contemplates nor de-

[1] Conference with the press, March 26, 1942.

sires to let Berlin have them, but might well use them to protect
French trade with the French dependencies. Since Laval would,
no doubt, permit Nazi penetration in those countries, an armed
naval clash with Allied forces might well result. Surely Laval
would foster transfer to Germany of French workingmen, but is
unlikely to try regaining De Gaullist territories (because too
difficult a problem) despite his pertinent announcement and the
opinion of De Gaulle himself." [2]

This evaluation of the situation was shown by the sequel
to have been sound and discerning. In Washington it had come
to be realized that in all probability the French fleet would
never be allowed to fall into German hands, if only because
it was too good a bargaining point for the Vichy government.
In reply to a question from a newspaperman Welles, even
before Laval's return, had stated that not more than fifty per
cent of the French naval officers and certainly not more than
ten per cent of the crews would obey German orders, even if
Darlan issued them. As a matter of fact, Admiral Auphand,
who was Minister of Marine under Darlan, was known to be
anti-Axis in his sentiments. Though serving with Laval, he
told the American naval attaché that the recent cabinet
changes would in no way affect the French navy: "The assurances repeatedly given the United States by Maréchal
Pétain still held—the French navy would never be turned
over to the Axis." Many French officers asserted that Darlan
himself would never issue orders to turn over the fleet, and
that even if he did, the orders would not be carried out. Our
naval attaché was firmly convinced that the fleet would never
be turned over to a foreign power. [3]

Concern for the fleet, therefore, was not uppermost in the
minds of American statesmen in the spring of 1942. The chief
anxiety was lest Laval should sell out to the Germans in other
respects. Speaking off the record to a press conference on May
5, 1942, Hull voiced his apprehensions. The main reason why
we had kept on with Vichy, he said, was in order to get in-

[2] Tels. (April 16, 23, 1942) from Matthews.
[3] Report from Vichy, April 27, 1942.

valuable information and to counteract the pro-Hitler elements:

"We found it awfully important to have a person on the ground with authority. He could point his finger every day to disloyal elements in the Vichy Government and insist that they not go beyond the terms of the armistice. He could use other methods and means that would prevent a folding up of the less pro-Hitler elements in the French Government and that would give them courage to hold up their end when undue pressure was brought to bear on them. We could have run out over there and cussed them out, as the saying goes, and we would not have gotten anywhere then. Admiral Leahy, who was a tower of strength to Pétain on desperate occasions of pressure, would have been absent. Then the whole thing would have gravitated straight into the hands of the worst and most disloyal elements in the French situation."

It is of course difficult to assess the importance of Admiral Leahy's presence in Vichy. Men like Darlan and Laval probably went their own way without reference to foreign influences, but there can be little doubt that Leahy's strong personality served as a deterrent to the extremists and as a reminder of American strength and courage and determination to the French government generally. His presence in Vichy gave aid and comfort to numerous French officials who were not disposed to sell out to the Axis and who dreamed of and planned for the day of liberation.

That being so, the admiral's departure for home necessarily represented a great and distinct loss. And yet there seems never to have been any thought of his return to Vichy, at least so long as Laval remained in power. We kept a skeleton staff at Vichy, but we no longer expected to accomplish much thereby. This explains why, early in May, we sent Rear Admiral John H. Hoover with Samuel Reber, the assistant chief of the Division of European Affairs in the Department of State, on a special mission to Martinique. The United States government was not prepared to yield to the vociferous demands of the press and seize control of the French Caribbean islands, but it was determined to make sure that any unfriendly plans that Laval might cherish would not have much chance of realization. From this time on we dealt with the high commissioner, Admiral Robert, much as we dealt with de Gaulle; we regarded him as the effective authority in the control of the islands and negotiated with him without reference to Vichy. Laval protested, but without avail.

In other words, our relations with the new French government were relations of ill-concealed enmity, which made any healthy co-operation impossible. A striking example of this was the exchange of notes in July with reference to the fate of the French warships that lay in the harbor of Alexandria. It will be recalled that Rommel's army had broken into Egypt and that there was real danger that the whole country would be lost. If Rommel were actually to reach Alexandria, the Germans would *ipso facto* come into possession of a strong naval force unless the ships were got away beforehand. The British view was that these ships were outside the scope of the Franco-German armistice of June 1940 and that therefore the Vichy government could dispose of them freely as it saw fit. The President consequently proposed to the Vichy government that these ships should be placed in the custody of the United States, that they should be sent through the Suez Canal and thence to some American or neutral port in the New World, with a guarantee that they would not be used by the American or British government, and that they would be returned to France at the end of the war. Though the President warned Vichy that, in the event of a refusal, the British would be justified in taking the ships away from Alexandria, Laval flatly rejected the proposal, as he did a further suggestion that the ships should proceed to Martinique for demobilization until the end of the war. Laval's idea was that the ships should go to some near-by French port, which, as Welles put it, was like saying that Martinique was not close enough to the Germans and Italians.[4]

[4] Roosevelt Records. The President thought that if the offer were refused, the French crews might at least be less disposed to resist British action in an emergency.

In dealing with the Vichy government it was difficult not to become as cynical as Laval himself. Much as he might protest his interest in the future of France, his actions belied his words and drove the French population itself further and further into revolt.[5] In accordance with Nazi doctrine, Laval introduced drastic measures against the Jews and initiated an extensive program of conscripting French labor for work in Germany. The Washington government registered vigorous protests against both these policies, but without achieving even the most meager effect. Laval's reply was merely to protest against the bombardment of French towns by American airmen.[6]

Considering the state of veiled hostility that now existed between Washington and Vichy, it is not surprising that the popular demand in the United States for a complete rupture and for out-and-out recognition of de Gaulle and the Free French movement should have grown apace. The two demands usually went hand in hand and seemed to many American liberals and radicals to be logical counterparts. But the problem for American diplomacy was not so clean-cut as some critics would have it. Apart from the fact that recognition of de Gaulle would have constituted a provocation of the Vichy government and a snapping of what many thought was our only connection with the mass of the French people, it must be particularly emphasized that the position of de Gaulle was by no means clear or his intentions certain. It was easy enough to say that de Gaulle represented the real sentiments of the French people and that he was our obvious ally in the campaign against the common enemy. But was that the fact? No one could say with certainty, for there was no way of sounding out French opinion. Our representatives in France did not believe it and neither did the Department of State. Only this much was clear: that de Gaulle had no man-

[5] On June 23 Laval committed what in French eyes was the most unpardonable crime: he stated in a radio address not only that he expected, but that he *desired* the victory of Germany (*Procès du M. Pétain*, pp. 201, 202, 336).

[6] *Documents on American Foreign Relations*, V, 539ff.

date from the French people, that his political program was
not really known, and that, as a matter of fact, even outside
France it was proving very difficult for French leaders to
work with him in building up a strong and impressive resistance movement.

From the welter of contradictory statements and frag-
ments of evidence one way or the other, it is worth while to
note at least a few items. Late in March Matthews cabled
from London saying that a certain prominent Frenchman
would soon return to the United States. This gentleman had
been working with de Gaulle for some time and was later to
be an influential member of the Fighting French cabinet. Yet
in the spring of 1942 he appears to have been entirely disillusioned. He told Matthews that de Gaulle and his entourage
were devoid of all "sense of realism." It was essential, he held,
that the seeds of resistance within France should be nurtured.
But "De Gaulle and his followers have no contact with 'the
people.'" The whole movement, he thought, was so preoccupied with petty squabbles that real leadership without
self-seeking had become impossible.[7]

Substantially the same views were expressed at about the
same time by one of the French generals, formerly commander
of the French air force in North Africa and a man who had
tried to work with de Gaulle in London. On his arrival in
this country in April this general declared that Gaullism represented something quite different from a symbol of resistance
to the Germans. De Gaulle, he said, was fighting Vichy more
than Germany. He was convinced that "De Gaullism is simply
the expression of one man's ambition."[8]

De Gaulle in the interval did nothing to dispel such
suspicions. No doubt he was nettled by the St. Pierre-Miquelon
incident or, better, by its consequences. No doubt he was also
piqued by the unceremonious occupation of New Caledonia

[7] Tel. (March 26, 1942) from Matthews; comments by Ray Atherton.

[8] OSS Files: memorandum of conversation with John Wiley, sent to the
President by General Donovan, April 21, 1942. There can be little doubt
that the spring of 1942 marked the low point in the Gaullist movement,
which was racked at the time by dissension and personal conflicts.

by American troops and by the British seizure of Diégo-
Suarez on Madagascar in May 1942.[9] None the less, it was
hardly diplomatic on his part to express himself freely and
publicly as he did. Thus, his London speech of April 17 was
nothing less than a challenge to Britain and the United States.
It began with a violent attack on Vichy and then went over
to a hardly less bitter attack on the Allies:

"Some crimes are so cunningly committed that even upright
men cannot refrain from a sort of melancholy admiration. Thus,
in the face of that foul masterpiece of Nazi strategy which constitutes the Vichy regime, we cannot help touching our hats as
a tribute to Herr Hitler.

"Fighting France means to go forward shoulder to shoulder
with her Allies, on the express condition that her Allies go forward with her. In fighting at their side, she means to regain her
independence, her sovereignty, and her greatness, provided they
are respected by her Allies. She is doing everything in her power
to promote an Allied victory, but on condition that this victory
should also be her own. Over a period of 1500 years she has become accustomed to being a great Power, and insists that everybody and first of all her friends, should not lose sight of this fact.
In short, Fighting France has only one reason and only one justification for finding herself in the camp of freedom; that of being
France herself, and treated as such by her co-belligerents."

It has often been said of de Gaulle that he believed it necessary to assert the dignity of France as against even the most
friendly powers, in order to counteract the charge that he
was simply a paid tool of the foreigner. Very likely considerations of this kind had some validity, and some allowance ought
further to be made for his difficult and precarious position.
Thus, Winant on one occasion cabled quite charitably concerning the French leader:

"I believe if we could talk with him occasionally, it would help
and enable us to get on a reasonable work basis with him. The
man in my judgment needs some sense of security. There is a
price on his head in his own country, and the exigencies of the

[9] Tel. (June 16, 1942) Winant to Hull.

war have not made his position easy either in relation to the British or ourselves." [10]

Yet it was hard to see how one could approach a man like de Gaulle, who was intemperate in word as he was in deed and whose pretensions went far beyond what many Frenchmen were willing to concede. Speaking to a press conference on May 27, he referred scathingly to American negotiations regarding Martinique. Dealing with Vichy, he remarked, was like dealing with Hitler and was certainly not representing general French interest as among allies. Furthermore, he roundly denied that the Fighting French movement was a purely military affair. "Fighting France," he declared, "fights for the general interests of France, which it claims to represent." [11]

This declaration was so extreme in its implications that it appears to have caused considerable opposition even within the ranks of de Gaulle's followers. At any rate the national committee at once sent a telegram to Tixier in Washington in the hope of counteracting the unfavorable impression of de Gaulle's words. The committee, it was pointed out, had never asked to be recognized as the government of France. This was a matter for the French people to decide. The committee regarded itself merely as a provisional authority, and its political role was merely to arouse and organize resistance in France and to administer liberated French territory. [12]

Before leaving this topic, it may be well to add one last bit of evidence. Early in May, Henry-Haye, the Vichy ambassador in Washington, reported to Laval that certain émigrés like Chautemps, Leger, and Cot were attempting to form a new party and alleged that Bullitt was backing this move with the President and the Department of State. This, thought Henry-Haye, probably explained the denial of recognition to de Gaulle and the Fighting French. [13] The facts

[10] Tel. (May 17, 1942) from Winant.
[11] Tel. (May 29, 1942) from Matthews.
[12] Dispatch (June 7, 1942) from Matthews.
[13] OSS Files (May 5, 1942).

of the matter, however, were quite different. An effort was evidently made at this time to induce Leger to take over the leadership of the Fighting French movement in the United States. But Leger refused to be associated with de Gaulle— an attitude in which he was supported by other prominent figures. Jacques Maritain, for example, is reported to have sent a message to de Gaulle warning him against his political activities, and to have told Aglion that he himself would have nothing to do with a "new Bonaparte experience." There appears to have been some talk of setting up a new committee under Maritain, from all of which we can at least infer that some of the most respected Frenchmen in this country were extremely critical of de Gaulle and unwilling to accept his leadership. Under the circumstances the hesitancy of the Department of State becomes the more understandable.[14]

Leaving aside, for the time being, the related problems of Vichy France and of de Gaulle's Fighting French, let us consider the further development of the North African question. It is not necessary to repeat what has already been stressed, that North Africa had become, with our involvement in the war, one of the most important strategic areas. German conquest of this region, or Sicily or Spain, would have been followed by the establishment of the enemy in West Africa, which in turn would have constituted a threat of the first order to the entire Western Hemisphere. It was of crucial importance, therefore, that North Africa should be kept in line, at the very least until we were in a position to initiate action there ourselves. Considerations of this sort conditioned our attitude toward Vichy to some extent. At any rate they determined our policy with respect to the famous Economic Accord, which was now entering upon the second year of its existence.

Brilliant though the conception of the Murphy-Weygand Agreement may have been, it could hardly be described as a success. Murphy, who had done his very best to implement

[14] OSS Files: report of a conversation between Allen Dulles and Raoul Aglion, sent to Murray by General Donovan (June 8, 1942).

it, was quite heartbroken by our failure to make a big thing of it. Writing to Secretary Hull in September 1942, he recalled his negotiations with Weygand and the expectations that had been attached to them:

"We hoped, counting on his proven anti-Nazi and anti-Axis sentiments, that he might succeed in developing in Africa an organization which would become an important element in combating the Axis, possibly leading to a resumption of hostilities by the French in that area. That ultimate hope has not yet been achieved, but we did benefit substantially by the sturdy resistance which Weygand offered to the Axis during many long months to November 1941, when, a victim of political combination and Axis pressure, he was cashiered." [15]

And now, as a result of Laval's return to power, we had to decide whether the accord should be scrapped completely or whether we should continue it in some form or other. We knew that Darlan had been evading past promises and that the French had allowed supplies to go forward to the German forces in Libya. We had struggled in vain to get assurances that we knew in advance would be next to worthless. Furthermore, we knew that the Axis was securing large quantities of strategic materials from North Africa by way of France and that, possibly, some of the oil that we were supplying was being used to fuel the ships that carried these materials to Marseille. To be sure, it was not a very edifying or encouraging picture. And yet the fact remained that we still had twelve control officers in North Africa and that these officers, if they did nothing more, were serving as valuable agents in what might soon be hostile territory. The official records are full of the reports of these men, who furnished systematic intelligence not only to the American authorities, but also to the British. Thanks to them, we at least knew what conditions were like in that area. We knew what supplies were going to France and what ships were carrying them from what ports. But beyond that our agents managed to create a measure of

[15] Murphy to Hull (September 26, 1942).

goodwill and succeeded in forwarding a great deal of military intelligence, order of battle information, aviation codes, port studies, and so on. In June 1942, for example, our vice-consuls at Oran sent in five long reports. One of these dealt with electric generating plants, with details as to capacities, localities served, types of current, voltage, frequencies, and so forth. Another furnished a complete list of hospitals. A third was a study of cold-storage and ice plants, while the others analyzed wheat-storage capacities, grist mills, and the like. Taken by itself, no one of these numerous reports may have been world-shaking. But in the aggregate they made an impressive body of up-to-date intelligence.

No wonder, then, that in May 1942 Murray, one of the originators of the Economic Accord, wrote a memorandum to Berle urging its continuance, if only in order to keep the control officers at their posts:

"Their continued functioning is perhaps the most important single advantage to be derived by the United States from resuming shipments to North Africa." They have supplied "the most valuable kind of information, including military, naval and economic data of great interest not only to this Department, but to the War Department and the British Government." [16]

That this was no exaggeration was shown by the fact that Murphy sent a letter from Wyndham White enclosing a statement from the British services testifying to the value of the information received, while the American Joint Intelligence Committee also went on record in favor of the system. The control officers, according to the J.I.C. report, were "of very substantial value." If they were discontinued, "there would be virtually a blackout of an entire and crucial region." [17]

In order to strengthen its position in North Africa, the Department requested letters from General Donovan, the Coordinator of Information, and from Secretary of War Stim-

[16] Memorandum of May 4, 1942 (*North African Economic Memoranda*, III, No. 344).

[17] Murphy's letter, April 30, 1942, and Berle's memorandum, May 4, 1942 (ibid., III, Nos. 347, 350).

son. General Donovan urged the resumption of shipments for propaganda purposes, if for no others:

"We believe this to be of incalculable importance to the war effort. It is needed to combat strong and increasing German propaganda pressure in that area, to keep critical materials out of German hands, to win friends among the French and Moorish populations, with special reference to French naval personnel stationed there." [18]

Stimson, quite naturally, stressed the military aspect, pointing out that the goodwill of North Africa might become of importance later and that the control officers were a valuable source of information: "It is believed advisable for military reasons to continue the small shipments contemplated and to maintain control officers therewith in North-West Africa." [19]

On the strength of these testimonials Secretary Hull on June 12, 1942 announced that shipments would be resumed. But no very extensive program was envisaged. The Board of Economic Warfare agreed only to ship 5,000 tons of sugar, 1,200 tons of cotton goods, 400 tons of tobacco, 3,000 tons of coal, 1,500 tons of kerosene, and a quantity of green tea, all of which could be carried in two bottoms.

To men like Murphy and Colonel Eddy the whole thing from the beginning had been miserly. Writing to Wyndham White, Murphy remarked:

"I am disappointed over the limited success of the program. I feel that we missed the boat during the Weygand regime. If the American program had worked out successfully in a really important way, I think his position would have been almost invulnerable. The results he attained under it, however, were so small that it became a weapon in the hands of his adversaries, who said it was nothing but a Trojan horse. It did, however, succeed in bolstering Weygand's own resistance to the Axis in this area over a period of many months."

[18] Donovan to Hull (May 28, 1942) in ibid., III, No. 361; comment by Henry S. Villard.
[19] Stimson to Hull (June 1, 1942) in ibid., III, No. 362 D.

Murphy felt that a real effort should have been made to render North Africa substantially self-sufficient. As it was, all we had done was to dangle a carrot before a donkey.[20] Colonel Eddy took much the same view and urged that we should really come to grips with the problem:

"He believes," wrote Paul H. Alling to Dean Acheson, "that we should now embark on a bold program of supply to North Africa, without too much bargaining as to details or as to formal conditions to be fulfilled by the French." [21]

The political officers of the Department of State were eager to go forward and even to extend the agreement to West Africa, so as to introduce control officers in that area also. Here again the Joint Intelligence Committee gave unanimous support.[22] But the obstacles in the way of real implementation of the program appeared to be hardly less than insuperable. In the Department itself the Office of the Economic Adviser continued to object and obstruct. At the same time both the British Ministry of Economic Warfare and the American Board of Economic Warfare fought valiantly and beclouded the issue. As Murphy remarked bitterly: "We have permitted ourselves throughout to be victimized by all sorts of vague suspicions and doubts leading to indecision." [23]

The fundamental trouble was that the agencies of economic warfare looked at the problem in a strictly professional way. While a British expert was declaring: "It is to the advantage of the United Nations to keep these territories poor," his American colleague echoed him and declared that it would be to our advantage to "disorganize as far as possible the transportation system in French North Africa." [24] All they could see was that North Africa was a source of important raw materials for the Axis, and that anything we might send would

[20] Murphy to White, May 12, 1942, in ibid., III, No. 350.
[21] Alling to Acheson, June 23, 1942, in ibid., III, No. 375.
[22] *North African Economic Memoranda*, III, Nos. 378, 382, 383.
[23] Murphy to Alling, July 19, 1942, in ibid., III, No. 393 A.
[24] Minutes of the North African Committee, July 22, 1942 (ibid., III, No. 395 E).

only make it easier for the French to drain off what was already there. Economically the argument was undoubtedly sound. Germany was dependent on North Africa for phosphate fertilizer. She relied on French Morocco for about sixty per cent of her essential supply of cobalt, and badly needed the high-grade, non-phosphoric North African iron ore. Huge quantities of these materials went to Marseille during 1941, and of these imports into France a large part found its way into Axis hands. Some of the ships that carried the cargoes to France then made return trips to Tunisia loaded with military supplies for Rommel's Libyan armies. No doubt North Africa was a major hole in the British blockade.[25]

Standing on these undisputed facts, the Ministry of Economic Warfare had long been pressing for a campaign of preclusive buying. The Axis was to be deprived of strategic materials from North Africa in return for any supplies we might send to that area.[26] The Board of Economic Warfare at once fell in with this scheme. Although the President himself had issued instructions on July 29 that the economic program should be carried out without further interruption or delay, the whole business came to hinge on the preclusive buying plan. The Board of Economic Warfare rather unrealistically demanded that thirty Allied purchasing agents be sent to North Africa to compete with the Axis agents. Thereby it was hoped that exports to the Axis might be reduced by fifty per cent.[27]

This particular matter was compromised by a joint grand conference between State Department and B.E.W. officials, presided over by Admiral Leahy, who had been appointed Chief of Staff to the Commander-in-Chief and presiding officer of the Joint Chiefs of Staff organization. Admiral Leahy inter-

---

[25] Memorandum by Finletter, August 3, 1942 (ibid., III, No. 410 A); B.E.W. Blockade and Supply Branch Report: *The Economic Contribution of French North Africa to the Axis* (September 12, 1942).

[26] *North African Economic Memoranda*, III, Nos. 322, 324 (March 19, 27, 1942).

[27] Finletter Memorandum, August 3, 1942 (ibid., III, No. 410 A).

preted the President's wishes and made it clear that the program should be put into effect without delay, the emphasis to be placed on speed and regularity rather than on quantity of shipments. No *quid pro quos* in the form of demands that the French traffic with Axis countries should be cut down were to be asked for, unless a much more extensive program were later to be approved.[28] Representatives of B.E.W. at once raised objections and began to quibble over details. Finally the meeting broke up in an almost disorderly way when Admiral Leahy rose and walked out. The bickering went on without respite, until the whole problem became an issue of interagency warfare. The French purchasing mission could not get on with B.E.W., while the Department of State had difficulties over every item in negotiation not only with B.E.W. but with the Treasury over such matters as the unblocking of funds. The whole business makes one of the dreariest chronicles imaginable, the details of which may mercifully be spared the reader. In the official records there are literally hundreds of documents dealing with every minute phase and every painful step. Surely no good purpose could be served by rehearsing all the detail, and no effort will be made to do more than sketch the main features of the story.[29]

In one of the State Department memoranda it was suggested that B.E.W. was trying to undermine the whole supply program in order to substitute therefor a plan for the preclusive buying of strategic materials. B.E.W., it was pointed out, seemed to want to get control of the whole North African economic problem.[30] These remarks serve to highlight one of the real difficulties in the situation. By the creation of the Board of Economic Warfare the Department of State had been deprived of one of the most effective weapons of modern diplomacy: namely, economic pressure, an instrument of

[28] B.E.W.: *The Economic Contribution of French North Africa to the Axis*, p. 24, record of the meeting of August 3, 1942.
[29] *North African Economic Memoranda, passim*; comments by Henry S. Villard and Cass Canfield.
[30] Memorandum by Alling (August 20, 1942), in ibid., III, No. 432.

action over which it was bound to try to regain control. In short, there was a fundamental conflict of jurisdiction that it was impossible to conjure away. In Britain the Ministry of Economic Warfare was closely tied to the Foreign Office, and the latter had the ultimate power of decision; but in Washington the situation was quite different. The Department of State could not enforce its policy against an independent agency that threatened to usurp a vital field of policy.

Under the circumstances it is altogether likely that insufficient guidance was given the B.E.W. with regard to the ultimate objectives of American policy. To be sure, one might think that by August 1942 almost any high official in an American war agency should have had an inkling of our intentions with respect to North Africa and should have been able to deduce for himself the relative importance of political or military factors as against the purely economic. But this does not appear to have been so with the B.E.W., which persisted in its errors till the very end.

This is the more remarkable in view of the fact that Admiral Leahy acted as mediator and in conferences with the parties to the dispute made the issue so plain that one who ran might read. A striking example of this was his discussion with Villard of the Department of State and with the chief of the blockade and supply branch of B.E.W. on September 7, 1942. On this occasion Admiral Leahy requested that the French in North Africa be sent whatever they needed—agricultural spare parts, kerosene, or anything else—without reference to assurances and returns:

"He said," reads the record, "that the objective of sending supplies to North Africa at this time was to please the French in every possible way and to remove any sources of irritation. In two or three months," he continued, "we may want to send everything we have to French North Africa, or, on the other hand, we may wish to send nothing at all. At the moment, however, it is our objective to help the population of French North Africa and induce the people to think that we are their friends.

. . . If a good feeling could be induced in French North Africa at this time, it might save thousands of American lives, which might otherwise be lost through delays and quibbling over small amounts of economic supplies that could not change the course of the war. Even at the risk of driblets of these supplies reaching the enemy, Admiral Leahy believed that we should proceed as rapidly as possible with getting supplies to the French which they needed. . . . Admiral Leahy repeated again the urgent necessity of pleasing and placating the French in every way possible at this time." [31]

It would be hard to imagine more plain and pointed talk than this, yet it appears to have left the B.E.W. unenlightened and unregenerate. At one after another of the weekly meetings of the North African committee the bickering continued, even though Murphy was himself present at one session and explained in detail what he thought ought to be done. On September 18 Villard, of the Department, again appealed to Admiral Leahy, and was told by Commander Freesman, the admiral's aide, that the attitude of the B.E.W. appeared altogether incomprehensible:

"He said the entire question was one of broad policy and that economic warfare considerations of a technical nature should not stand in the way of our attempts to induce a feeling of good will on the part of the North African population."

Admiral Leahy, he added, supported Murphy's recommendations as to what should be sent. Indeed, Admiral Leahy himself reiterated his stand to Canfield of the B.E.W.[32]

But nothing seemed to be of much avail. On October 1 one of the B.E.W. representatives, who had emerged as the *bête noire* of the entire program, was objecting to the shipment of two hundred tons of used clothing and two thousand tons of coal, as well as of spare parts for commercial planes and a hundred typewriters. This incident was fairly indicative of

[31] *North African Economic Memoranda*, III, No. 447.
[32] Ibid., III, Nos. 450, 459 A, 461, 462.

the level to which the discussion had sunk. All prospects of healthy co-operation had come to an end, and finally Berle felt obliged to take up the matter with Vice President Wallace, the titular head of the B.E.W. In Berle's own words:

"I went to see the Vice President this morning regarding the difficulties which the Department has been having with the Board of Economic Warfare in connection with the North African Agreement. Mr. Wallace said that he understood the situation perfectly. There was certain information available to him and probably available to the Department which had not been, and could not be, divulged to either Milo Perkins or to the men lower down."

He had already spoken to Perkins, he said, though it is hard to see why this should still have been necessary.[33] Even this conversation did not really break the log-jam, and even though the last meetings of the committee were fairly harmonious, not much headway was made with the program.

By this time we had reached the eve of the invasion, which automatically ended all dispute about the Economic Accord. But before leaving this topic reference may fittingly be made to one closing episode because it reflects all the antagonism and distrust that had been engendered over the preceding months. On November 10 Murray and Villard of the Department had a conversation with General Hull of the Operations Division of the War Department. In the course of this conversation General Hull expressed his regrets that two French ships, which had been trying to load at New Orleans since August, had not reached Casablanca a week or two before the invasion. "He said that if the ships had reached Casablanca in time, it was possible that they would have been an important factor in lessening the resistance encountered in Morocco by our forces, and consequently in reducing the unfortunate loss of life."[34] This was a startling statement, which seemed

[33] Ibid., IV, No. 497A. Berle's visit to Wallace resulted directly from protests of B.E.W. against unilateral discussions between State Department officials and Admiral Leahy (comments by Henry S. Villard).
[34] Ibid., IV, No. 517.

to tie the economic program right in with military operations. The B.E.W. later claimed that the delay in the shipments was due to failure of the French to complete the cargo, and furthermore that the ships could not leave the United States until two other ships had sailed from Casablanca.[35] Like almost everything else about the program, these claims were open to debate.

So high had feeling risen, however, that Berle, without examining further into the circumstances, on November 12 read to the North African Committee parts of the record of General Hull's remarks. Despite Berle's disclaimer, the B.E.W. representative chose to take this as direct criticism of his agency. Both the Department of State and the B.E.W. referred the matter once more to General Hull, who promptly toned down his original statement. To Villard he said on the telephone

"that the arrival of the vessels at Casablanca before the commencement of military operations might have had an important effect on the reception of our troops and on the attitude of the civil population. Whether the arrival of the ships would have had an effect on the French Army and Navy and thus lessen the resistance to our forces was not so certain." [36]

When confronted by officials from B.E.W., he retreated even farther:

"The General stated that in his opinion it could not be said that American lives had been lost because two ships failed to arrive before the invasion took place. In fact, the General stated that he did not believe the arrival of the ships prior to the invasion would have had any effect upon the military decisions taken by Generals Noguès and Michelier. It was recognized that their decisions would be followed by the French armed forces, and the degree

[35] B.E.W. record of conversation (November 18, 1942) between General Hull on the one hand and Canfield, Fleming, and Colonel MacDonald of B.E.W. on the other.
[36] *North African Economic Memoranda*, IV, Nos. 523, 524, 525.

of resistance actually encountered corresponded very closely to what the Chiefs of Staff had expected." [37]

And so the Economic Accord ended on a very sour note. As an economic policy it had never amounted to much, since we never got beyond the stage of dangling a carrot before the donkey, and at all times mention of the program had been a signal for argument, dispute, and recrimination. None the less, it was the entering wedge for our North African policy and proved itself handsomely as a device for getting intelligence. Not only that, it gave us an opportunity far beyond anyone's dreams for establishing contact with dissident groups in North Africa and thereby preparing the ground for the invasion that was to come in November 1942. We may therefore leave the depressing story of wrangling over the economic aspects and return to our narrative of the subversive activity carried on by Murphy, Colonel Eddy and their associates.

Our account of the dramatic doings of these men was brought down, in the preceding chapter, to about April 21, when the Joint Chiefs of Staff decided against the supply of arms to the French leaders, though they approved of the financial support that it was proposed to give them. At what time Murphy learned of this decision it is impossible to say, for he continued to send messages for some weeks beseeching the Department to act:

"My impatience will be appreciated," he cabled on April 18, "when you consider that there is a possibility of throwing French officers and non-commissioned officers and several hundred thousand trained men into the fight on the side of the Allies. If this is at all possible, I cannot urge you too strongly to enable me to give these people some immediate encouragement. This is an op-

[37] B.E.W. record of conversation between General Hull, Cass Canfield, H. K. Fleming and Colonel MacDonald (November 18, 1942). Despite the request of B.E.W., this record, sent at once to the State Department, was not included in the minutes of the North African Committee on the plea that Berle's remarks had been inaccurately reported. (Comments by Villard.) Another explanatory memorandum from B.E.W. may be found in *North African Economic Memoranda*, IV, No. 529.

portunity we should take at the time, I am convinced. It may be unfair to mention it, I know, but practically a year has elapsed without to my knowledge the offer as a practical encouragement of as much as a cap pistol to our friends in this area." [38]

Or again on May 3:

"I am informed by the group described in my March 14 that they may be obliged to abandon the matter unless we are prepared to give them some indication of our intentions. They state further that our long continued reticence is arousing suspicions on the part of the friendliest elements regarding our motives and they have returned to me the funds advanced by Coordinator of Information. I fear we cannot indefinitely hold them in a state of suspense, though we have done our best to encourage and hearten these people." [39]

And finally on May 6:

"I am informed by the leaders of the group that they are in contact with an Allied intelligence agent and, according to him, London is sending on May 20 a military expert to meet a representative of the group.

"As an example of what should not happen in French North Africa, the Madagascar operation has put the group in a state of effervescence. They urge that the technique of ultimata and debarkation without a prior accord with someone controlling an effective organization who is inside the country is costly and may prove disastrous in this area, and so they continue to plead for our cooperation in organizing an effective *coup d'état* in advance of any military intervention. . . . The group's earnestness of purpose and their potential usefulness impresses me very much." [40]

As a matter of fact, the patriot group was on the very verge of despair. It was feared that the British action in Madagascar might precipitate a German move on Tunisia, for which eventuality the Vichy orders were to make no resistance unless ordered to do so.[41] A new appeal was therefore addressed to

[38] Tel. (April 18, 1942) Murphy to Hull.
[39] Tel. (May 3, 1942) Murphy to Hull. Also Murphy to Eddy, May 4, 1942 (OSS Files).
[40] Tel. (May 6, 1942) Murphy to Hull.
[41] Tel. (May 6, 1942) Murphy to Hull.

Murphy and May 20 was set as the last day for receipt of an American answer. If the reply were negative, all attempts at further co-operation were to be abandoned. At the same time the British secret intelligence was informed that British aid would be accepted if forthcoming.[42]

That the British were much more ready to act at this time than the Americans is certainly true. Lord Gort, at Gibraltar, was willing and ready to build up supplies for the French leaders, while the British SOE was also eager to exploit the possibilities of the situation. In this connection Colonel Eddy went to London early in May, where he was joined by Colonel Solborg, the American assistant military attaché in Lisbon, whose real position was chief of special operations under General Donovan's office. Of the details of the discussions in London there appears to be but little record. It is clear, however, that the British SOE was anxious to pursue a more aggressive policy, and that it was agreed between British officials and Colonel Eddy to collect stores at Gibraltar and to assign six small boats to transport these stores to Algeria. The British chiefs of staff approved this program and issued a directive to this effect.[43]

Without a doubt the British were at this time ready to take over the entire operation. Colonel Eddy, on a brief visit to Tangier before going on to Washington, reported unenthusiastically that the War Office was planning to send a military expert to confer with the French leaders. He added that he feared the French group would disintegrate, in view of the vigorous purge that was being conducted by Laval's appointees and by Doriot's ruthless Parti Populaire Français. "With the hope of the French fading, I propose to approach Moorish leaders in Spanish Morocco regarding future sabotage of the Axis," he concluded gloomily.[44]

Murphy, too, seems to have been confused in his feelings. On May 22 he cabled to Colonel Eddy saying that Robin

[42] G. Lemaigre-Dubreuil: *France's Re-entry into the War*, etc.
[43] OSS Files (May 12, 1942).
[44] Tels. from Eddy (May 15, 25, 1942).

Hood (i.e., Colonel Van Hecke) had come around splendidly and had requested funds, which a short time before he had declined. Five hundred thousand francs had therefore been made available to him. On the other hand the British were going ahead with much more extensive plans: "On approximately June 1 he [Colonel Van Hecke] possibly at Casablanca, has scheduled a meeting with Uncle Charlie [i.e. d'Astier de la Vigerie] or another and British representative; furthermore, he said that communications are still being conducted and continued with the British." [45]

Murphy was fully empowered to disburse to the French leaders money which came from the Coordinator of Information. For the moment there was nothing more to be done, so Colonel Eddy proceeded to Washington, where he stayed through June. During that time he gave testimony before the Joint Chiefs of Staff, before General Patton, Admiral Cook, and other officers regarding the possibilities of the North African situation and concerning topographic aspects of the terrain. In a rather detailed memorandum prepared at this time he described the state of the French resistance and the forces that might be at the disposal of the Allied nations. He recalled that when he had left for Tangier in January 1942, he had been told that it might be not more than three months before the Axis powers, if not the United Nations, began operations in this area:

"My instructions were 1) to establish listening posts and sources of intelligence which could be left behind if the Americans should be excluded from the area, and 2) to prepare and to supply groups which would resist the Axis by sabotage, guerrilla warfare and organized armed resistance."

Much had been accomplished in a few months, for which the colonel gave Murphy the chief credit. Intelligence had been greatly expanded, among the French, the Poles, and the Spanish Republicans. "We are particularly fortunate in Algeria in having the cooperation of men who hold high official

[45] Tel. May 22, 1942, from Murphy to Eddy (OSS Files).

positions in the French diplomatic and military services." Furthermore, a secret radio chain had been constructed and was in operation: Tangier (code name, *Midway*), Casablanca (*Lincoln*), Tunis (*Pilgrim*), Algiers (*Yankee*), and Oran (*Franklin*) were all linked up: "Tunis has transmitted valuable intelligence to Malta (*Columbus*) regarding the departure and course of ships carrying war materials to the Axis in Libya." As for the resistance groups, Colonel Eddy claimed that we controlled about 5,000 Europeans in Morocco (mostly demobilized French army officers and men), and through the native chiefs about 10,000 native irregulars. But the heart of the movement was in Algeria: "The organization had the finest kind of leadership in a separatist movement led by French patriots, some of whom are Royalists." Their preparations were complete and they had full control of communications. Furthermore, they commanded 10,000 Europeans, 10,000 native irregulars, and 1,500 young Frenchmen in the Chantiers de la Jeunesse. The organization could hold the province of Oran for a week without outside help. But the leaders were being replaced at an alarming rate by Laval's henchmen, and the whole movement was disintegrating. The remainder were turning to the British for the supplies that we had refused them. Finally, as to Tunisia, there was no organized military resistance there, but there were "many sabotage and guerrilla groups." [46]

While Colonel Eddy was doing his utmost to call attention to the potentialities of resistance to the Germans and of aid from the French in North Africa, an incident occurred within the Office of the Coordinator of Information (Office of Strategic Services after June 13, 1942) that was to have unfortunate effects on the subsequent course of events. This incident turned upon the activities of Colonel Solborg, who, it will be recalled, was chief of special operations under General Donovan, though officially he functioned as assistant military at-

[46] OSS Files: memorandum: Eddy to Donovan (June 9, 1942). Conversation with Eddy (December 8, 1943); also memorandum on *Organization of Resistance Groups* (May 12, 1942), and the memoranda prepared by David King (June 22, July 25, 1942).

taché at Lisbon. Colonel Solborg had traveled widely in North and West Africa and had written a memorandum on the situation there in the autumn of 1941 that highlighted a number of the resistance leaders and called attention to the prospects in that region. Perhaps because of his connection with North Africa, the State Department had feared that if he returned there his life might be in danger and the entire American position might be compromised.[47] Consequently he had been sent to Lisbon, whence he more or less directed the activities of Colonel Eddy and served as co-ordinator of American plans with those of the British.

Apparently Colonel Solborg became impatient and decided to proceed on his own initiative to get the operation into swing. His great idea was that a prominent leader must be found for the French resistance movement in North Africa and that only then would the United States government give the movement full backing. It may be recalled that this idea had been prominent also in the mind of Murphy and that for a long time hopes had been pinned on General Weygand. The general had flatly rejected advances made by President Roosevelt himself in January 1942 and had thereby ruled himself out. But now a new star had appeared on the horizon in the shape of General Henri Giraud, an impressive and able military man who had the rare distinction of having been captured by the Germans and having escaped during both the first and the second World Wars. On April 17, 1942 he had made a dramatic break from the castle of Königstein and, after successfully evading the German secret police for a week, had finally crossed into Switzerland and thence into France. On April 27 he arrived in Vichy and had lunch with Marshal Pétain. Laval did his utmost to induce him to return to captivity, but without success. Instead he stayed at Vichy and prepared for Pétain a long memorandum on the causes of France's defeat.[48]

[47] Memorandum of Donovan to Colonel Goodfellow (March 23, 1942).
[48] A copy of this memorandum is in the Department of State and considerable portions of it have been published in the press.

General Giraud held much the same views as Pétain. He explained France's downfall chiefly on moral grounds and favored an authoritarian regime as the only hope for the future. But Giraud did not pose as a politician. He was a soldier first and foremost and an irreconcilable opponent of France's traditional enemy. He is said to have persuaded Pétain that the Germans could not win, and he appears to have devoted himself, from the very moment of his return to France, to laying plans for resistance and liberation.[49]

Naturally the arrival of so eminent a patriot and soldier caused a stir of excitement in France. S. Pinckney Tuck, our chargé d'affaires at Vichy, reported at once:

"A number of well-informed government officials who have heretofore mentioned Weygand as the possible leader of such a movement [against the Germans], now express the thought that Giraud, who is considered to have both the requisite qualities of leadership and the necessary prestige both with the Army and civilians, might possibly be the man for the job." [50]

No less attention was aroused elsewhere by Giraud's spectacular appearance. As soon as his arrival in Vichy was known, a prominent British statesman spoke about it to Matthews: "He said that the Prime Minister seems to have a feeling that Giraud and Pétain may fly over to North Africa and start a resistance movement." He himself doubted whether Pétain would go back on his decision of 1940 not to leave Metropolitan France. He had therefore suggested to Churchill that it would be better to get Giraud to England. "If we could get him here, we would have a real leader for the Free French government," he told Matthews.[51]

While all these ideas were hatching, Colonel Solborg too saw the possibilities. In May he therefore hurried off to London, where he conferred with de Gaulle and other French leaders. He reported adversely to General Donovan on de

[49] Many details may be found in G. Ward Price: *Giraud and the African Scene* (New York, 1944).
[50] Tel. (May 2, 1942) from Tuck.
[51] Tel. (April 29, 1942) from Matthews.

Gaulle himself, but said that he had sounded out de Gaulle regarding Giraud and had found that the Free French leader was enthusiastic. Giraud, de Gaulle was reported as saying, was one man under whom he himself could work.[52] This seems indeed to have been de Gaulle's attitude at the time. At a press conference on May 27, 1942 he spoke of Giraud in the following terms:

"I, like the whole French Army, have the highest esteem and admiration for General Giraud. Unfortunately I fear that General Giraud is at present unable to do anything, for he has put himself under the control, discipline and surveillance of Vichy. But I am personally sure that he is resolved to do what he can to enable France to do her duty in this war and resume the struggle. In fact, I have personal assurances of this." [53]

In a word, then, General Giraud seemed acceptable to everyone. Clearly he was the man of the future. Possibly Weygand recognized this and bethought himself of his own lost opportunities. Though it has no bearing on the further development of affairs, it may be worth while, as a piquant detail, to quote here a message that Weygand sent on to Tuck early in June. In this he argued that his failure to respond to President Roosevelt's advances was due to his loyalty to Pétain. But now, he went on, he had become disgusted by the treatment that Vichy had meted out to him:

"The General's feelings toward the Marshal," reported Tuck, "which were never at any time really friendly, have greatly changed and he now holds the Chief of State in contempt."

The general also gave his views on any projected action by the United States:

"General Weygand is of the opinion that any such military intervention should be effected in *continental* France, preferably in the occupied zone, and that it should be brought off at the moment we are ready—in fact, the quicker the better."

[52] Conversation with Colonel Goodfellow (August 14, 1943).
[53] Tel. (May 29, 1942) from Matthews.

The American forces, he urged, should bring arms and munitions to supply French volunteers. "General Weygand is *strongly opposed* to the idea of a military landing anywhere in North Africa for the following reasons: 1) The administrative and military structure of North Africa had deteriorated since his own departure in November 1941; 2) The morale of many French troops in North Africa was poor and therefore an American landing might be met with apathy if not hostility; 3) The possibility of the French fighting against the Americans must be avoided at all costs; 4) Civilian morale in North Africa was also bad; 5) The higher officials were preoccupied with petty jealousies and would be unable to work in the best interests of France." [54]

But to return to Colonel Solborg. According to his own account, it was decided during his stay in London that a meeting should be held between the French military leaders and American delegates to discuss ways and means of co-operating in North Africa and "to prepare the ground for an invitation to be issued to us by the French when the time comes for military intervention." This plan was cabled to General Donovan, who had some reservations. Colonel Solborg nevertheless went on to Africa, claiming later that he had authority from the War Department to do so.

Early in June Solborg crossed over to Tangier, where he consulted with J. R. Childs, the American chargé d'affaires. At Casablanca he met Murphy and Lemaigre-Dubreuil, one of the leaders of the Algiers resistance group. The latter was a close friend of General Giraud, whom he had just visited at Lyon. He had found that the general had long planned a resistance movement and was quite ready to become the leader of a war of revenge. In Lemaigre's words

"General Giraud's plan of action was a broad one. It consisted of launching a number of synchronized operations at a time when German enfeeblement was sufficiently far advanced: Re-entry of

[54] Tel. (June 5, 1942) from Tuck. If Weygand was still under consideration at this time, his objections to a North African operation certainly put the quietus on any hopes that may have been placed upon him.

France into the war, in the form of an offensive action of the army of France itself under the armistice, combined with a rising in the Occupied Zone and seizure of the depots under control. Direct support of the American landing corps on the Mediterranean coast, North Africa serving only as a base of operations; supplying of the Armistice Army of France itself with arms. Immediate support of the rearmed army of Africa. Extension of the rising of the Poles, Yugoslavs and Belgians."

Giraud planned all this for the spring of 1943, when the Germans would have suffered further attrition in Russia. The plan was an impressive one, but did not exactly suit Lemaigre and the North African conspirators. Lemaigre had argued with Giraud that open resistance in France would be impossible because of the presence of the German forces, but he had been unable to persuade Giraud to go to Africa at the very outset.[55]

Nevertheless, the North African patriots had enlisted Giraud in a vague way, and Lemaigre was therefore able to satisfy Colonel Solborg's demand for a "man." Solborg posed as an official representative of the United States government and went to Algiers with Murphy and Lemaigre for further conferences with the French leaders. Detailed plans were worked out for Solborg to take back to Washington, while Lemaigre was to get Giraud's approval of them. According to Solborg's account:

"The substance of the plan briefly is that the General would assume command of French forces in North Africa and would issue orders to receive our task force without opposition whenever the opportunity comes."[56]

Armed with this plan, Lemaigre set out for France during the second half of June. Being a very skillful manipulator, he stood well with both sides. By way of precaution he first went to Paris to sound out Laval. Murphy reported the substance of his conversations as follows:

[55] Lemaigre-Dubreuil: *France's Re-entry into the War*, etc.
[56] Solborg to Donovan, July 8, 11, 1942. Lemaigre's account.

"It is the opinion of our friend [i.e., Lemaigre] that the policy of concessions and obedience is only limited by the desire on the part of certain Germans to avoid a rupture between the United States and France. There is a belief in a German victory, and Laval, possibly to persuade himself that it is true, insists on it. The fear that he will be replaced by Doriot incites Laval to concessions and facilitates Marshal Pétain's agreement to these concessions." [57]

We may assume that Lemaigre found Laval unsuspecting; otherwise he would not have gone on to confer with Giraud at Lyon. The evidence on what passed between the two men is far from complete or clear. Apparently Giraud continued to be more interested in organizing resistance in France, supported by an American landing, than he was in any expedition to North Africa. Lemaigre seems to have persuaded him to entertain the second project as well as the first. In his recollections Lemaigre says simply that Giraud "confirmed his intention of preparing and carrying on the military operation in France at the same time as in Africa," the whole enterprise to be planned for the spring of 1943. On the other hand Lemaigre reported in somewhat greater detail to Murphy, who also got some indications from General Charles Mast, the chief of the 19th Army Corps at Algiers, whom Giraud named as his representative in North Africa. Reporting to Colonel Solborg, Murphy stated that Giraud hoped to become the pivot of resistance in Europe as well as in Africa:

"The group [in Algiers] is not informed whether circumstances will permit realization of a combined operation in Africa, France and certain other occupied territories. It is believed certain by our friend that military and political events may make an African operation essential at any moment. This explains why the interested principal [Giraud] is said to desire arrangements to insure his arrival here and has requested état major which he has established in North Africa to do whatever may be necessary in order that this area may be as well prepared as possible. It should be anticipated also that measures might be taken by the Govern-

[57] Lemaigre-Dubreuil, op. cit.

ment against the principal or against his assistants. Immediate action would under those circumstances be necessary. It is underscored by our friend that all plans would be subject to modification if Allied resistance in the Eastern Mediterranean should collapse."

And again:

"According to Mast, General Giraud is heart and soul for the resumption of hostilities against the Axis and will take command of the French forces either in France or North Africa. He believes that the action will start in North Africa."

Mast added that it was yet too early for staff talks, which might well be started in the autumn. Fourteen divisions could be counted on in North Africa.[58]

From such evidence as is here adduced we may, I think, conclude that while Giraud by no means gave up the idea of a Continental operation, he recognized that things might break at any time in North Africa or that action by Vichy might make it necessary for him to flee to North Africa. He therefore agreed to lead the North African movement, thinking of it, however, as only a part—in fact, a secondary part—of the larger and more ambitious project.

By the time Lemaigre returned from his mission to Giraud, Colonel Solborg was already on his way back to Washington, where he proposed to report in person both to General Donovan and to the Chief of Staff. On his arrival, however, he found that Donovan was infuriated by his failure to obey orders not to go to North Africa and that he would not even see him. Thereupon Solborg began a veritable bombardment of memoranda, partly to exculpate himself, partly to save the cause in which he was so deeply interested. These memoranda are of some interest for they give a broad picture of the entire transaction and add many related details of a rather startling nature. The argument ran like this: even if we could not then

[58] Tel. (July 8, 1942) from Murphy to Hull, enclosing his message to Solborg; also Murphy letter to Atherton (July 6, 1942).

think of sending a task force to North Africa, we should carry on staff talks with the French, if only to keep up their hopes:

"Contact has been established on the highest possible plane and the General in France has assumed command of preparation for a movement of insurrection and has agreed to invite our intervention when the opportune moment comes. It will be recalled that we have, on past occasions, repeatedly attempted to obtain just such a state of affairs from General Weygand without success. The General with whom I have been negotiating represents today the highest authority, overshadowing that of Weygand, De Gaulle and everybody else. He is a fighting general and a true and patriotic Frenchman. We should not let him down."

He then stressed the importance of Spain and Spanish Morocco—"the wide gaping flank." No expedition to Africa would be possible so long as this flank remained open. With the existing regime in Spain, it would be almost certain that Spain would attack, supported by German forces. But he had heard of plans for a change of government in Spain, to be engineered with the help of "all Spanish generals of note." All this was contemplated for August 1942. Since Giraud did not desire action in less than three months, everything would fit nicely together. Solborg further proposed that he himself should be named military attaché at Tangier to carry on staff talks at Casablanca. He urged that paramilitary supplies be made available to the French and that he should be allowed to co-operate with the appropriate British authorities. In conclusion Solborg stated categorically that he had made no promises to the French: "It is understood that the entire movement must be French and that our intervention could only take place at an express invitation from them." [59]

This long argument made but little impression on General Donovan, who suspected the accuracy of Solborg's report and raised numerous questions. Another, equally lengthy

---

[59] OSS Files: memorandum from Solborg to Colonel Preston Goodfellow (July 8, 1942).

memorandum still left him cold.[60] He dropped the colonel from the rolls of the Office of Strategic Services and refused to pursue the matter further. How justified this drastic action may have been need not be examined here. Solborg no doubt had been overeager and had taken too much upon himself. Possibly there was some exaggeration in his statement of the Algiers negotiations and plans. But the broad lines seem to have been clear enough and his reports are, in general, an accurate reflection of what was being hatched out by Murphy on the one hand and the French leaders on the other. Under the circumstances it was a pity that Solborg threw things out of gear by his independent proceedings.[61]

In the discussions carried on by Solborg and Murphy with the French leaders the idea constantly cropped up that the United States would ultimately take action in North Africa. In fact, that was the crux of all the plans that were drawn and of all the negotiations carried on with General Giraud. Actually there was no authority for such plans, for the decision to invade North Africa was not made until some weeks after the Algiers negotiations. In order to understand further developments, a few words about the genesis of the famous "Torch" operation will be in order.

The idea of an American operation against North Africa was one dear to President Roosevelt from an early date. The entire region was of obvious and vital interest to the United States and offered the possibility of establishing a base for operations on the continent of Europe. In December 1941 the President had sent Bullitt to North Africa and the Near East as ambassador-at-large, and Bullitt had sent back from Cairo a plan for invasion that had been worked out by General Catroux. Since Churchill was visiting in Washington at Christmas 1941, the two statesmen canvassed the possibility of action in North Africa in some detail and decided to go on with the scheme. Pretty extensive preparations appear to have been

---

[60] OSS Files: Donovan to Goodfellow (July 10) and Solborg to Donovan (July 11).
[61] I rely here on comments by Murphy, Eddy, and Matthews.

made, but in a matter of weeks the idea had to be abandoned, primarily because of the phenomenal advance of the Japanese in the southwest Pacific and the consequent necessity of diverting naval strength to that theater.

There were other considerations, however, that obstructed the North African plan. The Russians were in dire straits and their demand for the opening of a second front in Europe was becoming more and more insistent. The War Department regarded the Continental problem as far and away the more urgent and took the view throughout that American forces should be concentrated in Britain, partly to strengthen the British Isles against possible attack and partly to lay the foundation for a cross-Channel operation. In April 1942 General Marshall and Harry L. Hopkins went to London to initiate discussions of this problem. It was then decided to aim at the summer of 1943 as the date for a grand invasion of France, but to plan for a smaller, diversionary operation (*Sledge-hammer*) for the summer of 1942.[62]

There the matter stood when, in June 1942, Churchill came to Washington on a second visit. The discussions at that time were interrupted by the shocking news of the fall of Tobruk and of Rommel's advance on Egypt. In view of this serious threat it was decided in principle to give up the idea of a Continental operation in 1942 and to rush supplies to the Near East instead. The idea of operations in North Africa was quite naturally revived, for a campaign there would of necessity relieve the pressure on Egypt and would in a measure, at least, draw off German forces from Russia.

The President and the Prime Minister were in entire agreement on this program, but the War Department was still far from convinced. In the eyes of General Marshall the essential thing was still to get on with a cross-Channel attempt. Only so could the Soviet armies be given relief and the danger of Russia's defeat be exorcised. General Marshall, Admiral King,

[62] *Biennial Report of the Chief of Staff, July 1, 1941–June 30, 1943*, p. 18; *Biennial Report of the Chief of Staff, July 1, 1943–June 30, 1945*, p. 8; Churchill speech, November 10, 1942; comments by William C. Bullitt.

and Hopkins therefore went to London in July to arrive at agreement with their British colleagues. They fought hard for the original plan of invading the Continent by October, but found the British altogether opposed to opening a second front during 1942. The British were set on "getting on Rommel's tail" by landing in North Africa and cutting the German supply route through Tunisia. The American Chiefs of Staff were finally obliged to agree, albeit most reluctantly. To Churchill fell the unenviable task of going to Moscow and breaking the news to Stalin. Although the Soviet leader was naturally very disappointed, he was distinctly interested in the Allies' substitute plan, which had been christened "Torch." [63]

General Eisenhower was given definite instructions early in August to proceed with planning and at once came up against the political aspects of the problem. In the words of General Marshall:

"If our occupation of North Africa could be carried out without fatally embittering the French troops and authorities in that region, it would provide a setting for the reconstitution of the French army in preparation for its return in force to the homeland. The psychological effect of the conquest of North Africa would be tremendous." [64]

The political question was indeed beset by all kinds of difficulties. There was first the question of what attitude the French forces in North Africa would take; secondly, how would the Vichy government react? thirdly, should the Fighting French be brought into the picture? and, lastly, how should the danger of Spanish intervention and the possibility of German attack through Spain be dealt with?

With respect to the first question, Murphy's negotiations with the French leaders in North Africa had at least provided a starting-point. We shall have to revert to this aspect of the matter later. As for the Vichy government, there was little if

[63] *Biennial Reports* of the Chief of Staff, as cited above, and Captain Harry C. Butcher's diaries: *My Three Years with Eisenhower* (New York, 1946), entries for July 10, 19, 22, 24, 31, 1942.
[64] *Biennial Report, July 1, 1941–June 30, 1943*, p. 18.

any hope of concurrence or assistance. It was regarded from the outset as practically certain that the Germans would at once occupy the whole of France to prevent a landing in the south and would seize the French fleet at Toulon. Furthermore, it was recognized as all too possible that the Nazis would make a rush through Spain in an effort to cut our communications through the Strait of Gibraltar. But these were dangers that had to be faced and military plans had to be framed to provide against them. There remained the problem of de Gaulle and Fighting French, to which we must advert in at least a summary way.[65]

From the very beginning President Roosevelt took the initiative in all political decisions. It was his view that the operation should be staged at the earliest possible moment to minimize the danger of leakage from French sources. He held further that the invasion should be a predominantly American affair and that the United States should manage the political aspects. His correspondence with Churchill is very instructive on these matters. On August 30 he cabled the Prime Minister:

"I feel very strongly that the initial attacks must be made by an exclusively American ground force, supported by your naval and transport and air units. The operation should be undertaken on the assumption that the French will offer less resistance to us than they will to the British. I would even go so far as to say I am reasonably sure a simultaneous landing by British and Americans would result in full resistance by all French in Africa, whereas an initial American landing without British ground forces offers a real chance that there would be no French resistance or only a token resistance."

To this Churchill replied (September 1):

"We could not contest your wish if you so desire it to take upon the United States the whole burden, political and military, of the landings. Like you, I assign immense importance to the political aspect. I do not know what information you have of the

---

[65] *Biennial Report of the Chief of Staff, July 1, 1941–June 30, 1943,* p. 20; *Report of the Commanding General,* February 20, 1943; Butcher: *My Three Years with Eisenhower,* entry for August 22, 1942.

mood and temper of Vichy and North Africa, but of course if you can get ashore at the necessary points without fighting or only token resistance, that is best of all. We cannot tell what are the chances of this."

The President thereupon summarized the situation as he saw it (September 2):

"Our latest and best information from North Africa is as follows: A) An American expedition led in all three phases by American officers will meet little resistance from the French army in Africa. On the other hand, a British commanded attack in any phase or with De Gaullist cooperation would meet determined resistance. B) Maintenance of the French civil government is essential to friendly relations, and I have several experienced civilians who would be persona grata to accompany the landings and be charged with getting French civil cooperation. C) I am willing to risk explanation of British troops in Algiers by telling the French that they are not intended to remain in French territory but that their object is primarily to march into Axis-held Tripoli from the rear. Because of this information I consider it vital that sole responsibility be placed with Americans for relations with French military and civil authorities in Africa. As you and I decided long ago, we were to handle the French in North Africa, while you were to handle the situation in Spain." [66]

It was on the basis of these considerations that the staff plan was worked out and approved on September 5. In the sequel it proved impossible to adhere to it and British ground forces had to be employed to a certain extent. Nevertheless the principle stood and was recognized in the discussions with the French.

And now for the question of Gaullist co-operation or participation. This had been ruled out from the beginning by common consent of the President and the Prime Minister. The reasons for the decision were two. In the first place, the patriot leaders in Algiers were all men appointed by Vichy, men who, though violently anti-German, were conservative, authoritarian, or even royalist in their political views. Although a

[66] Roosevelt Records.

number of them desired and hoped for an eventual agreement with the Fighting French, they were flatly opposed to having either the British or the Gaullists take any part in the operation. Both at Dakar and in Syria the British had employed Frenchmen to fight Frenchmen. These incidents had left a very bad and almost indelible impression. The French in North Africa were determined to oppose any repetition of this situation, and there can be no doubt that the use of Fighting French forces would have led to civil war.

Then there was the added problem of security if de Gaulle were even informed of the projected operation. For this if for no other reason it was felt that the Fighting French must be excluded from the plan. In a draft letter to Churchill the President stated (September 16): "I consider it essential that De Gaulle be kept out of the picture and be permitted to have no information whatever, regardless of how irritated and irritating he may become." On the eve of the invasion the British Prime Minister suggested that he tell de Gaulle about the invasion one day before the operation was to start, explaining that it was an American affair and a military secret. But the President would not agree even to that. He wrote to Churchill (November 5):

"I am very apprehensive in regard to the adverse effect that any introduction of De Gaulle into the invasion situation would have on our promising efforts to attach a large part of the French African forces to our expedition. Therefore I consider it inadvisable for you to give De Gaulle any information in regard to the invasion until subsequent to a successful landing. You would then inform him that the American command of an American expedition with my approval insisted on complete secrecy as a necessary safety precaution."

The Prime Minister could not dissent from this position, and actually de Gaulle was not informed officially until the operation was already under way.[67]

[67] Roosevelt Records; also memorandum by Murphy: *Elements for Consideration in the French North African Situation* (September 4, 1942); Felix Cole: *Memorandum on North Africa* (January 26, 1943); comments by Matthews.

The exclusion of de Gaulle and the Fighting French from the North African venture was unavoidable for practical reasons. Yet it was bound to create tension and unpleasantness later. President Roosevelt was quite aware of this aspect of the problem and for that reason suggested to the British the possibility of his inviting General de Gaulle to pay a visit to Washington. But neither Eden nor Ambassador Winant thought the time an appropriate one. The British Foreign Minister commented (September 17) as follows on the subject:

"The President's object is presumably to keep relations between the United States and De Gaulle steady during preparations and execution of the invasion of North Africa. It would, however, take more than a contingent invitation to Washington to keep the General quiet if he got wind of what is afoot. Once the invasion starts we must face a major crisis in relations between both our Governments and De Gaulle. The whole Fighting French movement will bitterly resent being kept out of the operation and of subsequent administration of the country. . . ."

Winant pointed out the additional consideration that if de Gaulle were invited to Washington the impression made on the French leaders in North Africa might be very bad. So the matter was dropped for the moment, on the understanding, however, that after the invasion the general might be asked to come over.[68]

The reason why de Gaulle had to be so seriously considered in this connection was that during the summer he had made marked progress in securing for himself the leadership of the French underground resistance movements. Opposition to the Vichy government had grown apace after Laval's return to power, and the new German policy of labor conscription was already driving large numbers of Frenchmen into active resistance organizations. Since the beginning of the year 1942 both the British and the Fighting French were in contact with the leaders of the resistance and had already begun the work

[68] Roosevelt Records.

of supplying the movement. By June 1942 a French intelligence officer could report that while many Frenchmen still
believed in Marshal Pétain and still credited him with being
another Talleyrand who was outwitting not only the Germans
but also Laval, nevertheless de Gaulle was being commonly
looked upon as the chief who would reorganize France after
the Allied victory.[69]

How extensive this support of de Gaulle may have been,
and what it may have represented, of course remains debatable. The Fighting French and their sympathizers maintained
loudly that all French circles, from the Royalists on the one
hand to the Communists on the other, were uniting in a
common cause. Actually de Gaulle made a real effort to rally
the Leftist elements. In May he sent a statement to various
labor groups in France promising that after liberation a con-
stituent assembly would be summoned and that the time-
honored principles of liberty, equality, and fraternity would
be restored.[70] Despite all this, much doubt was always cast on
de Gaulle's assertion that French labor organizations were behind him. Some no doubt were, but others quite as certainly
were not. French labor elements in this country remained decidedly skeptical.

Notwithstanding the uncertainty of de Gaulle's position
and the constant friction that developed in relations with him,
the British government on July 3 for the first time recognized
Fighting France and the National Committee as the "symbol
of resistance to the Axis of all French nationals who do not
accept capitulation and who, by the means at their disposal,
contribute wherever they are to the liberation of France by

[69] OSS Files: report from David W. King (June 26, 1942). Also the
statements of André Fradin to Murphy, as reported by the latter on April
1, 1942. For a general review of this development, OSS: Foreign Nationalities Branch report: *De Gaulle, the Free French and the French Underground* (July 9, 1942); also a more recent study: *Lessons from the Resistance
to the German Occupation of France* (June 1945).

[70] Dispatch (May 9, 1942) from Matthews. According to a tel. from
Winant (June 24, 1942) this message was the entire so-called "agreement"
with the French underground. Further, the OSS study: *The Political Ideas
of General de Gaulle* (October 5, 1945).

the common victory of the United Nations." [71] The United States government, in line with its policy of supporting any forces that were fighting the Axis, almost immediately offered to make arrangements for consultation and co-operation between the American military authorities and those of the Fighting French.[72] The note handed to General de Gaulle on July 9 stated:

"The Government of the United States recognizes the contribution of General de Gaulle and the work of the French National Committee in keeping alive the spirit of French traditions and institutions and believes that the military aims necessary for an effective prosecution of the war, and hence the realization of our combined aims, are best advanced by lending all possible military assistance and support to the French National Committee as a symbol of French resistance in general against the Axis powers. The Government of the United States whole-heartedly agrees with the view of the British Government, which is also known to be the view of the French National Committee, that the destiny and political organization of France must, in the last analysis, be determined by free expression of the French people under conditions giving them freedom to express their desires unswayed by any form of coercion.

"In pursuing the common war objective, the Government of the United States will continue to deal with the local Free French officials in their respective territories where they are in effective control. Realizing the need for coordinating their common efforts the Government of the United States perceives every advantage in centralizing the discussion of those matters relating to the prosecution of the war with the French National Committee in London. An essential part of the policy of the Government of the United States for war collaboration is assistance to the military and naval forces of Free France, which is being extended under the terms of the President's statement of November 11, 1941, that the defense of those French territories under control of Free French forces is vital to the defense of the United States.

"In harmony with the foregoing observations the Govern-

[71] Tel. from London (July 3, 1942).
[72] Tel. (July 7, 1942) Hull to London.

ment of the United States is prepared to appoint representatives
in London for purposes of consultation."

General de Gaulle accepted this proposal with alacrity and
Admiral Harold R. Stark and Brigadier General Charles L.
Bolte were named at once as the American representatives.
The British Foreign Office was also pleased and relieved that
Washington had taken this further step. In the face of con-
tinued criticism, especially from British army and navy circles,
the Foreign Office had obviously been on the defensive,
Winant reported from London:

> "Its repeated insistence that ninety per cent of the French pub-
> lic is 'Gaulliste,' and on the military importance of the Free French
> territories in Africa have not silenced its critics here."

Therefore the appointment of American representatives came
as welcome support. In the words of the *Manchester Guard-
ian*: "In the general, as distinct from the technical sense, full
recognition is at least given to the fact that Fighting France is
the real France and that General de Gaulle is its leader." [73]

Actually the new departure contributed little if anything
to the clarification or improvement of the situation. Military
consultation, as we have seen, did not extend by any means to
the plans for the North African invasion. De Gaulle evidently
took the American gesture to be more serious than it was intended to be. He promptly put forward proposals for the provision of supplies for the resistance movements in France, and
appears to have assumed that he would be taken into the
councils of the Allied powers. Not only that, he clearly expected some sort of *de facto* recognition in the political
sense. When none of all this materialized, he was naturally
disappointed and resentful.[74] Winant reported that the Free
French wanted to be asked to join the United Nations pact:
"They feel that such an adherence is necessary in order to
make them appear as the French *provisional government* (and

[73] Tel. (July 10, 1942) from Winant.
[74] OSS Files: memo. reviewing the problem (February 18, 1943).

the United Kingdom Foreign Office backs their views, hoping in this way to create greater unity among the French)." [75]

And so the French problem continued in an atmosphere of scarcely concealed distrust. In Syria the British found themselves in no end of trouble with the Free French leaders, de Gaulle himself taking a prominent part. Indeed, the general poured forth all his bitterness during a visit to Syria in September. Speaking to William M. Gwynn, the American representative at Beirut, he made it clear that he had got wind of the North African plan and that he resented his exclusion from it. He said frankly that he had no confidence in the State Department's policy toward his movement. For a time it had seemed that the Department was more favorably inclined, but that had changed very soon:

"This he attributed to projects entertained by the American Government to launch an attack or attacks on French Africa at Casablanca or Dakar or both in the near future, and to its intention of doing so independently of him. He was to be disregarded because the American Government had been advised, mistakenly in his opinion, that the garrisons and populations of these regions would offer little resistance to the Americans alone, but would resist bitterly if the Fighting French were a party to the attack. This he thought was a grave error. He would willingly admit that the French in Vichy France and the Colonies had much more friendship for the Americans than for the British; however, he had most reliable information that they looked to him as their real leader. The thing that would turn these French people definitely against the English and Americans would be the conviction or the mere suspicion that these latter were inclined to belittle him and his movement and to disregard or jeopardize the rights of France, whose champion he is. Such an attitude would throw the French into the Vichy and German camp, and the Americans if they then attacked would be painfully surprised at the reception they would receive."

Openly criticizing the United States policy toward Vichy, he then asserted:

[75] Tel. (August 21, 1942) from Winant.

"Our whole policy was badly inspired by the advice of Admiral Leahy, Bullitt and Donovan, who were well intentioned but mistaken."

If the French fleet had remained inactive, it was because Laval and Darlan would never dare, for fear of the French people, to order it to attack the enemies of Germany.[76]

In London a representative of de Gaulle lodged an equally strong protest against the American plans, which he said he had learned from Vichy, New York, and two other unnamed places.[77] No doubt the *démarche* occasioned considerable uneasiness in London. Murphy, when he heard of de Gaulle's remark to Gwynn, was quite upset:

"The question arises whether General de Gaulle, who has adopted a hostile and arrogant attitude toward Great Britain recently over the Syrian question, would be capable of treachery should the United States undertake military intervention in French North Africa. It would appear the part of wisdom to exclude the Fighting French at the moment from knowledge of your current discussion." [78]

The discussion that provoked this uncomplimentary suggestion from Murphy was that which, at this very time, was being conducted by representatives of the Office of Strategic Services with delegates from the French resistance movements who had been smuggled out of the country and had gone to London for the purpose. The problem under consideration was whether aid should be furnished to the French underground through the Fighting French organization. Naturally this issue raised the further question to what extent the resistance movement recognized de Gaulle and the Fighting French. It is therefore interesting and decidedly worth while at least to summarize the evidence and the conclusions that emerged from the negotiations.

The leaders of the resistance (representatives of groups like

[76] Tel. (September 1, 1942) from Gwynn.
[77] OSS Files: letter from Eddy to Donovan, from London (September 2, 1942).
[78] OSS Files: memorandum of Murphy to Donovan (September 5, 1942).

Libération and *Combat*) all denounced the Vichy regime and insisted that it was hated throughout France. The French people, they declared, would never accept Pétain, Laval, Chautemps, General Giraud ("who is a pure Fascist") or any other of the former leaders. During the preceding six months, they claimed, the whole of France had been reborn and Frenchmen were looking more and more to de Gaulle, "who represents a continuity of the French democratic form of government." The Leftists had accepted him and even the Communists had given their word to co-operate. Within the preceding months "all resistance movements within France have accepted De Gaulle as their leader, and for the duration, at least, will work unitedly in their resistance efforts under his direction." Fully ninety per cent of the population were now supporting him.

"General de Gaulle," continues the report, "and his associates believe that there is a strong group in the State Department and around the President—Mr. Bullitt's name was mentioned in this connection—who were exercising their influence to bring about in France after the war a 'middle of the road' Government, which might even include Pétain."

This would mean civil war, they declared.

From all this the American negotiators concluded that "the De Gaullist movement is the most powerful in France," though they doubted if it was as widely supported as the Fighting French claimed. None the less, so far as the projected North African expedition was concerned, they conceded that

"It would be difficult to persuade our military authorities that, for the sake of a logical conclusion, they should sacrifice any reasonable prospect of securing the aid of certain of the officers and troops in French North Africa." [79]

It is interesting to note that much the same view was taken by Admiral Stark's aide, Lieutenant Commander Kittredge,

[79] Memorandum of conversations between OSS representatives and the Fighting French in London, September 3-10, 1942.

after his conversations with these same French leaders. Commander Kittredge prefaced his report by pointing out that

"In general, the British are opposed to working with or through the Fighting French undercover resistance organization. . . . The British feel that there are leaks in the Fighting France organization, which have resulted in the Germans receiving advance notice of various plans and operations."

As for the sentiments of the French people, Commander Kittredge reported:

"The French mass, now without leadership and organization, is said to be practically unanimous, not only in opposition to the Germans, but in their conviction that France must have a new political organization and leadership when liberated. . . . To the mass, De Gaulle is merely a symbol of resistance for keeping France in the war. They approve of his symbolic manifestation of the continuance of French participation in the war; they do not expect, and are not prepared to accept, any political leadership from him or his supporters, either now or after liberation." [80]

Finally, still further to reinforce these impressions or conclusions, Walter Lippmann brought back even more decided convictions from his talks with the French leaders in London:

"The evidence is, I am now convinced, clear and the proofs are conclusive that General de Gaulle and the French National Committee are the true leaders of the French Nation. . . . There is no shadow of doubt that General Charles de Gaulle is today as much the acknowledged leader of the French war of independence as General George Washington was the acknowledged leader of the American. . . . The crucial question about General de Gaulle is not whether he is the unanimous choice of all Frenchmen, but whether he is the practical, effective commander of those Frenchmen who mean to fight the enemies of France." [81]

To wind up this aspect of the story, it must be recalled that the purpose of the London discussions was to make arrange-

[80] Report from London (September 23, 1942).
[81] Walter Lippmann: address before the French-American Club (October 28, 1942).

ments, if such seemed desirable, for supplying the French resistance groups through the Fighting French organization. An agreement to this effect was actually recommended by the representatives of the Office of Strategic Services and appears to have been approved by General Eisenhower's delegate, General Dahlquist. The British SOE also was prepared to enter upon a tripartite agreement.[82] In support of this plan another memorandum was written to lay before the Joint Chiefs of Staff in Washington. In this document it was argued that both the Department of State and the European Theater Command tended to look on de Gaulle too much as a creation of the British. Actually there had been much misunderstanding and friction, and the British were inclined to ignore de Gaulle, especially because of his political pretensions:

"What is of far greater significance and importance for us," the memorandum continued, "is the fact that in recent months there has been a solidification of the active Resistance Groups in France behind De Gaulle, not as a man—he is virtually unknown to them—but as *the* symbol of French resistance."

For a long time Unoccupied France and French North Africa had looked to Pétain, Weygand, and even Darlan for eventual leadership in driving out the Germans. But since Laval's return all this had changed and the French people had begun to look outward, where they saw only de Gaulle. The French hated collaborationists almost more than they hated the Germans. Even Giraud was being looked upon as tainted and identified with other Vichyites.

"There is a very serious risk that the leaders of the best organized Resistance Groups would look upon any movement led by Giraud, or other generals who have 'ridden along' with Vichy, as merely representing the Vichy ideology under a somewhat different cloak—an attempt to save the regime and maintain its elements in power."

[82] OSS Files: memorandum by W. A. Roseborough: *Possibilities of Cooperation with the Fighting French Secret Intelligence and Subversive Operations Services* (September 28, 1942); note by Roseborough of October 23, 1942; note of Roseborough to Donovan (October 22, 1942).

To be sure, Giraud may have been maturing plans of his own, and he and his associates might represent a potential of resistance that should not be overlooked. But they might act too late. In the meanwhile de Gaulle had at his disposal some twenty-five thousand to fifty thousand men. It therefore seemed wisest to support and supply de Gaulle, but the author urged also that an effort be made to reconcile opposing French groups, especially de Gaulle and Giraud.[83]

Although the recommendations submitted in this memorandum received the support of the OSS Planning Group, nothing appears to have come of the project, at least before the invasion of North Africa.[84] On October 6 the President had issued instructions that in future lend-lease aid to the Fighting French should be given directly to the authorities of the French National Committee and not as heretofore by way of retransfer from the British government.[85] That is as far as the United States government got in its approach to the Fighting French movement and de Gaulle.

This whole problem has been examined and discussed at such length because, from the very beginning, it was the counterpart of the problem of our relations with Vichy France. For months the Department of State and the United States government had been violently attacked by American liberal and radical newspapers not only for not breaking with Vichy, but also for not recognizing and openly espousing the cause of de Gaulle. For those who saw the situation simply, the thing could be stated in a few words: in contrast with the Vichy collaborators, the Fighting French were irreconcilably opposed to the Germans and were prepared to fight them at every turn. The British had recognized and adopted

[83] OSS Files: memorandum by W. A. Roseborough: *The Present Position of the Fighting French with relation to Resistance within France and our Policy toward the French* (October 21, 1942).

[84] OSS Files: memorandum by the Foreign Nationalities Branch: *Considerations in regard to Proposals for a Closer Military Collaboration with the Fighting French* (October 30, 1942); memorandum by the OSS Planning Group: *Proposed Limited Collaboration with Fighting French* (October 31, 1942).

[85] This was done at Welles's suggestion (Roosevelt Records).

de Gaulle, and, according to his proponents, the great majority of the people in France—certainly the great majority of the resisting elements—had accepted his leadership by the summer of 1942. Why, then, did the State Department have to hang back? The answer of these critics was simple: the State Department was either stuffed with appeasers or else could not bring itself to deal with popular forces. The conservative tradition was too strongly entrenched. Even if our diplomats were able to recognize and gauge a popular movement, they could not bring themselves to accept it. They would have no truck with revolutionary forces or with a movement of the masses. Their business was, as it always had been, with the upper classes, and in the case of France this meant the royalists, conservatives, and even the authoritarians and fascists of Vichy.[86]

Actually, of course, the situation was by no means so simple and transparent. Some features of it have already been discussed in other connections. De Gaulle was notoriously hard to get along with and at no time succeeded in rallying many prominent French leaders to his cause. The British, who had broken relations with France, accepted him and supported him despite the fact that on many occasions he tried their souls and left them hopeless and disgusted. As a matter of fact, even the British were careful to draw the line when it came to military operations. The War Office appears never to have put much reliance on de Gaulle or to have had much hope of effective aid from his movement. Where collaboration was tried, as in Syria, it led only to squabbling and grief. So the British unceremoniously left the Fighting French out of the Madagascar expedition, as they were prepared, from the outset, to debar him from any participation in the North African enterprise.

As for our policy, it must be remembered that the St. Pierre-Miquelon episode was still fresh in many minds and that it had been decided that the cultivation of Vichy was worth while. This in turn implied the impossibility of espousing the

[86] Cf. the strictures of Pertinax: *Les Fossoyeurs*, II, 262.

Fighting French cause. But there were at least two other factors that determined our policy. One was that the Department of State, following the lead of the President, was firm in the decision not to meddle in French domestic affairs, and the second was the refusal to believe that de Gaulle really enjoyed much popular support in France. The first item requires no further discussion, since it was in keeping with general principles of American policy. As for the second, it will perhaps always be impossible to adduce conclusive evidence one way or the other. It is certain that a number of the more important resistance groups in France fell into line behind de Gaulle in the course of the year 1942, but just what this falling in line, this acceptance of leadership, may have involved at that time it is utterly futile to speculate upon. We are told again and again that de Gaulle was virtually unknown in France—in other words, that he was merely a name. The phrase that most commonly occurs is "symbol of resistance," and that no doubt he had become by the autumn of 1942. But a symbol frequently means all things to all men. No one knew what de Gaulle's exact position was or would be. Very likely he scrupulously concealed his views in order to prevent dissension. That he had political ambitions was clear then and has become clearer since. But as for his programs and plans, they were still quite obscure. For some he was the coming man on horseback, the dictator of the future, while for others he was the herald of the new revolution, the sponsor of the Fourth, socialized Republic.[87]

In all this welter of conflicting evidence and claims it was hard to know which way to turn. The question was never really whether de Gaulle represented resistance, but rather how strong the forces of resistance behind him would be— how large and effective his following. The British military authorities evidently held a low opinion of him in this respect,

[87] It is worth recalling that de Gaulle, who started as an exponent of almost fascist doctrine, adjusted his views Leftward in 1942, only to revert to a pretty conservative line in 1944.

and so did our own commanders. Possibly we were merely taking our cue from the British, but more probably we were more influenced by the demands of the job before us. So far as North Africa was concerned, there was every reason to think that de Gaulle's following was insignificant. If at one time there was such a following, it had long since been eradicated or driven underground by the officials and agents of Vichy.[88] On the other hand, there was a substantial resistance movement in North Africa, and we knew all about it. Its leaders, for whose ardor and sincerity Murphy and Colonel Eddy were willing to vouch, were for the most part military men, appointed by Vichy and holding important posts. They were patriots, of that there could be no doubt. Most of them were also royalists and conservatives, of that also there could be no doubt. But we did not associate with them because they were politically on the Right. Our interest was merely in the fact that they were violent opponents of collaboration with the Germans, that they were determined to defend North Africa from German or Italian infiltration or invasion. Because they were bound by their oath to Pétain and because as Frenchmen they were sticklers for legality, they had no use for dissidence. Some there were among them who hoped that ultimately agreement could be reached with the Fighting French, if not with de Gaulle. But for the time being they were determined to resist any effort at conquest by the Fighting French and they refused flatly to have anything to do with any projects that might involve de Gaulle. These were the facts. We did not create them, neither could we do anything to change them. We had made the decision to attempt the invasion of North Africa, as we had made the decision not to attempt a second front on the Continent for the time being. Such being the case, de Gaulle's following in France was, in the military sense at least, of little importance for the moment.

[88] De Gaulle told Murphy somewhat later that he knew he could not count on more than ten to fifteen per cent of the French North African population. See also Kenneth Pendar: *Adventure in Diplomacy*, p. 84.

But the resistance group in North Africa was of major significance. The leaders of this group were in a position to help us or harm us. It therefore behooved us to exploit their aid and, so far as French affairs were concerned, to accede to their terms. How this problem was worked out will be the subject of the following chapter.

CHAPTER VIII

The "Torch" Operation

IT IS NOT the purpose of this study to discuss in detail the preparations for the invasion of North Africa. That task will undoubtedly be performed by the historical section of the general staff, which will have at its disposal the complete files of military records. We are concerned here with these preparations only in so far as they involved political issues or affected American policy with respect to French affairs. This leads us back once more to the conditions in North Africa and to the story of the underground resistance movement, which was to be an important factor in our military calculations.

We left this phase of the problem as it was in July 1942, when Robert Murphy and Colonel Solborg had completed their negotiations at Algiers, when Lemaigre-Dubreuil had gone to France to enlist the aid of General Giraud, and when Solborg had returned to the United States to report to General Donovan. This entire episode had ended in distrust, irritation, and disavowal. Colonel Solborg thenceforth dropped out of the picture, and the whole finely spun plan threatened to fade out.

On July 11 Colonel Eddy returned to Tangier, only to be met with sad and discouraging news. Only two weeks before, more than three hundred people had been arrested in Morocco for forming a secret organization that, according to the police, menaced the security of the French state. Some of those arrested were army, navy, and aviation officers. Their plans to carry on propaganda for the American cause and to sabotage the French defense arrangements in the event of an American intervention had been betrayed to the German armistice commission. Thereby an important and active branch of the resistance movement had been lopped off, and any revival of the movement was hardly to be hoped for. The fascist Parti Populaire Français was organizing and arming a strong-arm squad to break up all political demonstrations and "to act as key men at strategic points in the event of an American invasion of this territory." [1]

This was bad enough, but even worse was the collapse of all the hopes that had been pinned on the Algiers conference. Apparently Colonel Eddy knew nothing of all this until his return to Tangier.[2] In accordance with earlier instructions, he at once offered to support the French leaders financially and with supplies of small arms from Gibraltar, but this, of course, was far below what Solborg had indicated might be expected.[3] Finally, giving way to despair, Murphy sent a message to Solborg, through the Department of State:

"Failure to receive some word from you since your arrival in Washington has disturbed our friends.'

With this message he sent the translation of a memorandum from Lemaigre:

"Should a debarkation of Anglo-American forces [in Occupied France], accompanied by De Gaullist elements operating without previous accord with those who effectively are heading the resistance against Germany occur, such debarkation would be opposed by force by French troops."

This declaration had been forwarded from Lyon, where Lemaigre was carrying on further discussions with General Giraud. The latter, according to Lemaigre, would be much embarrassed if he had to dissociate himself from such an enterprise. To this Murphy added:

"From my conversations with these people I gather that they fear that an early, large-scale commando operation against the Occupied Zone is being planned by the De Gaulle Movement."

[1] OSS Files: report from Tangier (July 11, 1942).
[2] Tel. to Eddy, evidently from Murphy (July 14, 1942).
[3] OSS Files: Tel. from Eddy (Juy 14, 1942).

This the French resistance leaders thought would be premature and would be resisted by fifty per cent of the French
population.[4]

On receipt of this message Colonel Solborg made a last appeal to General Donovan, urging that this unique opportunity
to achieve a bloodless victory in North Africa should not be
forgone:

> "I take this opportunity of again repeating that no promises
> were made, nor hopes held out to the French in North Africa,
> and that their present request is simply to agree to carry on staff
> talks without commitments and to supply them with an insignifi-
> cant quantity of paramilitary equipment. If we wait for the out-
> come of the situation in the Middle East, our agreement with the
> French leaders may come too late, for it is to be borne in mind
> that staff talks and preparations will take the better part of two
> months. . . . We must not let the big man down, for there is
> nobody else on whom we could depend." [5]

No reply whatever appears to have been made either to this
appeal or to Murphy's message. Thereupon Murphy decided
to go to Washington himself, but at the crucial moment Colonel Eddy returned from a short visit to London and brought
news that revived all spirits.[6] Eddy had gone to London in
the hope of making some arrangement with the British for
furthering the patriot cause in North Africa. As it turned out,
however, his presence was to prove very fruitful to the American side. General George V. Strong, the assistant chief of
staff, G-2, was in the British capital in connection with the
staff conferences and expressed a desire to check Solborg's
report by what Colonel Eddy might have to say. Colonel
G. Edward Buxton, the assistant director of the OSS, arranged a dinner party on or about July 24 at which General
Strong and Colonel Eddy met for the first time. General
George Patton and later General James Doolittle were also
present on this occasion.

[4] Tel. (July 21, 1942) from Murphy to Hull for Solborg.
[5] OSS Files: memorandum of Solborg to Donovan (July 23, 1942).
[6] Lemaigre-Dubreuil: *France's Re-entry into the War*, etc.

General Strong began the conversation by warning Colonel Eddy that any misrepresentation or stretching of the facts might lead later on to huge loss of American lives. The United States army was not interested, he said, in any vague programs or good intentions. What he wanted was accurate and reliable information. Thus cautioned, Colonel Eddy proceeded to give a detailed, factual account of the French resistance, its numbers, organization, leadership, and potentialities. The generals were much impressed with what they learned and evidently were prepared to put faith in what Eddy reported. At any rate, General Strong at once brought the entire situation to the attention of General Eisenhower's staff, and from this time onward the French resistance movement in North Africa was integrated with the plans for the invasion. Colonel Eddy himself was drawn repeatedly into the planning work and became the army's liaison officer with Murphy and the French leaders.[7]

When Colonel Eddy returned to Africa at the end of July, he went at once to Algiers, where he conferred with Murphy for some days, after which he returned immediately to Gibraltar and London. The only record we have of this period is a letter that he wrote to General Donovan. In this he urged the importance of Murphy's dispatch to Atherton of July 6, in which the negotiations with Solborg had been reported. He then went on to say:

"The organization of resistance in Algeria is obviously so full and complete that we have no reason to delay the establishment of a route for supplies."

With Murphy's approval, he added, he would try to secure a small shipment from the British SOE stores at Gibraltar.

"There will be no problem at all about reception of the merchandise, since our partners practically control the Province of Oran, as well as other sections of the coast. All they ask is an

[7] Conversation with General Strong and Colonel Buxton, June 14, 1944; notes by Colonel Eddy.

early delivery to reassure both sides that the traffic can flow." [8]

Colonel Eddy was successful in making arrangements at Gibraltar, after which he went on to London. Murphy meanwhile proceeded to Washington, and Lemaigre returned to France for further conferences with General Giraud.[9] Eddy was plunged at once into staff work, having brought with him the estimates of French forces that had been drawn up by General Charles Mast, the Algiers representative of Giraud.[10] He then went on to Washington, where he conferred with General Donovan, and arranged for co-ordination of OSS activities with the military plans. The result was a preliminary memorandum setting forth proposed action on D-day. North Africa leaflets and posters were to be distributed and wireless communication between Gibraltar, Tangier, and the American convoys was to be established. The guerrilla groups were to be supplied after the arrival of the troops. Plans were to be perfected for disposing of the German and Italian armistice commissions in Morocco and Algeria just as soon as the landing took place. French agents were to take care of this delicate job. For the rest, Colonel Eddy urged that staff talks with the French leaders should be initiated. In conclusion he wrote as follows:

"The highest military, diplomatic and political influences should be brought to bear to exclude British as well as Free French from landing on French territory in North Africa. If this proves impossible, there must at least be a promise by the highest American authority that the British troops included in the campaign are there only for the purpose of fighting the Germans and Italians, and are really in transit to their ultimate destination of Tripoli, Libya and Sicily. In any case, the essential point is the assurance to the French that there will be no occupation and annexation of French territory by the British, otherwise we will certainly forfeit the benefit of general cooperation by the French Army." [11]

[8] OSS Files: Eddy to Donovan (August 3, 1942).
[9] Lemaigre-Dubreuil memorandum.
[10] Conversation with Colonel Eddy, December 8, 1943.
[11] OSS Files: memorandum of Eddy to Donovan (August 26, 1942).

Eddy's concrete recommendations were submitted to the Joint Chiefs of Staff on August 27 and were, in the main, approved (September 11). The Joint Chiefs, however, assigned control of the entire operation to General Eisenhower and disapproved staff talks with the French leaders, "as the danger of information leaking out by staff talks with Separatists appears too great." [12]

Once again Colonel Eddy proceeded to London, where he drafted a number of recommendations for General Gruenther, of Eisenhower's staff. He proposed that Frederick P. Culbert, the vice-consul at Casablanca, and John C. Knox, the vice-consul at Algiers, be called to London so that they might accompany the task forces. David W. King, the chief organizer in Morocco, was to remain at Casablanca, and Leland L. Rounds at Oran. He recommended further that Carl Clopet, of Eddy's Tangier staff, be summoned to London and Washington. Clopet was a hydrographer who for eight years had been captain of a salvage-tug company in Morocco: "He knows every rock and buoy and wreck, as well as being an expert on the very treacherous swell which is perhaps the chief hazard for any landing party." Eddy concluded with reference to plans for getting rid of the Axis armistice commissions and to specific sabotage operations:

"Our groups are prepared to destroy key power stations, tunnels and bridges connecting Morocco with Algeria and they are prepared to isolate from reinforcement the Port of Fedalah and the Port of Lyautey. These preparations were in anticipation of Axis aggression and will presumably not be necessary if we occupy the territory first.

"It is, of course, in general true that we can count on the submission or active support of the French Army as we must also count upon the determined resistance of the French Navy and of the aircraft under the Navy's control." [13]

[12] OSS Files: note on the above-mentioned document.
[13] OSS Files: memorandum from Eddy to General Gruenther (August 30, 1942).

It is extremely difficult and probably unnecessary to trace all the many strands that ran through the planning for the North African campaign. Murphy had reached Washington on August 30 and had been called into conference with Admiral Leahy, Admiral King, and General Marshall, after which he was invited to Hyde Park for discussions with the President. It was at this time that he first learned of the decision to send an expeditionary force to North Africa; the President enjoined him, however, not to discuss these plans with the Department of State or with any but authorized army or navy officers.[14]

At that time Murphy set down his views in a detailed memorandum entitled: *Elements for Consideration in the French North African Situation.* In this he pointed out that North Africa had never since the armistice had either the resources or the military strength necessary for its defense. In other words, the fate of the region depended in the last analysis on the decision of the Germans. Local officials could do little until it was clear what the United States might do. If American action was decided on, co-operation of the administration, police, and army in North Africa would be certain. The French group had worked out a program that would be effective if the United States would:

1. Recognize a provisional government in North Africa.
2. Provide transport to take troops and supplies from Dakar to North Africa.
3. Arrange for the immediate shipment of arms and munitions.
4. Send an expeditionary force of at least twelve divisions.
5. Guarantee complete restoration of the French Empire after the conclusion of hostilities.
6. Accept French command of the forces in North Africa.
7. Send naval units to Bizerte if and when French Africa proclaimed its independence.

The French, Murphy pointed out once more, did not want to have anything in the way of British intervention; neither

[14] Murphy notes.

did they want anything to do with de Gaulle. He then proceeded to review French needs and requirements and discussed the desirability of conversations regarding them:

"The French group hopes for a consolidation of all French nationals in an effort to resist the Axis, but understands that the British Government will never abandon General de Gaulle. It does understand, however, that the British Government will promise formally that the National Committee will not participate in any action in French North Africa. . . . They hope that contact with General de Gaulle would only be established after the intervention in French North Africa had been realized."

Murphy then noted General Giraud's readiness to lead, and pointed out that General Mast had informed him:

"that the ideal of this group of French officers, including General Giraud, would be a general resumption of hostilities by the French in Metropolitan France and North Africa in the spring of 1943."

In conclusion he stressed once more the French demand for leadership:

"It is important to note that these representatives consistently emphasize that action in French North Africa must be under *French*, as distinguished from foreign leadership; that if the United States intervenes, it should be at French invitation, avoiding the appearance of a violation of French sovereignty and with our formal assurances of respect for French territory." [15]

The substance of this memorandum was submitted by General Donovan to the Joint Chiefs of Staff as a program for psychological warfare in North Africa. It was recommended in this document that we wait until the patriots were ready— that is, till March or April 1943, so far as France was concerned, though action in North Africa might be feasible somewhat earlier. Furthermore, it was proposed that we ac-

[15] Murphy memorandum of September 4, 1942. No doubt Murphy's views explain in part at least the President's insistence on American leadership and the exclusion of the Fighting French.

cept the conditions laid down by the French, and that we promise assistance.[16]

Closely related to this program, but more specific and more indicative of the stage reached by the staff planners, was the joint OSS-SOE plan worked out in London at the same time, probably with the aid of General Donovan himself, who was in the British capital for a short visit. The preface to this plan stated:

"Plan envisages three simultaneous landings at A., B. and C. It is considered essential operation should be entirely American in first instance. Consequently all troops will be American, but will be assisted by Royal Navy and Royal Air Force. Obviously impossible to disguise Royal Navy, but R.A.F. support will be disguised as American."

The plan then listed a number of OSS-SOE tasks in order of priority:

a). During assault: 1. light beaches; 2. neutralize batteries; 3. put out infra-red detectors.
b). Safeguard dock installations from Arab destruction.
c). Safeguard wireless installations from Arab destruction.
d). Sabotage enemy air forces by any means.
e). Temporarily block roads and rails.
f). Damage French naval forces if they resist.
g). Provide guides for forces after landing.

This program was sent to Colonel Eddy at Tangier. He commented on it that his organization could carry out e) and g), but that the other items involved preparations and activity that had been strictly forbidden him while he was in London; a), b), and f), he noted, assumed access to French navy yards and port defenses, which access it would be impossible to secure; as for b) and c), there was no danger of such destruction by the Arabs. Eddy would be willing to attempt a) if so ordered; b), c) and e) he thought could be arranged; d) would be planned with pleasure; f) he considered inadvisable

[16] OSS Files: *Memorandum on Psychological Warfare for North Africa* (September 8, 1942).

—it would be better to let the French fight it out with the French.[17]

Discussion of these plans was to continue for some time until a definitive program was decided on. In the meanwhile various related decisions were being arrived at. On September 9 General Eisenhower was asked by Washington whether he would need civil-affairs officers for his forces.[18] In his reply (September 12) he answered affirmatively, pointing out that some work had been done on this problem in London, but that he desired more trained personnel from the United States. A few days later Murphy left Washington for London, taking with him a draft directive from the President appointing him adviser for civil affairs under General Eisenhower. This draft had caused General Marshall some concern, since it seemed to give Murphy political authority as distinct from the military. General Eisenhower and Murphy himself agreed that everything must be done to avoid the impression of a division of authority, and the President finally agreed that Murphy should act under the commanding general.[19]

During his brief secret visit to London Murphy discussed the political aspects of the situation in great detail in conference with General Eisenhower and his staff and in the presence of Ambassador Winant, Averell Harriman, and H. Freeman Matthews, who was to continue as acting chief civil-affairs officer while Murphy returned to Algiers. Unfortunately neither Murphy nor anyone else could give reliable information on what the Spanish might do or what might happen in France itself. Murphy reported that the Americans could count on the French army in North Africa and that in his opinion the best time for action would be the spring of 1943. He pointed out that the French would be very sticky

[17] OSS Files: tel. London to Tangier (September 10, 1942) and Tangier to London (n.d.).

[18] H. Freeman Matthews had already been detailed to General Eisenhower's staff from the London Embassy to serve as political adviser and counterpart of Mr. Mack of the British Foreign Office.

[19] War Department: tels. of September 9, 12, 15, 19, 1942; Roosevelt Records.

on the question of command, but it was decided that that would have to wait. Murphy was authorized to tell the French leaders that the initial operation would comprise 150,000 men and that eventually there would be a force of 500,000 in North Africa.[20]

On September 22 General Eisenhower cabled to the War Department his decision regarding subversive work in North Africa before D-day and his arrangements for civil affairs after the invasion: General Donovan was to provide one or more specialists to Eisenhower's headquarters, to be incorporated in the staff section. Donovan would be instructed as to what activities his organization should undertake and was to do nothing without Eisenhower's approval. Murphy was to head the civil-affairs section of the staff after the operation had started. Until that time Matthews was to be Murphy's deputy, remaining with the commanding general and available at once if anything should happen to his chief. Furthermore, until the time of the invasion Murphy was to be the sole agent in North Africa in charge of all political maneuvering there. He was to suggest what projects OSS might carry out, and submit them to General Eisenhower.[21]

On the very same day the President issued his revised directive to Murphy. Since this is a basic document, parts of it, at least, should be quoted verbatim:

1). "Upon the occupation of French North Africa by American Military Forces, you will act as the Operating Executive head of the Civil Affairs Section and Advisor for Civil Affairs under General Eisenhower. . . .

2). "You will work in close cooperation with General Eisenhower, U. S. Army, Allied Commander-in-Chief, European Theater, in the preparation and execution of plans of a civil and political nature for the occupation of French North Africa by American Military Forces. . . .

3). "You will at an early date contact personally and through

[20] Murphy notes; Butcher: *My Three Years with Eisenhower*; General Julius Holmes: "Eisenhower's African Gamble" (*Collier's Magazine*, January 12, 1946).

[21] War Department: message from Eisenhower (September 22, 1942).

your Psychological Warfare and other assistants those French nationals whom you consider reliable, and give them the following information:

"Information having been received from a reliable source that the Germans and Italians are planning an intervention in French North Africa, the United States contemplates sending at an early date a sufficient number of American troops to land in that area with the purpose of preventing occupation by the Axis and of preserving French sovereignty in Algeria, and the French administrations in Morocco and Tunisia.

"No change in the existing French Civil Administrations is contemplated by the United States.

"Any resistance to an American landing will, of course, have to be put down by force of arms.

"The American forces will hope for and will welcome French assistance.

"The American forces will provide equipment as rapidly as possible for those French troops who join in denying access to French North Africa to our common enemies.

"Money, in addition to that provided by French sources, will be made available for additional expense incurred through co-operation with American forces.

"The American Government will guarantee salaries and allowances, death benefits and pensions of those French and other military, naval and civilian officials who join with the American expeditionary forces.

"The proposed expedition will be American, under American command, and it will not include any of the forces of General de Gaulle.

"After the necessary preparation is made by French patriots in French North Africa, which should be accomplished with the utmost expedition, at least 24 hours' notice will be given our friends of the time of landings, and in your discretion of the approximate places." [22]

There is no need to follow here all the details that were worked out with respect to civil affairs. By October 14 General Eisenhower was calling for as many as sixty officers for this work. Proclamations were drafted and approved by

[22] President's directive to Robert D. Murphy (September 22, 1942).

Murphy and by the President. Murphy was provided with a clandestine radio transmitter, so that he could communicate in special code with the commander-in-chief and the task-force commanders.[23] Furthermore, all special operations of OSS were put under G-3, which was to maintain liaison with the civil-affairs section. Colonel Eddy was put at the head of joint OSS-SOE activities, but was to take instructions from Murphy regarding any modifications or changes in plans or in timing of operations.[24]

Plans for these secret operations had been worked out further in Washington by Murphy and General Mark W. Clark, in consultation with the task-force commanders. Summarized, they were as follows:

Algeria: One hour before the assault a number of coast-defence batteries were to be destroyed or put out of action. These batteries, all near Algiers, were listed and described.

On D-day, the instructions read: Break electrical connections between infra-red detector stations and coast-defense batteries. Seize Blida and Maison Blanche airdromes and destroy French planes. Secure and immobilize tanks. Seize and preserve intact the main civil broadcasting station, also the main telephone and telegraph exchanges. Prevent destruction of cable huts and cables, main power stations and docks. Provide guides for Algiers. Prevent damage to key road and railroad bridges and tunnels. "Arrange, in so far as consistent with maintaining secrecy, for seizure or neutralization of German and Italian armistice commissioners."

On D-day plus 1, and thereafter, United Nations prisoners were to be released.

Similar instructions were issued for the Casablanca and Oran regions.[25]

All these discussions eventuated in a series of general orders that were issued about the middle of October. One of these

[23] War Department: messages of October 3, 6, 14, 1942.
[24] War Department: message from General Eisenhower (October 15, 1942).
[25] OSS Files: letter of General Mark W. Clark to Murphy (September 23, 1942).

(No. 4) was a political directive, signed by Brigadier General
W. B. Smith. This stated in so many words:

IIIa. "The principle upon which all relations with the civilian
authorities is to be based, is that, regardless of resistance, the
French are friendly and are to be maintained in their government.

IVa. "In the assault stage, the idea of American command kept
to the front.

b. "Murphy is United States representative, and will function as Chief Civil Administrator in North Africa. Before operations he will arrange for taking over authority throughout
French North Africa when operations begin by Frenchmen
who are friendly.

c. There is reason to believe that at least a part of the French
Army and French Air Force will welcome the arrival of American forces. It seems certain that the French Naval Forces will
resist." [26]

General Order No. 5 dealt with a related problem:

"Maintain existing form of government in territories under
control. Retain civil governments and officers and employees in
present positions, so far as consistent with military mission and
policy of commanding general. To supplant persons not in accord with war aims of U. S. and Ally, with local personnel, or
with military personnel in event there is hostile action."

"Agreed by U. S. and British that civil administration shall be
entirely American controlled." [27]

And finally the instructions to Colonel Eddy regarding
secret operations: This directive pointed out that there would
be three task forces: one at Algiers, one at Oran, and one at
Casablanca.

"From Algiers, Eastern Task Force is to advance with all speed
into Tunisia with the object of forestalling any German or Italian counter-moves."

[26] OSS Files: General Order No. 4. Allied Force Headquarters (October
11, 1942).
[27] OSS Files: General Order No. 5. (October 12, 1942).

"The joint **OSS-SOE** organization will assist by subversive action the landing and subsequent operations of the three Task Forces and the subsequent advance of the First Army into Tunisia."

Eddy was to be a member of Eisenhower's staff and to be chief of OSS-SOE operations:

"By order of the President, Mr. Murphy has been charged with carrying out certain preliminary negotiations with French leaders in North Africa. The success of these negotiations may greatly reduce, or even make unnecessary, the tasks given you in these instructions."

Therefore Eddy was to take directions from Murphy, who might want to control operations in Algeria and Tunisia himself. On or about D-day minus 3, Eddy was to transfer from Tangier to Gibraltar. Actual date of landing was not to be disclosed to agents until the last possible moment. There followed a detailed list of assignments along the lines already indicated above.[28]

By this time all agents in North Africa were already feverishly at work. They sent back to London sheafs of reports dealing with harbors and beaches and with all aspects of landing operations. Above all, they watched the German and Italian armistice commissions, which Colonel Eddy and his associates were particularly anxious to eliminate.[29] They labored also with the problem of enlisting Moorish help in case the Spanish or French authority should break down. For this eventuality it was proposed that the renowned Riff leader, Abd-el-Krim, be brought back from his exile on Reunion

[28] OSS Files: S.O. Operations Instructions to Lieutenant Colonel W. A. Eddy, from the commander-in-chief (October 14, 1942), with Eddy's comments on feasibility of each item.

[29] OSS Files: report from Eddy (September 23, 1942), reporting that the commissioners were fearful and had already reserved rooms in a hotel at Meknès: "The Germans in Fedala and Casablanca now keep their effects ready packed and have been trained to clear from the hotels, complete with baggage, within 15 minutes." (Note from D. W. King, September 23, 1942.)

Island, and that another Moorish leader, Allal-el-Fasi, be brought from Brazzaville. These men would be invaluable for raising a revolt against Spain if that country should prove hostile.[30]

By this time the situation in North Africa had become extremely tense. A message from Tunis, which was repeated to Gibraltar, London, Washington, and Algiers, reported that an attack by the Italians was expected momentarily. In such an event the French forces would probably fall back on Algeria. But the French had only about ten thousand poorly equipped troops and less than one hundred military planes. The attack, it was thought, would come from Sicily. The furious assault by air upon Malta was probably only a mask for a combined operation in the Mediterranean. Five thousand troops had been flown to Libya within the past ten days, and many more had been transported by destroyers.[31]

Under the circumstances everything depended on the completion of arrangements with the French leaders. Murphy had arrived in Casablanca on October 11, where he met the inevitable Lemaigre-Dubreuil. According to the latter, the American diplomat remarked jubilantly:

"I am bringing back to you more than anything you could have hoped. We are expecting an intervention by 500,000 men, 2000 airplanes, a hundred supporting warships, battleships, airplane carriers, etc." [32]

On September 22 similar indications had been given to General Giraud, to whom General Eisenhower was able to send a message. This message appears to have been approved by the President and is of some importance in connection with later pourparlers. It read (in paraphrase): "Both Allied governments extend cordial greetings. In the near future concrete

[30] Tels. from Eddy (September 21, 1942); also OSS Files: Eddy to Donovan (September 23, 1942). These negotiations were carried on chiefly by Dr. Carleton S. Coon and Gordon Browne. The project was finally given up lest it arouse suspicion.

[31] OSS Files: tel. Springs to Eddy (October 15, 1942).

[32] Lemaigre-Dubreuil: *The Re-entry of France into the War*, etc.

proposals will be sent you in which you will be contemplated
as the leader of the French effort, which is to be fully supported by the Allies. In future messages we will refer to you
as General Guignan." [33]

By this time Murphy was back at his Algiers post and had
resumed his conversations with the local French leaders. The
plot began to thicken, and at a rate that soon became uncom-
fortable. Giraud, as we have seen, had been fixed on as the
man to lead the French forces in North Africa. For months
Lemaigre-Dubreuil had been flitting to and fro between Algiers and Lyon, carrying messages from Giraud's representative, General Mast, and trying to induce the French hero to
assume leadership. Thus far, however, he had got from Giraud
only a broad, general assurance that he would lead a movement of insurrection against the Axis. There the matter
rested, despite the fact that the American military leaders
knew full well that Giraud's thoughts centered on a revolt
in France itself and in other occupied countries and that the
general expected to be the commander-in-chief of the movement, which he was planning for the spring of 1943. It was
certainly unfortunate that Giraud was not more fully informed of the American plans until just before the invasion,
but the American staff attached so much importance to the
element of surprise that it was considered too risky to take
the French leaders completely into our confidence.

Then, just as Murphy was about to embark on the final
stage of negotiation, an unexpected name was rocketed into
the problem. Emissaries of Admiral Darlan appeared in Algiers and indicated that the renowned exponent of collaboration—the man of the Paris Protocols—might be willing to
shift his allegiance to the Allied side. They told Murphy that
the Vichy authorities had learned from both German and
Japanese sources that the United States was planning an early
assault on Dakar or Casablanca or both. Vichy had been urged
to offer all-out opposition and had been promised Axis aid.
This prospect had determined Darlan to join the Allies and

[33] War Department: message of September 22, from Eisenhower.

bring over the fleet, provided he could command the French forces in North Africa.[34]

This development raised the whole question of Darlan's views and objectives, which, needless to say, are still shrouded in considerable obscurity. It is more than likely that the admiral, who had been in at least partial eclipse since Laval's return to power in April, had lost his confidence in a German victory and that, as a good opportunist, he had begun to shift his ground. It has been suggested that he was in touch with Giraud from the very time of the latter's escape from Germany, and that he secretly participated in the plans for a revolt in France. It has also been pointed out that there were a number of pro-Americans in his entourage, and that he himself appointed General Delattre de Tassigny, an ardent supporter of the Allied cause, to be commander of the coastal region of France from Marseille to the Italian frontier. It seems altogether likely that he knew what was afoot in both France and North Africa and that he was intent on establishing his position under the new dispensation. In the meanwhile he continued to appear to play the German game. In the second half of October he made a tour of inspection of North Africa as far as Dakar, ostensibly to assure himself that all defenses were ready to prevent a successful American attack.[35]

Be that as it may, Darlan's advances were not to be taken lightly. He was, after all, commander-in-chief of all French forces—land, sea, and air—and his authority over the fleet was unquestioned. Since the chief opposition to an American landing was expected from the French naval forces, Darlan's assistance might be crucial. Murphy therefore recommended

[34] Butcher: *My Three Years with Eisenhower*, entry for October 17, 1942.

[35] See Sumner Welles: *The Time for Decision*, p. 165, and Renée Gosset: *Le Coup d'Alger*, pp. 133ff. It is most interesting to note that ten days later Paul Guérin, the French representative in Washington in connection with the economic program for North Africa, spoke to Henry S. Villard about the probable position of Darlan. He described the admiral as a bitter enemy of Laval and also of the Germans. Above all, he said, Darlan was a believer in superior force, and if he could be shown that the United Nations could act with sufficient strength, he might be prepared to assist. Since Darlan commanded the French fleet, he might be a man worth approaching. (Memo. of conversation, October 26, 1942.)

that he be encouraged, on the basis of co-operation with Giraud. He also suggested this procedure in his conferences with General Mast, but only to find the latter unsympathetic. It was probably for this reason, and because of the lateness of the hour, that Darlan was dropped from consideration for the time being. But Murphy's discussions with Mast were so important that his record of them must be given in full. In the first report to General Marshall, Murphy stated that he had found General Mast genuinely alarmed about the possibility of an invasion of North Africa by the Axis:

"General Mast stressed the delicate internal political situation and asked whether we are prepared to launch an operation on a large scale at the present time. He stated that Giraud insists that only he be dealt with and that no negotiations be carried on with Darlan, who, he believes, is not to be trusted, but is desirous only of opportunely joining a successful operation. Mast believes that the Army in North Africa will follow Giraud and that the Fleet will go along with the Army, despite the fact that it is commanded by Darlan. Murphy brought out that the success of the venture depends upon cooperation of the French forces with the United States.

"Mast made inquiries as to our ability to undertake operations on a large scale, and Murphy assured him that we were prepared to do so. Mast further asked whether the United States would be prepared to react immediately in case of an Axis invasion, and Murphy replied that he was confident that we could do so, but that this being a technical military problem of which he was not in a position to judge, he could not give him definite assurance.

"Mast requested that a conference be arranged for at once between five American officers to be sent from General Eisenhower's staff and a similar number of French officers, at the conference to take place on 21 October at a point 150 kilometers to the West of the city of Algiers. He requested that of these American officers one be a general. He asked that these officers be immediately selected and sent to Gibraltar to await further and fuller details as to the manner, time and place of their reception.

"Mast brought up the necessity of furnishing small arms to the French. Murphy informed him and his subordinate leaders that

the Americans have been waiting for some time for the designation of the time and place and that, because of the phase of the
moon, that time is limited. The French stated that the delay is
due to the fact that they had been awaiting Murphy's return
from the United States, and that the necessary data relative to the
initial delivery of small arms and other equipment would be furnished by late tonight. Mast suggested, based upon information
received yesterday from Giraud via Mast's messenger, that the
occupation of some portion of the unoccupied part of France by
the French Army be planned in conjunction with the North African operations, and that the French Army be supplied by the
United States. This idea is very important to General Giraud,
since during the past months he has been working on a plan for
combined action in Europe and Africa next spring. General Giraud appreciates that early action is urgent and believes consideration should be given to the possibility of including in the North
African plans a project of establishing a bridgehead in France
before the Axis can have time to occupy and organize the presently unoccupied area. Mast raised the question, which is delicate
because of French susceptibilities, as to a unified command under
which Eisenhower would retain complete command of American
forces and would be subordinate to the supreme command of
Giraud. He felt that French command is necessary, due to the
superior knowledge of the terrain possessed by the French and
in order to permit the Allied forces to move through French
North Africa with rapidity to a contact with the enemy in Tunisia. In this regard he again emphasizes the great masses of Axis
forces on the Libya-Tunisia frontier and reported that they may
number as high as 250,000." [36]

This report must be supplemented with a further message
from Murphy, which was quoted in a cable sent from Washington to General Eisenhower on the same day:

"Murphy suggested, in conversation with Mast, that the matter of supreme command in Northwest Africa was technical
rather than political, but Mast insisted strongly that it was of a
political nature and must be settled in advance. Murphy requests
a formula for settlement of this delicate point which he may pre-

[36] War Department: paraphrase: Murphy to Marshall (October 16, 1942).

sent to Mast, a formula which will leave the command effectively
in General Eisenhower's hands, but will still permit the French
to regard the operations as being theirs, while requiring them to
provide the maximum aid to us. Mast states that he can gain entry
into Northwest Africa by means of Giraud's name, with no fighting, and that Giraud insists that the Embassy at Vichy, the Legation at Berne and other possible contacts be instructed that all
negotiations with Giraud will be routed through other channels,
since Giraud wishes his contacts with United States continued
through his representative, Mast. It is the opinion of General
Mast that we should send an American submarine to pick up
Giraud and party by night at a point somewhere on the southern
coast of France. Only as a last resort should Giraud be forced to
travel by plane." [37]

These discussions brought us face to face with a most
difficult situation. The fact is that although all preparations
had been made for subversive work under Murphy and Colonel Eddy, it was hardly more than three weeks before the
invasion that General Mast and through him General Giraud
was given any concrete indication of our plans. The result
was that at this late date such knotty and dangerous questions
as that of the supreme command were thrown up.

General Eisenhower was evidently much disturbed by the
reports of Murphy's conferences. Replying to Washington
he proposed a compromise:

"He suggests as a possible formula for the delicate command
situation in North Africa the following: The Allied expedition
to be commanded exactly as now contemplated. Giraud to be
recognized as the principal French collaborator, and that it be
proposed that he assume a position of French governor of all
French North Africa immediately upon occupation; that he be
protected and supported by the Allied forces.

"General Eisenhower intends, in order to satisfy the French
leaders as to the ultimate Allied intentions, to propose to them
that eventually the entire military command of all North Africa
pass to the French. The timing for this passing of command

[37] War Department: message to Eisenhower (October 16, 1942).

would be based upon the attainment by the French forces—
ground, air and sea—of a strength and efficiency capable of defending North Africa against Axis aggression without any further assistance from the United States and the United Kingdom,
other than equipment and supplies. It is calculated that such a
situation will develop only after several months. In anticipation
of the time when the French can assume command, the French
would be invited to commence the setting-up of their organization and staffs to take over such a command, with the immediate
functions of collaboration and cooperation with the Allied Commander-in-Chief.

"General Eisenhower states that it is obvious if we should receive the extensive collaboration implied by the accomplished
conversations with the French, that the various American contingents could be concentrated rapidly and prepared for coordinated
action much sooner than we have hitherto anticipated. The immediate solution after such consolidation had been accomplished
would be to set up the American Fifth Army and to assign General Clark as the commanding general, thus making it possible to
designate either Darlan or Giraud as Deputy Commander-in-
Chief. Such action would give added assurance that we are hon-
estly working toward the time when French can take over the
command. We would make provision for the future use of the
whole area as an allied base for offensive action against Axis territory even after the French had assumed military command of
the Northwest Africa area.

"In conference with the British, General Eisenhower will discuss primarily, first, whether they will support some such arrangement as to the command as he has outlined above. Second,
whether they can escort some few shiploads of equipment and
supplies to the Mediterranean for delivery to the Metropolitan
French at Marseilles almost simultaneously with the landing in
North Africa. Third, the question of British appraisal of the
present capabilities of hostile activity in the Mediterranean. General Eisenhower is instructing Clark to make, in his conference
with the French, only statements of principle and not to attempt
at this time to go into such details as could later result in confusion and possible misunderstanding." [38]

[38] War Department: message from Eisenhower (October 17, 1942).

As the sequel was to show, General Eisenhower and his staff—perhaps even Murphy—underestimated the tenacity of the French, particularly in the matter of the supreme command. None the less, it was clear that some of these issues would have to be solved at once and that the French leaders, if they were to give real co-operation, would have to be informed of many things that they did not know. These leaders, from the outset, had left no doubt that the movement as they envisaged it must be a French movement and that the Americans were to come in merely by invitation. They had also stated categorically that they would have nothing to do with an operation that involved de Gaulle and the Fighting French and that, furthermore, they did not wish the British to have any part in it. We on our side had ignored their wishes with regard to leadership and, though we had made up our minds to leave de Gaulle out of the picture, we had concluded that British aid was essential and we had planned a combined operation. This unpleasant item now had to be revealed to Mast and his associates. General Eisenhower was therefore advised to instruct General Clark:

"to bring out the fact in his conference with the French that in view of the present situation in the Pacific it is clearly necessary that British Air and Naval support be given our operations in the Mediterranean and that it may be necessary for British ground troops to enter the area after the initial landings. To emphasize the fact that the African operation is primarily an American enterprise and under American control, and that British participation is in the nature of support of the United States and not of direction." [39]

This brings us to the dramatic story of the mission of General Mark Clark and his associates to the territory that they hoped soon to invade. Several more or less detailed accounts of this thrilling episode have already appeared in the public press. They give an accurate account at least of the external

[39] War Department: message to Eisenhower (October 18, 1942).

aspects of the mission, which we may therefore safely omit here.[40]

General Clark left London for Gibraltar on October 19, accompanied by General Lemnitzer, Colonel Hamblin, Colonel Julius Holmes, and Captain Wright (U.S.N.). On October 20 Colonel Eddy was instructed from Gibraltar: "Please advise G.B. 6005 [Murphy] most immediately that X [General Clark] and four staff officers as requested by him intend to rendezvous at point fixed on night Wednesday, October 21." The message continued:

"Reception party should therefore be at rendezvous from 21.00 hours G.M.T. October 21 and be prepared to remain there till dawn October 22.

"In the event weather preventing landing night 21/22 request G.B. 6005 arrange alternative plan to conduct conference aboard submarine at time and place to be determined by G.B. 6005 and communicated to X via Gibraltar.

"If neither plan operates on night 21/22, landing party will attempt landing on night 22/23." [41]

At the other end Murphy had arranged with General Mast to hold the secret meeting at a farmhouse near the shore, about seventy-five miles west of Algiers, between Cherchell and Gouraya. On the evening of October 21 Murphy and Knight, together with General Mast, d'Astier de La Vigerie, and Colonel Jousse drove to the rendezvous. They watched all night in vain, only to get a message that the British submarine had arrived at dawn, too late to make a landing. The meeting had to be postponed until the following night. Murphy and his friends thereupon returned to Algiers for the day and then

---

[40] See Captain Godfrey B. Courtney: "General Clark's Secret Mission" (*Life*, December 28, 1942); Frederick C. Painton: "Secret Mission to North Africa" (*Readers' Digest*, May 1943); Ridgeway B. Knight: "General Clark's Secret Mission to Algeria" (*American Foreign Service Journal*, March 1943); Demaree Bess: "The Backstage Story of Our African Adventure" (*Saturday Evening Post*, July 3, 1943); Wes Gallagher: *Back Door to Berlin* (New York, 1943), pp. 26ff.; G. Ward Price: *Giraud and the African Scene* (New York, 1944), pp. 92ff.; Renée Gosset: *Le Coup d'Alger*, chap. iv; N. L. A. Jewell: *Secret Mission Submarine* (New York, 1944).

[41] OSS Files: tel. from Gibraltar to Eddy (October 20, 1942).

reappeared at the rendezvous in the evening, excepting for General Mast, who arrived the next morning with Rigault and Colonel Van Hecke. This time the arrangements worked out better. The American party, together with three British commando officers (Captain Livingston, Captain Courtney, and Lieutenant Foote) landed after midnight. After the arrival of General Mast, early in the morning of October 23, conferences began between him on the one hand and Murphy, General Clark, and General Lemnitzer on the other. The discussion went on throughout the day, until at about six p.m. General Mast, Colonel Van Hecke, and Rigault departed. The rest of the party sat down to dinner, but were interrupted by news that the local police were on the way to investigate the suspicious goings-on. "One would have thought that fifty dead skunks had been thrown on the table at the speed with which most of our French friends disappeared," remarked General Clark later. The general and his party hastily concealed themselves in the wine cellar, where their presence was almost betrayed by a violent coughing fit that overcame one of the group. In the meanwhile Murphy, Knight, the owner of the farm, and one of the French organizers remained above, playing poker dice. Fortunately the police were stupid enough to be put off with a cock-and-bull story and the situation was saved. Later in the night the visiting Americans and British attempted to re-embark. As fate would have it, the surf was running high and it was only after several abortive attempts that the party finally got off in kayaks, several members without their full apparel or equipment.[42]

More important than the circumstances of the visit were the substance and outcome of the discussions. The lesser players spent their time going over various operational mat-

[42] One of the best accounts is that of Knight, in his report of January 12, 1943, but see also the reports of Queyrat and Karsenty, who were present, in *Les Cahiers français*, No. 47 (August 1943). It is simply astounding what discrepancies there are among the various accounts, even as regards dates. The above account has been pieced together from all the available sources and has been checked by Murphy and General Julius Holmes.

ters: tonnage capacity of the North African ports, locations
of batteries and arsenals, plans of the French naval forces, data
on French airfields, and so on.[43] Meanwhile the really crucial
negotiations were those between Generals Clark and Mast.
The latter revealed himself in favor of early action—"the
sooner the better"—since he and his associates were much
disturbed by the concentration of Axis troops in Libya,
Sicily, and Sardinia. This corresponded to the American plans,
some idea of the magnitude of which was given the French
general. The two soldiers then discussed strategic and tactical
objectives and ultimately arrived at the thorniest questions of
all: who should lead and who should exercise the supreme
command. General Mast felt reasonably sure that General
Giraud could be counted on, though he emphasized Giraud's
insistence on a simultaneous operation on the southern coast
of France and stressed the French demand for supreme command from the very outset. None of these questions was
definitively disposed of.

Clark made it clear that a landing in southern France would
be impossible until after the invasion of North Africa, though
he thought Allied support of such a venture might be feasible
later on. As for the question of command, the American general stated that he could not commit himself beyond saying
that it was the desire of the Allies to turn over control of
North Africa to French command as soon as the situation
permitted. It was finally agreed to send a messenger to
Giraud, from whom Mast hoped to have an answer by October 28. If Giraud accepted the conditions, he was to be
taken off the French coast by submarine. Mast having stated
that, given four days' notice, he could guarantee that there
would be little or no resistance from French military or air
forces and that naval resistance would cease after successful
landings, Clark promised to give such notice, though he refused to divulge the probable date of the operation. American
lack of confidence in the French sense of security was evi-

[43] See especially Painton's account, which seems to me to exaggerate
somewhat the importance of the intelligence obtained.

dent throughout the discussions. For example, at no time before the beginning of the operation were the French informed on what beaches the landings would be made.[44]

When one stops to consider that on October 23, the very day of the Cherchell conference, the first slow convoy set out from Britain for Algiers, the crowded drama of these days becomes all too evident. It was hardly two weeks before the day set for the landings. Yet some of the most important questions, such as those of French resistance or collaboration and those of the supreme command, were still in suspense. Following General Clark's negotiations with General Mast, the French leaders at once sent off Lemaigre-Dubreuil to consult further with General Giraud. The French emissary found the general hesitant but none the less impressed with the scope of American plans. He finally agreed in principle with the Allied propositions, but made his final consent contingent upon his acceptance of a written text to be submitted by Murphy. Furthermore, he was still unwilling to give up all thought of an operation on the southern coast of France. He gave Lemaigre a long statement on the necessity for an Allied bridgehead in France, which would enable the French army to keep open possibilities for the future, provided it could be supplied by American equipment. Finally he sent a letter to Murphy restating his view about the character of the operation in North Africa:

"I attach the greatest importance to the fact that, in case of combined military operations on French territory (either in Metropolitan France or overseas) which is not occupied under the terms of the Armistice Conventions by the Axis Powers, that the expeditionary force of the United Nations which would come to collaborate with local French troops should be an expedition es-

[44] War Department: message from Eisenhower (October 25, 1942); message from Marshall to Eisenhower, suggesting that the French be given twenty-four, but preferably forty-eight hours' notice (October 26, 1942); message from Eisenhower to Murphy (October 27, 1942); messages from Eisenhower (October 27, 28, 1942); message to Eisenhower (October 31, 1942); report of the commanding general (February 20, 1943); General Julius C. Holmes: "Eisenhower's African Gamble" (*Collier's Magazine*, January 12, 1946); notes by Murphy.

sentially American, placed under American command. It must not involve any participation by French dissident elements. Only in consequence of and as a result of understanding between the local French authorities and the American authorities may non-American formations, Allied or Dissident French, in case of need be brought onto French territories." [45]

Murphy replied almost at once to the above letter by saying that the views expressed by General Giraud were in harmony with those of the American government. This may seem like a pretty misleading assurance in view of the fact that British participation had long since been decided on. Murphy of course knew of the plans, but it was his understanding that the first wave of the invasion would be principally American and that if British forces were included, they would be in United States uniforms. He was convinced, furthermore, that the anti-British feeling in North Africa was an artificial thing, the result of systematic Vichy propaganda. He proved right in his view that after the landings a reconciliation of French and British would come easily and quickly.[46]

On the larger issue of the supreme command Murphy, knowing General Eisenhower's views, had already drafted a letter to General Giraud, which was approved by General Eisenhower with some emendation. General Eisenhower had reiterated his conviction that the American command in North Africa could not be relinquished by the Allies until the military situation was secure.[47] He had expressed his doubts, therefore, whether agreement could be reached with Giraud and had decided that General Mast should be accepted as deputy to the chief of staff whether Giraud assumed the leadership or not.[48]

Murphy attempted to bury the issue under a mass of quali-

[45] OSS Files: letter of Murphy to Giraud (November 2, 1942) quoting Giraud's letter of October 28; see also Lemaigre-Dubreuil: *France's Reentry into the War*, etc.; War Department: message from Murphy (October 26, 1942).

[46] Notes by Murphy.

[47] War Department: message from Eisenhower (October 27, 1942).

[48] War Department: Eisenhower to Murphy (October 27, 1942).

fying verbiage. His letter of November 2, 1942 to General Giraud was a basic document, the full text of which ran as follows:

"Referring to the declarations made on various occasions by President Roosevelt and to the engagements already entered upon by the American Government as well as by the British Government, I am in a position to assure you that the restoration of France, in all her independence, in all her grandeur and in all the area which she possessed before the war, in Europe as well as overseas, is one of the war aims of the United Nations.

"It is well understood that French sovereignty should be re-established as soon as possible over all territories, Metropolitan as well as colonial, over which the French flag waved in 1939.

"The Government of the United States considers the French nation as an ally and will treat it as such.

"I add that in case of military operations on French territory (either Metropolitan or colonial), in all instances where the French collaborate, the American authorities will in no way intervene in affairs which are solely the province of the national administration or which derive from the exercise of French sovereignty.

"So far as the command is concerned, the Government of the United States has no thought or desire but to put the military command of the region in the hands of the French as soon as possible. However, during those phases of the operation that involve the landing, establishing the security of French North Africa and providing the necessary bases, it is considered essential that the American command organization which has been set up with so much effort and difficulty for this special operation should remain unchanged. (The clause above derives from the recent conference between American and French representatives. It was drafted before the receipt of your note of October 27 which reads as follows:

" 'It is altogether normal and well understood that all the operations of debarkation shall be directed by the general staff of the American Army. The Interallied Command shall begin to function after the debarkation, that is to say, at each point of debarkation 48 hours after the hour fixed for the beginning of the landing operations of the first convoy. So far as further op-

erations are concerned, the American troops will pass under the
Interallied Command as soon as they reach land.'

"I am communicating your suggestion to the General-Staff of
the American Army and I am certain than an acceptable formula
will be found. During this period, the Government of the United
States will bend its efforts to furnish the French forces with arms
and modern equipment. While the equipment and organization of
the French forces is thus proceeding, the details of command can
be concluded in such a way that the French may be able to assume
the supreme command at the desired moment. It would be desirable, in order to facilitate the direction of operations, if a general
of the French Army could be attached to the Commander-in-
Chief immediately after the debarkation." [49]

In the meanwhile the French leaders in North Africa were
on pins and needles. General Mast was pressing for the date
of the operation, arguing that Giraud, being in virtual charge
of the French general staff, would need time to contact many
officers before he departed. Eight to ten days, he thought,
would be necessary to make the arrangements. And in this
connection he once more reiterated the importance of com-
bining the establishment of a beach-head in southern France
with the North African invasion.[50] To this General Eisenhower replied that General Clark had made it perfectly clear
to General Mast that a landing in southern France, con-
temporaneously with the invasion of North Africa, was impossible, and that any Allied support for such an operation
would have to come later. Churchill, he remarked, was much
interested in such a move and was earnestly attempting to
find some way of supporting a possible operation by the
French armistice army designed to prevent a German advance to the Mediterranean coast of France. Nevertheless,
General Eisenhower considered that such an operation could
not be carried through as an incident of the North African

[49] OSS Files: letter of Murphy to Giraud (November 2, 1942). A summary of this letter is given in the article of Demaree Bess (*Saturday Evening Post*, July 3, 1943). This correspondence did not reach the Department of State until long after it was written, in the spring of 1943.
[50] War Department: message from Murphy (October 27, 1942).

invasion. To ease the situation, he authorized Murphy to notify Giraud at once that the North African landing would take place early in November, so that the general might realize the need for speedy arrangements for his departure. A British submarine, under American command, was being sent to the Gulf of Lion to take him off.[51]

The news of the impending operation struck the French leaders like a thunderbolt. Giraud, when advised, declared that it would be utterly impossible for him to depart from France before November 20. General Mast, too, argued heatedly with Murphy, who finally cabled General Eisenhower:

"I am convinced that the invasion of North Africa without favorable French High Command will be a catastrophe. The delay of two weeks, unpleasant as it may be, involving technical considerations of which I am ignorant, is insignificant compared with the result involving serious opposition of French Army to our landing."

The very idea of postponement struck General Eisenhower as fantastic. After all, the first convoys were already at sea. He therefore cabled General Marshall:

"It is inconceivable that Murphy can recommend such a delay with his intimate knowledge of the operation and the present location of troops and convoys afloat. It is likewise inconceivable to me that our mere failure to concede such demands as have been made would result in having the French North African Army meet us with serious opposition. Recommend the President advise Murphy immediately that his suggested action is utterly impossible in view of present advanced state of operation and that we will proceed to execute this operation with more determination than ever."

The President accepted General Eisenhower's view at once and Admiral Leahy wired Murphy on behalf of the Chiefs of Staff: "The decision of the President is that the operation will be carried out as now planned and that you will do your

[51] War Department: message from Eisenhower (October 28, 1942).

utmost to secure the understanding and cooperation of the French officials with whom you are now in contact." [52]

In the stress of the moment the ever ready Lemaigre-Dubreuil was packed off once more to France, carrying Murphy's letters of November 2. His interview with General Giraud he described as stormy—"an avalanche of reproaches." Yet in the end Giraud decided to go on, and to leave France at once for Gibraltar. "He designated a leader in France and hoped that he could obtain from the Allies the immediate sending of forces in order to support resistance in France, which he did not want to abandon. [53]

Giraud was scheduled to leave the French coast on the evening of November 4. Actually, because of failure to make contact, the submarine was unable to take him off until the evening of November 5. At sea he was transferred to a flying boat, but he did not reach Gibraltar until the late afternoon of November 7. [54]

Pending the final discussions at Gibraltar, things were moving apace in North Africa. General Juin, commander of the French ground forces and a man who had always been well disposed toward the United States, was much concerned lest the Axis forces should attack first. His orders were to resist, but he had doubts whether the Vichy government would stand by these orders. He therefore suggested the possibility of American aid, if called for, and proposed that he and Murphy keep in close touch. [55] At the same time in Morocco General Béthouart, who also had been friendly to the Ameri-

[52] War Department: message from Murphy (November 1, 1942); message from Eisenhower (November 1); message from Leahy to Murphy (November 2). Also Roosevelt Records.

[53] Lemaigre-Dubreuil: *France's Re-entry into the War.* Also War Department: message from Murphy (November 4, 1942).

[54] War Department: message from Murphy (November 4, 1942); message from Murphy (November 5, 1942); messages from Eisenhower (November 7, 1942). The story of his escape is told in detail in Wes Gallagher: *Back Door to Berlin,* pp. 31ff.; in G. Ward Price: *Giraud and the African Scene,* pp. 119ff.; and in N. L. A. Jewell: *Secret Mission Submarine.*

[55] War Department: message from Murphy (October 20, 1942) and another message of November 5, 1942.

cans, decided to co-operate. A message from King at Casablanca reported:

"French General Staff at Casablanca entirely in agreement with operation, and are preparing landing between Safi and Port Lyautey. They propose landing north and south of Casablanca and auxiliary landing at Safi. There would be no resistance. Then advance from north on Port Lyautey and Casablanca in order to cut off resistance of naval forces. Advance from south to Azemmour and Mediouna to surround Casablanca from the rear. Occupation of airfields at Rabat Sale, Casablanca, Mediouna and most likely Meknès. Then negotiations with French Navy and opening of ports. French troops will occupy Rabat two hours before landing, surround Residency and take Noguès. They will seize telephone, telegraph and radio at Casablanca and Rabat." [56]

The time had now come for Murphy to give Mast the promised notice.[57] Actually the general had only three days for making his final dispositions. As General Eisenhower said, the decision as to what methods he would use to assist the American landings would have to be governed by his judgment as a trained soldier.[58] Matters had become pretty thoroughly snarled up in these last days, for Giraud's belated arrival at Gibraltar made it impossible for him to get to Africa on the evening of November 7. Therefore arrangements had to be made to have his important statement to the French in North Africa broadcast from Gibraltar.[59]

Actually things turned out even worse than anticipated. Giraud, having arrived at the Rock, went into conference with Generals Eisenhower and Clark in their subterranean quarters. The discussions lasted for six hours and made very little progress. Captain Butcher's diary gives an amusing account of a situation that at the time was quite devoid of comic relief. First, he notes, "Ike" worked for an hour on the gen-

---

[56] OSS Files: message from King to Eddy at Gibraltar (November 5, 1942); another message to Gibraltar of the same date.
[57] War Department: message from Murphy (November 4, 1942).
[58] War Department: message from Eisenhower (November 5, 1942).
[59] War Department: message from Eisenhower (November 7, 1942).

eral, after which Clark took over, "offering him the governor-
ship, virtually the kingship of North Africa." But the old
general declined in seven languages, all of them meaning
"prestige." He wanted to know what the French people, what
his own family, would think if he were less than commander-
in-chief. But General Eisenhower's report gives a much fuller,
albeit more sober account:

"Giraud initially refused to issue any statement for broadcast
tonight, either from Gibraltar or from London or Washington.
He insisted specifically that no radios should emanate from either
national capital or from Allied Headquarters which would connect his name in any way with the operation in North Africa.
Giraud flatly refused to participate in the operation in any other
capacity than that of Supreme Allied Commander. He insisted
upon a position which would make him completely independent
to carry out his own strategic and tactical conceptions. He demanded this position at once and stated categorically that by
November 10 all forces then ashore must come under his command and that thereafter all forces landing in North Africa
should come under his command upon debarkation. He was
willing that General Eisenhower retain control of base and administrative facilities near the ports and take care of the arrival
of Allied reinforcements, including supplies, but insisted that he,
Giraud, alone have the sole authority to make all decisions respecting the tactical and strategic employment of all Allied
troops.

"General Eisenhower explained to Giraud the impossibility of
such an arrangement and assured him that it was the honest
intention of the Allies to recognize him promptly as military and
civil head of all French affairs in North Africa and that the Allies
would assist him in developing French forces that he could use
as he saw fit, even to the extent of re-entering France from the
South and engaging the Germans in that area.

"Giraud is obsessed with the idea of an immediate move into
France and implied that if he were made commander he would
promptly use the entire airforce coming into North Africa for
the neutralization of Sardinia and to protect the transportation
of troops into southern France; that he would transfer the fighter
and bomber units thereafter to airfields in southern France.

"Both Eisenhower and Clark urged Giraud to go along with us temporarily on the basis previously outlined and under assurances that the President had already made respecting French sovereignty and territorial integrity and pointed out to him the promise already made to turn over to him eventually the supreme command and that the pressing problem of the moment was the establishment of secure bases and the development of land and sea communications activities which would require at least several weeks.

"Giraud was deaf to all arguments. His final position was that he must be Commander-in-Chief without responsibility to the American and British Combined Chiefs-of-Staff, and that Eisenhower's function should be that of obtaining necessary reinforcements of personnel and supplies from the Allied Governments." [60]

Here indeed was an impasse hard to break. Giraud, who was an honest and straightforward soldier, proved to be an obstinate one as well. Still, it must be admitted that he had a grievance. The plans he had been working on for so long, which he regarded as sound plans, were to be entirely scrapped. It was something to expect him to yield against his best judgment. And it was something more to expect him to accept something less than what had been indicated in Murphy's letter of only a few days before. Whatever may be said against him, he played fairly and squarely. The Allies were about to invade French soil and were asking him to cooperate. This he would do only if he were given undisputed, supreme authority and command, and he made no bones about saying that once he had that command, he would reverse the entire plan and direct the main effort toward France itself.

Naturally Eisenhower could not accept any such arrangement. The American-British expedition was a colossal one, with a very definite end in view. The objective was closely connected with the British advance from El Alamein, which had just begun. There could be no thought of changing the command at this late date, and there was not the slightest

[60] War Department: message from Eisenhower (November 8, 1942). Butcher: *My Three Years with Eisenhower*; Renée Gosset: *Le Coup d'Alger*, pp. 243ff.

possibility of altering the basic plan. If anyone had to yield, it had to be Giraud. And yield he finally did. In a further message General Eisenhower reported:

"Eisenhower at Gibraltar has finally brought Giraud to an agreement which in substance is as follows:

"Giraud is recognized as the leader of the effort to prevent Axis aggression in North Africa, as the Commander-in-Chief of all French forces in the region and as governor of the French North African provinces. Eisenhower, as Commander-in-Chief of the Allied American-British forces, will co-operate with Giraud to the fullest possible extent, and will work in the closest collaboration with him.

"Giraud will leave Gibraltar tomorrow for North Africa, where he will do all in his power to stop all French resistance to the Allied forces and to begin the organization of French forces for use against the Axis." [61]

At just what time of the night the agreement was arrived at we do not know. But at one thirty A.M. on November 8 the operations off Africa began. This is not the place to review the military events or to trace the vicissitudes of the three task forces that appeared off Casablanca, Oran, and Algiers. The convoys, especially those from the British Isles, had been at sea for a long time and had fortunately evaded the German submarine packs off the Bay of Biscay. Luckily, too, they had been able to pass through the Strait of Gibraltar without interference. In this connection a word should be said about Spain and the Spanish danger.

In all the discussions and planning for the expedition Spain had loomed as a great question mark. The Franco regime, which was considered notoriously pro-Nazi, might easily have decided to throw in its lot with the Axis or at least have taken the opportunity to seize a part of coveted French Morocco. At Algeciras, across from Gibraltar, were the great Spanish shore batteries, which were able to blast the one airfield through which the Allied air forces had to be funneled and

[61] War Department: message from Eisenhower (November 8, 1942). Butcher: *My Three Years with Eisenhower.*

could at will have closed the strait by gunfire. In order to provide against all dire eventualities, General Eisenhower had organized a British force under General Morgan to be in readiness to take action against Spanish Morocco if Spain should become hostile. But this did not remove the threat to the convoys, which was particularly great after an unhappy incident that occurred late in October. A special messenger bearing plans for the invasion from London to Gibraltar failed to arrive at his destination. Presently word was received from Spanish authorities that his plane had been downed and his body washed ashore. The corpse was turned over to the British and in the inside pocket of the officer's coat were the secret papers, apparently untouched and untampered with. The question then arose whether the sealed envelope had been opened or not, and whether, under the circumstances, prudence did not dictate a change in the plans. But the most stringent tests revealed nothing and it was finally decided that the risk would have to be run.[62]

None the less General Eisenhower continued to take precautions. He requested that General Mast be advised through Murphy not to allow French commanders to take retaliatory action in the event of incidents created by the Spanish on the Moroccan frontier, no matter how provocative these incidents might be. Even an advance by Spanish troops into French territory, wrote General Eisenhower, would not justify measures by the French that might bring Spain into active collaboration with the Axis.[63] The War Department seems to have thought that this was going somewhat far, for it raised the question whether it would be advisable to ask the French not to resist in case of an actual Spanish invasion, inasmuch as such an invasion might tend to reduce or eliminate any French resistance to the American forces.[64]

However, on this point General Giraud stood with General Eisenhower. He informed Murphy that he thought the

[62] This story was told J. Rives Childs, the American consul at Tangier, in the late spring of 1943. Childs relayed it to me on May 4, 1944.
[63] War Department: message from Eisenhower (October 28, 1942).
[64] War Department: message to Eisenhower (October 31, 1942).

Americans should do everything possible to placate the
Spaniards, in order to avoid a winter campaign in the Riff.
Indeed, he favored yielding even so far as to allow the Span-
iards to take French Morocco as far as the Ouergha River.[65]

Actually nothing happened, to the immense relief of all
concerned with the success of the venture. Many months later
Churchill recalled with gratitude the position then taken by
the Madrid government. Before the invasion of North Africa,
he pointed out:

"the situation of Spain and Spain's power to injure us was at its
very height. For a long time before this we had been steadily
expanding our airfield at Gibraltar and building it out to sea, and
for one month before the zero hour on November 7, 1942 we had
sometimes 600 airplanes crowded on this airfield in full range
and full view of Spanish batteries. It was very difficult for
Spaniards to believe that all these airplanes were intended to reinforce Malta, and I can assure the House that passage of these
critical days was very anxious indeed. However, the Spaniards
continued absolutely friendly and tranquil. They asked no questions and raised no inconvenience." They simply ignored the
situation at Gibraltar, "where, apart from the aircraft, enormous
numbers of ships were anchored far outside neutral waters inside
the Bay of Algeciras, always under command of Spanish shore
guns. We should have suffered the greatest inconvenience if we
had been ordered to remove these ships. If we had been, I do
not know how the vast convoys could have been marshalled and
assembled." [66]

But to return to the events of November 8. Our task forces
all arrived safely at their appointed stations. Everywhere they

[65] War Department: message from Murphy (November 3, 1942).
[66] Churchill: speech in the House of Commons (May 24, 1944). Carlton
J. H. Hayes: *Wartime Mission in Spain*, pp. 87ff., has revealed that for a
time it was planned to seize the Canary Islands as a precautionary measure.
This idea was abandoned as a result of the ambassador's protest, and instead
assurances were given the Spanish Foreign Minister on November 2 that
Spanish territory would be rigorously respected. None the less, the situation continued so delicate that preparations were made to move the American Embassy to Gibraltar on short notice. Anxiety about Spain is fully reflected in Butcher's diary, cited above.

were met by gunfire from coastal batteries and from units of the French fleet. There was nothing surprising about this resistance for it had been clear all along that hostility from the French naval forces was to be expected. The alarming thing was the extent of French *military* resistance, which was insignificant at Oran and not very impressive about Algiers, but on the Moroccan coast was substantial and menacing. The fact was that the subversive work that had been planned was only partially successful. The time had been too short for final arrangements, supplies had failed to reach the patriot groups, and the time schedule was somewhat off. According to Murphy, he and Colonel Eddy have always been at a loss to explain the failure of supplies for the patriot group to arrive. Evidently the American command felt that there was a risk that our plans would be disclosed or that the arms might be used against our own forces. Added to this was the failure of General Béthouart in the role of conspirator. At eleven p.m. on November 7 he had had news of the impending landings flashed on the cinema screens of Rabat and Casablanca, along with the announcement that at seven o'clock the next morning General Giraud would broadcast his assumption of the command and his welcome to the Americans. At midnight Béthouart arrested General Noguès, the French resident-general, and called on the troops to revolt against Vichy and aid the Americans. Unfortunately he was naïve enough to allow Noguès to remain in his own home. Noguès had a private telephone, on which he called Admiral Michelier at Casablanca. Convinced that the Americans were staging only a commando raid, he ordered Michelier to resist any landing. Since the Giraud broadcast did not materialize on time and since the Americans failed to appear at Rabat, as Béthouart had promised, the insurgent leader was left in the air. Loyal troops presently arrived at Rabat from Meknès, arrested Béthouart, and left Noguès once more in command.[67]

Despite the Moroccan debacle, things went somewhat bet-

[67] Notes by Colonel Eddy, who feels that it was a tragic mistake not to have informed Béthouart more fully of the Allied plans.

ter elsewhere. Throughout North Africa the secret communications network set up by the OSS functioned admirably and made it possible for American agents to communicate with one another and to keep in touch with the task-force commanders. At Algiers the patriot movement started with great élan. Several hundred patriots, chiefly young men of the Chantiers de la Jeunesse, seized the key positions in the city. All would have been well if the American forces had landed and reached Algiers by about two a.m. Sunday, as planned. Unhappily the eastern task force landed at a point nearly four and a half miles farther west from Algiers than its real objective. In the darkness the troops, failing to locate their positions on the maps, lost their way so that the first patrols arrived in the city only at three thirty p.m.—that is, over thirteen hours late. During these anxious hours the small groups of insurgents could not hold out against the regular police authorities. Everything was out of kilter. Giraud had not arrived and, before long, Frenchmen were fighting Frenchmen as well as resisting the invaders.[68] If the plans to take over Morocco and Algeria and then press on to the occupation of Tunisia were to be adhered to, something had to be done to end resistance and secure French co-operation.

It was at this point that Admiral Darlan emerged as the man of the hour. It will be recalled that at the end of October he had made a tour of inspection of North and West Africa and that he had already taken soundings in both Algiers and Washington looking toward his leadership of a patriot movement in support of the Americans. His advances had not been accepted, but his name was at least on the books as a possible alternative to Giraud. As fate would have it, at the most crucial moment, a couple of days before the landings, he was summoned to Algiers to the bedside of his son, who had been stricken with paralysis and was not expected to live. Darlan's presence, Murphy reported at first, might be embarrassing,

[68] See the very detailed account as given by one of the leaders, José Aboulker, in *Les Cahiers français*, No. 47 (August 1943); Renée Gosset: *Le Coup d'Alger*, chap. v. Notes by Murphy.

but it was thought that he would depart before the landings took place.[69]

Time and again the suggestion has been made that Darlan's arrival in Algiers was prearranged, but there is absolutely no evidence to substantiate this theory; neither is there any truth in the charge that secret arrangements had been made with him beforehand. It is not impossible that, having got wind of what was about to happen, he decided to be at the right spot at the right time. But the fact remains that his appearance on the scene was a disagreeable surprise to Murphy and probably to the French leaders, who hoped that he would leave at once. The story goes that Darlan did in fact plan to return to France on November 7, but that at the last moment he decided to stay another day. In any event, the arrival of the expeditionary forces near Algiers found him peacefully asleep at the villa of Admiral Fenard.

The sequel of developments thenceforth can best be given from Murphy's own notes:

"As in his directive Mr. Murphy was led to expect that the Allied landing would be made in the vicinity of Algiers at any time after 2 a.m. November 8, he gave orders to the Algiers patriots to seize the city at 12.30 a.m. At that time he proceeded to the home of General Juin, who was then occupying General Weygand's former residence 'Les Oliviers' in El Biar, a suburb of Algiers close by the Fort l'Empereur on a hill overlooking the city. This is the same residence later used by General de Gaulle.

"When Mr. Murphy called, General Juin, who commanded the land and air forces in French North and West Africa, was sound asleep. He came to the living room in his pyjamas and Mr. Murphy informed him that the landing of a large American expeditionary force (a reference was made to 500,000 men, although the first wave actually only included about 100,000 men) was expected momentarily; that he desired to convey this information in the first instance to General Juin because he was convinced after his several conversations with General Juin that the latter was a patriotic Frenchman who desired to see the liberation of

[69] War Department: message from Murphy (November 5, 1942).

his country and who knew that France's interest lay with the Allies.

"General Juin was startled and shocked. He ejaculated: 'What! You mean that the convoy we have seen in the Mediterranean is going to land here?' When Mr. Murphy replied in the affirmative Juin said: 'But you told me only a week ago that the United States would not attack us.' Mr. Murphy replied that the American expeditionary force was not coming to attack the French, but was coming at French invitation to collaborate with the French in working for the liberation of France. General Juin inquired who gave the invitation. Mr. Murphy replied that General Giraud had extended the invitation. Juin demanded to know whether Giraud was in Algiers and he was informed that General Giraud was expected momentarily.

"It should be remembered at this point that the Allied fleet approaching French North Africa was maintaining radio silence so that our representatives on the shore had no means of knowing at what exact time the landings would be effected. The clandestine radio network maintained by our American representatives continued to keep the fleet informed of developments on shore.

"General Juin paced the floor for a number of minutes, making references to the grave situation which was thus presented and regretting vehemently that he had not been taken into our confidence before. To these regrets Mr. Murphy pointed to the fact that General Juin had taken an oath of allegiance to the French Government and that it had not been desired to place him in a situation embarrassing to an army officer, but that knowing his sentiments we were confident of his support when the time came.

"General Juin then said that if the matter were entirely in his hands there would be no resistance on his part to the American landing, but that, as Mr. Murphy knew, Admiral Darlan had arrived at Algiers unexpectedly incident to the grave illness of Darlan's son who was at that moment in Algiers in a hospital with advanced infantile paralysis. Juin said that no matter what decision he himself might make, it could be immediately overruled by Darlan who commanded all French land, air and sea forces. Mr. Murphy said: 'Very well, let us talk to Darlan.'

"General Juin telephoned Admiral Darlan, who was stopping at the home of Admiral Fenard, about a mile away, informing Darlan that Mr. Murphy had an urgent message for him. Darlan

arrived in about twenty minutes and Mr. Murphy immediately
announced the news to him. His first reaction was to turn purple,
exclaiming: 'I have known for a long time that the British were
stupid, but I always believed that the Americans were more intelligent. I begin to believe that you make as many mistakes as
they do.' (Admiral Darlan explained this later to Mr. Murphy,
saying that what he had in mind was that the French Government in Vichy very possibly would have asked the American
Government, when it considered the time opportune and when
the United States would be able to conduct a simultaneous operation in France and North Africa, for its assistance. The surprise
of the North African landing in his opinion had deprived the
United States of the effective cooperation of the French.)

"Admiral Darlan paced the floor for at least fifteen minutes,
during the course of which Mr. Murphy tried with every argument he could advance to persuade Darlan that it lay both in the
interest of France and in his own interest to seize this golden opportunity. That Admiral Darlan was taken by surprise and torn
by great inner strife Mr. Murphy has no doubt. Among other
arguments advanced, Mr. Murphy reminded Admiral Darlan that
in July 1941 he had stated to Admiral Leahy that if ever the
United States would be prepared to send 500,000 equipped American soldiers and several thousand tanks and planes to Marseille,
to talk to him, Admiral Darlan. Mr. Murphy said to Darlan: 'That
moment has now arrived and it is your responsibility that no
French blood will be shed incident to the massive landing of
American forces which is now about to take place in French
North Africa.' At the end of half an hour Darlan said: 'I have
given my oath to Marshal Pétain and for the past two years I
have preached to my men in the Navy and to the nation unity
behind the Marshal. I cannot now deny my oath.' Mr. Murphy
asked him whether he would cooperate if Marshal Pétain authorized him to do so. To this he replied he would, whereupon
Mr. Murphy suggested that he radio Marshal Pétain and ask him
for the authorization. This Admiral Darlan agreed to do and sat
down in the presence of Mr. Murphy, General Juin, Admiral
Fenard and Admiral Battet, and drafted a radio message to
Marshal Pétain at Vichy, stating that an American landing operation involving half a million men was happening in French North
Africa and requesting the Marshal to give him liberty of action.

"It is obvious from what transpired later that Marshal Pétain, when he received this message, believed that Admiral Darlan was an American prisoner. It had been decided to send this message by the French naval radio from the station in the port of Algiers. When the messenger came to leave the house, however, he found it surrounded by a group of young men armed with rifles. To General Juin's inquiry they replied that no one was to leave the house except a representative of the American consulate. Admiral Darlan and General Juin thereupon concluded that they were prisoners. However, the message was delivered by Vice Consul Kenneth Pendar to the French naval officer in charge in the port of Algiers, who took Pendar into custody. Whether Marshal Pétain ever received this message is not clear. It was never acknowledged.

"Mr. Murphy remained with Admiral Darlan and General Juin until 6.30 a.m., and during that period had opportunity for a comparatively friendly discussion of the possibilities involved. Admiral Darlan grew more relaxed and evidently began to take a passionate interest in the undertaking as he saw its possibilities. He discussed General Giraud with great impartiality, but his analysis of Giraud was simply: 'He is not your man, for politically he is a child. He is a good divisional commander, nothing more.'

"Mr. Murphy began to grow more anxious as the hours went by and there was no sign of the arrival of the American forces. He began to believe that there was an error of date or that things had gone amiss. Radio messages were sent to Gibraltar and the fleet requesting information. The several hundred young men who had seized the city after some violence began to grow apprehensive and the military police and French divisional headquarters in Algiers were activated. It was impossible for the small group of badly armed young men to hold the city indefinitely. At 6.30 a.m., a detachment of 50 Gardes Mobiles armed with machine guns rushed the residence of General Juin, chased away the volunteers after capturing several of them and took Mr. Murphy and Vice Consul Pendar into custody. They were promptly released, however, and at Admiral Darlan's request remained in the house with Admiral Fenard while Darlan and Juin proceeded to Fort l'Empereur, saying that they would communicate with Murphy after they had had an opportunity to obtain information regarding the arrival of our forces which they began to doubt seriously. A telephone call was received shortly saying that the landings were in process all along the Algerian and Moroccan coasts and that there was no doubt that it was a large scale operation. This naturally afforded great relief to the American representatives in Algiers."

In the afternoon General Juin telephoned Murphy from Fort l'Empereur asking him to get in contact with the Allied commander and inform him that the French wished to cease resistance. Murphy at once passed this information on to Major General C. W. Ryder, whose troops were already on the outskirts of the city. Negotiations were opened with Darlan and Juin and an agreement was reached that all resistance should end in the Algiers area at seven p.m.[70]

But these arrangements were purely local and depended in part on the attitude and reaction of Vichy. President Roosevelt had sent to Marshal Pétain a special message explaining the North African enterprise and giving him assurances regarding American intentions:

"My clear purpose is to support and aid the French authorities and their administration. . . . I need not tell you that the ultimate and greater aim is the liberation of France and its Empire from the Axis yoke."

The marshal's reply was immediate and completely uncooperative:

"You knew that we would defend the Empire against any aggressor. . . . You knew that I would keep my word. We have been attacked, and we shall defend ourselves. That is the order I am issuing."[71]

Pétain's reply to the President was probably meant for the record. The story goes that he handed it to Pinckney Tuck,

[70] Notes by Murphy. See also Kenneth Pendar: *Adventure in Diplomacy*, chap. x, and the accounts in *Les Cahiers français* (August 1943), pp. 44-5, and in Renée Gosset: *Le Coup d'Alger*, chap. v.

[71] Released by Radio-Lyon at 7.40 a.m. on November 8, 1942. The full text of these letters is given in *Procès du M. Pétain*, pp. 333-4.

the American chargé d'affaires, with a knowing tap on the shoulder. In any case, the evidence we have of the happenings at Vichy all points to the conclusion that the marshal wished the Allied operation well. There can be no doubt that he knew in advance that something was brewing. On October 30 General Bergeret had let him into the secret of the French plans in North Africa and had urged him to leave Vichy at once to take over the leadership. In the following weeks many others attempted to persuade the marshal to flee to North Africa, but he insisted on sticking by his decision of June 1940 to stay with his people, come what may. He did, however, at once summon General Weygand from Cannes for conferences and seems throughout to have done what he could to obstruct action against the Americans.[72]

The Germans were certainly taken by surprise by the Allied landings in Algeria. They had expected some operation against Dakar or Casablanca, but not in the Mediterranean. Even when the convoys had begun to pass through the strait, they had concluded that a landing would be tried in Rommel's rear or that the Allied effort was designed to relieve hard-pressed Malta.[73] When finally their eyes were opened, they decided at once to put up a fight for Tunisia. Vichy was immediately asked for the right to send German air forces across the unoccupied zone and to grant airfield facilities in Africa. This question was debated by the French cabinet during the day of November 8, the majority of the ministers favoring the German request, while Admiral Auphand, the Minister of Marine, was violently opposed and Pétain supported him. In the end Laval granted the Germans what they asked, without informing the marshal. But by that time a much more serious decision was called for. In the evening Herr Krug von Nidda, the German representative near the marshal, submitted a proposal from Hitler for an out-and-out alliance between Germany and France. The details are not

[72] *Procès du M. Pétain,* p. 139 (Weygand's testimony); pp. 262–3 (General Bergeret).
[73] *Biennial Report of the Chief of Staff, July 1, 1943–June 30, 1945,* p. 3.

known, but the suggested alliance was characterized by the German phrase *"durch dick und dünn"* and according to Laval called for *"une sorte d'intimité totale."* This was too much even for Laval, who set out for Munich on November 9 to beg off. On leaving, Laval gave instructions that no decisions be made regarding North Africa pending his return.[74]

Of further developments at Vichy during November 8 and 9 we have no knowledge. Laval had left for Munich and Pétain, supported by Weygand and Auphand, was permitting events to take their course. We may therefore return to the negotiations that were carried on at Algiers. It will be recalled that Darlan had finally issued an order to cease fire in the Algiers area, but fighting continued elsewhere and was really serious in Morocco. It was imperative that some more comprehensive agreement be arrived at.

General Eisenhower, at Gibraltar, had been taken aback by the news that Darlan was ready to negotiate. The question was what to do with Giraud, who had only just accepted the American terms. Could Giraud and Darlan be brought to work together? Giraud was at once bundled off to Algiers by plane (November 9), followed in the afternoon by General Clark and his advisers. In the meanwhile General Eisenhower issued a statement that proved to be entirely too optimistic:

"General Henri Giraud has arrived in Algiers from France. It can be expected that his presence there will bring about a cessation of scattered resistance, which is tragic between soldiers who have the same enemy. General Giraud has assumed the leadership of the French movement to prevent Axis aggression in North Africa and will organize the French North African Army, again to take up the fight side by side with the forces of the United Nations for the defeat of Germany and Italy and the liberation of France and her Empire. The Allied Commander-in-Chief has agreed to support General Giraud in this theater with the strong forces under his command. The

[74] *Procès du M. Pétain*, p. 202 (Laval's testimony); pp. 279–82 (Captain Archambaud); 308–9 (Lavagne).

Government of the United States has pledged itself to assist in providing arms and equipment for this new French Army."

Actually General Giraud received a very chilly reception from his fellow officers, who refused to have anything to do with him. The French officer corps felt strictly bound by its oath and completely boycotted all those, like General Mast, who had had dealings with the Americans. There was no room in Algiers for "*généraux de dissidence*," and Giraud had to admit from the outset that his following and authority was nil. When General Clark arrived in Algiers, he had to seek out Giraud from a temporary hiding-place in order to bring him into conference with Darlan and Juin.[75]

The conference of General Clark with the French leaders on the evening of November 9 led to no agreement. The general demanded the cessation of hostilities throughout North Africa and tried to bluff Darlan into believing that great numbers of troops were already ashore. But Darlan and Juin were unconvinced. They complained that they had been taken completely by surprise and maintained that if only the Americans had waited two more weeks a French proposal would probably have been made officially that would have obviated French resistance and would probably have secured French co-operation.[76]

On the morning of November 10 the discussions were resumed, this time without Giraud, in deference to the objections of a number of high commanders who had refused to confer in his presence. Darlan stated that he had sent a message to Pétain saying that resistance was futile and asking authority to conclude an armistice. But he would have to wait for authority from Vichy. To this General Clark replied in his usual salty manner: "Tell him that Pétain is nothing in our young lives. He has today broken relations with the United

[75] Notes by Matthews; War Department: message from Eisenhower (November 10, 1942); Pendar: *Adventure in Diplomacy*, pp. 116–17.
[76] OSS Files: message from Algiers (November 9); War Department: message from Eisenhower (November 10); General Julius Holmes: "Eisenhower's African Gamble" (*Collier's Magazine*, January 12, 1946),

States and declared this landing as an act hostile to France. He ordered resistance. As far as we're concerned, we don't recognize any authority of Pétain in North Africa." Darlan still backed and filled but finally, under threat of arrest and given half an hour to make up his mind, he agreed to issue orders to cease firing everywhere. He agreed further to issue orders to the French fleet to be ready to move at once from Toulon in case the Germans proceeded to occupy all of France. In the meanwhile he assumed complete authority over North Africa "in the name of the marshal" and ordered all military and civil officials to remain at their posts.[77]

Darlan's decision was at once communicated to Vichy, where both Weygand and Auphand urged Pétain to approve it. The marshal agreed at once and it was decided further to order the fleet to sea and to instruct the French garrisons to take to the hills. But unfortunately Darlan's message had been intercepted by the Germans, who at once confronted Laval with it. Laval phoned Vichy in a panic, threatening to resign and forecasting all sorts of dire reprisals by the Germans unless Darlan were disavowed and new orders issued to resist. Thereupon Pétain reversed himself, did Laval's bidding, and, on the theory that Darlan was no longer a free agent, named General Noguès as commander-in-chief in North Africa. At the same time, however, he sent a message in a special secret naval code indicating to Darlan that he approved his action and continued to have confidence in him.[78]

Unluckily Darlan received the first of these messages before the second. The result was a final flurry. The admiral announced that he must rescind his order, since he lacked authority to maintain it. To this General Clark replied: "Damned

---

[77] War Department: message from Eisenhower (November 11, 1942); General Julius Holmes: "Eisenhower's African Gamble," as above. The account in Wes Gallagher: *Back Door to Berlin*, pp. 68–9, is evidently based on information from General Clark. Demaree Bess (*Saturday Evening Post*, July 10, 1943) is less accurate. See also Churchill's statement at a secret session of the House of Commons, December 10, 1942 (*Life*, February 4, 1946).

[78] *Procès du M. Pétain*, p. 139 (Weygand's testimony); pp. 262–3 (General Bergeret); 279–82 (Archambaud); 299–301 (letter of General Juin); 308–9 (Lavagne).

if you do," whereupon Darlan stated that he would have to consider himself under arrest. Things were now in a complete mess. Darlan refused to budge and Giraud was helpless. It was at this crucial moment that Pétain's secret message arrived and, what was even more important, word was received that the Germans were proceeding to the occupation of all France.[79]

Even after the final victory over Germany in 1945 General Eisenhower confessed, in a press conference, that his most anxious moment had been in the night of the North African landings. "We hoped," he remarked, "that if we made a show of overpowering strength the Germans would not hold that part of France that was then unoccupied and would let it alone. In other words, if the French could show that it was impractical for them to make a great fight down there, it would give them an out." [80] Actually the chances of this were so slight as to have been negligible and the German occupation of all France had been discounted in advance in the Allied plans. We know from Count Ciano's diary that Hitler's decision was taken almost at once. On November 9 he said that he would listen to Laval but that nothing would shake his determination to occupy all France, land in Corsica, and establish bridgeheads in Tunisia.[81]

Under the circumstances Laval's visit to Munich was futile. The Führer told him that he was shocked at Giraud's conduct and declared that France had the choice between two courses: either final and definitive attachment to the Axis, or loss of her entire colonial empire. The Anglo-Saxons, he added, would get it all. Would France accept Axis aid? But Laval, be it said to his credit, avoided committing his country to an alliance. He agreed that Britain would not keep her promises, and said that he had never expected Giraud to keep his word. On the other hand, he had persuaded Pétain to disavow Darlan's action and he was sure that Noguès was reliable. There

---

[79] Butcher: *My Three Years with Eisenhower*; General Julius Holmes: "Eisenhower's African Gamble" (*Collier's Magazine*, January 12, 1946).
[80] *Washington Post*, June 16, 1945.
[81] Ciano *Diary*, entry for November 9, 1942.

followed some acrimonious debate about collaboration, which Laval tried to show had been far more extensive than Hitler supposed. The Führer, however, was dissatisfied and told Laval that he would occupy the rest of France and demand bases in Tunisia. Laval promised to urge Pétain to accord them, but suggested that it would be better for the Germans simply to take them. In closing he stressed his "fanatic resolution" to do everything possible to help Germany in the struggle against Bolshevism.[82]

So even Laval was presented with a *fait accompli* so far as the occupation of France was concerned. At Vichy, Weygand and others induced Pétain to publish at once a vigorous protest, and this went on the air before Laval could return to stop it.[83]

But let us return to the North African scene. General Eisenhower had at once cabled the news of the German advance and had urged General Clark to get Darlan, Giraud, and Juin to telephone Admiral Esteva in Tunisia begging him to seize all Axis personnel and equipment and hold on until the Allies could rush troops and supplies to his assistance. Darlan was also to get the French fleet to Gibraltar.

The news from France simply electrified Darlan and the other French leaders. They could now argue with a clear conscience that the marshal was a prisoner of the enemy, and Darlan, with a reassuring telegram in his pocket could reason that it was his duty to take control of North Africa in the marshal's name. All he had to do was to square the situation with General Noguès, whom Pétain had officially named to the command.

Conferences went on almost without a break. On the afternoon of November 11 Darlan agreed to appeal to the French fleet and to order resistance to the Germans in Tunisia. That same evening Darlan and Giraud met for the first time in conference and agreed tentatively that Darlan should be the

[82] Captured German Documents: record of the meeting of Hitler, Ribbentrop, Ciano, and Laval at Munich, November 19, 1942.

[83] *Procès du M. Pétain*, pp. 279–82 (Archambaud's testimony); 209 (Laval).

political chief, while Giraud should hold the military command of the French troops.[84]

Another day was lost, however, in dispute and recrimination, due apparently to the unwillingness of many French officers to accept Giraud. There were threats from General Clark and appeals from General Eisenhower and finally, on the evening of November 12, Noguès arrived from Morocco. He willingly returned his mandate to Darlan, but argument on the command question continued into the following day, when General Eisenhower arrived from Gibraltar and induced all the French leaders to accept the arrangement worked out between Darlan and Giraud.[85]

At Vichy the double play continued. Laval, on his return, ordered Admiral Esteva to co-operate with the Germans, as unfortunately he did. At the same time Pétain was obliged to issue an order to Darlan to continue the resistance. Giraud was branded "a rebel chief and a felon" who had broken his oath as an officer.[86] But by most secret code a second message was sent to Darlan by the marshal (of course without Laval's knowledge) indicating approval of his assumption of authority.[87] This message naturally reassured Darlan and his associates and enabled them to bring Boisson, the Governor-General of West Africa, to the Allied side. General Bergeret at once flew to Dakar with the message and induced Boisson to declare his adherence in principle (November 14). But the wary Governor insisted on sending his own officers to Algiers to test the authenticity of the message. His emissaries were entirely satisfied and so reported to their chief. Boisson went through the formality of appealing to Vichy for instructions, but, having been told to resist to the uttermost, he

[84] War Department: messages from Eisenhower (November 11, 12, 1942), and the full account in Gallagher's book and in General Holmes's article. See also Churchill's statement to the House of Commons, December 10, 1942 (*Life*, February 4, 1946).
[85] War Department: messages from Eisenhower (November 12, 13, 14, 1942); General Holmes's article and Butcher's diary, as cited above. See also Gallagher's book and Demaree Bess's article already referred to.
[86] *Procès du M. Pétain*, pp. 139, 209.
[87] Ibid., pp. 279–82 (Archambaud); 299–301 (Juin's letter).

threw in his lot with Darlan and the Allies (November 22).[88] This was a great and unqualified victory for the Allied cause, for it gave us security in the rear and enabled us to open new and better air supply lines across the Atlantic to our fighting forces. Darlan's recognized authority, together with the secret approval of Pétain, served to turn a trick that would otherwise have been impossible.

But however clear Darlan's usefulness may have been, the emergence of his name had at once caused a storm of protest in both Britain and the United States, a storm that de Gaulle fanned to the best of his ability. We shall have to return to this aspect of the problem later, but right here and now it should be said that all the Americans, from General Eisenhower downward, accepted the Darlan solution with the greatest reluctance. Yet this solution was forced on us by the French themselves, who would have none of Giraud, but were only too ready to accept Darlan because he had legality on his side. General Eisenhower assumed full responsibility and undertook to explain his stand in great detail. His message of November 14 is so explicit, and for that reason so important, that despite its length a paraphrase of it must be given here. The general prefaced his remarks by saying that he could well understand the bewilderment in London and Washington, but then went on to explain:

"Existing French sentiment in North Africa does not even remotely resemble prior calculations and it is of utmost importance that no precipitate action be taken which will upset such equilibrium as we have been able to establish.

"The name of Marshal Pétain is something to conjure with in North Africa. From highest to lowest, everyone attempts to create the impression that the shadow of the Marshal's figure dominates all his actions and, in fact, his very life. The military and naval leaders, as well as the civil governors, agree that only one man has the obvious right to assume the mantle

[88] *Procès du M. Pétain*, pp. 262–63 (General Bergeret); 279–82 (Archambaud); General Holmes: "Eisenhower's African Gamble" (*Collier's Magazine*, January 19, 1946); notes by Matthews.

of Pétain and that man is Admiral Darlan. Even General Giraud clearly recognizes this over-powering consideration and he has modified his own ambitions and intentions accordingly.

"The initial resistance to our landing was due to the fact that all concerned believed such action to be in keeping with the Marshal's desires. General Giraud, in fact, is deemed guilty of at least a touch of treachery in urging non-resistance to the Allied landing. However, all concerned now profess themselves ready to support the Allies provided Admiral Darlan tells them to do so. They are absolutely not willing to follow anyone else. General Noguès stopped fighting in Morocco on Darlan's order; Admiral Esteva, in Tunis, says he will obey Darlan. We cannot escape recognition of Darlan's position in this respect.

"Briefly, the current agreement provides that the French in North Africa will do what they can at once to assist us in taking Tunisia. They will organize French North Africa for effective cooperation. General Giraud will begin reorganization of local French military forces for active participation in the war. Admiral Darlan will exhaust every expedient in an effort to get the Fleet at Toulon. On our part, we will support him in controlling and pacifying the country and in helping equip French military forces. Details are still under discussion.

"Our hope of gaining in North Africa a supporting and organized population and in securing the early conquest of Tunisia cannot be realized without acceptance along the lines of this general agreement. General Giraud, fully aware of his inability even with Allied military and moral support to do anything by himself, has accepted cheerfully the post of Military Chief in the Darlan group. Complete military occupation, the cost of which in time and resources would be tremendous, will be necessary unless we can deal with a strong French Government of some kind in North Africa. In Morocco alone, General Patton estimates 60,000 Allied troops would be required to control the Moroccan tribes. The effect which tribal disturbances would have on Spain is only a part of the problem. While hostilities in Morocco ceased on orders of Darlan and not by full military conquest, the situation in that area is still such as to be capable of causing us additional trouble. Noguès, who will obey no one but Darlan, may choose to influence the tribes. The results of such action on Spanish Morocco are obvious.

"I assure you that only after incessant examination of the important factors have these agreements been made. They are essential in order to get on with the military objectives against the Axis and advance the interests of the Allies in winning this war.

"General Giraud's name must not be associated publicly with this movement at present. However, you may assure any of the Free French, to whom it is necessary to impart this information, that General Giraud is an enthusiastic participant in this arrangement and has expressed himself to me as pleased with the turn of events. The fact that our Governments have commitments to certain elements of the French people throughout the world is clearly realized. We are not attempting to extend the local agreement beyond the areas in which it is necessary to do so. In this connection, however, the Darlan group firmly believes that permission to send an emissary to Dakar will eventuate in drawing French West Africa into this organizational arrangement very quickly. Thereby, that area can be made secure to the Allies. In view of the fact that the French group is committed to going along with us, defeating Germany, and staying in the war until the end, it would appear that I should be authorized at once to assist the Group in sending an emissary to Dakar.

"Admiral Cunningham has had a personal conversation with Darlan and they have agreed upon a final appeal to the Toulon Fleet. I am convinced that Darlan is making a determined effort to get the French Fleet. Even if he fails, it should be realized that he is not empty-handed, so far as affairs in North Africa are concerned. Mr. Murphy, who has done a grand job, will, as head of my Civil Affairs Section, be very close to Darlan. Mr. Mack and other capable men will cooperate with him.

"It must be understood that if we repudiate Darlan and attempt from the outside to dictate the personnel of the coalition to run North Africa, the following will be the consequences:

a. French armed forces here will resist us passively and, in certain instances, actively.

b. The hope of securing cooperation in this area will be lost at great cost to us in stagnation of operations and in requirements for additional troops.

c. The opportunity for gaining some assistance from remaining French naval and military units in North Africa will disappear.

d. The last glimmer of hope with respect to the Toulon Fleet will be gone.

e. Admiral Esteva, in Tunis, will not cooperate and our hope of getting Tunisia quickly will not be attainable. Admittedly, Esteva may already be helpless, but there is still a chance of his being able to assist.

"Admiral Cunningham and General Clark, together with my full staff, have assisted me in making what we consider to be the only possible workable arrangement desired to secure advantages and avoid disadvantages. No one who is not on the ground can have a clear appreciation of the complex currents of prejudice and feeling that influence the local situation. Also, it should be clear that General Giraud's earnest participation in this arrangement indicates the necessity for the agreements we have made.

"In the event the British and U. S. Government, after analysis of this radio, are still dissatisfied with the nature of the agreement made, I suggest that a mission of selected U. S. and British representatives (including the Free French if deemed advisable) be dispatched immediately to Algiers, where they can be convinced in short order of the soundness of the moves which have been made." [89]

This lengthy apologia leaves very little to be said, but in reviewing the developments recounted in this chapter a few

[89] War Department: message from Eisenhower (November 14, 1942).

general observations may be in order. In the first place it
should be pointed out that the arrangements first with Giraud
and then with Darlan were arrangements made by the Army—
that is, by General Eisenhower and those working under his
command. The Department of State had nothing to do with
them. In fact, the Murphy-Giraud letters of November 2 did
not even find their way into the Department until long afterward. From the standpoint of the military leaders it was essential that resistance by the French forces in North Africa
be avoided or at least reduced to a minimum. Under the circumstances it must be regretted that this problem was tackled
so late in the planning stage. When finally the question was
faced, there was nothing to do but approach the resistance
group with which Murphy and Colonel Eddy had been dealing for some time. De Gaulle and the Fighting French were
impossible from the outset because it was generally recognized
that they had no following in North Africa and that their appearance on the scene would have inevitably meant civil war.
North Africa, though it was anti-German, was passionately
devoted to Marshal Pétain and the Vichy government.

Giraud was the choice of General Mast and the rest of the
Algiers patriot group. There was no other group and there
was no other leader. Unfortunately the decisive negotiations
were initiated at a very late date, too late really to make effective action possible. Unfortunately, too, the sentiments of
General Mast and his associates were by no means the sentiments of all commanders and high officials in French North
Africa. And, finally, equally unfortunate was it that General
Giraud was not as ready to lead the French in the North
African enterprise as was his spokesman in Algiers. There is
no evidence whatever that Marshal Pétain had been initiated
into Giraud's far-flung schemes for a great rising in Metropolitan France in the spring of 1943, but there can be no doubt
that these plans were being elaborated and it seems likely that
Giraud would have brought the marshal into them at the
proper moment. At any rate, Giraud appears to have felt
bound by his promises to the marshal, and he was certainly

wedded to his own Continental plans. Militarily, no doubt
these plans were sound. The trouble was that they were not
feasible at the time nor in connection with the North African
campaign. It is not the least bit astonishing, though, that
Giraud should have been loath to give them up. Neither is it
to be wondered at that he objected to accepting a subordinate
part in a plan elaborated by foreigners, by much younger and
less experienced commanders. His insistence on having the
supreme command is understandable from the French viewpoint as well as from the personal angle. The remarkable thing
is not that Giraud should have advanced these claims, but
rather that he should ever have abandoned them. Since General Eisenhower was unwilling to give Giraud and the French
leaders more than a few days' notice of the beginning of the
operation, it was inevitable that serious complications should
ensue. To the difficulties inherent in the situation were added
the complications resulting from lack of time.

The upshot of it all was that when the landings were made,
Giraud was not on the spot. In fact, his leadership had not
even been announced to the North African forces. In the
long run, however, this appears to have made little difference.
It is most unlikely that even if Giraud had issued his proclamation and had appeared on the scene at the right moment,
things would have been any better. Most of the important
French commanders—men like Noguès, Juin, Esteva, Fenard, Chatel, and others—were not in the group about General Mast. Most of these commanders were undoubtedly anti-
German and patriotic, and several of them were to play
prominent roles later in the campaigns against the Nazis. But
these men were appointees of Vichy. They were loyal to the
marshal and they took their orders from the Vichy government. Their orders were to resist attack from whatever quarter. They thought at first that the Allied operation was
nothing more than a series of commando raids, but the
chances are that even if they had known the magnitude of
our forces, they would none the less have obeyed their orders. Nothing is more revealing than the fact that these men

would have nothing to do with Giraud when he appeared. For them he was a traitor and a rebel, who had no authority whatever to give commands.

Under the circumstances it was nothing less than a miracle that Darlan happened on the scene, for Darlan was the legally appointed commander of all French forces, on land and in the air as well as on the sea. The officer corps recognized his authority and was ready to follow him. As for Darlan himself, it seems reasonably clear that on this occasion, as on so many others, he acted as a simon-pure opportunist. So long as he had reason to suppose that the Allied forces were small, he refused to have anything to do with the business. Only after he had learned the truth of the matter did he begin to waver. And even then he tried to act within the framework of his constituted authority. He appealed to Vichy on everything. Whether he would have proceeded on his own and whether the other commanders would have accepted his lead, had it not been for Pétain's secret messages and the total occupation of France by the Germans on November 11, we shall probably never know. At any rate, the new German move gave him an excuse, for it clearly deprived Vichy of all independence and made it possible for Darlan to take the protection of French interests into his own hands. The argument and dispute of November 11–13 had, in reality, nothing to do with this fairly simple proposition. The issue of the long and heated negotiations was simply whether Giraud should be given any part in the new undertaking and whether positive assistance should be given to the invaders. Since we ourselves had drawn Giraud out of retirement and had offered him the leadership of the French, we could hardly abandon him. Giraud himself, being ready to accept the authority of Darlan, made it all the more imperative that we continue to support him. But when the agreement was finally arrived at, the whole situation had been revolutionized. As the conclusion of our long-term policy of maintaining relations with Vichy, we found ourselves now in North Africa as the associates of one of the most notorious of the men of

Vichy. It was an awkward business and one that would require a good deal of explaining. But, as General Eisenhower said in his report, the decision to treat with Darlan was "dictated by considerations of sheer military expediency." Since we were at war, military expediency was of necessity paramount.

CHAPTER IX

The Darlan Interlude

THE INVASION of North Africa was planned and executed in conjunction with General Montgomery's breaking of the Nazi lines at El Alamein, which prefaced the spectacular British march through Libya. Taken together, the two operations marked the turning of the tide in the war against Germany. In the Pacific the Americans had taken the offensive at Guadalcanal in August, and now the Allies had seized the initiative at the gates of Europe also.

At first everything seemed to proceed under the most favorable auspices. The Germans had been badly misled by the direction of the Allied convoys toward Malta and were therefore taken by surprise. The Spanish government maintained a neutrality that, if it was cold, was none the less welcome. French resistance was, at its worst, not too formidable. A thrill of excitement and hope ran through Britain and through the United States, to say nothing of the conquered countries of Europe. President Roosevelt's messages and appeals set the tone for the great adventure. In his radio message to the French people he declared:

"We come among you to repulse cruel invaders who would remove forever your rights of self-government, your rights to religious freedom, and your rights to live your own lives in peace and security.

"We come among you solely to defeat and rout your enemies. Have faith in our words. We do not want to cause you any harm.

"We assure you that once the menace of Germany and Italy is removed from you, we shall quit your territory at once." [1]

[1] Radio message of the President, November 7, 1942.

In like manner the President appealed to Marshal Pétain, explaining that the American action was taken merely to forestall an Axis conquest of North Africa, which would have constituted a menace to the Western Hemisphere:

"I am making all this clear to the French authorities in North Africa," he wrote, "and I am calling on them for their cooperation in repelling the Axis threats. My clear purpose is to support and aid the French authorities and their administrations. That is the immediate aim of these American armies.

"I need not tell you that the ultimate and greater aim is the liberation of France and its Empire from the Axis yoke. In so doing we provide automatically for the security of the Americas." [2]

To be sure, Pétain responded to this appeal in uncompromising terms:

"You invoke pretexts which nothing justifies. You attribute to your enemies intentions which have not ever been manifested in acts. I have always declared that we would defend our Empire if it were attacked; you should have known that we would defend it against any aggressor, whoever he might be. You should have known that I would keep my word." [3]

As we have seen in the preceding chapter, Pétain's official pronouncements did not reflect his real views, but in any case the public had its own ideas about the marshal and few if any expected him to subscribe to the American action. His refusal to do so only bore out the widespread impression that he was merely a tool of the Nazis, whose occupation of all Metropolitan France on November 11, 1942 was more or less anticipated. By and large, the final rupture of relations with Vichy was hailed in the American press as the final liberation from a hated bond.

Secretary Hull seized this occasion to settle accounts with the many opponents of the government's past policy. In his press conferences of November 8 and 9 he interpreted recent events as a justification of what had gone before. The libera-

[2] Message of the President to Marshal Pétain (November 8, 1942).
[3] Message of Pétain to President Roosevelt (November 8, 1942).

tion of North Africa, he argued, carried forward the various purposes and objectives that the government had had in pursuing its policy toward Vichy—a policy that had been directed to the ultimate liberation of France. The more important of the government's purposes, he went on, had been the following: (1) opportunity for the government of the United States to get from week to week highly important information virtually from the inside of German-controlled territory and from North Africa regarding Axis subversive activities and other important aspects of the international situation; (2) the maintenance of close relations with the French people and encouragement of leadership in opposition to Hitlerism wherever it existed; (3) the keeping alive of the basic concepts of freedom of the French people, looking toward ultimate restoration of free institutions for France as they existed before the German occupation; (4) the retention of the closest personal touch on the ground with all phases of the French and German situation under the armistice prevailing between Germany and France; resistance to increased German pressure on France to go beyond the armistice provisions and to collaborate with Germany; constant effort to prevent delivery of the French fleet or any part of it into German military hands or to give military support to German arms; that also included French bases all along the Mediterranean and Atlantic coasts; and (5) last, but most important, paving the way and preparing the background, in the most effective manner possible, for the planning and sending of the military expedition into the western Mediterranean area, and assisting the movements supporting present British operations farther east.

These explanations satisfied the larger part of American opinion, if only on the theory that all's well that ends well. Coming to Secretary Hull's support, the *New York World-Telegram*, like many other papers, declared:

"Because our Secretary of State had the brains to keep contact with France and her African colonies through diplomatic representation, he was smeared as an 'appeaser,' a 'Fascist' who should resign or be fired by the President. Today, thanks to the Hull policy of maintaining friendship with the French people, even at the price of recognizing the Pétain-Laval regime, most Frenchmen at home and in Africa welcome instead of oppose the American offensive of liberation." [4]

Only the die-hards raised questions. Walter Lippmann queried whether our policy had prevented France from joining the Axis, whether it had immobilized the French fleet, and whether it had opened up North Africa to us. "The foundation of all these things," he maintained, "has been the increasingly organized and ever more vehement resistance of the people of France, and we must not approach the tremendous problem of France with any illusion that the tail has been wagging the dog." [5] Other writers and papers of liberal persuasion challenged the Secretary on the same grounds, the implication being always that our Vichy policy had confused the French rather than comforted them and that the "basic concepts of the freedom of the French people" had been fostered by de Gaulle and his followers rather than by the Department of State. The *Nation* bemoaned the fact that de Gaulle had been left out of the picture, while the *New Republic* declared "it is certain that the [American] policy frittered away much good will on the part of the anti-Fascist French, and raised doubts all over the world about our war aims." [6]

But even many of those who were prepared to accept the wisdom of past State Department policy were shocked and horrified by the emergence of Darlan as the man of the hour, the more so as acceptance of Darlan blasted all hope of associating the de Gaulle forces with the effort to liberate French territory. Churchill, it will be remembered, had been anxious to inform de Gaulle at least a day or two before the

[4] *New York World-Telegram*, November 10, 1942.
[5] *Washington Post*, November 12, 1942.
[6] See Dorothy Thompson's column (November 13, 1942); the *Nation* (November 14, 1942); the *New Republic* (November 16, 1942).

invasion, in the hope of reconciling him to the situation and paving the way to co-operation between the Fighting French and the followers of Giraud. The President had vetoed any discussions prior to the invasion, so it was only on November 8 that the Prime Minister and Anthony Eden could take the general into their confidence. The results were eminently satisfactory. De Gaulle declared that he put the interests of the French people above all other considerations and regarded it as imperative to avoid the development of two competing Free French movements. In his opinion, Giraud was well qualified to play the part assigned to him, for he was not tainted by the armistice, was well known in North Africa, and would enjoy support of the army. If he succeeded in bringing over North Africa, de Gaulle would be ready to arrive at an agreement with him.[7]

Lord Halifax was so pleased that he communicated this message at once to Secretary Hull, adding his congratulations to the Department for its part "in the work of establishing and carrying out our policy toward Vichy." In view of previous British criticism and obstruction, Hull thought this a mite gratuitous. He expressed his thanks, but added his opinion that the British government "might well give an expression of approval after having concealed its position over all these months."[8]

In the meanwhile Churchill cabled the President to say that he felt under a definite obligation to see that de Gaulle got a fair deal and that it was necessary at all costs to prevent the formation of rival French émigré governments, one backed by Britain and the other by the United States. The President agreed and replied at once (November 11):

"In regard to De Gaulle, I have heretofore enjoyed a quiet satisfaction in leaving him in your hands. Apparently I have now acquired a similar problem in brother Giraud. I wholly agree that

[7] Message from London (November 8, 1942).

[8] Note of Hull on the above telegram. In his statement to the House of Commons on December 10, 1942, the Prime Minister also recognized the value of the American relationship with Vichy (*Life*, February 4, 1946).

we must prevent rivalry between the French émigré factions and I have no objection to a De Gaulle emissary visiting Giraud in Algiers. We must remember there is also a catfight in progress between Giraud and Darlan, each claiming full military command of French forces in North and West Africa. The principal thought to be driven home to all three of these primadonnas is that the situation is today solely in the military field and that any decision by any one of them, or by all of them, is subject to review and approval by Eisenhower." [9]

But all thought of co-operation between de Gaulle and Giraud was at once exploded by Giraud's eclipse and Darlan's rise. In both Britain and the United States a howl of indignation went up at the news of Allied dealings with that "stinking skunk." This "shameless dickering" with a notorious Quisling was an outrageous betrayal of Allied ideals. The de Gaullists added their voices to the din, and before long André Philip, the Fighting French delegate for foreign affairs, announced publicly: "We and we alone have the right to speak for France and we know that France wants to have nothing more to do with the traitors of Bordeaux and Vichy, who sold their country once and are now trying to sell it again to the highest bidder."

So violent was the public reaction that General Clark felt impelled to restate once more the case for the deal with Darlan. In a message to General Eisenhower he pointed out:

"It would have been perfect chaos had we attempted to force Giraud to the top against this seething opposition. I want you to know, and Murphy, Matthews and Holmes concur, that if we had to do this over again, we would be forced to deal with Darlan as a military expediency in order to be free to move our troops to the East, unhindered by strife and disturbance in our rear areas. I have made it clear to Darlan in no uncertain words that we are dealing with him only as long as he does exactly as we say." [10]

[9] Roosevelt Records.
[10] General Julius Holmes: "Eisenhower's African Gamble" (*Collier's Magazine*, January 12, 1946).

General Eisenhower did not need convincing, neither did the President. Even Churchill gradually came to accept the military viewpoint. But the public on both sides of the Atlantic continued in furor until on November 17 the President issued a public statement explaining the situation and particularly the position of Darlan:

"I have accepted General Eisenhower's political arrangements made for the time being in Northern and Western Africa.

"I thoroughly understand and approve the feeling in the United States and Great Britain and among all the other United Nations that in view of the history of the past two years no permanent arrangement should be made with Admiral Darlan. People in the United Nations likewise would never understand the recognition of a reconstituting of the Vichy Government in France or in any French territory.

"We are opposed to Frenchmen who support Hitler and the Axis. No one in our Army has any authority to discuss the future Government of France and the French Empire.

"The future French Government will be established, not by any individual in Metropolitan France or overseas, but by the French people themselves after they have been set free by the victory of the United Nations.

"The present temporary arrangement in North and West Africa is only a temporary expedient, justified solely by the stress of battle.

"The present temporary arrangement has accomplished two military objectives. The first was to save American and British lives, and French lives on the other hand.

"The second was the vital factor of time. The temporary arrangement has made it possible to avoid a 'mopping-up' period in Algiers and Morocco which might have taken a month or two to consummate. Such a period would have delayed the concentration for the attack from the West on Tunis, and we hope on Tripoli. . . .

"Admiral Darlan's proclamation assisted in making a 'mopping-up' period unnecessary. Temporary arrangements made with Admiral Darlan apply, without exception, to the current local situation only.

"I have requested the liberation of all persons in North Africa who have been imprisoned because they opposed the efforts of the Nazis to dominate the world, and I have asked for the abrogation of all laws and decrees inspired by Nazi governments or Nazi ideologists. Reports indicate that the French of North Africa are subordinating all political questions to the formation of a common front against the common enemy." [11]

This statement helped to quiet the agitation on this side of the ocean and made it possible for the Combined Chiefs of Staff (November 22) to put their stamp of approval on the Clark-Darlan agreement. Even then the President refused to have the document described as a *protocol*, because that word might imply official government commitment. The whole thing was to be kept on a strictly military basis: "It is not desired to recognize Darlan, either expressly or by implication, as a national plenipotentiary." [12]

Nevertheless, in Britain criticism and protest continued unabated. On November 26 a motion was introduced in the House of Commons to this effect:

"That this House is of the opinion that our relations with Admiral Darlan and his kind are inconsistent with the ideals for which we entered and are fighting this war; furthermore, that these relations, if persisted in, will undermine the faith in us among our friends in the oppressed and invaded nations and impair the military, social and political prospects of the final and complete triumph of the cause of the United Nations."

The situation was serious. Ambassador Winant informed the President that Eden might have to make a statement. The President hoped that this would not be necessary but that if it were unavoidable it might be restricted to something like this:

"The United States Government takes the position that the operations in North Africa are purely military in character. A desperate battle for the control of Africa is in progress. General Eisenhower is in command of our Allied armies. He will give out

[11] Statement of President Roosevelt (November 17, 1942).
[12] War Department: message to Eisenhower (November 19); Roosevelt Records.

all information that is consistent with the security of the armed forces." [13]

In the end Eden made no statement, but the Prime Minister read the President's explanation of November 17.[14] None the less, criticism of the Darlan deal continued right down to the admiral's assassination.

Looking at the other side of the shield, it should be noted that the President's statement was a severe blow to Darlan, who at once wrote an aggrieved letter to General Clark:

"*Monsieur le Général*:

"Information from various sources tends to substantiate the view that I am 'only a lemon which the Americans will drop after they have squeezed it dry.'

"In the line of conduct which I have adopted out of pure French patriotic feeling, in spite of the serious disadvantages which it entails for me, at a moment when it was extremely easy for me to let events take their course without my intervention, my own personal position does not come into consideration.

"I acted only because the American Government solemnly undertook to restore the integrity of French sovereignty as it existed in 1939, and because the Armistice between the Axis and France was broken by the total occupation of Metropolitan France, an occupation against which the Marshal solemnly protested.

"I did not act through pride, ambition or calculation, but because the position which I occupied in my own country made it my duty to act.

"When the integrity of France's sovereignty is an accomplished fact—and I hope that it will be in the shortest possible time—it is my firm intention to return to private life and to end my days, in the course of which I have served my country ardently, in retirement.

"If it is in this sense that I may interpret the declaration attributed to President Roosevelt that an agreement with me can only be temporary, I entirely share this point of view.

[13] Roosevelt Records.
[14] Churchill's statement at a secret session of the House of Commons on December 10, 1942 (published in *Life*, February 4, 1946) was a brilliant review of the entire political problem in North Africa.

"But I venture to think—the claim is perhaps excessive—that
in present circumstances it is about my name, associated with
the names of men like General Giraud, General Noguès,
Governor-General Boisson, Admiral Michelier, that the union of
Africa can be realized, with a view to frank and loyal co-
operation between the French forces and the population and the
Allied Armies. This co-operation is an essential element in the
success of the cause of the United States in Africa.

"In these conditions the task of rallying all Frenchmen which
I am undertaking, would be made very difficult for me if the
Allies of France were themselves to sow doubt in the minds of
Frenchmen regarding the scope and importance of this task.

"I hope I can count on a realization of this by the United
States Government and that, were it only in view of the result
to be expected in the struggle into which French Africa is returning, they will not give Frenchmen the impression that the
authority of the leader which has brought it back into the struggle is a diminished one." [15]

According to Captain Butcher's diary, Churchill was quite
touched by this letter when he saw it, and suggested that a
friendly reply be made to it. In all fairness it must be said
that Darlan had a grievance. He had not offered his help to
the Allies, but rather had been pressed into service by them.
Yet here, even before his agreement with General Clark had
been officially approved, he was being disavowed and de-
flated. And despite all this the American authorities were
making extensive demands on him and he was meeting them
to the best of his ability. In the picturesque words of General
Clark: "Once we got him into the box for our side, he pitched
big-league ball." [16] His cease-fire order had without question
saved many American lives, and his quick action had put at
our disposal French forces for the campaign in Tunisia. Furthermore, it was his position and influence that induced Boisson to come into the Allied camp, giving us security in West
Africa. And, finally, he had made repeated efforts to persuade

[15] War Department: letter of Darlan to General Clark (November 21,
1942).
[16] General Julius Holmes, as cited above; notes by Matthews.

the French fleet at Toulon to come to North Africa. In this, to be sure, he had been unsuccessful, but the fault was in no way his. A few words of explanation will clarify this point.

Darlan's influence and control of the French fleet had always been the basis of his power and there was every reason to suppose that his orders to the fleet would be obeyed even if all others were ignored. Furthermore, Admiral Auphand, the Vichy Minister of Marine, was his friend and was a confirmed antagonist of the Germans. There can be no doubt whatever that both Auphand and Weygand persuaded Pétain that the fleet should at least flee Toulon as the German forces approached. Unfortunately the French commander at Toulon, Admiral de Laborde, hated Darlan and replied to his appeals with the one inelegant word *"Merde."* Since the Germans discreetly left a small unoccupied zone around Toulon, Laborde bided his time. Auphand, in disgust, resigned from his post, and when finally the Germans proceeded to seize the fleet the French commanders scuttled it, in conformance with the instructions issued in June 1940. Why Laborde chose this course may never be known. It has been claimed that the ships were in no condition to go to sea and that they lacked fuel; furthermore, that the Germans had mined the waters off Toulon and that they would have dive-bombed the ships the moment they attempted to leave. These explanations may be valid, but it should be noted that a strong British naval force (three battleships, two carriers, four cruisers, and fifteen destroyers) had been stationed off Toulon and Italy to watch the Italian fleet and give the French ships aid if they tried to escape. However, the fleet was scuttled. If the Allies failed to get it, so did the Germans.[17]

But even though Darlan did his best to give the Allied cause all possible support, he conducted a policy in internal affairs that bore no relationship whatever to the democratic ideals advanced by the Allies. Pétain had publicly disavowed him

[17] See the valuable testimony of Captain Archambaud, who was Auphand's aide, in *Procès du M. Pétain,* and General Julius Holmes's article in *Collier's Magazine* (January 19, 1946). I am indebted also to notes by Murphy.

and declared him an outlaw, but the admiral, arguing conveniently that the marshal was no longer a free agent since the occupation of all France, insisted and continued to insist that he remained faithful to Pétain and was acting in his name. In the colorful words of Churchill:

"All this is done in the sacred name of the Marshal and when the Marshal bleats over the telephone orders to the contrary and deprives Darlan of his nationality, the Admiral rests comfortably upon the fact or fiction, it does not much matter which, that the Marshal is acting under the duress of the invading Hun, and that he, Darlan, is still carrying out his true wishes. In fact, if Admiral Darlan had to shoot Marshal Pétain, he would no doubt do it in Marshal Pétain's name." [18]

So Darlan set himself up as "chief of state" and established an imperial council, consisting of Giraud, Noguès, Bergeret, and Chatel. In short, he pretended to have succeeded the helpless marshal as the head of *the* French government and made no pretense of changing the nature of that government. He and his supporters were all men of Vichy. Assuming that they were genuinely anti-German, they nevertheless subscribed to the Vichy form of government, a form of government, incidentally, that appears to have been quite to the liking of the French population of North Africa. In the last analysis, then, the Allies discovered themselves committed to a new edition of the Vichy regime. Temporary it might be, and the product of military expediency; but it was nonetheless objectionable, and certainly was an uninspiring prelude to the great crusade of freedom.

Under pressure of public opinion the United States government and General Eisenhower continued to wrestle with this problem to the best of their abilities. On December 3 General Eisenhower was instructed that when the agreement with Darlan was ready to be published, it should be dubbed a "joint announcement" rather than an "agreement," and the words "French Imperial Federation" should be omitted:

[18] Churchill's statement in Parliament December 10, 1942 (*Life*, February 4, 1946).

"It is not desired that any act of ours can be understood as recognizing any particular government set-up except such a provisional one as is locally necessary for the carrying out of the current military operations." [19]

Again, a few days later, the general was advised to explain orally to Darlan the attitude of the American government:

"That the United States Government fully appreciates the important military contribution which Darlan has made and is continuing to make to the Allied effort in North Africa,—an effort which is only a prelude to the complete liberation of all French people in Europe and in the Empire. That it is the policy of the American Government to welcome the active cooperation of all Frenchmen in resistance to Axis aggression and to the extension of Axis domination and control. That until these purposes are achieved, other considerations must be held in abeyance and for subsequent determination, and that military unity of purpose must not be weakened by a dispersal of effort. That as long as the efforts of Admiral Darlan are directed to the specific end of resisting the Axis, it is felt that he is making a positive military contribution to our United effort. That this will not be the case if he devotes his efforts to the building up of an organization not directly concerned with the military effort. And that this Government has no intention of disregarding the sovereignty of France and of the French people by attempting to predetermine the choice which the French people will eventually have to make in the selection of their leader." [20]

Thereupon General Eisenhower had a frank talk with Darlan. In this he "made it perfectly clear that anything that could be interpreted as political maneuvering on his (Darlan's) part to extend the scope of his influence outside French Northwest and West Africa would react definitely to his disadvantage in his relations with the American army and government." To which Darlan replied that he had "no intention of trying to achieve political influence in other countries,"

[19] War Department: message to Eisenhower (December 3, 1942). Roosevelt Records.
[20] War Department: message to Eisenhower (December 7, 1942).

and promised complete co-operation in the local military effort
and in any other way desired by the United States government.[21]

All this was very well, but Darlan and his associates continued on their established course. Indeed, a large number of
those who had been friendly and co-operative with the American enterprise had been thrown into concentration camps
and were still there. In Morocco, under the patronage of
Noguès, the hooliganism of the S.O.L. went on unchecked.
Vichy was enjoying a renaissance in North Africa.

It was this situation that continued to supply fuel to those
who agitated against the Darlan regime. The President had
therefore suggested to Churchill that some consideration be
given to the appointment of one Britisher and one American
"to whom would be given authority, not to administer civil
functions, but to hold a veto power over French civil admin-
istrators and to direct them in rare instances to follow out certain policies." This suggestion eventuated in the appointment
of Murphy as the President's personal representative on Eisenhower's staff with the rank of minister. At the same time
Churchill named Harold MacMillan to an analogous position.[22]

In view of Darlan's authoritarian policy, an agreement between the Fighting French and the North African regime had
become impossible. De Gaulle, who had been genuinely willing to pool his efforts with Giraud, would have nothing whatever to do with Darlan. Representatives of the French committee, who had been sent to negotiate with Giraud, were recalled early in December and discussions that were held at
Gibraltar eventuated in the conviction that Darlan must go.
It was decided, however, that it would be better to induce him
to resign, allowing him to nominate a successor. This, it was
thought, should not be difficult, "as Darlan has more wits than
guts." [23]

But Darlan escaped this humiliation. On December 16 he

[21] War Department: message from Eisenhower (December 12, 1942).
[22] Roosevelt Records.
[23] State Department: three telegrams from General Mason McFarlane
(December 13, 1942).

gave an interview to some newspapermen, in which he defended his policy under Pétain and as the marshal's successor:

"The aim of all I did while in the French cabinet was to keep within due limits the power which Germany had gained over France, and to save all that could be saved in my unfortunate country and its empire.

"During fifteen months of my vice-presidency of the Council of Ministers nothing—absolutely nothing—essential was ceded to the Axis. One makes politics with realities and not with sentiment. When a defeated country is alone in the world and at the mercy of the victor, there are no arms with which to defend oneself other than negotiation. We were unable to apply a policy of force. We negotiated and we loyally safeguarded everything which could be safeguarded."

And as for the present situation, he added:

"I am simply managing French interests in French Africa, in the name of the prisoner Chief of State. I am acting as a trustee of authority, the trustee of a national treasure." [24]

Having made his apologia, Darlan was assassinated as he entered his office on Christmas Eve. Whether the assassin was an agent of the royalists or whether his act was that of a lone fanatic need not concern us here. There were curious circumstances surrounding the assassination, and the murderer was hurried to his execution amidst much secrecy.[25] Anyway, the assassin had succeeded in cutting short the spectacular career of Admiral François Darlan. Unfortunately, however, the shots that killed the man did not kill the problem he had raised. When the question of his successor arose, General Bergeret, who had been Deputy High Commissioner under Darlan, brought out a secret ordinance, supposedly signed by Darlan on December 2. This provided that General Noguès should become High Commissioner in case Darlan were unable to perform his functions, but that in a case of prolonged incapacity

[24] Broadcast by Radio Maroc, December 24, 1942.
[25] The matter is discussed in some detail by General Julius Holmes: "Eisenhower's African Gamble" (*Collier's Magazine*, January 19, 1946); also Kenneth Pendar: *Adventure in Diplomacy*, pp. 126ff.

on his part, the imperial council should choose a successor. This was a bit too much for General Eisenhower, who, when asked for his personal opinion, stated flatly that Noguès would not be acceptable and that General Giraud was the only possible choice. He then went on to say "that he felt that now was the time to break definitely with the notion that Vichy legislation was necessary to establish the legality of the functioning of a regime established in North Africa for the prosecution of the common Allied war effort." [26]

The commanding general was instructed at once from Washington that Giraud was to be appointed as High Commissioner, in charge of both military and civil affairs, and this was the solution arrived at on the very same day.[27] It was the only sensible solution under the circumstances. In fact, it promised at last to resolve the awkward situation into which military expediency had plunged the American authorities. But even this solution, like others that had gone before, did not prove final. Darlan, in the words of the *New Statesman*, had "left in French North Africa a political cesspool whose stench not merely infected the cause of the Western Allies, but threatened, unless there be plain speaking and better understanding, to poison Anglo-American relations." [28] Giraud, it was hoped, would correct many of the local evils, though Giraud too was anything but a liberal or democrat at heart. But even then there remained the French problem itself, centering more and more on the question of the relation of the French regime in North Africa to the French National Committee in London. De Gaulle had always maintained his readiness to arrive at an agreement with Giraud, as distinguished from Darlan and his associates. On Giraud's appointment, de Gaulle reiterated his intention to co-operate, and when President Roosevelt and Prime Minister Churchill met at Casablanca, late in January 1943, every effort was made to effect a compromise. Despite outward cordiality no agreement was reached. On the con-

[26] War Department: message from Eisenhower (December 26, 1942).
[27] War Department: messages to and from Eisenhower (December 26 1942); Roosevelt Records.
[28] *New Statesman and Nation* (January 9, 1943).

trary, the French problem merely entered upon a new and if anything more bitter phase, which, even at the time of the invasion of Normandy, eighteen months later, was far from resolution. But this is a question apart and one which cannot be examined in this study. For us the death of Darlan and the appointment of Giraud closes the narrative, as the defeat and fall of France opened it.

CHAPTER X

Conclusion

THE SO-CALLED Vichy policy drew more criticism of the Department of State than almost any other issue of foreign affairs during the war years. In the United States it generated no end of indignation and bitter feeling and led to charges that frequently went beyond the limits of decency and reason. Ultimately the Vichy policy became the butt of attack by liberals and radicals who tried to make out that the Department, under a New Deal administration, was a citadel of reaction and the breeding-ground of fascism. The President, though he obviously took a great interest in French affairs and certainly was responsible for all the basic decisions, was rarely called personally to account. But Secretary Hull, though a democrat of the democrats and a liberal if ever there was one, became the target of a merciless onslaught. The best that was said of him by the opponents of the Vichy policy was that he was the innocent victim of his reactionary subordinates and advisers, most of whom were unceremoniously stamped "appeasers" and enemies of popular liberties. All that this government had done even before Pearl Harbor to further the cause of those who were fighting the Axis was conveniently forgotten. None of it counted as against the crime of the Vichy policy.

In the preceding chapters the course of our relations with France and our policy toward the French problem have been examined in considerable detail, with occasional comment and criticism. But it may be well, at the end of this long and involved narrative, to review some aspects of the question in a broad way and to attempt some evaluation of the aims, procedures, and results of our policy.

It should be noted, first and foremost, that almost all of

[382]

the criticism of the Vichy policy was based on ideological considerations. In the eyes of the critics, the Pétain government was a fascist government, by nature fundamentally akin to the regimes of Mussolini and Hitler, a system that was authoritarian through and through and a menace to popular rights and liberties.

As a matter of fact, this interpretation was substantially correct. Pétain and his chief associates were fascist in their views and had long yearned for an authoritarian regime to put an end to what they considered democratic chaos and corruption. But it should be remembered that in the beginning, when our decision to maintain relations was taken, the Vichy regime was in its infancy and had not yet revealed itself in its worst aspects. In any event, the United States government could hardly have based its policy toward France on considerations of the form of government. Throughout history our sympathies have naturally been on the side of the liberal, democratic states, but rarely before this had it been argued that we should not maintain relations with governments of which we disapproved. Throughout the nineteenth century we continued to deal with the Ottoman despotism, while our relations with the Russian autocracy were for the most part distinctly friendly. In the period after 1919 not only did we maintain relations with the Italy of Mussolini, but we ultimately accorded recognition to Bolshevik Russia, which was at the other end of the ideological scale. We did not regard the victory of Hitlerism in Germany as a justification for breaking relations, and our connection with militaristic Japan was not ended until the bombs fell on Pearl Harbor. No one seriously agitated for a policy of quarantine, and, indeed, if our foreign policy in the modern world were to be based exclusively upon ideological affinity, we should probably find ourselves cut off from many of the most powerful and important nations. In short, the purely ideological approach to the Vichy problem could never be a realistic or practicable one. The task of the Department of State is to protect American interests abroad, not to sit in judgment on other governments.

But closely connected with the ideological argument was the further consideration that the Vichy government collaborated with Germany. From this it appeared to follow that since Nazi Germany was recognized as a threat to this country, and since we were doing our utmost to aid and comfort the opponents of Nazi Germany, it was illogical to tolerate the collaborationism of Pétain, Laval, and Darlan. This entire approach to the problem is apt, however, to leave us in a morass of contradictions. One of the most unfortunate and baneful misapprehensions current in this country was the idea that everyone connected with the Vichy government was a collaborationist and a friend of Germany. A critical examination of the situation shows that within the Vichy ranks there was every conceivable gradation.

Let us begin with Marshal Pétain himself. In the summer of 1945 he returned from his captivity in Germany to present himself for trial. His attorneys appealed to Admiral Leahy, among others, to make a statement in the old soldier's behalf, and the admiral, in what was necessarily a carefully considered reply, wrote as follows, referring to the period of his ambassadorship to Vichy:

"I had then, as I have now, the conviction that your principal concern was the welfare and protection of the helpless people of France. It was impossible for me to believe that you had any other concern. However, I must, in all honesty, repeat my opinion as expressed to you at the time that positive refusal to make any concessions to Axis demands, while it might have brought immediately increased hardship to your people, would, in the long view, have been advantageous to France." [1]

The record of the Pétain trial is a volume of almost four hundred triple-column pages, containing a vast amount of valuable evidence from those who were involved, from Reynaud and Weygand and Laval down to mere secretaries. I have read every word of this record and find it hard to believe

---

[1] *New York Times*, August 2, 1945. The testimony of another neutral observer, Stucki, the Swiss minister at Vichy, was almost identical (*Procès du M. Pétain*, p. 378).

that anyone who has done likewise could regard the conviction of the marshal as anything but a political judgment. Not that the trial clinched the case for the defense. Pétain remains an enigma and about all that an impartial person can say is that he evidently tried to serve France according to his lights. He presssed for an armistice in 1940 because he considered it the only sane thing to do. He favored the national revolution because he distrusted democracy and held it primarily responsible for France's defeat. In the autumn of 1940 he probably regarded some measure of collaboration with Germany as unavoidable because he despaired of Britain and the United States. After that he changed his mind once and for all and did what he could to hold collaboration to a minimum.

But it must not be forgotten that Pétain was dealing with much younger men—men like Laval and Darlan, who were politically adroit, blatantly opportunist, and frequently quite ruthless. There can be no question that they often withheld full information from him and that they dragooned him into certain courses of action by drawing lurid pictures of the reprisals that the Germans, if they were thwarted, would take against the French prisoners and the French people generally. So Pétain's policy looks bad on many individual scores for reasons that can rarely be stated with certainty. He was a vain old man, full of solicitude for his people. At times he did not grasp all that was involved and at other times he was unduly fearful. But over the years he stood firm and his achievement was substantial: he maintained France as a going concern, he kept the French fleet out of the enemy's clutches, and he fended off the danger to North Africa, which was to serve as our gateway to Europe.

Really about the only sincere collaborationists in France were the industrial interests like the Banque Worms group. They not only accepted collaboration—they yearned for it and worked for it. As a matter of fact, they did a thriving business and came off extremely well. Laval and Darlan made full use of these people and sponsored economic collaboration of large dimensions. According to what Laval told Hitler in No-

vember 1942, France had spent for Germany 125 billion francs
industrially, 40 billion francs agriculturally, and 425 billion
francs in a purely financial way. Furthermore, France had
sent 320,000 workers to Germany, had contributed 200,000
men to the Todt organization for German military work in
France, and had put another 350,000 to work on armaments
production for Germany.[2]

Laval and Darlan were both opportunists. They were intensely anti-British and deeply convinced that Germany
would win. The thing was for France to be in the good graces
of the Führer and secure a leading position in his new Europe
of the future. Both men kept plaguing Hitler for some assurance as to France's future position and carefully abstained
from far-reaching political or military commitments until they
had some substantial guarantee. Hitler, as we know, had no
long-range plan for France. He would hear nothing of a peace
treaty or a definitive commitment until the war was won,
which led Laval on one occasion to make a politically very
discerning remark to the man who was sure he knew it all:
"You want to win the war in order to organize Europe; you
would do better to organize Europe in order to win the war."[3]

The opportunism of Laval and Darlan meant that, both for
themselves and for their country, they were intent on being on
the winning side. In the case of Darlan it is likely that the
entry of the United States into the war made him wobble and
that the return of Laval to power decided him. As for Laval,
there is no doubt that long beyond the American invasion of
North Africa he still believed in an ultimate victory of the
Germans. When he changed his mind it is hard to say, but at
any rate he waited too long.

Returning to the larger issue, it must be emphasized that
the group of opportunist collaborators was at all times more
than counterbalanced by innumerable Frenchmen, mostly
nameless, in low positions as well as in high places, who felt

[2] Captured German Documents: record of the meeting of Hitler and
Laval at Munich (November 10, 1942).
[3] State Department: interrogation of Dr. Paul Schmidt.

that they could best serve France by standing behind the venerated figure of the marshal and protecting national interests as best they could. From the ministries in Vichy down to the petty *fonctionnaires* there were countless Frenchmen who hated and detested their German conquerors, who dreamed only of the resurrection of France, and who, while awaiting the day of liberation, did their best to obstruct the demands of the Germans and to aid the cause of France's traditional friends. Nothing could be more unjust than to condemn all those who were connected with the Vichy regime or to club them all together as collaborationists and traitors. Until November 1942, at least, the vast majority of patriotic Frenchmen felt that they could serve best by staying in France. It was most unfortunate that the Fighting French were unwilling to recognize this and that, through their propaganda, they aroused a considerable antipathy within the country.

This leads us at once to one of the most important factors in the entire Vichy policy. The Department of State, though it could not announce the fact from the rooftops, realized from the very outset how valuable contact with the Vichy government could be. As aforesaid, Vichy itself was full of men, notably officials of the Foreign Office and officers of the army, with whom we had had dealings over the years and whom we knew for what they were. From start to finish these men furnished us political and military information of the highest value and order. Vichy meant to our Department of State not only a helpless old man and a collection of unscrupulous intriguers. It meant also a large number of friends, on whom we could rely and through whose aid we could learn more about the enemy than through perhaps any other source. The experience and the connections of many men in the Foreign Ministry were at our disposal, while the military intelligence service of the French army, which was clandestinely reorganized after the defeat, was freely available to us. It would have been perfectly idiotic to cut ourselves off from this vital spring of information. When the last word is said, one can hardly escape the conclusion that for intelligence purposes, if for no others, the Vichy policy was completely justified.

The policy of the North African Economic Accord was, at bottom, based upon similar considerations. The President and the Department recognized at an early date the great importance of this area and the necessity for doing everything possible to deprive the enemy of any pretext for intervention there. The initial idea was to stave off an economic crisis in the North African area, thereby preventing unrest among the natives and at the same time facilitating the task of General Weygand, whose objective was to make the French Empire strong enough to resist aggression. But very soon the intelligence possibilities became evident and began to overshadow all other considerations. Through the American vice-consuls we were afforded golden opportunities not only to follow developments in North Africa, but to observe and evaluate enemy activity throughout the western Mediterranean.

Our whole North African policy must be described as an unqualified success, despite the fact that it was never well implemented or exploited to the full. From start to finish it was hampered and obstructed by the British and by other American agencies. Indeed, it may be taken as a classic example of jurisdictional conflict and confusion at its worst. No doubt the different parties to the dispute would want to allocate the blame in different quarters. The argument of the Board of Economic Warfare was that the Department of State never gave sufficiently clear policy directives. There is something in this claim, though it is impossible to accept it as applying to the later and more crucial period of the program. Fundamentally the problem appears to have been different, going back to the unhappy separation of economic warfare from political warfare. The Department of State never had anything like the measure of control over the Board of Economic Warfare that the British Foreign Office exercised over the Ministry of Economic Warfare. This, certainly, was a situation that should be avoided in the future. If there had been full authority and singleness of direction in our North African policy, it might have been carried much farther. Even as it was, it proved to be one of the cleverest and most fruitful moves we could have made. Our investment was ridiculously small, and the returns were very substantial.

Among the claims occasionally made for the Vichy policy by spokesmen of the Department was the claim that it had enabled us to save parts of the French Empire from falling into the hands of our potential enemies, and that, furthermore, it had kept the French fleet from becoming an instrument of Hitler and Mussolini. This claim is at best debatable—though our role was probably a substantial, contributory one. So far as the French colonial possessions are concerned, it is impossible to deal with them as a unit. The French possessions in the Western Hemisphere were kept from the Axis by the near-by power of the United States. We were long-suffering with Admiral Robert at Martinique, but we could afford to be lenient, because in case of a real threat we could have acted promptly and effectively. Under the circumstances it would have been folly to provoke a crisis that might easily have led to reprisals elsewhere. Other French colonies or mandates (like Syria and Madagascar) were dealt with militarily by the British. French Indo-China fell into the lap of the Japanese, without our being able to do much to prevent it. As for the remainder, they were taken over by the de Gaullists or else remained under Vichy rule until we ourselves occupied them.

In this whole confused situation we followed a sensible, purely opportunist policy. We gave as much recognition to de Gaulle as the circumstances warranted, yet we managed to avoid antagonizing Vichy to the point of open hostility. North and West Africa were, of course, the great danger spots and we rightly encouraged any official, like Weygand, who tried to put them in condition to defend themselves. As it happened, the Germans abstained from occupying them, for reasons we have already examined. If they had chosen to act in that area, neither Vichy nor Britain nor the United States could have stopped them at any time prior to the autumn of 1942. In the autumn of 1940 or during the ensuing winter they might have had a pretty easy time of it. But then Spain was opposed and German action might well have led to the collapse of the Pétain government and have obliged the Germans to take over a much larger administrative job in a much more restless country. In the later period the Germans would have come up against stronger resistance in North Africa and at Vichy, for we had begun to support Weygand, and Admiral Leahy was at Pétain's side. We were able to throw all our weight against Darlan's Paris Protocols and in general to bring real pressure on the marshal, who was constantly confronted with the danger of a break of relations with us. The old man put great store by his personal prestige and popularity, and the one thing he was anxious to avoid above all others was being responsible for American hostility. That, he knew, the country would neither understand nor excuse.

The question of the French fleet was simpler, though its importance was even greater. After the fall of France the French squadrons more or less held the balance between British sea power and Axis naval strength in European waters. The British recognized this fully and therefore did not hesitate to take the most drastic measures, as at Mers-el-Kébir, to keep it out of German hands. We realized it, too, and without a doubt decided to keep on good terms with Vichy in the hope of swaying the Pétain regime to resist any German designs or demands. Our anxiety on this score was immediate, intense, and serious, but it proved to be more or less superfluous. The evidence is conclusive that the French, even at the time of the armistice, were determined not to surrender the fleet and to scuttle it if any attempt were made to seize it. The fleet was really the only substantial force the French had left. It was an excellent fleet, of which the French were very proud. It is altogether unlikely that they would ever have given it up, either to the Germans or to the British.

As we know, the Germans were fully aware of this. They made no serious effort to get control of the fleet until after the invasion of North Africa. At that time not even Darlan succeeded in getting the ships to leave for Algiers. When it

came to a showdown, the fleet was scuttled, as the logical conclusion to the whole knotty problem. The French kept their
fleet out of foreign hands as long as they could. They did it
for their own good reasons. When ultimately it became impossible to deny the Germans, they sent the ships to the bottom. There is no reason to suppose that they would not have
done the same thing at any time between 1940 and 1942, without reference to our Vichy policy. On the other hand, it must
be remembered that at the time no one could be sure of the
ultimate solution. There was no guarantee that if the collaborationists won out, Vichy France might not join in the war
against Britain and put the fleet at Hitler's disposal. After all,
there was nothing sacred or eternal about the orders issued in
June 1940. It therefore behooved us to be constantly on the
alert and to use every last ounce of our influence to oppose
collaboration. Any other course would have been tantamount
to criminal negligence.

Perhaps the most widely debated claim of the State Department was that by maintaining the tie with Vichy we were
able to keep contact with the people of France, to remind them
of the past friendship between the two countries, to keep alive
the sentiment of liberty and equality, to maintain hope of
deliverance, and to stimulate resistance to the conqueror. Time
and again the reply to this claim was made that by our Vichy
policy we only discouraged and confused the French people.
How could our dealings with the fascist regime of Pétain appeal to the French love of liberty? How could we pose on the
one hand as the friends of the collaborationist government of
the marshal and on the other as the exponents of democracy?
In what way were we keeping alive the hope for deliverance,
and in what way were we stimulating resistance? Would it
not have been more effective and more straightforward, say
the critics, to have come out openly and whole-heartedly for
de Gaulle and the Free French movement? After all, it was de
Gaulle and the Free French who had raised the standard of
resistance, and it was de Gaulle who enabled the French to
maintain their self-respect and their hope of ultimate victory.

Admittedly the question is a controversial one to which a simple answer can probably never be given. A large number of factors entered into the situation. On the one hand it must be confessed that we were unable to maintain much contact with the French population, especially in the Occupied Zone. There really is no way to gauge what feeling and opinion in the rank and file may have been. If a generalization is to be made, it should probably be along these lines: the great bulk of the French population undoubtedly detested the conqueror and all his works. But for a long time the French people were lost in despair and hopelessness. With almost no prospect of deliverance, the attention of the population was focused almost entirely on the problem of keeping body and soul together. Interest in the form of government appears to have been very slight indeed. Pétain was deeply revered, and throughout this period enjoyed the affection of thousands of Frenchmen, whatever his deserts. The Republic, rightly or wrongly, was discredited. Under these circumstances it is impossible to suppose that the population, by and large, staked their hopes upon the United States. Many there were, no doubt, who prayed that Britain might ultimately win, with the help of the United States. But the chances of Britain holding out were slim, and there was little reason to think that the United States would intervene in time to be really effective. In the first year of France's debasement it was probably fairly accurate to say that neither Britain nor the United States enjoyed much prestige or following, and that de Gaulle was generally unknown. What hope there was centered on the marshal, who, according to many, would finally outwit the Germans and save France from complete annihilation.

The situation changed gradually as Britain warded off the German air attack, as the United States came out openly in support of Britain, and as the Vichy regime became avowedly collaborationist. This was the period of Admiral Leahy's mission to Vichy. We may safely assume, I think, that during most of 1941 American influence was real and effective. Darlan and his supporters, to be sure, gave way to German demands on a large scale. To all appearances Pétain was unable to check the policy of his subordinates, as, in the long run, Weygand was unable to maintain his opposition. None the less, Admiral Leahy's presence in Vichy undoubtedly strengthened the hand of the old marshal and gave aid and comfort to innumerable patriot Frenchmen, within the Vichy government as well as in the country at large. Naturally it is impossible to evaluate such influence in detail. It is not something that can be measured with a yardstick. But it stands to reason that the interest of the United States, as well as the growing evidence of American might and American determination to challenge the domination of Hitler, must have reacted favorably on many Frenchmen.

During 1942 the situation changed even more rapidly. The spirit of resistance began to mount high as the Russians checked the German advance. At the same time opposition to the Laval system in France became much more pronounced. Our entry into the war no doubt played a part in this French revival, but we cut a sorry military figure at first and with Admiral Leahy's departure were no longer in a position of direct influence. It was only at this time, in the spring of 1942, that de Gaulle's star came into the ascendant. Many resistance groups rallied to him in a general way, though without committing themselves to any particular political program. De Gaulle became a symbol of resistance, but he was not yet an accepted leader.

What conclusion, then, can be reached with respect to United States policy? So much certainly is clear: we had three alternatives, and no more. We could maintain relations with Vichy and encourage resistance in this way. We could break off relations with Vichy, wash our hands of the whole French problem, and go our own way. Finally, we could disown Vichy and espouse the cause of de Gaulle. Actually very few people ever suggested or recommended the second course. The issue was always between Vichy and de Gaulle. We chose the first policy to begin with because at that time it seemed to have real advantages and because at the outset de

Gaulle hardly offered an effective alternative. We continued our policy during 1941 because Admiral Leahy's mission really paid off, because we were getting rich returns in intelligence and because through General Weygand we were establishing a valuable position in North Africa. De Gaulle was a hireling of the British, who caused the latter no end of trouble in Syria. He had no demonstrable following in France, or even among Frenchmen outside France. Everywhere he had the reputation of being a man personally vain and ambitious, self-centered and almost impossible to deal with. When finally he burst upon the American scene, it was to present us with the St.Pierre-Miquelon crisis, which he had timed most awkwardly for the Christmas following Pearl Harbor. De Gaulle would have had to have much greater promise, much more enthusiastic and far-reaching support, to make him attractive to the United States government. He appealed, of course, to the heroic sentiments of many Americans, but the Department of State could hardly have been expected to deal in terms of sentiment. As a political reality he had but little to offer us.

The one really debatable phase in this whole complex situation was the one that arose in the spring and summer of 1942, when de Gaulle did succeed in building up a substantial following in France and when he did become a symbol of resistance not only to the invader but to the fascist Vichy regime. Perhaps at that time we might have thrown over Vichy and given de Gaulle and the Fighting French our undivided and unequivocal support. We did not do so for a variety of reasons. In the first place, the Department seems to have underestimated the extent of de Gaulle's following. More important, however, were other considerations: to adopt de Gaulle would have meant a rupture with Vichy, and with it the loss of the intelligence we were getting from France and from North Africa. This would have been a tremendous blow at a time when we were already at war with Germany and when we were already laying plans for action in North Africa. These considerations were in themselves compelling, but to them must be added the skepticism of the President and of the

Department with respect to de Gaulle and his entourage. We were determined to leave the future of France to the decision of the French themselves, after their liberation. We were equally determined not to aid and abet the political hopes and plans of the Fighting French. We distrusted them and we distrusted their program, such as it was. We tried to find some other leader, some prominent French figure who represented more nearly the traditions of patriotic France. At one time we had thought of Herriot, and at another time we had turned to Weygand. Ultimately we were led to Giraud, whom both the British and we ourselves accepted with alacrity. But at no time were we willing to stake much on de Gaulle. There was never any thought of associating him and his movement with the North African enterprise. Possibly if we had treated de Gaulle differently, if we had thrown ourselves behind his movement, the man himself might have become less rambunctious and his following might have become more comprehensive and united. But all this is purely speculative. The fact is that we adopted another policy for what appeared to us good and sufficient reasons. Sentiment played no role in the decision. We were not partial to the fascism of Vichy and we were not unsympathetic to French aspirations. Our objective was to safeguard our own interests, among which was the liberation and re-establishment of France. No doubt there were different conceptions of how this might be done. But we could choose only one, and it remains an ironic detail that in the summer of 1942, just as de Gaulle was coming into his own, we had to discard him in the interests of the North African venture.

We come then finally to the last of the claims made for our Vichy policy: that it provided the groundwork for the invasion of North Africa. This is really the heart of the matter and in the last analysis is pretty much beyond controversy. Reynaud's plans made it clear that North Africa was nothing but an extension of Metropolitan France, the obvious refuge for the French in the hour of extremity. The importance of that strategic area escaped no one and therefore we, as well as the

French, were intent on keeping it from the enemy's clutches. In other words, our interest was to support the interest of the French in this matter and to fight a diplomatic delaying action until the day when we could use North Africa as a springboard to Europe. And so we used all possible influence to keep Vichy in line and prevent the sacrifice of French interests. At the same time we began to work constructively with economic weapons. The Economic Accord was a masterstroke and, even though its implementation left much to be desired, its advantages were real and obvious. Murphy was a happy choice for the position he was called to fill. The various vice-consuls, too, were without exception well-qualified, intelligent, and courageous men. They not only watched the course of shipments within the country and to French ports, but collected a large body of information on the region and established useful contacts with the various patriotic groups that were scattered all the way from Casablanca to Tunis. Later, when Colonel Eddy and his staff arrived to conduct the operations of the Office of Strategic Services, the closest co-operation was effected between Murphy and those whose function it was to develop subversive plans. The relation of these men to each other was beyond praise. Through them an almost perfect connection was established between the Department of State and the military services.

This leads us to the concluding phase of the entire policy, that phase which was the prelude to armed action. Properly speaking, this part of the story might well be left out of account, since it belongs rather to the history of military plans and operations than to political programs. Nevertheless, Murphy played so large a role in the story and was so closely tied to both the political and military activities that some comment is in order.

In a word it may be said that the War Department was slow in taking advantage of the opportunities that had been prepared in North Africa. In the spring of 1942 some sort of action had already been discussed, but little effort was made to follow up the problem of French resistance and possible

French assistance. Although there was a real and continuing danger that the Germans might proceed to the occupation of North Africa, and although it was a foregone conclusion that neither Britain nor the United States could do much to prevent such occupation, nothing much was done to encourage and equip the resistance groups. Supplies, to be sure, were badly needed elsewhere, but the requirements of the North African French were so modest that somewhat more consideration might have been given them. Fortunately the Germans did not take the offensive. But if they had, the degree and extent of French resistance might have been a crucial factor.

As for the later period, when the invasion was definitely decided on and plans were in processs, the high command was again slow in appreciating the importance of the French attitude. The negotiations at Algiers came only on the very eve of the invasion. They hinged very largely on the leadership of Giraud, yet they left that general barely time enough to pack his bags. Because of the fact that everything was hastily arranged at the last moment, it was inevitable that there should have been misunderstandings and confusion. The army evidently had no conception of the strength of Vichy loyalty among the high officials and officers of North Africa. For a few days we were really in a dangerous dilemma, from which Darlan extricated us most providentially. The point of this whole business was, of course, not the cessation of hostilities in itself. We could almost certainly have suppressed resistance in a short time. But we could never have gone on safely so long as the high authorities in North Africa were opposed to us. Darlan's great achievement and real contribution was to bring the leaders to our side. For that he deserves full recognition.

We arrive, then, at the end of a long and complicated story. The most appropriate question to ask at this point is this: If we had the whole thing to do over again, would we do it differently? The answer is certainly in the negative. The Vichy policy was, at the outset, a *pis aller*. We continued our relations with Vichy because there was no good reason why we should break them off. As time went on, the policy crystallized around certain fairly obvious advantages. From the standpoint of American interests, the policy was always a substantially sound one even though it may have been an unattractive one. The only real arguments against it were arguments of a sentimental or ideological character. Such considerations are dangerous if they are made the basis for foreign policy. They have validity only if they can be made to coincide with real national interests. In the popular mind it all reduced itself to the choice between the authoritarian regime of Vichy and the heroic crusade of de Gaulle. But unless one can demonstrate that de Gaulle and his movement could have contributed more effectively to American interests than could the connection with Vichy, the whole argument against our policy falls flat. To a possible solution of this question this history, it is hoped, will have added something.

APPENDIX I

THE MURPHY-WEYGAND ACCORD

Memorandum d'une Conversation entre le Général Weygand et Mr. Murphy, February 26, 1941

LES CONDITIONS générales du ravitaillement de l'Afrique du Nord Française en produits essentiels au maintien de la structure économique de cette région ont été discutées. Au cours de cette conversation il fut souligné que tout accord à ce sujet doit naturellement faire l'objet d'une négociation entre le Gouvernement du Maréchal Pétain et le Gouvernement des Etats-Unis à Washington.

Toutefois, en vue de marquer immédiatement les progrès accomplis au cours des conversations de Lisbonne et de Tanger se rapportant à cette question, et afin de permettre l'envoi immédiat de certains produits particulièrement nécessaires, il fut estimé utile de préparer ce memorandum qui sera soumis naturellement à l'approbation du Gouvernement du Maréchal Pétain.

La proposition du Gouvernement Américain, que la Général Weygand est disposée à recommander au Maréchal, envisage:

1.—que le ravitaillement de l'Afrique du Nord n'aura pas pour résultat la constitution de stocks excessifs,

2.—que des dispositions seront prises en vue d'assurer que ces produits et les produits similaires seront consommés en Afrique du Nord Française et ne seront réexportés sous aucune forme,

3.—qu'en vue de réaliser ce qui précède, le Gouvernement Américain sera autorisé à désigner des représentants chargés du contrôle dans les ports et sur les chemins de fer,

4.—qu'en cas de violation de l'accord relatif à la non-réexportation, la coopération économique entre les Etats-Unis et l'Afrique Française du Nord prendra fin automatiquement et définitivement.

Il fut entendu que le Gouvernement Américain est disposé à faciliter le ravitaillement du Maroc français et aussi de l'Algérie et de la Tunisie en produits essentiels, ainsi qu'à débloquer à cet effet les fonds nécessaires sur les avoirs français aux Etats-Unis, si les conditions précédentes sont respectées.

En vue du succès de l'exécution de cet accord, il fut également trouvé désirable qu'un expert économique et commercial au courant des questions de l'Afrique Française fût nommé aux Etats-Unis. Cet expert serait attaché à l'Ambassade de France à Washington.

Alger le 26 Fevrier, 1941
M. W.
R. D. M.

II

French State
Vichy, March 10, 1941

Ministry of Foreign Affairs
10/RB
Commercial Relations
C.857
—————
11

Mr. Ambassador:

Referring to the conversations which have just taken place between the French and American Governments, with a view to ensuring the supplying of French North Africa with products originating in the United States, I have the honor to inform Your Excellency that the French Government attaches vital importance to the supplying of Algeria, Tunisia and Morocco with overseas products. It is therefore disposed to take, in Territories of French North Africa, the measures necessary to ensure the execution of the provisions which, in the opinion of the Federal Government condition this supplying, that is to say:

1.—No accumulation of surplus stocks in Algeria, Tunisia or Morocco;

2.—Consumption of the products imported and of similar products in French North Africa, and no reexportation of these products under any form whatsoever;

3.—Control by American representatives in ports and on railways, of the above undertakings.

The French Government, moreover, takes note of the fact that the American Government is disposed to facilitate the supplying of French North Africa with essential products and, for this purpose, to free from French holdings in the United States the sums necessary to finance the purchases which will be effected on the American market in behalf of North Africa.

The French Government believes that its assent to the dispositions indicated above in paragraphs 1, 2 and 3, will, within a very short time, permit the effective importation into North Africa of the products which correspond to the most urgent needs of Algeria, Tunisia and Morocco. These products appear in the enclosure hereto. The French Government therefore would greatly value knowing at what date the first shipment of merchandise corresponding to these needs will be effected.

It would be desirable if negotiations might be undertaken in Washington as soon as possible with a view to deciding upon the modalities which will permit, in effect, the supplying of all of the North African requirements in foodstuffs.

I should appreciate it if Your Excellency would be good enough to acknowledge the receipt of this letter.

Accept, Mr. Ambassador, the assurance of my high consideration.

F. DARLAN

His Excellency
   Admiral Leahy
      United States Ambassador to France

APPENDIX II

TEXT OF THE PROTOCOLS SIGNED AT PARIS
MAY 27–28, 1941 [1]

DANS LE CADRE des négociations politique actuellement en cours entre les Gouvernements Français et Allemands, des négociations d'ordre militaire ont eu lieu, du 20 au 26 mai 1941, à l'Ambassade d'Allemagne à Paris, entre les Hauts Commandements Allemands et Français et ont abouti aux accords ci-après:

I.—*Accord relatif à la Syrie et à l'Irak* [a]
II.—*Accord relatif à l'Afrique du Nord*
III.—*Projet d'Accord relatif à l'A-O. et à l'A.E.F.*

I—SYRIE—IRAK

1—Le Gouvernement Français s'engage à donner satisfaction aux désirs suivants du Haut Commandement Allemand:

a)—Accord de principe sur la cession à l'Irak, contre paiement, du matériel de guerre stocké en Syrie, jusqu'à concurrence des ¾ de l'ensemble dudit matériel, ainsi qu'il a été fixé antérieurement. Exception est faite en vertu d'accords particuliers, pour les armes nécessaires à la défense immédiate de la Syrie.

b)—Pendant la durée de l'état de choses actuel en Irak, escale et ravitaillement dans la mesure du possible, des avions allemands et italiens avec octroi à l'Armée de l'Air allemande d'un point d'appui dans le Nord de la Syrie (Alep).

c)—Utilisation de ports, routes et voies ferrées syriens pour livraison à destination de l'Irak.

d)—Sur instructions précises à donner par le Haut Commissaire Français, instruction donnée en Syrie, à des soldats irakiens, en ce qui concerne le maniement des armes françaises cédées.

e)—Transmission au Haut Commandement Allemand (à charge de réciprocité) de tous renseignements recueillis par le commandement français sur les forces et sur les mesures de guerre anglaise dans le Proche-Orient.

[1] The text of these protocols, here published for the first time, has become available from a French source of unquestioned reliability.

[a] Cet accord signé à Paris le 27 Mai n'est que la confirmation d'accords verbaux qui avaient conclus à Berchtesgaden, et à Paris, les semaines précédentes.

Le Gouvernement Français déclare, en outre, que le Haut Commissaire Français accordera des prestations nouvelles, selon la situation et dans la mesure du possible, sur demande des services allemands locaux; il affirme, par ailleurs, que, en vue de maintenir en Syrie et au Liban la Souveraineté Française, il est décidé à défendre ces territoires contre toute attaque, avec tous les moyens dont il y dispose.

2—En égard à la situation dans le Proche-Orient, le Haut Commandement Allemand est d'accord pour que les mesures immédiates suivantes soient prises, en dehors des clauses de la Convention d'Armistice.[b]

a)—Destockage d'un quart de l'ensemble du matériel de guerre stocké en Syrie ainsi que des quantités supplémentaries qui seront concédées au Commandement Français en vertu de tractations particulières.

b)—Transfert en Syrie d'un groupe de 3 batteries lourdes de D.C.A. avec 5 dotations normales en munition et 150 hommes par prélèvement sur les unités autorisées dans la Métropole. Remplacement de ces pièces par prélèvement sur les matériels stockés dans la Métropole.

c)—Transfert en Syrie d'un groupe motorisé de 36 pièces de canons de 25 contre avions, avec 5 dotations normales en munition et 150 hommes, par prélèvement sur les unités autorisées dans la Métropole. Remplacement de ces canons par prélèvement sur les matériels stockés dans la Métropole.

d)—Transfert en Syrie de 24 pièces de 25 anti-chars et de 7.200 coups par prélèvement sur les matériels stockés dans la Métropole.

e)—Transfert en Syrie de 24 pièces de 75 par prélèvement sur les matériels stockés dans la Métropole. Ces pièces seront à l'arrivée restockées en Syrie, sous contrôle italien; leur destockage ultérieur, en vue de leur emploi, rest subordonné aux nécessités de la situation.

f)—Transfert de 80 T. de matériel (pièces de rechange pour avions).

g)—Transfert de la Métropole en Syrie de 150 spécialistes pour le renforcement du personnel de 3 batteries fixes de 75 D. C. A. qui y sont installées.

[b] Sous réserve de l'accord italien, dans le mesure où ces dispositions touchent à des interêts italiens.

Note pour les paragraphs b) à g):

Dans le cas exceptionnel où ces transports (ainsi que les transports allemands de ravitaillement à destination de la Syrie) seraient effectuées par mer, leur sécurité dans les zones dangereuses sera à la charge:

—de l'Allemagne jusqu'à Castellorizzo
—de la France entre Castellorizzo et la Syrie.

Dans le cas du transport par voie de terre, celui-ci sera réglé par les soins de l'Allemagne à travers les territoires qui lui sont soumis.

h)—Transfert d'Afrique du nord en Syrie d'un groupe renforcé de chasse, avec quelques avions de transport, avec escale à Brindisi, Athenes ou Larissa et Rhodes.

i)—Renforcement de la défense aérienne de la Syrie par des mitrailleuses à prelever sur le matériel destocké, conformément au paragraphe a) ci-dessus.

En principe, le *Haut Commandement Allemand* est, en outre, prêt à complèter, dans la mesure du possible, les stocks de carburants et de lubrificants existant en Syrie, et, en cas de transport par mer à assurer en Grèce le ravitaillement en carburant des transports français, et, là où c'est nécessaire, celui des escorteurs. A cette fin, dans la mesure du possible, du tonnage français de pétroliers pour être affrêté par l'Allemagne.

II—AFRIQUE DU NORD

1—*Le Gouvernement Français* s'engage à donner satisfaction aux désirs suivants du Haut-Commandement allemand:

a)—Utilisation du port de guerre de Bizerte comme port de déchargement des ravitaillements et des renforts en matériel pour les troupes allemandes en Afrique, avec un personnel réduit d'accompagnement (en civil). Comme ports de chargement, on utilisera les ports du sud de l'Italie et, dans le cas d'emploi de tonnage français, autant que possible Toulon. La Marine de guerre française assurera, en cas de nécessité, la protection des transports effectués par bateau français de Toulon à Bizerte (voir aussi paragraphe b).

b)—Affrêtement de tonnage se trouvant aux mains de la France pour les transports de ravitaillement en matériel et en carburant et pour le cabotage en A. M., à la demande de l' Allemagne.

c)—Utilisation de la voie ferrée Bizerte-Gabès pour le transport en transit vers la Lybie des ravitaillements allemands en matériel et en vivres.

d)—Le personnel allemand d'accompagnement utilisé à Bizerte pour le transport consécutif vers la Lybie, ainsi que les marchandises elles-mêmes, sont dispensées de toutes les formalités douanières et du contrôle habituellement en vigueur pour les importations et les passages de frontières.

e)—Accord de principe pour la cession, contre paiement, d'artillerie lourde, de pièces d'artillerie de côte et de quantités correspondantes de munitions à prélever sur les stocks existant en A. N. Pour le moment les stocks suffisants seront laissés dans les Parcs pour permettre, en cas de besoin, de renforcer la défense de *l'Afrique du Nord Française*.

f)—En supplément des véhicules actuellement en cours d'achat en Afrique du Nord, à savoir:

—1.100 camions
— 300 voitures de transmission
— 300 Motos
—   30 autobus
—   10 camions-ateliers

cession, contre paiement, de 400 autres camions en état de marche en provenance de la Métropole; transport de ces camions en A. N. à destination de la frontière lybienne, par bateau français ou par voie de terre, jusqu'à un port de l'Italie du Sud.

g)—Accord de principe pour la cession de marchandises destinées au chargement des véhicules achetés par l'Allemagne à destination de la Lybie. Ces marchandises seront remplacées par des livraisons allemandes.

2—*Le haut commandement Allemand* est d'accord pour que les mesures immédiates soient prises en dehors des clauses de la Convention d'Armistice.[e]

a)—Maintien, en supplément des effectifs accordés jusqu'à ici, de l'un des trois groupes d'artillerie légère dont la dissolution avait été prévue (groupe hippo).

b)—Destockage des parcs de la Métropole d'un total de 33

---

[e] Sous réserve de l'accord italien dans la mesure où ces dispositions touchent aux interêts italiens.

pièces anti-chars de 25 m/m avec 33.000 coups, dans la mesure
où ces pièces existent dans les parcs. Onze de ces pièces sont
destinées au renforcement de la défense des côtes.

c)—Destockage des dépôts d'A. N. de 140 mitrailleuses, pour
le renforcement de la défense contre avion en A. N.

3—*Le Haut Commandement Allemand* est, en outre, d'accord en ce qui concerne les mesures suivantes:

a)—Transfert de 200 Officiers et de 6.000 sous-Officiers et
hommes de troupe de l'Armée de Terre, de la Métropole en A. N.
pour combler les déficits en effectifs des unités de l'Armée de
terre qui y sont autorisés.

b)—Transfert de 50 officiers, 1.600 sous-officiers, 3.000 hommes
de troupe de la Métropole en A. N. et A. O. F. en vue de combler
les déficits des effectifs des unités de l'Armée de l'Air qui y sont
autorisés. Les déficits ci-dessus comprennent également les civils
nécessaires au titre du personnel non navigant.

c)—Limitation aux militaires seuls du contrôle mixte germano-
italien dans les ports français de la Méditerranée; sous réserve que,
pour les civils, les mesures actuellement appliquées restent en
vigueur.

d)—Extension des possibilités de déplacement de la marine de
guerre française.

aa)—Les forces navales et aériennes reçoivent liberté de mouvement pour l'escorte et la couverture du trafic moyennant simple
déclaration aux Délégations locales ou aux Commissions d'armistice.

Sous réserve d'en informer les Commissions d'armistice les
itinéraires utilisés pour le trafic commercial seront laissés au libre
choix des autorités maritimes françaises en fonction de la situation générale.

bb)—Les unités non libérées comme force d'escorte et de
couverture reçoivent liberté de mouvement pour le cas de menace
anglaise effective, et s'il y a nécessité de parer à cette menace.
Les mouvements envisagés à cet effet sont à communiquer aux
organes de contrôle locaux et aux commissions d'Armistice, au
plus tard au moment de l'envoi des ordres d'engagement; les
organismes ci-dessus doivent être tenus au courant des actions
et des mouvements.

La traversée du Détroit de Gibraltar par le Groupe Strasbourg (dans les deux sens) est subordonnée à l'assentiment des deux commissions d'armistice.

cc)—La liberté de mouvement aux fins d'exercice est accordée, sous réserve d'un préavis de trois jours avant la sortie des unités, dans des zones limitées, à l'intérieur desquelles aucune gêne ne serait apportée à des projets allemands ou italiens.

e)—Remplacement du groupe de chasse envoyé en Syrie par destockage du matériel correspondant, placé sous dépôts dans la Métropole ou en A. N.

f)—Remplacement en nature des carburants ou du lubrifiant utilisés pour le transport par mer des ravitaillements allemands en matériel et en vivres et pour la couverture de ces transports.

4—Quant aux *demandes françaises suivantes*, la décision est différée jusqu'à plus ample informé:

a)—Maintien des forces de police indigènes qui devaient être dissoutes (goumiers, chaouch, etc. . . .)

b)—Libération de captivité de 961 officiers (dont le général JUIN), 3.200 sous-officiers et soldats, 2.686 spécialistes, pour l'armée de transition de l'Afrique du Nord.

c)—Destockage des dépôts Nord-Africains de 62 chars de combat pour l'armée de transition de l'Afrique du Nord.

Note pour I et II.
Tous les details découlant du présent P. V. seront réglés par les Commissions d'armistice.

Paris le 27 mai 1941
Pour le Haut Commandement allemand:
signé: VARLIMONT

III—*AFRIQUE OCCIDENTAL ET EQUATORIALE*

1—Le Gouvernement Français se déclare prêt, en principe, à permettre aux navires de guerre et de commerce allemande d'utiliser comme point d'appui le port et les installations de DAKAR et à accorder dans cette zone un point d'appui pour l'Armée de l'Air allemande. Cet accord doit d'abord se traduire, au cours d'une *première période* commençant le 15 juillet 1941, par le fait que des sous-marins allemands seront ravitaillés dans le port de DAKAR par un bateau ravitailleur et que des navires de commerce allemand pourront y faire escale.

Au cours d'une *deuxième période*, conformément aux accords généraux consignés dans le procès verbal complémentaire ci-après de nouveaux points, notamment l'utilisation du point d'appui également pour des *forces de surface*, l'utilisation des *installations portuaires* et la concession *du point d'appui pour l'aviation* seront réalisés. *Le Gouvernement Français* se charge d'assurer, par ses propres moyens, la défense desdites organisations utilisées du côté allemand, ainsi que celle de l'ensemble des possessions françaises en A. O. et de résister à toutes attaques, même en passant le cas échéant, à une action offensive contre les points d'appui ennemis d'où sont parties les attaques en question.

2—*Le Gouvernement Français* estime que le renforcement préalable de ses forces d'Afrique Occidentale, tel qu'il est défini ci-après, est absolument indispensable pour lui permettre de réaliser les mesures mentionnées au chiffre I, 2me alinea.

1)—*Armée de terre*:

a)—recomplètement du déficit en personnel de groupe mobile renforcé (motorisé) d'A. O. déjà accordé antérieurement par la libération de captivité de:

        154 officiers
        594 sous-officiers
     1967 hommes de troupe (spécialistes)
        154 officiers et compte tenu des
        346 sous-officiers
           dont la libération est déjà accordée.

b)—Destockage de:

      32 auto mitrailleuses (M. G. AUF KRAFTWAGEN)
      15 sections de canons de 25 anti-chars à 3 pièces avec chenillettes et le personnel nécessaire à préciser
       2 équipages de pont (modèle 35) pour le franchissement du Niger
  28.000 cartouches de pistolet
646.000   "   de 7,5
   5.000 obus de rupture de 7,5
 52.000 grenades V. B.

3.000 coups de 81 m/m
2.800 coups de 60
67.500 coups de 25
6.500 coups de 25
    ainsi que munitions complémentaires à préciser en vue
    du recomplètement des stocks.
  56 camions-citernes
   4 camions avec remorque
 100 camionnettes
 174 motocyclettes
  50 voitures de parc à 3 chevaux avec les harnais
 100 fourgons à deux chevaus.

2)—*Marine de guerre*:
  a) Libération d'environ 6.000 prisonniers de la Marine de guerre
française.
  b) Armement et mis en service des forces navales ci-après
avant le 15 juillet 1941:
  2 contre-torpilleurs (Kersaint, Verdun)
  3 torpilleurs (Pomone, l'Iphigénie, Bombarde)
  2 sous-marins (Diamant, Argonaute)
    en plus de l'armement de ces deux sous-marins, porter le
    groupe de relève (armé à 15%) de 9 à 12;
à partir du 15 juillet 1941:
  4 torpilleurs (Vautour, Gerfaut, Vauban, Aigle)
  3 autres contre-torpilleurs (Panthère, Tigre, Lynx, suivant les
    possibilités en personnel).
  4 torpilleurs (Casque, Siroco, Foudroyant, Trombe)
    croiseurs (remplacement des bâtiments gardiennés)
  1 cuirassé (Provence)   ⎫ suivant les possibilités en
  1 porte-aéronef (cdt. Teste) ⎬ personnel.

3)—*Armée de l'Air.*
  Porter de 13 à 17 le nombre des avions des groupes de bombardement en A. O. F.
  Destockage de:
 18 batteries de 75 D. C. A. (8 fixes, 10 mobiles)
 65 sections de 2 pièces D. C. A. de petit calibre (25 ou 20
    m/m) (dont 35 fixes et 30 mobiles) avec personnel et
    quantités de munitions à préciser.
 26 pièces 20 m/m D. C. A. avec 20.000 coups.

4)—En outre, *les nouvelles mesures*, ci-après, dont une partie vient en complément du procès-verbal du 21 mai 1941, sont considérées comme nécessaires:

a) autorisation de recruter en zone occupée des volontaires pour l'armée française, étant extendu qu'on devra renvoyer en zone occupée un nombre de soldats libérés sensiblement égal à celui des volontaires ainsi recrutés.

b) réouverture de l'Ecole de l'Air de SAINT-RAPHAEL.

c) doublement des contingents de carburants accordés jusqu' ici pour les Marines françaises de guerre et de commerce (mazout, gaz-oil, charbon).

5—Communication, à charge de réciprocité, des informations recueillies par le Haut Commandement Français sur les forces et les mesures de guerre anglaises en A. O. F. et A. E. F.

3—*Le Haut Commandement Allemand* note que en vue de rétablir la souveraineté française dans les territoires de l'A. E. occupée par les troupes gaullistes le Gouvernement Français estime nécessaire que lui soient consenties les mesures supplémentaires suivantes, destinées au renforcement des forces de l'A. O. et A. E. et qui, en égard à la menace pouvant peser ultérieurement sur DAKAR, devraient être réalisées pour l'essentiel, avant le mi-juillet 1941:

(1) *Armée de terre*:
Constitution de quatre nouveaux groupes mobiles renforcés (motorisés).
A cet effet, il serait nécessaire de:
—libérer de captivité

614 officiers
2376 sous-officiers
7868 hommes de troupe blancs
11660 sénégalais

—stocker le matériel de guerre nécessaire pour les 4 groupes motorisés.

(2) *Armée de l'Air*:
Constitution nouvelle de:

4 escadrilles de reconnaissance
2 groupes de bombardement
4 groupes de chasse

ou destockage des matériels de guerre correspondants nécessaires à cet effet.

Augmentation de la part revenant à la France sur les productions du programme franco-allemand de construction aéronautiques, les appareils supplémentaires ainsi accordés devant être stockés pour le moment.

(3) *Carburants*

En vue des opérations en question, mise à la disposition des quantités de carburants nécessaires, savoir:

300.00 hectolitres de carburant auto
60.00 hectolitres de carburant avion.

(4) Le règlement de tous les détails découlant des mesures fixées ou projetées dans le présent procès-verbal ci-contre à la Commission Allemande d'Armistice.

Paris, le 28 mai 194.

Pour le Haut Commandement Allemand
Le Général de Brigade

signé: VARLIMONT

A la suite et au sujet des accords militaires ci-dessus, L'Ambassadeur d'Allemagne à Paris et le Vice-President du Conseil des Ministres Français sont convenus du

PROTOCOLE COMPLEMENTAIRE

ci-après:

Le Gouvernement Français doit escompter que le droit d'utiliser le port de Bizerte, fixé dans l'accord sur l'Afrique du Nord et la *protection* des transports de matériels débarquant dans ce port à destination de l'Armée allemande d'Afrique, ainsi que l'aide à accorder aux forces de la Marine allemande prévu dans l'accord sur l'Afrique Occidentale Française et l'Afrique Equatoriale Française peuvent conduire à un conflit armé immédiat avec l'Angleterre ou avec les Etats-Unis.

Le Gouvernement Français doit donc obtenir la réalisation des conditions militaires et politiques qu'implique cette situation.

Les concessions allemandes fixées et prévues dans l'accord sur *l'Afrique du Nord* en vue du renforcement de l'état défensif sur terre, sur mer et dans les aires permettent d'assurer immédiatement les risques que comportent les facilités accordées du côté français et en ce qui concerne BIZERTE.

Les grands dangers que comporte l'octroi, par les Français, des facilités prévues dans le projet d'accord sur *l'A. O. F. et l'A. E. F.* exigent toutefois de subordonner l'exécution pratique de ces mesures, convenues, en principe, aux conditions suivantes:

1) Le Gouvernement Allemand accordera *préalablement* les renforts nécessaires en vue d'augmenter l'état défensif de l'A. O. F.

2) Le Gouvernement Allemand fournira au Gouvernement Français par la voie de *concessions politiques* et *économiques* les moyens de justifier devant l'opinion publique de son Pays, l'éventualité d'un conflit armé avec l'Angleterre et les Etats-Units.

Paris, le 28 mai 1941
signé: DARLAN
Vice-Président du Conseil
des Ministres Français

signé: ABETZ
Ambassadeur d'Allemagne
à Paris

INDEX

[i]

A NOTE ON THE TYPE

This book was set on the Linotype in Janson, a recutting made direct from the type cast from matrices made by Anton Janson some time between 1660 and 1687.

Of Janson's origin nothing is known. He may have been a relative of Justus Janson, a printer of Danish birth who practised in Leipzig from 1614 to 1635. Some time between 1657 and 1668 Anton Janson, a punch-cutter and type-founder, bought from the Leipzig printer Johann Erich Hahn the type-foundry which had formerly been a part of the printing house of M. Friedrich Lankisch. Janson's types were first shown in a specimen sheet issued at Leipzig about 1675. Janson's successor, and perhaps his son-in-law, Johann Karl Edling, issued a specimen sheet of Janson types in 1689. His heirs sold the Janson matrices in Holland to Wolffgang Dietrich Erhardt, of Leipzig.

The book was composed, printed, and bound by Kingsport Press, Inc., Kingsport, Tennessee.